DECOLONIZING FEMINISMS
Piya Chatterjee, *Series Editor*

ASIAN AMERICAN
FEMINISMS
AND WOMEN OF
COLOR POLITICS

EDITED BY

LYNN FUJIWARA AND

SHIREEN ROSHANRAVAN

UNIVERSITY OF WASHINGTON PRESS
Seattle

UNIVERSITY OF WASHINGTON PRESS
www.washington.edu/uwpress

LIBRARY OF CONGRESS CATALOGING-IN-PUBLICATION DATA
Names: Fujiwara, Lynn, 1964– editor. | Roshanravan, Shireen, editor.
Title: Asian American feminisms and women of color politics / edited by Lynn Fujiwara and
    Shireen Roshanravan.
Description: Seattle : University of Washington Press, [2018] | Series: Decolonizing feminisms |
    Includes bibliographical references and index. |
Identifiers: LCCN 2018011126 (print) | LCCN 2018012662 (ebook) | ISBN 9780295744377 (ebook)
    | ISBN 9780295744360 (hardcover : alk. paper) | ISBN 9780295744353 (pbk. : alk. paper)
Subjects: LCSH: Feminism—United States. | Asian American women—Political activity. |
    Minority women—Political activity—United States.
Classification: LCC HQ1421 (ebook) | LCC HQ1421 .A85 2018 (print) | DDC 305.420973—dc23
LC record available at https://lccn.loc.gov/2018011116

Cover illustration © Vesna Asanovic
Cover design by Katrina Noble

This book is dedicated to:

Thomas Akira Fujiwara and Yetsuko Sakamoto Fujiwara,
may your journey be peaceful

Melisa and Leo, for the faithful witnessing and the love
that makes transformation possible

CONTENTS

ACKNOWLEDGMENTS

We are grateful to our friends, colleagues, and institutions who supported this project. Our greatest appreciation goes to our contributors for their fine work, politically engaging conversations, and willingness to be part of this collection. We are indebted to the scholars who generously participated in roundtable discussions at the Association for Asian American Studies conferences: Alice Kim, Sharmili Majumdar, Juliana Pegues, Judy Wu, Lani Teves, Kimberly McKee, Angie Chung, Tom Sarmiento.

Special thanks to the Department of Ethnic Studies (especially Donella Elizabeth-Alston and Amy Thomas), the Center on Diversity and Community in the Division of Equity and Inclusion, the College of Arts and Sciences, the Oregon Humanities Center, and the Women of Color Project at the Center for the Study of Women in Society at the University of Oregon. We are eternally grateful to Larin McLaughlin and Piya Chatterjee for their unwavering encouragement and support from start to finish and to the rest of the amazing team at the University of Washington Press for bringing this book to life. Also thanks to David Martinez for our index.

We could not have done this without the love and support of our dear friends who gave us support and feedback along the way. Special thanks to Michael Hames-García, Ernesto Martínez, Shari Huhndorf, Priscilla Pena Ovalle, Laura Pulido, Sharon Luk, Alai Reyes-Santos, Charise Cheney, Dan HoSang, Lani Teves, Dana Takagi, Deborah Vargas, Monisha Das Gupta, Patti Duncan, Martin Summers, Karl Mundt, Melisa Posey, Isabel Millán, Norma Valenzuela, April Petillo, Rabab Abdulhadi.

We wish to thank our families for their patience and cheerleading.

Lynn: The years we worked on this book were shaped by enormous personal change and growth. I am so grateful to the Morozumi family for their love and support. I express my deepest gratitude to my siblings (Mitch, Mark, and Melissa), cousins, and aunties who shared a deep connection in the past year caring for our mother. My parents' passing bookends the beginning and completion of this collection, and the love of my family, Steve, Kyra, Joanna, and Martin held me throughout.

Shireen: I want to thank María Lugones for encouraging me to explore what it means to identify politically as an Asian American and a Woman of Color feminist, Lisa Yun for introducing me to Asian American studies, and Joshua M. Price for shaping the interdisciplinary conversations that connected me with Jen-Feng Kuo—dear friend, collaborator, and thinking partner on Asian American feminist methodologies at the intersection of Women of Color and transnational feminisms. Nelima Gaonkar and Liz Philipose accompanied and guided me to trust my capacities during some of my lowest lows. Melisa Posey, thank you for the sustaining conversations, laughter, and commitment to living a radical Asian American politics that is also always in solidarity with Women of Color feminisms. Finally, I thank Leo Tyree for all of their love and support.

Most of all, our thanks to each other—Shireen Roshanravan and Lynn Fujiwara. Together, this process was kind, caring, supportive, empowering, and politically motivating. Collaboration is not always easy, but this was truly a collaboration of love and friendship.

ASIAN AMERICAN FEMINISMS AND WOMEN OF COLOR POLITICS

INTRODUCTION

LYNN FUJIWARA AND SHIREEN ROSHANRAVAN

AS FEMINISTS WHOSE INTELLECTUAL AND POLITICAL DEVELOPMENT emerged through Women of Color feminisms, our own connections and experiences with Asian American feminist work have been inspiring, informative, and hopeful. Important contributions by Asian American feminists (Mitsuye Yamada, Genny Lim, Nellie Wong) in the first edition of *This Bridge Called My Back* (1981) established an Asian American feminist voice among Women of Color feminists challenging white feminist hegemony and heteropatriarchal nationalisms. Since *This Bridge*, critical publications focused on Asian American women's histories, experiences, and feminist perspectives have appeared in collections like *Making Waves: An Anthology of Writings by and about Asian American Women* (1989), *The Forbidden Stitch: An Asian American Women's Anthology* (1989), *Making More Waves* (1997), *Dragon Ladies: Asian American Feminists Breathe Fire* (1999), *Asian / Pacific Islander American Women: A Historical Anthology* (2003), and *Asian American Women: The Frontiers Reader* (2004). For those of us searching for company in the gap between hetero-masculine Asian American and white racist feminist studies, these anthologies provide important ground for claiming and making sense of the specific impact of racialized gender oppressions on the lives of Asian American women and our communities. We found in them articulations of potential intellectual and political communities from which to teach and engage the concerns specific to Asian Americans with a growing feminist and antiracist consciousness.

The very possibility of imagining and generating this collection thus emerges from the Asian American feminist work of so many who offer analytics that enable us to think how race, gender, sexuality, class, and citizenship have shaped Asian American communities and politics. Historians such as Shirley Hune, Judy Yung, and Valerie Matsumoto provide us with a gendered lens through which to make sense of the role and presence of

Asian American women in "first wave" Asian immigrant histories. Influential scholarship by Evelyn Nakano Glenn, Catherine Ceniza Choy, Yên Lê Espiritu, Rhacel Salazar Parreñas, and Linda Trinh Vo historically and contemporaneously examine the global economy of racialized gendered labor, family, and citizenship. Literary and cultural studies scholars such as Lisa Lowe, Elaine Kim, Chandra Mohanty, Trinh T. Minh-ha, Gayatri Gopinath, Candace Fujikane, Jasbir Puar, Grace Hong, and Laura Kang forged analytics that gave us the language to name and examine racialized gender dynamics of Asian American negotiations of multiple oppressions. We honor these and the many more Asian American feminist scholars who have left indelible marks on the emergence and advancement of the intellectual and political ground for an Asian American feminism.

While the question "What *is* Asian American feminisms?" motivates this collection, we are also attentive to what should not be subsumed within Asian American feminisms. During the 2002 Association for Asian American Studies meetings in Salt Lake City, Utah, a ballot initiative to change the AAAS to include Pacific Islanders (AAPIAS, Association for Asian / Pacific Islander American Studies), ignited a contentious debate about the historical practice of erasing or subsuming Pacific Islanders within the racial category *Asian American*. In the name of inclusion and coalition, the initiative met strong resistance from Pacific Islander scholars who astutely pointed out a history of erasure and dissimilarity, as well as structural differences in notions of citizenship, migration, sovereignty, and indigeneity (see Hall 2008; Diaz 2004). J. Kēhaulani Kauanui articulated the politics of this problematic in her article "Asian American Studies and the Pacific Question," where she states: "Asian America, and Asian American Studies more specifically, has derived some power and legitimacy by not acknowledging the degree to which their own have participated in the further marginalization of Pacific Islanders—and Pacific Islander Studies, through their self-promotion as both decision-maker and speaker on behalf of Pacific peoples" (Kauanui 2005, 138). Heeding Kauanui's (and many others') concerns, we recognize Asian American feminist studies and Pacific Islander feminist studies as two distinct fields in need of comparative engagement rather than false inclusion.

GENERATIVE BEGINNINGS

The idea for this edited collection materialized at the 2014 Association for Asian American Studies (AAAS) meeting in San Francisco, where we noticed minimal Asian American feminist content in the many sessions, plenaries, and roundtables. Though we were both faculty members in women's and gender studies, we were in various stages of moving our positions to ethnic studies departments. Thus we possessed a keen sense of intellectually engaging an Asian American feminism in both ethnic studies and women's and gender studies spaces and classrooms. We regularly teach Women of Color feminist theory courses and lamented the absence of more contemporary edited collections akin to Chicana feminisms or Indigenous feminisms readers that grapple with both theoretical and conceptual frameworks of the field as well as specific and particular issues. Asian American feminisms, as a field of scholarly and political inquiry, has yet to be presented in a conceptual manner or through an epistemological approach.

It just so happened that our initial conversation about our desire to see a collection that confronted the messiness, indefinability, and contentious strains of what one may call an Asian American feminist framework was with Larin McLaughlin, editor in chief at University of Washington Press. She was inspired by our riffing and gave us the support and encouragement to make this collection happen. Our goal was to create a teachable collection with an intentional focus on the dynamics, tensions, and parallels between Asian American feminisms and Women of Color feminisms. This collection is not intended to be a survey of Asian American women. We did not anchor the collection in questions that seek different Asian American perspectives foregrounding "gender" to understand an issue like "immigrant families." Instead, we conceptualized this collection as offering responses to questions that require a mapping of the historically and culturally specific logics and theoretical frameworks constitutive of what we could call a distinctly Asian American feminist reading of resistant possibilities, violent realities, and political solidarities.

Accordingly, we asked each contributor to consider the following questions as they wrote their chapters: What theoretical interventions, resistant strategies, and epistemic shifts shape the field of Asian American feminisms? More specifically, how are these central concepts, theories, and praxical strategies in dialogue with the coalitional politics of Women of Color and US Third World feminisms? What tensions or disconnections push against and redefine or reimagine the possibilities for an Asian American feminist politics? This collection offers the beginnings of what we hope will become an enduring engagement with these questions. In doing so, we also consider why these questions need to be asked and remain difficult to answer, and we consider the possibility that Asian American feminisms as a field is situational, uncontained, and always in dialogue with shifting tensions within Asian America. Our concern here is to leave the reader with a clearer and broader perspective of the politics at stake: What is an Asian American feminist politics as a conceptual lens, a praxical strategy for resistance, and a nexus for Women of Color solidarity?

In her 1981 article "Invisibility Is an Unnatural Disaster: Reflections of an Asian American Woman," Mitsuye Yamada calls for Asian American women to make themselves meaningfully visible in coalition with Women of Color activism. Core to this collection is the question of an Asian American feminist visibility accountable to the (tentative, relative, and illusory) institutional privileges of model-minority racial constructions that sustain today's racial and settler-colonial landscape. As Grace Hong has theorized, Women of Color or US Third World Women formations emerged purposefully as "coalition through difference" (Hong 2006, xvi); however, in today's neoliberal technology of power, those differences drive protection for some and death for others (Hong 2015, 1–25). How does an Asian American feminism engage in a coalitional praxis of visibility within heterogeneous Asian American communities and in solidarity with Women of Color resistant communities, responsibly and with accountability to different forms and urgencies of violence and threat?

The word *politics* as we use it in the phrase *Women of Color politics* references the maneuvers, mobilizations, movements, tactics, and strategies used to actively negotiate and resist the ongoing legacies of power and domination in their myriad manifestations across time and space. In this regard, we do not understand "politics" as something taking place only at the level of law and policy or street-level issue-based organizing, nor do we presume these realms of political work to be divorced from the politics of knowledge generation. The language, concepts, and theoretical frameworks that shape what, when, and how we perceive violence inform policies and organizing strategies in realms more readily identifiable as where "the real political work" happens. Indeed, *Women of Color* as a political identification exemplifies the necessary politics of creating language that can name what (neo)colonial projects do not want us to identify, address, and change. Kimberlé Crenshaw's (1991) theorizing of "intersectionality" reveals the impossibility of identifying violence against women of color insofar as the law cannot account for the simultaneous experience of gender violence shaped by racial violence and vice versa. This impossibility at the level of the law is reflected in the failure of mainstream public antiviolence movements, which either tend only to white English-only, middle-class cis heterosexual women or cis heterosexual men of color (see Critical Resistance and Incite! 2016, 227–30). Insofar as *Women of Color* names an impossible reality that simultaneously references violence unseen at the intersection of race and gender, it also opens avenues for imagining an impossible politics that refuses the false separation of "race" and "gender" embedded in our cultural and political frameworks (Crenshaw 1991; Hong 2006). Accordingly, the chapters in this collection intentionally emphasize conceptual, methodological, epistemic, and historical analyses as an urgent political project to offer ways of identifying injustice and strategies that can better inform an Asian American feminist praxis.

Of course, political projects of knowledge generation are liberatory only if they are informed by on-the-ground struggle. The terrain of struggle can and should vary to maximize and sharpen the production of multiple tools for liberation. All of the contributors in this collection, including ourselves, write in and through our specific geo- and body politics of struggle, in tension with, and beyond, the colonial confines of the university and its disciplinary mandates. We are clear about the stakes involved in remembering histories and generating analyses that Asian Americans were never meant to remember, elaborate, or enact. We are scholars who have engaged in scholarly activist research that works to challenge, rework, and reshape knowledge production in the academy. Several of us have engaged in participatory action research in local Asian immigrant and refugee communities toward organizing or mobilization efforts. Still others have worked toward meaningful social change and transformation in academic spaces that are often hostile to women and queer people of color. Several of our contributors examine particular "on-the-ground" Asian American feminist political mobilizations, like Partners in Healing, Af3irm, the Asians4BlackLives network, working through broader conceptualizations of solidarity, coalitional possibilities, settler colonialism, heterogeneity, and difference as ways to consider the possibilities of an Asian American feminist praxis. While we would like to avoid binaristic and overly dichotomous distinctions between "academic feminism" and "on-the-ground feminism," we do not profess this book to be a community activist handbook or community activist narration. But we do offer it as an incitement to methodologies and frameworks that are more accountable to the various intellectual, political, social, and familial communities and collectives with whom we seek to build violence-free ways of living, thinking, and loving.

Through the course of putting this collection together we held numerous roundtables with contributors and audience members interested and invested in the further development of the field. Contributor Judy Wu reestablished the feminist caucus in the AAAS, which convened at the 2017 meetings in Portland, Oregon. Needed conversations about the meaning of Asian American feminisms revealed that we struggle to name and examine our different political entry points into whatever we considered to be constitutive of an Asian American feminisms. We hope that the chapters in this book will work as a point of departure for future conversations and more dialogue on the methodological and political groundings of our Asian American feminist orientations.

WHY WOMEN OF COLOR POLITICS?

Given that Women of Color feminisms provide our point of departure for the dialogues initiated by the chapters in this collection, we want to be clear on how we are understanding the political identification, principles, and genealogy of the term *Women of Color*. While the identity *women of color* is often used as a demographic descriptor for those legally classified in the United States as "nonwhite" and "female," we use the identification in its cross-racial feminist coalitional meaning and historical emergence at the intersection of the 1960s US civil rights, antiwar, gay and women's liberation movements. We do so intentionally and with a keen awareness of its political and intellectual relation with, and distinctions from, "transnational" or "global" feminist projects. As part 1 of this collection addresses, the Third World Women's Alliance, one of the first Women of Color political formations, materialized through an emergent consciousness that total liberation requires acknowledging and addressing what Crenshaw (1991) came to theorize as the "intersectionality" of oppressions. Crenshaw's now widely used and cited framework of intersectionality names the experience of multiply marginalized peoples who become invisible on multiple fronts of struggle when singular privileged identity markers overdetermine antiviolence priorities, approaches, and agendas. Made invisible by the racism in the 1960s women's and lesbian movements and by the (hetero)sexism in the racial justice and civil rights movements, Black, Puerto Rican, Chicana/o, Native, Arab, and Asian American women came together in a coalitional commitment to address the interdependence of all oppression and liberation efforts. In using the capitalized terms *Women of Color politics* and *Women of Color identification* in this collection, we invoke cross-racial feminist coalitions and the cultural, scholarly, and activist work they generated.

The institutional eclipsing of Women of Color feminisms by "transnational" or "global" feminisms resonates with what Sau-Ling Wong (1995) theorizes as the "denationalization" of Asian American studies into Asian diasporic studies at the turn of the twenty-first century. Characterizations of "Asian American" studies and "Women of Color" feminisms as a "narrow" US-centric phase that must give way to, or be absorbed into, a more sophisticated and encompassing "transnational" or "global" focus evidences a "forgetting" of the anti-imperial radical organizing and political consciousness grounding these *political* identifications. Those who came to forge the intellectual and activist genealogies of Women of Color feminisms did do so within the belly of the beast, but their specific US geo- and body politics advanced an unequivocal refusal to abide by the carceral, (settler-) colonial, imperialist and heteropatriarchal logics of US empire. Relatedly, the identity *Asian American* emerged in cross-racial coalition with other US communities of color against white supremacy and US imperialism. Jettisoning the "Asian American" or US "woman of color" as a "narrow" subject of ethnic studies or feminist inquiry facilitates an evasion of political grappling with one's subjection to, and complicity in, US empire. It allows one to escape into what Chandra Mohanty and M. Jacqui Alexander have called the "cartographic difference of the transnational as always elsewhere" (Mohanty and Alexander 2012, 33), thereby enabling the recentering of white scholars as saviors of the now prioritized "foreign" non-US, non-English-speaking Third World subject. Such evasion from the contradictory US subject of color assuages apolitical preferences to study ethnic experiences of peoples descending from different Asian origins where "race" or "white supremacy" cease to be salient analytics. Given the model-minority racial project's overdetermination of Asian Americans as white supremacy's favorite apolitical pawns, we emphatically join Sau-Ling Wong in "claiming America," not in a patriotic celebration but in a Women of Color commitment to accountability for all violence constitutive of the US settler-colonial state.

When and how Asian American feminisms heed this Women of Color call to "claim America" requires careful attention to the various settler-colonial, imperial, racial, and sexual borders of violence that shape one's historical present in (resistance to) the US settler-colonial state. To this end, Asian American feminist thought must learn from Indigenous theorizing of sovereignty and Black theorizing of freedom in the face of ongoing genocide and enslavement, as well as Chicanx and Latinx feminist theorizing on the politics of borders and borderlands. Our shared, though distinct, racialization as "foreigners" and "illegals" presumed to speak no or poor English and with a penchant for doing work whites/Anglos will not do, especially for the wages offered us, makes Chicanx and Latinx feminisms particularly rich theoretical ground for the borders that Asian American feminisms must navigate. Similar to Chicanx and Latinx feminist scholarly compilations, we worked consciously to approach an Asian American feminisms project as critically heterogeneous and marked by multiple and divergent histories and experiences. The editors of *Chicana Feminisms: A Critical Reader* state in their introduction, "Chicana feminist writers recognize that women of Mexican origin constitute a diverse community that requires varied theoretical frameworks and methodological approaches to understand all facets of Chicana experiences" (Arredondo 2003, 3). As Claire Jean Kim (2004) notes, Asian America constitutes an extraordinarily diverse people across language, religion, and histories of colonization and Euro-American imperialism. We thus follow Chicanx and Latinx, Indigenous, and Black feminisms to articulate an Asian American feminist project that refuses any monolithic prescription or description and situates our historical ground of complicity and resistance, to open coalitional possibilities in ongoing struggles for social justice.

Born of political agendas that utilize difference as a tool of division and subordination, Women of Color politics is decidedly coalitional and actively engages "difference" as a site of knowledge that can amplify and sharpen any arsenal of resistance. Political identification with Women of Color feminisms thus requires openness to engage differences as they reflect back our own (unwitting) complicity in the oppression of others. Accordingly, we began this project in a commitment to engage Indigenous Pacific Islanders, Southeast Asian Americans, and Arab Americans in their critiques of Asian American studies. Their distortions, marginalizations, and/or erasures by and within Asian American intellectual and political formations—via imperialist "forgetting" or settler-colonial absorption—compel any Asian American feminist politics to center its perspectives in generating a truly liberatory praxis. Centering those historically and systemically marginalized or erased as knowing subjects is a key methodological and epistemological principle of Women of Color feminisms. This requires us to consider not only who is present in our circles of solidarity but also who is absent and why. Although we did reach out to, and invite contributions from, Arab American and non-Hawaiian Pacific Islander scholars, their absence from our collection nevertheless evidences our own complicity in the institutionalized marginalization of their scholarship. Whom did we not know to invite? What ways of relating in and beyond the academy construct this ignorance? Their absence also evidences the enormous weight these already marginalized scholar-activists bear in the struggle to exist in the face of poor infrastructural academic support and aggressive targeting by US empire and its ongoing commitments to settler colonialism. For example, the persistent barrage of right-wing Zionist attacks by organizations like Lawfare Project informs the absence of Rabab Ibrahim Abdulhadi, professor and chair of Arab and Muslim Ethnicities Diasporas (AMED) at San Francisco State University, from this collection. Professor Abdulhadi's absence from our collection is thus inextricable from daily on-the-ground struggles for Palestinian rights to exist against aggressive US-backed Israeli settler colonialism. The US academic ouster of Steven Salaita further demonstrates in no uncertain terms the targeting of Palestinian Americans who dare speak against the US-backed Israeli occupation of Palestine and the genocide of their peoples. The enormous toll these battles for existence claim on one's well-being cannot be overstated. We must be accountable for the ways the genocidal logics of settler colonialism are inextricable from what Boaventura de Sousa Santos calls "epistemicide": the derailing, silencing or other destruction of Indigenous knowledges, memories, and relations to other cultures (Santos 2016, 18). We hope this collection breaks ground in building a robust and outspoken Asian American feminist praxis that commits unequivocally to the struggle for Palestinian and all Indigenous self-determination. Such commitments are the roots of US Third World and Women of Color feminist politics.

READING ROUTES: MAPPING MULTIPLE
CONCEPTUAL CONSTELLATIONS

We organized the twelve chapters into five possible constellations that emerge at the intersection of Asian American feminist engagement with Women of Color coalition politics. This mapping of the chapters offers one of multiple routes for reading the chapters in relation to each other. Each part title invokes a concept, methodology, or epistemic principle central to Women of Color feminist scholarship.

Part 1, "Re-membering Our Present: Asian American Genealogies in the Emergence of Women of Color Formations," invokes M. Jacqui Alexander's concept of "re-membering" as a Women of Color feminist methodology that resurges genealogies to expand our historical ground and give voice to yearnings for a large sense of a resistant self in community. Judy Wu and

Grace Kyungwon Hong enact this methodology of "re-membering" Asian American feminist participation in the early formations of Women of Color politics. In doing so, they open possibilities for how we might imagine Asian American feminist horizons of liberation as deeply tied to an anti-imperial, cross-racial, and anticapitalist coalitional consciousness.

Wu's and Hong's projects of "re-membering" Asian American feminist participation in Women of Color political genealogies ground the intimate politics of Tom Sarmiento's and erin Khuê Ninh's explorations of Asian American feminist ways of knowing, being, and desiring. In part 2, "Erotic (Dis)Connections: Epistemologies of Asian American Sexual Politics," both Ninh and Sarmiento foreground the ontological and epistemological dimensions of Asian American intersubjectivity shaped by the heteropatriarchal forces of neocolonialism and racism. Their chapters center modes of desiring that Asian American women and queer subjects manifest to interrogate avenues for understanding and undoing self-destructive logics of (neo)colonialism and its racial projects. As such, they enact a central Women of Color methodology that emphasizes how different understandings of our self emerge through what Audre Lorde calls "erotic knowledge"—"our deepest and nonrational knowledge" (Lorde 1981, 53).

The decolonial refusal to enact an Asian American feminist subjectivity that remains complicit in (neo)colonial and white supremacist logics, especially settler-colonial logics, is the Women of Color methodological principle organizing part 3. In "Decolonial Investments: Centering Indigeneity and Orienting against Settler Complicities," we hold Asian American feminisms accountable to tensions between Asian American settler colonialism and dialogues with Pacific Islander feminisms. The chapters in this part outline and enact concrete methodologies for an Asian American feminist praxis that invests in a decolonial refusal to think and act in complicity with settler-colonial logics. Lani Teves and Maile Arvin generously elaborate the violence that Asian Americans enact when they absorb Pacific Islanders into their organizational, intellectual, and political projects with disregard for their settler-colonial complicities in Pacific Islander oppressions and erasures. Tamsin Kimoto and Sunera Thobani offer analyses and methodologies for doing Asian American and Asian Canadian feminism that heed Teves's and Arvin's call to accountability.

The "re-membering" enacted in part 1 includes Asian American feminist challenges to coloniality's framing of the "civilized West" against the "backward East" in the revaluing of the Asian woman as symbolic warrior of decolonizing nations. This revaluation is a central epistemic shift enacted by Women of Color coalition politics in its stand against the demonization or dismissal of non-Western ways of knowing. In part 4, "Beyond 'Culture Clash' Reductions: Organizing against State and Interpersonal Violence," Priya Kandaswamy, Gina Velasco, and Ma Vang challenge the ways the Asian-Backward/US-Progressive binary silences or erases the nuances of Asian/American and Asian refugee complexities. Re-seeing these subjects beyond these "culture clash" reductions, they argue, is crucial to generating an Asian American feminist praxis that centers the non-English-speaking Hmong refugee, the Filipina migrant worker, or the pregnant unmarried Indian American woman as agentic subjects of knowledge in the struggle to end state and interpersonal violence endemic to US empire.

In part 5, "Incommensurability and (In)Visibility: Theorizing an Asian American Feminist Praxis," Lynn Fujiwara and Shireen Roshanravan center Women of Color coalitional politics as a way to forefront accountability for power differentials animated by the incommensurability among those with whom we seek solidarity. Both Fujiwara and Roshanravan dwell in Asian American moments of (unwitting) complicity in the harms perpetrated against Asian refugee/migrant and Black communities to identify and motivate the political consciousness necessary to enacting expansive coalitions. This last part thus returns to a Women of Color politics of "remembering" and its call to *practice* the expansion of our political sense of selves in relation to those with whom we became, and are becoming, Asian American feminists.

We encourage the reader to explore the various conceptual constellations that may emerge when the chapters are read along routes different from the one we offer above. The chapters in this book could easily be read through other critical logics or political threads. For example, different modes of problematizing the conceptualizations of "home" in Asian American feminist theorizing emerge when reading across the chapters by Stephani Nohelani Teves and Maile Arvin, Tamsin Kimoto, and Sunera Thobani. While Teves and Arvin reaffirm Oceana as home to Indigenous Pacific Islanders and Kimoto questions the meaning of home for Asian Americans, Thobani exposes immigrant resistance movements that unquestioningly struggle for inclusion (*home*) into the Canadian nation-state as complicit with the dispossession and genocide of Indigenous peoples. Centering settler colonialism and reaffirming existing critiques of Asian American scholars who incorrectly subsume Pacific Islander interests, Teves and Arvin actively "dislodge the perceived affinities of the Asian and Pacific Islander racial category" in their chapter "Decolonizing API: Centering Indigenous

Pacific Islander Feminism." To be clear, they state, "The acronym *API* fore-closes genuine possibilities for allyship by erasing differences between and among Asian Americans and Pacific Islanders," marginalizing Indigenous struggles under an Asian American politics. Oceania, while a space of mul-tiple overlapping sites of colonization, has been and always will be the cul-tural and organizing force of Pacific Islander communities. "Oceania is more than a Magellanic space of transit," not a shore for strangers to arrive on. Asian Americans residing in the Pacific Islands are settler colonials as are other nonindigenous peoples; they do not get to claim Hawaiʻi as their *home*. Foregrounding Pacific Islander feminisms, Teves and Arvin decol-onize "API" by mapping out the historical, political, and geographical differences between Pacific Islanders and Asian Americans; they present a series of concrete recommendations for Asian American feminists to consciously practice solidarity with Pacific Islander politics. As Native Hawaiian feminist intellectuals working within Pacific Islander feminist collectives, they provide this list of recommendations based on their political, personal, and intellectual experiences. It is a sharply written, pointed approach that intentionally ignites the very emotional stakes for Asian American feminists hearing the ways they may have been complicit in Pacific Islander erasure.

Tamsin Kimoto and Sunera Thobani attempt to do the work that Teves and Arvin call out, recommending that Asian American feminists be con-scious and accountable to Indigenous politics. Growing up in Hawaiʻi as an Asian American settler colonial, Tamsin Kimoto begins their chapter, "Becoming Restive: Orientations in Asian American Feminist Theory and Praxis," with an auto-ethnographic politics of questioning *home*. Work-ing through their own accountability to Indigenous struggles for self-determination and the contradictory positionality of Asian Americans as settlers-of-color, Kimoto suggests that Asian American feminists adopt a restive orientation in practicing several of the recommendations set forth by Teves and Arvin. Kimoto's theoretical intervention of restive orientation "allows us to think in two directions simultaneously: to unsettle the place one is in while also remaining on the move toward another place and to remain in a certain place while unsettling that toward which one is ori-ented." By adopting a restive orientation, then, Asian American feminists take up the call to disrupt settler-colonial logics in a reorientation of notions of home and place before attempting to work toward liberation alongside Indigenous peoples.

In "Navigating Colonial Pitfalls: Race, Citizenship and the Politics of 'South Asian Canadian' Paradigms," Sunera Thobani enacts dimensions of Kimoto's restive orientation as she works through a South Asian Canadian feminism that interrogates the importance of home, belonging, and rights for Muslims in post-9/11 anti-Muslim movements in North America. She argues that the configuration *South Asian Canadian* has yet to come to terms with the colonial logic of power that is foundational to North America in its settler formulation and its relation to the making of "South Asia" as a colonial/imperial formation. At the core of her analysis are the workings of gender and sexual violence that shaped the dispossession of Indigenous peoples and the erasure of this genocidal violence in the nation's foundation in contemporary South Asian feminist activism against racial, gendered, and sexual violence of South Asian women. Because South Asian resistance movements have privileged citizenship over interrogation of the violence entailed in the sovereignty organized by the state, the politics articulated in the "South Asian Canadian" paradigm have been unable to challenge the dehumanization of the Muslim figure.

Filipinx American scholars echo the political and intellectual distinctions between Asian American and Pacific Islander feminisms established by Teves and Arvin. In their chapters, Thomas X. Sarmiento and Gina Velasco critique the lack of political specificity in Asian American feminist studies to adequately capture the undercurrents of Filipina and Filipina queer context that speak not to a connection with Asia but rather to a neocolonial Philippines. In "Peminist and Queer Affiliation in Literature as a Blueprint for Filipinx Decolonization and Liberation," Sarmiento theorizes a decolonial queer *peminist* framework that engages the complexity of Filipinx diasporic literature through Jessica Hagedorn's oft-cited *Dogeaters* and *Gangster of Love*. To analyze the possibilities for queer women of color solidarities among Hagedorn's characters, he utilizes *peminisms* as defined by Melinda de Jesús: "A specific form of feminist theory rooted in the *Filipina American* experience—an experience very different from the implicit (and thus explicit) subject of white liberal feminism"—that "describes Filipina American struggles against racism, sexism, imperialism, and homophobia and struggles for decolonization, consciousness, and liberation" (de Jesus 2005, 5). Contextualizing the historical marginalization of Filipina/o American studies within Asian American studies, his reading of Hagedorn through a peminist lens amplifies the complexities of decolonial queer Filipinx subjectivity in the Philippine American global context. Sarmiento makes clear that "while peminism stands in solidarity with Asian American and Women of Color feminisms more broadly, to not make space for the particularities of diasporic Filipina/x experience reinforces structural inequality within subjugated populations, which of course is an extension of colonial domination." Sarmiento's peminism reads queer-hetero relationships within Hagedorn's stories as imaginative ways for enacting peminist and queer affiliation. In tending to a Women of Color coalitional politics, he highlights the peminist-queer coalitional politics that Hagedorn's novels promote as an alternative to postcolonial Filipinx nationalism.

Gina Velasco shifts from the realm of diasporic literature to the globalized circuits of Filipina migrant labor to further unpack layers of the uneasy inclusion of Filipina/o Americans into the project of Asian America. The violent colonization of the Philippines by US finance capital and militarization, supplanted by neoliberal neocolonial interdependencies, resulted in distinctive experiences for Filipinx living, working, and resisting in the imperial center. In her chapter, "Negotiating Legacies: The 'Traffic in Women' and the Politics of Filipina/o American Feminist Solidarity," she calls for a Filipina/o diasporic feminist approach that centers the nation-state, globalization, and transnational labor to capture the complexity of Filipina migrant workers surviving and mobilizing in the United States. Drawing from global economic feminist approaches that center US empire and neoliberal forces that shape global inequality and service sector work—or as Pierrette Hondagneu-Sotelo puts it, "domestic apartheid" (2001)—Velasco critiques feminist resistance efforts that rely on sexual morality. To challenge trafficking narratives overly reliant on sexual exploitation and victimization, she argues that a Woman of Color coalitional politics of solidarity must engage the manifestations of empire and global economic politics to establish a diasporic Filipina/o feminist solidarity accountable to the transnational inequities engendered from neoliberalism. Given Filipina American feminists' positionality to US imperialism and neoliberalism, her concern is how a Filipina American feminist can be in solidarity with Filipina diasporic feminists in struggles for workers' rights for Filipina migrant women. According to Velasco, Filipina and Asian American feminisms must move beyond notions of exclusion/inclusion and incorporate US imperialism and colonization as queer, race, and sexualized projects that shape the political realities for Third World women workers.

Reading Sarmiento and Velasco's chapters together also reflects generative differences in their respective theorizing of how sexuality functions in a Filipina/x American feminist praxis of solidarity. For Velasco, the axis of sexuality functions prominently in its heteropatriarchal iterations to advance a morality discourse that hinders, rather than advances, more expansive transnational feminist solidarities between Filipina American and Filipina migrant women. By distinction, Sarmiento's intervention lies in a retheorizing of queerness as primary for solidarity and inherently inseparable from other identity locations where *peminisms* captures the multiplicity of identity and centrality of sexuality for neocolonial subjects. Considering these two frameworks together leads us to ask: How do we generate an on-the-ground praxis that simultaneously fosters the possibilities of a boundary-crossing queer affiliation of *peminism* that also challenges the impact of neocolonial mandates for a heteronormative morality as the salve for postcolonial struggles? How have sexuality studies impacted Asian American feminisms, and how can we situate sexuality more centrally?

Chapter author erin Khuê Ninh amplifies this question by boldly asking whether and how Asian American women can speak, know, and enact our own desires when model-minority logics infiltrate cultural imperatives to produce us as subjects wired to always please others. In "Without Enhancements: Sexual Violence in the Everyday Lives of Asian American Women" she writes, "What is consent for a subject whose algorithm for all things is to identify and meet the standards set by others? For whom the question of yes or no has been ontologically supplanted by the question of success or failure?" Answering these questions, Ninh explains, requires acknowledging how our internalization of racist values organizing the model-minority racial project produces us as desiring subjects whose core understandings of worth and success orient us to desire, first and foremost, the fulfillment of other people's directives. Following M. Jacqui Alexander, she compels us to ask: How have we assimilated alienation (Alexander 2002, 96)? For Ninh, then, an Asian American feminist praxis that effectively addresses the date rape, sexual harassment, and abuse experienced every day by Asian American women must foreground the epistemological and ontological question of what it means for us to "present sexually." Dismissing the model-minority racial project as a state-imposed racist myth with no impact on our subject formation *as Asian Americans* consigns us to modes of desiring self-abnegation rather our own well-being.

Ninh's chapter speaks to the collection's mission to explore the complexities of an Asian American feminist resistance that communicates our specific loci of struggle and projects of self-creation without reinforcing the racist and heteropatriarchal logics of the model-minority racial project. This requires grappling with the model-minority racial project as it shapes

possibilities integral to politically redefining our Asian American subjectivity as expansively coalitional. Shireen Roshanravan joins Ninh in the
assertion that an Asian American feminism must grapple with the model-
minority racial project as more than an externally imposed racist myth in
need of debunking through public testimony of the different ways Asian/
Americans are also oppressed racial minorities. In her chapter, "Weapon-
izing Our (In)Visibility: Asian American Feminist Ruptures of the Model-
Minority Optic," Roshanravan argues that we must foreground a politics
of accountability to the ways we have internalized and reinforced the racist
optic of our racial construction as "the model minority." Drawing on the
lessons of coalitional genealogies of Asian American resistance from Yuri
Kochiyama and Grace Lee Boggs to the contemporary Asians4BlackLives
campaigns, she suggests that any Asian American feminist project of visibility must negotiate the racist model-minority optic and the communicative barriers imposed by the model-minority racial project toward
cross-racial coalition. Accordingly, Roshanravan concludes that a Women
of Color feminist project of Asian American visibility bears a *coalitional
imperative* to disrupt the anti-Black and heteropatriarchal insular logics of
the model-minority racist optic. This coalitional imperative does not seek
public visibility and recognition by the racial state but rather invests in
horizontal coalitional communication of cross-racial solidarity with those
against whom we have been racialized.

While Yuri Kochiyama and Grace Lee Boggs are perhaps two of the
better-known Asian American activists who committed their life's work to
cross-racial solidarity, Judy Wu and Grace Hong shore up genealogies of
Asian American feminist commitments to cross-racial solidarity that were
integral to early Women of Color political formations. These re-memberings
of Asian American participation in early Women of Color political formations provide the ground for imagining an Asian American feminist political subjectivity rooted in, and routed through, a consciousness of the
interdependence of all oppressions and possibilities for liberation. Wu's re-
membering includes highlighting the importance of Japanese American
Patsy Mink, the first woman of color US legislator, in what we would call
"liberal feminist" efforts to pass legislation that would guarantee equal educational opportunities for girls/women and paid child care for working
mothers. While Roshanravan suggests that Asian American feminist visibility oriented toward inclusion in state politics cannot communicate the
coalitional imperative of Women of Color feminist politics, Wu argues for
the importance of Asian American feminist visibility in all political realms,

including those aimed at liberal reforms and state inclusion. Doing so, she notes, embraces the principle of multiplicity at the heart of what Chela Sandoval (2000) calls the "differential consciousness" of US Third World feminist methodology. Reading Wu and Roshanravan together thus moves us to ask: How does an Asian American feminist praxis enact the "differential" mode of embracing multiple resistant tactics and strategies against oppression while being accountable to the racist US state's selective absorption of us as weapons against Indigenous and Black-led movements for self-determination?

Lynn Fujiwara and Grace Hong amplify Wu's invocation of the importance of Women of Color methodological emphasis on multiplicity in their formulations of an Asian American feminist intervention in shaping a politics of solidarity attentive to the heterogeneous loci of struggle constitutive of Asian America. While Judy Wu's concept of "radical Orientalism" situates the "Asian woman" as the radical symbol of liberation and inspiration for US Third World liberation politics, Fujiwara theorizes the ways such associations, even in their radical articulations of solidarity, can dismiss the specific geo- and body politics of Asian American struggle and epistemic resistance. In "Multiplicity, Women of Color Politics, and an Asian American Feminist Praxis," Fujiwara identifies such a dismissal of her own loci of struggle as a third-generation Asian American US Woman of Color in a journal reviewer's painful comments labeling her honest reflections on a methodological misstep in an early approach to interviewing refugee and migrant women as "unforgivable." Through an auto-ethnographic theorizing of her politics of location, Fujiwara reworks Lisa Lowe's foundational theorizing of "multiplicity" to challenge this dismissal and instead outline a conceptual framework that "strives for coalitional formations with accountability to differing, conflicted, and incommensurable positionalities." She thus offers the conceptual framework of "multiplicity" as a way of illuminating the factors informing her methodological misstep in an attempt to do research aimed at advancing social justice agendas centering the struggles facing Asian migrant and refugee women. Central to this framework is an understanding of the need to engage the tensions emerging from our encounters with the incommensurabilities ever present in the vast heterogeneity of Asian America. Doing so, Fujiwara argues, allows us to access crucial sites of resistant knowledge formation that carry the potential to expand our resistant self-understandings as interdependent with those differently located but nevertheless bound to our possibilities for a violence-free world.

Grace Hong historicizes Fujiwara's methodological emphasis on a politics of solidarity routed through an engagement of incommensurable differences, rather than through their erasure, in her chapter, "Intersectionality and Incommensurability: Third World Feminism and Asian Decolonization." Drawing on the archived issues of the Third World Women's Alliance newsletter, *Triple Jeopardy*, and interviews with former members, Hong demonstrates how "the role of Asian American women in the organization reveals an ethos of multiplicity, heterogeneity, and juxtaposition that challenges us to recognize the alternative, relational analytic of comparison also produced by this organization." In dialogue with Judy Wu, Hong theorizes how Asian and Asian American women participating in Third World liberation movements motivated differential logics of coalitional identification. While the symbol of the Asian woman, animated as symbol of an anti-imperialist internationalist politics, inspired an identification based on a sense of commonality, the Asian American women who chose to identify with the Third World Women's Alliance reveal a politics of identification motivated by the incommensurable differences encountered in the organization. As Hong underscores in her interview with Christina Choy, one of the few Asian American members of the Third World Women's Alliance, the decision to identify in coalition with Puerto Rican and Black women was born of specific structures of violence that shaped Choy's Asian American genealogy. Her attraction to the Women of Color political formation was born not of a sense of sameness as much as a shared sense of the complexity of interdependent multiple oppressions. Like Fujiwara, Hong illuminates how the Third World Women's Alliance, and the politics of intersectionality it advanced, relied on a willingness to interrogate difference and incommensurability as they manifested politically among members of their organization. Fujiwara and Hong thus amplify Wu's emphasis on multiplicity as an Asian American feminist methodological commitment by underscoring how the radical coalitional politics that is the hallmark of Women of Color feminist praxis commits to engaging incommensurabilities and grappling with tensions that arise even among those we may presume to share our perspectives or modes of reading power.

Engaging rather than dismissing or assimilating incommensurable differences is also a central component of decolonial feminist praxis that allows the centering of Women of Color frameworks otherwise denied by the colonial mono-logic of Eurocentrism. In "The Language of Care: Hmong Refugee Activism and a Feminist Refugee Epistemology," Ma Vang uses an "ethnography of care" to illustrate the life-saving potential of an Asian American feminist praxis that engages the incommensurable non-Western refugee worldviews lived through languages Indigenous to refugee home-lands. She documents the work of Hmong refugee activist Moua, and her founding of Partners in Healing in Merced, California, to navigate the gaps in care between social welfare and medical institutions and the local Hmong refugee community. Vang shows the decolonial epistemic commitments of Moua's work to center Hmong refugees as knowing subjects whose world-views offer more effective and revolutionary modalities of care that "empha-size the importance of social relationships to counter individualized notions of care." The Hmong language in this refugee activism and the worldviews it illuminates cease to be "barriers" to Hmong access to health-care and instead become the bridge to accessing care that is not about man-agement but rather about honoring Hmong refugee ways of being well in the world.

Vang thus joins Fujiwara in exploring the communicative politics of an Asian American feminism that centers the perspectives of Asian/American refugee communities and the violence they endure at the hands of the very US institutions heralded by the state as agencies of care. Priya Kandaswamy extends this analysis to the case of Purvi Patel, a twenty-three-year-old Indian American woman charged in 2015 in the state of Indiana with feti-cide and neglect of a dependent for what the state determined to be the ter-mination of her pregnancy. In this case involving the first woman to ever be convicted of feticide for self-induced abortion, pro-choice feminist activ-ists mobilized to advance their efforts against legal restrictions on abor-tion. Kandaswamy challenges these "pro-choice" rallying cries on behalf of Patel and instead elaborates an Asian American feminist lens through which to read Patel's criminalization as inextricable from medical and legal realms of institutional violence. Instead of presuming, as news coverage of her case did, that Patel's "decision" to terminate her pregnancy was due to a presum-ably "backward" heteropatriarchal Hindu culture that forbade sex before marriage, Kandaswamy traces the relation between the economic and social vulnerabilities Indian and other Asian immigrant communities endure because of racist and xenophobic state laws and Patel's sense of her restricted options for self-care. In dialogue with Ninh, Kandswamy argues for an Asian American feminist lens that would make sense of Patel's actions in terms of the racist state's impact on her subject formation within an immi-grant community struggling to be well. She insists that such a lens must link the "racist stereotypes of Asian women as deceptive, manipulative, and inconceivably foreign" that contributed to Patel's criminalization with the hypercriminalization of Black women and the mass incarceration of their communities. If we are to address all the dimensions of violence that shaped the circumstances of Patel's story, Kandaswamy contends, we must mobilize an Asian American feminist praxis that seeks to forge new subjectivities while confronting the state violence that both targets Asian/American communities and solicits our complicity in state-sanctioned violence against other communities of color.

ON THE POLITICS OF LIMITATIONS, PARTIAL BEGINNINGS, AND EXTENDED INVITATIONS

The politics of anthology making involves confronting and negotiating limits—word limits, resource limits, and time limits but also, and most importantly, the limits of our own perspectives, knowledges, and locations in relation to the heterogeneous communities of struggle to whom we seek accountability in elaborating an Asian American feminist politics. This edited collection, like all collections, is a partial and limited effort to begin what we hope will be a sustained intellectual and political commitment to grow the theoretical groundings of an Asian American feminist praxis that animates Women of Color coalition politics. We stand ready to do the work necessary to address the limits of this collection as we attempt to live the politics we theorize. In the meantime, we offer you this partial beginning as an invitation to join us in forging a fierce feminist and decolonial defiance of the presumed compliance, silence, and complicity imposed on Asian Americans.

REFERENCES

Alexander, Jacqui M. 2002. "Remembering This Bridge, Remembering Ourselves: Yearning, Memory, and Desire." In *This Bridge We Call Home: Radical Vision for Transformation*, edited by Gloria Anzaldúa and Analouise Keating. New York: Routledge.

Alexander, Jacqui M., and Chandra Talpade Mohanty. 2012. "Cartographies of Knowledge and Power: Transnational Feminism as Radical Praxis." In *Critical Transnational Feminist Praxis*, edited by Amanda Lock Swarr and Richa Nagaar. New York: SUNY Press.

Arredondo, Gabriela F. 2003. *Chicana Feminisms: A Critical Reader*. Durham, NC: Duke University Press.

Asian Women United of California. 1989. *Making Waves: An Anthology of Writing by and about Asian American Women*. Boston: Beacon Press.

Choy, Catherine Ceneza. 2003. *Empire of Care: Nursing and Migration in Filipino American History*. Durham, NC: Duke University Press.

Crenshaw, Kimberlé. 1991. "Mapping the Margins: Intersectionality, Identity Politics, and Violence against Women of Color." *Stanford Law Review* 43 (6): 1241–99.

Critical Resistance and Incite! Women of Color against Violence. 2016. "INCITE! Women of Color against Violence." In *Color of Violence: The Incite! Anthology*. Durham, NC: Duke University Press.

de Jesús, Melinda L. 2005. "Introduction: Toward a Peminist Theory, or Theorizing the Filipina/American Experience." In *Pinay Power: Peminist Critical Theory: Theorizing the Filipina/American Experience*. New York: Routledge.

Diaz, Vicente M. 2004. "To 'P' or Not to 'P'?: Marking the Territory between Pacific Islander and Asian American Studies." *Journal of Asian American Studies* 7 (3): 183–208.

Espiritu, Yên Lê. 1997. *Asian American Women and Men: Labor, Laws and Love*. Thousand Oaks, CA: Sage Publications.

Fujikane, Candace, and Jonathan Okamura. 2008. *Asian Settler Colonialism: From Local Governance to the Habits of Everyday Life in Hawai'i*. Honolulu: University of Hawai'i Press.

Glenn, Evelyn Nakano. 2002. *Unequal Freedom: How Race and Gender Shaped American Citizenship and Labor*. Cambridge, MA: Harvard University Press.

Gopinath, Gayatri. 2005. *Impossible Desires: Queer Diasporas and South Asian Public Cultures*. Durham, NC: Duke University Press.

Hall, Lisa Kahaleole. 2008. "Strategies of Erasure: U.S. Colonialism and Native Hawaiian Feminism." *American Quarterly* 60 (2): 273–80.

Hondagneu-Sotelo, Pierrette. 2001. *Doméstica : Immigrant Workers Cleaning and Caring in the Shadows of Affluence*. Berkeley: University of California Press.

Hong, Grace Kyungwon. 2006. *The Ruptures of American Capital: Women of Color Feminism and the Culture of Immigrant Labor*. Minneapolis: University of Minnesota Press.

———. 2015. *Death beyond Disavowal: The Impossible Politics of Difference*. Minneapolis: University of Minnesota Press.

Hune, S., and Gail M. Nomura, eds. 2003. *Asian/Pacific Islander American Women: A Historical Anthology*. New York: New York University Press.

Kang, Laura Hyun Yi. 2002. *Compositional Subjects: Enfiguring Asian/American Women*. Durham, NC: Duke University Press.

Kauanui, J. Kēhaulani. 2005. "Asian American Studies and the Pacific Question." In *Asian American Studies after Critical Mass*, edited by Kent Ono, 123–43. New Jersey: Wiley Blackwell.

Kim, Claire Jean. 2004. "Asian Americans Are People of Color, Too . . . Aren't They? Cross-Racial Alliances and the Question of Asian American Political Identity." *AAPI Nexus: Policy, Practice and Community* 2 (1): 19–47.

Kim, Elaine H., Lilia V. Villanueva, and Asian Women United of California, eds. 1997. *Making More Waves: New Writing by Asian American Women*. Boston: Beacon Press.

Lim, Shirley, and Mayumi Tsutakawa, eds. 1989. *The Forbidden Stitch: An Asian American Women's Anthology*. Corvallis, OR: Calyx Books.

Lorde, Audre. 1981. *Uses of the Erotic: The Erotic as Power*. Tucson, AZ: Kore Press.

Lowe, Lisa. 1996. *Immigrant Acts: On Asian American Cultural Politics*. Durham, NC: Duke University Press.

Matsumoto, Valerie J. 2014. *City Girls: The Nisei Social World in Los Angeles, 1920–1950*. Oxford: Oxford University Press.

Minh-ha, Trinh T. 1989. *Woman, Native, Other: Writing Postcoloniality and Feminism*. Bloomington: Indiana University Press.

Mohanty, Chandra Talpade. 2003. *Feminism without Borders: Decolonizing Theory, Practicing Solidarity*. Durham, NC: Duke University Press.

Moraga, Cherríe, and Gloria Anzaldúa, eds. 1981. *This Bridge Called My Back: Writings by Radical Women of Color*. New York: Kitchen Table Press.

Parreñas, Rhacel Salazar. 2001. *Servants of Globalization: Women, Migration and Domestic Work*, Stanford, CA: Stanford University Press.

Puar, Jasbir K. 2007. *Terrorist Assemblages: Homonationalism in Queer Times*. Durham, NC: Duke University Press.

Sandoval, Chela. 2000. *Methodology of the Oppressed*. Minneapolis: University of Minnesota Press.

Santos, Boaventura de Sousa. 2016. *Epistemologies of the South: Justice against Epistemicide*. London: Routledge.

Shah, S. 1997. *Dragon Ladies: Asian American Feminists Breathe Fire*. Boston: South End Press.

Takagi, Dana Y. 1994. Maiden Voyage: Excursion into Sexuality and Identity Politics in Asian America." *Amerasia Journal* 20 (1): 1–17.

Võ, Linda Trinh, and Marian Sciachitano, eds. 2004. *Asian American Women: The Frontiers Reader*. Lincoln: University of Nebraska Press.

Wong, Sau-Ling C. 1995. "Denationalization Reconsidered: Asian American Cultural Criticism at a Theoretical Crossroads." *Amerasia Journal* 21 (1–2): 1–27.

Yamada, Mitsuye. 1981. "Invisibility Is an Unnatural Disaster: Reflections of an Asian American Woman." In Moraga and Anzaldúa, *This Bridge Called My Back: Writings by Radical Women of Color*, 35–40.

Yung, Judy. 1995. *Unbound Feet: A Social History of Chinese Women in San Francisco*. Berkeley: University of California Press.

PART ONE

RE-MEMBERING
OUR PRESENT

Asian American Genealogies in the Emergence

of Women of Color Formations

CHAPTER 1

INTERSECTIONALITY AND INCOMMENSURABILITY

Third World Feminism and Asian Decolonization

GRACE KYUNGWON HONG

THIS CHAPTER EXAMINES ACTIVIST ENGAGEMENTS WITH ASIAN American communities along with the importance of the figure of the Asian woman freedom fighter in the New York chapter of the Third World Women's Alliance (TWWA). TWWA, an organization formed in 1971, brought together Black, Puerto Rican, and Asian women in socialist anti-imperialist solidarity projects. Through readings of the TWWA periodical *Triple Jeopardy*, an interview with TWWA member Christine Choy, and analyses of archival materials from TWWA organizational records, I trace the role and representation of Asian women in this early Third World women's organization so as to reflect on the possibilities and limits of leftist Third World solidarity politics. *Triple Jeopardy* expressed a deeply internationalist Third World solidarity that highlighted US imperialism and connected it to state violence in the United States. While the group often mobilized a logic of commensuration in which the Third World was imagined as connected via imperialism, a logic advanced by their investment in the figure of the Asian woman freedom fighter in the pages of *Triple Jeopardy*, an analysis of the role of Asian American women in the organization reveals an ethos of multiplicity, heterogeneity, and juxtaposition that challenges us to recognize the alternative, relational analytic of comparison also produced by this organization. In so doing, they mobilized a variety of analyses and critiques so as to challenge the various mechanisms of capitalism and imperialism. TWWA connected a Black radical internationalist tradition with a feminist analysis, a potent combination that enabled them to produce a complex and contradictory definition of solidarity based on both a narrative of unity and one that took seriously the differences, inequalities, and hierarchies between and within racialized groups and anti-imperialist histories. Examining TWWA in this way suggests that feminist organizations provided new and different analytics of comparison, and also provides an analytic to apprehend latent or unrecognized analytics of incommensurability as inherent to Third Worldist internationalist politics as a whole.

At the heart of these analytics and tactics is the idea of founding movements *on* rather than *in spite of* difference, an idea that many have observed is foundational to US Women of Color feminism. Women of Color feminists' theorizations of what Kimberlé Crenshaw has termed "intersectionality" are profoundly relational and comparative, connecting power relations on seemingly disparate scales and registers (Crenshaw 1989). That is, the complexities of race, gender, and sexuality meant the persistence of hierarchies of power within racial groups, even within antiracist, decolonizing movements. As such, intersectionality meant challenging the ideas that communities are brought together by commonality and that identification is the only or even the primary basis for collectivity. Intersectional feminist practice engaged the affective and interpersonal relations within movements, relations where power relations are both replicated and contested. Women of Color activists, writers, and artists have developed an analytic of difference that became the foundation for their relationships within movements. They have addressed the ways languages of struggle did not, and still do not, translate across geographical contexts and historical trajectories, but asserted that solidarity and coalition could still be based on, rather than built in spite of, these incommensurabilities.

TWWA began through discussions in the New York chapter of the Student Nonviolent Coordinating Committee (SNCC), through the efforts of co-founder Frances Beal. A lifelong activist and icon of Black and Third World feminism, Beal is perhaps best known for her foundational essay "Double Jeopardy: To Be Black and Female," which was originally published as a pamphlet in 1969, and then included in Toni Cade's groundbreaking anthology *The Black Woman* as well as Robin Morgan's *Sisterhood Is Powerful*, both published in 1970 (Beal 1970a, 1970b). During the period in which she worked with SNCC and established TWWA, Beal worked at the National

Council for Negro Women. She later moved to the San Francisco Bay Area and worked as a journalist and associate editor of *The Black Scholar* (Beal 2005, preface). Beal recounts that the politicized space of SNCC allowed Black women to begin to theorize their concerns as structural rather than individual (Beal 2005, 35). At the same time, she recounts, some male members of SNCC started to gravitate toward the Nation of Islam and started "talking abortion was genocide" (Beal 2005, 36). Having almost died herself because of an illegal abortion that she underwent at the age of seventeen and profoundly affected by other Black women who had likewise suffered, Beal pushed back, along with others, and in 1968, SNCC voted to create a Black Women's Liberation Committee to investigate "the conditions under which black women function" (Beal 2005, 27, 37).

By 1970, a number of women who had no affiliation to SNCC had joined them, and they became an independent organization, changing their name to the Black Women's Alliance. Beal recounts that they focused on reproductive rights, connecting abortion rights to sterilization abuse, which seriously affected Puerto Rican women (Beal 2005, 37). As such, their efforts around reproductive justice were not simply confined to abortion, unlike mainstream white feminist reproductive rights discourses; instead, they were actually one of the earliest feminist organizations to address sterilization abuse against Women of Color. In 1971, perhaps inspired by this focus, a group of Puerto Rican women approached them, asking to join, and they became the Third World Women's Alliance.

In 1971, one of the New York TWWA members, Cheryl Perry (then Cheryl Johnson), moved to the Bay Area and started a chapter there (Burnham 2005, 19). In the early 1980s, the Bay Area chapter transformed into the Alliance against Women's Oppression (AAWO), allowed white women to join, and focused on women's reproductive rights, women's health, and welfare (Burnham 2005, 24).[1] AAWO dissolved in 1989, and member Linda Burnham, whom Johnson had recruited to TWWA, went on to found the Women of Color Resource Center in 1990 (Burnham 2005, 30). The archival record for the New York and Bay Area chapters is uneven, with documentary evidence from the New York chapter consisting mainly of issues of its periodical, *Triple Jeopardy*. More of the Bay Area chapter's organizational records survived because they were archived at the Women of Color Resource Center until it closed in 2011; the records were then donated to the Sophia Smith Collection at Smith College.

As Judy Wu observes in her essay in this volume, the role of Asian and Asian American women in Women of Color feminist politics has been underexamined in the scholarship. We see this tendency in the small but significant literature on TWWA, which has mainly been situated as a Black feminist organization. Historian Stephen Ward rightly points out the important ways in which TWWA originated as a Black Power organization (Ward 2006). Emerging out of SNCC, which by the late 1960s had dropped the *Nonviolent* part of its name in favor of *National*, TWWA's stated concerns overlapped with those of SNCC, including a critique of state violence, both domestically and internationally, a commitment to self-determination, and a willingness to entertain militant imagery and principles, if not as actual tactics. For example, the first issue begins with a discussion of watershed events for Black radical movements: the violent suppression of the Attica prison riot in September of 1971 and the murder of Black Panther political prisoner George Jackson two weeks prior to the Attica prison riot ("Now Attica!!" 1971, 2; "Murder at San Quentin" 1971, 3). While this is certainly true, TWWA demonstrates the capaciousness of Black feminist organizations; they could be both Black feminist and Third World feminist organizations at the same time, because of their radical re-envisioning of Blackness. Advancing the internationalist aspect of Black Power movements, TWWA connected US state violence against domestic populations with imperialist violence all over the world. Further, the organization offered a distinctly Third World feminist analysis, highlighting both the gendered nature of imperialistic ventures and Third World women's importance to anticolonial struggles.

While the small numbers of Asian American women in the era before the 1965 Immigration and Nationality Act meant that Asian representation in the organization was limited, Asian and Asian American women were integral to the organization. In the pages of *Triple Jeopardy*, the New York chapter of TWWA imagined itself as part of a worldwide struggle against imperialism in which Asian anticolonial struggles played a significant role. The Bay Area chapter engaged in a number of activist projects in Asian American communities, including working with United Farm Workers (UFW) and Katipunan ng mga Demokratikong Pilipino (KDP) to help build a facility for retired farmworkers, and participating in an antiwar demonstration organized by the Union of Vietnamese in the United States on Ho Chi Minh's birthday, among many other efforts.[2]

Triple Jeopardy's overall internationalist focus was impressively wide-ranging and comprehensive. During its four-year run, the journal featured stories about women's revolutionary struggles in Puerto Rico, Vietnam, China, North Korea, the Sudan, Ecuador, Mexico, Palestine, Chile, Oman, and many others. According to Beal, connecting US imperialism and militarism abroad with racialized and gendered exploitation and violence domestically was a priority for TWWA; she credits that position to SNCC and the civil rights movement more broadly: "So the very fact that SNCC was breaking through on the international issue, was, I think, a very important contribution that SNCC made to the people's movement as a whole. . . . So I think that was one of the big contributions that the civil rights movement of the '60s eventually made to our understanding of the link between international affairs and domestic affairs" (Beal 2005, 40).

The idealization of Third World women engaged in anticolonial struggles is present everywhere in *Triple Jeopardy*. The anticolonial struggles of women in Asia—in particular, Vietnam, China, and to a lesser extent, North Korea—were prominently featured in issues of *Triple Jeopardy* and were an important part of TWWA's transnational and cross-racial solidarity politics. Indeed, the cover to the inaugural issue of *Triple Jeopardy* featured an illustration of three women of color, featuring front and center a woman in a *qipao*-style dress holding a rifle, an image that could reference both Chinese and Vietnamese revolutionary soldiers. Throughout its run, *Triple Jeopardy* frequently depicted Chinese and Vietnamese women, in particular emphasizing their importance to socialist anticolonial revolutions.

The image of revolutionary Asian women often served as inspiration for US-based feminists, a part of a larger turn toward Asia as an alternative model for radicalism. As Robin Kelley and Betsy Esch observe in their essay "Black Like Mao," for the radical Black movements of the 1960s and 1970s in the United States, the idea of a socialist republic established not by European proletariats, as Marx had declared, but by racialized, formerly colonized, agrarian peoples was immensely inspiring (Kelley and Esch 1999). They write that W. E. B. DuBois's 1959 trip to China convinced him that "China will lead the underdeveloped nations toward socialism," a view shared by many Black radical organizations and individuals (Kelley and Esch 1999, 8). In *Radicals on the Road,* Judy Wu documents a tendency toward what she calls "radical orientalism" among US-based leftist activists (Wu 2013). The perceptions of US leftists like Bob Browne, Eldridge Cleaver, Elaine Brown, Alex Hing, and Pat Sumi, among others, "were refracted through idealized projections of the decolonizing Third World," in particular their romanticization of Vietnamese, Chinese, and North Korean societies that they met in their travels to Asia (Wu 2013, 4). Wu notes that this form of orientalism subverted the hierarchies manifested in classical orientalism as defined by Edward Said, in that US leftists "idealized the East and denigrated the West." Yet, in so doing, radical orientalism maintained the notion of a separation between the two (Wu 2013, 5).

US- and Canada-based feminists were not impervious to radical orientalism. Wu describes the historic Indochinese Women's Conferences (IWC) organized by North American feminists, which brought a delegation of women from North and South Vietnam and Laos to Vancouver and Toronto in April of 1971. While the differing political orientations of the main North American feminist groups organizing the conference led to disagreements and the formation of factions, Wu finds that the North American women were unanimous in their admiration for the Southeast Asian women delegates: "The political leadership of Indochinese women inspired an array of American sisters to combat American militarism and imperialism. . . . The idealization of Southeast Asian women, which was expressed broadly among the North American attendees and not just among Asian Americans, reflects a radical orientalist sensibility" (Wu 2013, 258–59). As Wu notes in her piece in this volume, "The political heroism of women in socialist Asia played a central role in creating Third World feminism in the United States."

The case of TWWA supports Wu's contention. Indeed, TWWA was one of two Third World organizations that the mainly white organizers invited to help organize the IWC. The TWWA did not send representatives to the major planning meeting held in Budapest but did eventually participate in the IWC by organizing with other Third World women (Wu 2013, 224–25). While TWWA's participation in the conference was limited, we can see many of the hallmarks of radical orientalism in *Triple Jeopardy*'s representation of Asian women. In contrast to liberal feminist perspectives on women in Vietnam and other Asian nations as victims requiring saving, *Triple Jeopardy* represented these women as heroes and models, and the United States as a prerevolutionary society in need of tutelage, particularly in terms of gender equality. In a cover-page article called "Puerto Rican Woman Visits China," Geneveva Clemente depicts China as a revolutionary example for a still-colonized Puerto Rico: "While Puerto Rico, a small island in the Caribbean, is still a colony of US imperialism, China is a vast country in Asia with a population of about 800 million people. All over China, women can be seen working alongside men and doing all kinds of jobs" (Clemente 1972, 1). Clemente recounts the advances that Chinese women have made under a Communist regime, including equal pay, access to family planning and abortion, paid maternity leave, socialized child care, and access to traditionally male professions. While Clemente observes some inequities in professions like politics, education, and medicine, she confidently asserts that these conditions are residual and that Chinese society under Communism will eventually eradicate them.

Another article, "Korean Women," which carries no byline and reads much like a North Korean news release, proclaims that under the leadership of Kim Il Sung, "the Korean women have grown up rapidly on the road of revolution. . . . Bringing the revolutionary spirit of self-reliance into full play, the Korean women on the industrial front have made together with the man-comrades important contributions to the rapid development of industrial production" ("Korean Women" 1972, 4). The same issue also features a statement by the Committee for Solidarity with the Korean People that provides the history of Japanese and US imperialism in the Korean peninsula, outlines the official state of war still governing relations between North and South, and likens Korea to Vietnam ("Korea = Vietnam" 1972, 3). A two-page spread, "Filipino Women and the Revolution," centers Filipinas in the movement against "the imposition of martial law by the US-Marcos dictatorship" (Roja 1973, 8).

Unsurprisingly, however, it was Vietnam that was most often referenced. Nearly every issue of *Triple Jeopardy* includes some reference to Vietnam, whether it be a critique of US Third World people's role as cannon fodder in the Vietnam War or an excoriation of US imperialist policy abroad. Most significant were the tributes to Vietnamese women freedom fighters as figures of revolutionary struggle. Two articles exemplify this position. One is a statement by activist Pat Sumi, who, as Wu documents, was part of the Black Panther delegation to China, North Korea, and Vietnam in the summer of 1970 and a central organizer of the IWC (Wu 2013, 186). Sumi writes, "The example of Indochinese and Vietnamese women shows us the way. . . . We must draw on our courage and follow the women of the world in throwing this system onto the rubbish heaps of history" (Sumi 1972, 8). Less than two years after her travels to socialist Asia and just over a year after the influential meetings with Vietnamese and Laotian women at the IWC, Sumi's words register the ways in which "American radicals who protested the war in Southeast Asia sought inspiration and political instruction from Third World socialist leaders" (Wu 2013, 188).

The second is the publication of a speech made by a TWWA representative at a Washington, DC, rally organized by the Peoples Coalition for Peace and Justice. That the speech situates Vietnamese women as role models is manifest in the article's title, "Live Like Her," next to a photograph of a young Vietnamese woman smiling into the camera with a rifle in her hands. The text of the speech proclaims that while "the role of women in liberation struggles has only been questioned here in America . . . [i]n China, Cuba, Vietnam and Guinea-Bissau it is assumed that women are a vital part of the revolution, and that no revolution can be or has been successful without them" ("Live Like Her," n.d., 14). Vietnamese women in particular are "the best example of what the role of women can be in liberation struggles" ("Live Like Her," n.d., 14).

While admiration for revolutionary women was consistent in the pages of *Triple Jeopardy*, we also see complex and sometimes contradictory analyses about the relationship among Third World women in various contexts. On the one hand, it certainly articulated a theory of Third World leftist internationalism predicated on common cause against US and Western imperialism and capitalism. In articles discussing women fighters in the Sudan or North Vietnam, for example, there is no explicit analysis of how people of color in the United States might be complicit with empire, or how some Third World nations might be structurally situated to benefit from the colonial expropriation and extraction of others. Much of *Triple Jeopardy*'s analysis of Third World feminism highlights commonality within the category "Third World," focusing on how women are colonized and exploited in similar ways. A two-page spread in the centerfold of the first issue, a reprint of material from a booklet that TWWA created to give context to its emergence and to describe its politics, describes Third World women as experiencing the "same general oppressions" ("Women in the Struggle" 1971, 8–9). As examples, they list industries that target Third World women for exploitation as domestic workers, hospital workers, factory workers, farm laborers, and garment workers; stereotypes; and endemic drug abuse within their communities. The frequent images of revolutionary women in the Third World are, of course, not inherently feminist, as Maylei Blackwell observes (Blackwell 2005).

On the other hand, even in the early 1970s, they developed an analysis of the differences and hierarchies that may occur between racialized groups. As Blackwell argues, the organization's attention to the relationship between the international and the local implied a diversity of struggle. She writes, "The TWWA was aware of how it was situated within geopolitical struggles and it localized a transnational imaginary of third-world solidarity among women to forge coalitional politics among women of color locally" (Blackwell 2015, 285). Blackwell argues that in contrast to the abstract, generalizing notion of "global sisterhood," TWWA "refused claims to universality by working from their own situated struggles, their political locations" (Blackwell 2015, 285). Likewise, rather than making "Third World" a universal category of oppression, *Triple Jeopardy* produced an alternative relational logic that highlighted the differences among contexts and imagined new and complex terms for building solidarity.

Thus, even as they steadfastly developed anti-imperialist socialist connections with women all over the world, their focus on gender and their resolutely feminist analysis required an immensely complex notion of racial solidarity. Nothing illustrates this more clearly than Beal's description of how the Black Women's Alliance became the Third World Women's Alliance. When Puerto Rican women asked to join, the request precipitated serious discussions weighing the importance of pursuing issues and concerns specific to Black communities against the imperative of a broader Third World solidarity. Beal recounts:

> So we had a big debate in the organization. And what we were essentially dealing with here was, what were the things that were particularly African American as opposed to what were the things that were specifically Puerto Rican. . . .
>
> And when we looked at the Puerto Rican sisters, we saw that they were trying to deal with both their national oppression of living within the United States and a kind of racial and class thing that was separate from just being a part of America as a whole, and how does your gender fit in when you have this other overriding oppression. And then black women were essentially trying to deal with the same thing: how do you deal with the question of race and class and gender. . . .
>
> So we finally decided that the two forms of oppression, while not precisely exactly the same—race versus, say, nationality—but the idea of the complexity of women's liberation in that context was fundamentally the same. (Beal 2005, 39–40)

As we know, the coalitional impulse won out, and the group changed its name to the Third World Women's Alliance. Beal's comments underscore how a complex and nuanced theorization of relational racialization and colonization was integral to the group's very founding. That is, bringing Black and Puerto Rican women together in a category of Third World women was predicated not on an emphasis on their similarities but rather on a nuanced understanding of their different relationships to racialized state violence and US imperialism, which Beal marks with the term *nationality*. Beal writes that what brought them together was not a uniformity or commensurability, but rather the exact opposite, that what they had in common was the

"idea of the *complexity* of women's liberation in [each] context." We can recognize her analysis—"How do you deal with the question of race and class
and gender?"—as that which Kimberlé Crenshaw decades later named
"intersectionality." Intersectionality connects them, but what *intersectionality* inherently means is the recognition of difference rather than a demand
for uniformity.

The circumstances through which an Asian American feminist ended
up as part of TWWA exemplifies the idea that identification with racial categories is not natural or presumed. The New York chapter included Christine Choy, who is credited as the art director of *Triple Jeopardy*.[3] In my
telephone interview with Choy, I found her disarmingly frank and funny,
speaking a mile a minute in her signature gravelly smoker's voice and pull-
ing no punches. Being the art director, she explained, meant that she drew
many of the graphics that were such an important part of the publication's
aesthetic.[4] She also participated in many of the TWWA's actions and campaigns and, as I will outline in more detail later, found in them a like-minded
community of leftist and revolutionary activists with whom she felt more
camaraderie than with other Asian immigrants. She later became an
acclaimed Oscar-nominated documentary filmmaker, the director of such
now canonical Asian American films as *Who Killed Vincent Chin?* and *Sa-
I-Gu*, and a pioneer in independent film distribution as one of the founders
of Third World Newsreel.

Choy's unusual life history made her an uneasy fit with Asian American communities and organizations of that era, and she found that she was
more comfortable with the Black and Puerto Rican women in TWWA than
she was with other Asian Americans. Born just a few years after the Chinese Revolution, Choy was raised in Shanghai by her mother, a brilliant and
educated woman who spoke several languages fluently. Her father was
Korean, born to a family that had fled Japanese colonial rule to Shanghai,
where the Provisional Government of the Republic of Korea had been established. Choy's father left Shanghai for South Korea after the Korean War, and
Choy and her mother eventually joined him. Succeeding academically
in South Korea, Choy received a scholarship offer from a Catholic high
school in Manhattan. Captivated by American films, she romanticized the
United States, and she moved to New York, alone, at the age of fifteen. She
spent a year at Princeton and then transferred to Columbia, earning a combined BA/MA degree. During her time at Columbia, she became involved
with TWWA. At the time, Choy had started working with Newsreel, a network of radical filmmakers. Choy would later be instrumental in turning

the New York chapter of Newsreel into the long-running film production and distribution organization Third World Newsreel. Having met Frances Beal and other members of SNCC through her activist work in New York, Choy offered Newsreel's office as a meeting space for TWWA once they split from SNCC. Because of Choy's background in art and architecture, they recruited her to draw graphics for *Triple Jeopardy*. Word of her facility for graphics spread, and Choy recounts drawing for publications produced by the Young Lords and the Black Panthers as well as TWWA.

Although for a time Choy was the only Asian American woman in TWWA (she recalls a Filipina joining later), she felt more camaraderie and ease among their ranks than she did with Asian American organizations. Partly this was because of her unusual upbringing. Choy's peripatetic life had exposed her to a variety of ideologies and forms of governance, with which she was able to cultivate a critical engagement:

> I was born under communism. Then we moved to Hong Kong which at that time was a colonial state. Then we moved to South Korea. I was bewildered by the amount of American GIs stationed in the middle of the 5th Avenue of Seoul. And then of course you see the division of white GIs and Black GIs very clearly. Clearly, clearly separate. Separate and not equal. My early upbringing was Marxism-Leninism, and I ended up in South Korea, which was against communism. It was rather confusing and then I went to Japan, which was a monarchy, right? Then I came to United States; there's capitalism. At a young age, I tasted all different "isms."

At the time, Choy explains, international students from the PRC were rare; the other recent Chinese immigrants in New York were largely from Taiwan and Hong Kong and were suspicious of her politics and background. She also recounts interpersonal antipathies. Her memories of Communist China were favorable, in particular because of its possibilities for a proto-feminist politics. She recounts, "Mao Zedong says women hold up half the sky. That really made a big impression on me when I was a kid. Women are no longer allowed to [have] bound feet, and feudal ideologies such as men can have several wives got wiped out when I was growing up in China. I also witnessed that my mother was very happy at the time. She felt she was really contributing to the country, and she spoke a lot of languages, so she already did shorthand and translation for the party, for the agencies."

Her pro-China politics clashed with the more conservative, anti-Communist Taiwanese international students in New York at the time. She notes that "Taiwan was Chiang Kai-shek. I grew up against the Kuomintang." She found the students from Hong Kong alienating for other reasons: "Then people from Hong Kong, they were colonials." In contrast, the anticolonial, leftist, revolutionary politics of TWWA resonated with her, and she found in them a welcoming community: "I ended up with a group of people who really believes [in] independence. Vietnam independence, Cuban independence, independence of Angola, Botswana, Mozambique." Choy found a community of like-minded people: "And the Newsreel people and the Panthers, Lords and Third World Women's Alliance, they took me very, very seriously. I appreciated that because my thinking was so different than most young people at that time, you know. . . . I've seen so much poverty. I've seen literally exploitation, the women being exploited in Korea as prostitutes and the GIs were using like PX and selling black market."

Choy's experience undermines any assumption of solidarity or shared experience based on racial categorization, as she found she had less in common with other Chinese immigrants than she did with radical Black and Puerto Rican women. At the same time, we must understand her experiences as not simply idiosyncratic or individual, for they were formed by the historical and material conditions of US and Japanese imperialism and wars both hot and cold that shaped Asian geopolitics in the twentieth century. While Choy's life story is certainly unique, it helps us understand the heterogeneity of Third World feminist organizing at the time. While TWWA understood the necessity of a rhetoric and discourse of commonality as the basis for solidarity, the women in the organization forged relationships based on a theory and practice of difference. We see that while the *figure* of Vietnamese and Chinese revolutionary women was ubiquitous, the presence of Asian American women in TWWA was more anomalous. Both examples, however, are instructive insofar as they help us understand the different and simultaneous understandings of collectivity and coalitions that TWWA forged at the time.

While TWWA's vision was global and international, *Triple Jeopardy*'s cogent and pointed analyses of the differing interests among individuals or factions *within* movements highlight the interpersonal as well as geopolitical stakes of theorizing collectivity based on heterogeneity. While in the main *Triple Jeopardy* did not comment on internal organizational politics, instead focusing on informational essays and articles, one early editorial stands out as a departure. In this editorial, published within the first year of *Triple Jeopardy*'s run, TWWA members expose a "serious and potentially dangerous situation" ("Editorial" 1972, 4). A member of SNCC, Mohammad

Hunt, had created a list of supposed government agents or these agents' pawns within TWWA and other SNCC-related organizations and had surreptitiously circulated this list among their friends and co-workers. Many of the accused women had turned down Hunt's sexual advances, and many of the men on his list were partnered with these women. They also reported that Hunt had been physically violent to two women who had criticized him.

The editorial goes on to detail the manner in which they attended to Hunt's activities once they discovered what he was doing: they convened a meeting at which they decided to inform their community of Hunt's actions and also to develop an analysis of "how a person like Mohammad Hunt was able to create this much turmoil and divisiveness so that other organizations can learn from our mistakes" ("Editorial" 1972, 4). The majority of the editorial, rather than detailing Hunt's activities, is devoted to their own analysis, in which they taxonomize three types of actors who jeopardize movement politics, whom they call "Agents, Opportunists, and Fools" ("Editorial" 1972, 4). And indeed, it is not inconceivable that Hunt was an agent of the state since SNCC had been infiltrated by government agents. Neither was TWWA immune: Kimberly Springer writes that COINTELPRO put the TWWA under investigation from 1970 to 1974, and that in addition to surveilling TWWA and *Triple Jeopardy*, COINTELPRO had infiltrated their meetings (Springer 2005, 50). The TWWA archives at the Sophia Smith Collection at Smith College contains the file the FBI maintained on the TWWA, uncovered through Freedom of Information Act requests.[5] The first issue of *Triple Jeopardy* featured an article appealing for funds for TWWA member Kisha Shakur, who was imprisoned because she had gotten caught up in a case against her husband, a case that turned out to be orchestrated by COINTELPRO (Springer 2005, 91).

Regardless of whether Hunt was an agent provocateur or simply a predator in the movement, TWWA make perfectly clear the stakes of a feminist analysis of antiracist and anti-imperialist struggle. They use this example as a case study that supports their analysis in the statement above, that antiracist and anti-imperialist struggles without a feminist analysis hinder their own growth and effectiveness and are thus "counterrevolutionary." The editors write, "The actions of Mohammad's began to have a disastrous effect on our organization. Essential tasks were not completed or done in a slipshod manner. Working and personal relationships between sisters became strained and a mass paranoia began to creep into our midst and poison our ability to function in an effective manner. Insinuations were made against the leadership of the Alliance and people were afraid to talk to each other. Criticisms raised were handled in a superficial manner. Two essential ingredients of any revolutionary organization were damaged in the Alliance: Honesty and Trust" ("Editorial" 1972, 4).

The publication of this editorial outlines a very different understanding of what solidarity, community, and organizing might look like. It presents no narrative of resolution or of failure, nor the story of an organization broken by these betrayals and violences, nor one that triumphantly overcame them. Instead, the editorial performs a contingent gesture to a future possibility, but one that is certainly not premised on an idealized utopian narrative of coming together. Instead, it presents a brutal analysis of how even within movements, some actors stand to gain more than others. We might find that this affectively difficult but politically useful insight offers a different definition of coalitional politics, one that proposes a new approach to understanding conflict within and across social movements. Rather than approach conflict and fracture as detrimental to collective organizing and solidarity movements, this editorial prompts us to ask what might happen if we took seriously what US Women of Color feminists advanced: that conflict even to the point of the demise of an organization can itself be understood as an organizing practice, something to be not overcome but utilized.

TWWA's theorization of the hierarchies of gender and patriarchy *within* racial and radical groups lends itself to theorizing solidarity *across* racial groups and histories. TWWA examined the important differences between groups of women, even as they highlighted a shared history of racialized and colonial violence. At the same time, because of their historical moment, their political and activist practice was predicated on an understanding of Third World women as sharing common concerns because of the global nature of capitalist imperialism. That is, the *historical* development of a post–civil rights era Black middle class or an Asian technical and managerial class or the neocolonial capture of newly independent nation-states by transnational capital had not taken hold enough to be reflected in their class analyses. However, by reading their feminist critiques of masculinist and patriarchal power *within* their racial groups, and analyzing the heterogeneous aesthetic of their periodical as an expression of political common sense, we can read for an incipient alternative political practice of solidarity that acknowledges differences of power and hierarchy within and across racialized and (neo)colonized groups. The role of Asian American and Asian women within these movements can help illuminate the politics of difference that might otherwise be implicit or overlooked.

NOTES

Acknowledgments: My gratitude goes to the many interlocutors who read versions of this chapter in earlier iterations, first and foremost LOUD Collective, who provided not only generous and rigorous intellectual engagement but support, care, and kindness over many years. I thank in particular LOUD members Maylei Blackwell, Dayo Gore, Sarah Haley, Jodi Kim, Shana Redmond, and Tiffany Willoughby-Herard for their attention to this essay, Special thanks go to Maylei Blackwell for introducing me to the Third World Women's Alliance and providing me my first set of copies of *Triple Jeopardy*. I also thank the UCHRI Residential Research Group on Transnational Feminisms for their careful reading of and enthusiastic support for this project. I am indebted to, once again, Maylei Blackwell, Judy Wu, Karen Leong, Monisha Das Gupta, Zeynep Korkman, Rana Jaleel, Rachel Fabian, and Jessica Millward. I thank the UCLA Council on Research's Faculty Research Grant, the UCLA Center for the Study of Women, and the UC Humanities Research Institute, which funded this research. I also thank Stephanie Santos, research assistant extraordinaire, as well as Christine Choy for graciously agreeing to be interviewed. All errors are my own.

1   A smaller chapter was also established in Seattle, but existing records of this chapter are sparse and consist mainly of reports filed to the TWWA national organization, copies of which were sent to the Bay Area chapter and are preserved in their records.

2   "Agbayani Work Brigade," Box 5, Folder 4; "Katipunan ng mga Demokratikong Pilipino (KDP)," Box 5, Folders 16–18; "Union of Vietnamese in the US," Box 5, Folder 23, Third World Women's Alliance Records, MS 697, Sophia Smith Collection, Smith College, Northampton, MA.

3   *Triple Jeopardy* 3 (4) (March–April 1974): 2. She was credited as Chris Choy.

4   Christine Choy, telephone interview with the author, February 20, 2017.

5   "FBI File of TWWA," Box 4, Folders 11–12, Third World Women's Alliance Records, MS 697, Sophia Smith Collection, Smith College, Northampton, MA.

REFERENCES

NEWSPAPER ARTICLES

"Editorial." 1972. *Triple Jeopardy* 1 (7) (September–October): 4.
"Korea = Vietnam." 1972. *Triple Jeopardy* 1 (5) (April–May): 3.
"Korean Women." 1972. *Triple Jeopardy* 1 (5) (April–May): 4.
"Murder at San Quentin." 1971. *Triple Jeopardy* 1 (1) (September–October): 3.
"Now Attica!!" 1971. *Triple Jeopardy* 1 (1) (September–October): 2.
"Women in the Struggle." 1971. *Triple Jeopardy* 1 (1) (September–October): 8–9.

OTHER SOURCES

Beal, Frances. 1970a. "Double Jeopardy: To Be Black and Female." In *The Black Woman*, edited by Toni Cade. New York: New American Library.

———. 1970b. "Double Jeopardy: To Be Black and Female." In *Sisterhood Is Powerful: An Anthology of Writings from the Women's Movement*, edited by Robin Morgan. New York: Vintage.

———. 2005. Oral history by Loretta Ross. Voices of Feminism Oral History Project, Sophia Smith Collection, Smith College.

Blackwell, Maylei. 2005. "Bearing Bandoleros." In *Beyond the Frame: Women of Color and Visual Representation*, edited by Angela Y. Davis and Neferti Tadiar. New York: Palgrave MacMillan.

———. 2015. "Triple Jeopardy: The Third World Women's Alliance and the Transnational Roots of Women-of-Color Feminism." In *Provocations: A Transnational Reader in the History of Feminist Thought*, edited by Susan Bordo, M. Cristina Alcalde, and Ellen Rosenman. Berkeley: University of California Press.

Burnham, Linda. 2005. Oral history by Loretta Ross. Voices of Feminism Oral History Project, Sophia Smith Collection, Smith College.

Clemente, Genoveva. 1972. "Puerto Rican Woman Visits China." *Triple Jeopardy* 2 (3) (March–April): 1.

Crenshaw, Kimberlé. 1989. "Demarginalizing the Intersection of Race and Sex: A Black Feminist Critique of Antidiscrimination Doctrine, Feminist Theory, and Antiracist Politics." *University of Chicago Legal Forum* 140 (1): 139–67.

Kelley, Robin, and Betsy Esch. 1991. "Black like Mao: Red China and Black Revolution." *Souls* 1 (4): 6–41.

Roja, Clarita. 1973. "Filipino Women and the Revolution." *Triple Jeopardy* 3 (1) (September–October): 8–9.

Springer, Kimberly. 2005. *Living for the Revolution: Black Feminist Organizations, 1968–1980*. Durham, NC: Duke University Press.

Sumi, Pat. 1972. "Vietnam." *Triple Jeopardy* 1 (6) (July–August): 8.

Ward, Stephen. 2006. "The Third World Women's Alliance: Black Feminist Radicalism and Black Power Politics." In *The Black Power Movement: Re-thinking the Black Power–Civil Rights Era*, edited by Peniel E. Joseph. New York: Routledge.

Wu, Judy. 2013. *Radicals on the Road: Internationalism, Orientalism, and Feminism during the Vietnam Era*. Ithaca, NY: Cornell University Press.

CHAPTER 2

ASIAN AMERICAN FEMINISMS AND WOMEN OF COLOR FEMINISMS

Radicalism, Liberalism, and Invisibility

JUDY TZU-CHUN WU

> Pregnant, married, white, yellow, black, brown, red. . . .
> Women stretching their arms way above the clouds
> . . . in San Francisco / Along the Mekong
> —GENNY LIM, "WONDER WOMAN," IN
> *This Bridge Called My Back*

THE POEM "WONDER WOMAN," WRITTEN BY CHINESE AMERICAN poet, playwright, and performer Genny Lim, explores the divisions but also the potential unity among women of different body types, marital status, racial identities, and national locations. Published in *This Bridge Called My Back,* the poem was part of a collection of "writings by radical women of color" in the early 1980s that sought to consolidate and further advance a Third World feminist politics. Building upon racial liberation, decolonization, and women's movements of the post–World War II era, particularly the 1960s and 1970s, Third World feminism sought to create "a broad-based US Women of Color movement capable of spanning borders of nation and ethnicity" (Moraga and Anzaldúa 1983). Such a movement, primarily located in the United States, nevertheless had an internationalist imaginary. Asian American, African American, Chicana/Latina, and American Indian women (the "yellow, black, brown, red" in Lim's poem) cared about and critiqued apartheid in South Africa as well as US-led and supported militarism in Honduras, El Salvador, Chile, Grenada, Beirut, and the Philippines. As Cherríe Moraga, a Chicana writer and co-editor of the anthology, stated, "We . . . see ourselves as refugees of a world on fire" (Moraga and Anzaldúa 1983, ii).

The roles of Asian and Asian American women as theorists of gender oppression and activists for social justice have been understudied in women's, gender, and sexuality studies as well as Asian American Studies. Accordingly, this chapter examines women of Asian ancestry who actively participated in multiple realms of feminist politics, from the formation of Women of Color political alliances in Third World liberation movements to the passage of crucial US legislation for women's equal rights. Focusing on radical Asian/American feminism recognizes Asian women both in the United States and globally as agents of change (rather than victims of rescue), producers of intersectional feminist scholarship, and coalitional actors in Women of Color political alliances that emphasized commonalities.

Although Women of Color feminism tends to be overwritten as limited to radical feminist ideology, this chapter also highlights and analyzes Asian American feminist contributions in the liberal feminist realm. Recognizing the contributions of Asian American women in liberal feminisms complicates the simplistic binaries of "radical" versus "liberal" and the associations of the former with Women of Color and the latter with white women. Such complication is central to Women of Color feminist methodology, which, as Chela Sandoval argues, operates through a "differential consciousness" that refuses any singular approach to resisting multiple intersecting oppressions" (Sandoval 1991).

Both the radical and liberal strands of Asian American feminisms, which exist in tension with one another, have largely been overlooked, rendered invisible, in historical as well as contemporary understandings of US feminisms. Ignoring these multilayered and complex activisms produces inaccurate and simplistic accounts of Asian American feminism. These partial stories, in turn, create academic and activist canons that label certain groups and forms of activism as less legitimate and less worthy of study. In an effort to animate the differential mode of Asian American feminist contributions, this chapter analyzes the heterogeneous, if tense and conflicting, interventions in feminist politics. Doing so allows us to take up Mitsuye Yamada's call to "finally recognize our own invisibility [so as] to finally be on the path toward visibility" (Yamada 1981, 40).

ASIAN/AMERICAN WOMEN AND RADICAL
THIRD WORLD FEMINISM

Asian American women co-created Third World feminism through two simultaneous and intertwined processes. They formed alliances with other Women of Color in the United States by sharing interpretations of their mutual and divergent experiences of racialization and patriarchy as well as identifying and working toward common political goals. At the same time, Asian American women and other Women of Color in the United States discovered political inspiration and expressed political solidarity with women in the Third World. Asian women in decolonizing and newly created socialist societies, such as Viet Nam, China, and even North Korea, served as hypervisible role models for women in the United States during the 1960s and early 1970s. Both at the 1955 Bandung conference and increasingly after the Sino-Soviet split, which began in 1960, the People's Republic of China (PRC) cultivated connections with Third World movements. The PRC championed the liberation of oppressed people, particularly people of color, around the world, including African Americans in the United States (Frazier 2015; Gore 2016; McDuffie 2011; Scarlett 2016). As part of the Chinese revolutionary iconography that circulated globally, Chinese peasant women overturning feudalism and patriarchy served as activist role models. Their political biographies and images appeared in the underground newspapers of US activists and tended to be popular within women's and Asian American movements.

In addition, the Viet Nam War played a central role in politically inspiring US activism and critique of American imperialism and militarism. The phrase *liberation front*, adopted by ethnic studies activists in the San Francisco Bay Area and elsewhere, was popularized by the National Liberation Front in South Viet Nam and by other oppositional movements throughout the Third World. Again, as part of the revolutionary images and messages that circulated in the antiwar movement globally, Vietnamese peasant women epitomized revolutionary heroism. They represented the ultimate underdogs who nevertheless challenged US global dominance and helped fight the most powerful military state in the world to a standstill. The hypervisibility of Asian female revolutionaries helped Asian American women to create their own political subjectivity and to subvert their political invisibility (Wu 2010, 2013, 2015). In other words, the political heroism of women in socialist Asia played a central role in creating Third World feminism in the United States.

The oral history of Donna Kotake, a Japanese American who became a political activist during the early 1970s, demonstrates this convergence of racial, international, and gender political consciousness among Asian American women. Kotake was raised in a farming community in San Francisco's South Bay. She was attending San Jose State University when she decided to travel to Vancouver, Canada, to participate in the 1971 Indochinese Women's Conference (IWC). Held in both Toronto and Vancouver, these conferences provided an opportunity for approximately one thousand women from the United States and Canada to meet with six women from Southeast Asia who were living through and fighting against the United States presence there. Kotake explained how her political awakening was connected to discoveries about her racial identity as Asian American, her political alliances with other people of color, and her international awareness of socialist Asia. Growing up in the United States, she said,

> your whole identity was not Asian. Your identity was just, like, you
> wanted to be a white person. . . . So, to us at that point, . . . identifying
> ourselves as Asian Americans, wanting to learn more about our own his-
> tories, and you know, being proud of the histories . . . and I think really
> hooking up with other non-whites was a really big deal. . . . So, you know,
> there's the identity going on as being Asian and there's a third world com-
> ing, coalitions coming together, and there's this international thing with
> Vietnam, and at the same time people talking about China and seeing
> what a shining example of, you know, what it could be like to be free,
> people who care about . . . people and a country that provides . . . for
> everyone. (Kotake 2006)

Kotake and other activists of her generation were discovering their racial identity as Asian Americans. She recognized herself as a member of a resistant pan-ethnic group that had a distinct history and culture connected to Third World struggles in the United States and around the world.[1]

Kotake and other Asian American women activists not only developed a racial and internationalist consciousness, but they also experienced a profound political and gendered connection with the Indochinese women in Vancouver. Asian American women were rendered largely invisible in American social movement circles in the 1960s. Cast as the "model minority" by the popular media, Asian Americans generally came to represent a counterpoint to social activism, a minority group seemingly altogether disengaged from politics. Mirroring similar conclusions regarding Japanese Americans, for example, *US News and World Report* argued in 1966 that "at a time when it is being proposed that hundreds of billions be spent to uplift Negroes and other minorities, the nation's 300,000 Chinese-Americans are moving ahead on their own—with no help from anyone else" ("Success Story," 6). For Asian American women, this image of the model minority was compounded by projections of hypersexuality and submissiveness (Espiritu 1996). Asian American women were racialized and gendered as the antithesis of political activism.

However, Kotake and other Asian American women who became activists found visible role models in Vietnamese women fighting the US military. They shared racial and gender status as well as anti-imperialist politics. When asked how the IWC influenced her, Kotake responded, "Just feeling the strength of the women and realizing how much women can do, and it really made me feel incredibly proud about being a woman" (Kotake 2006). Another Japanese American woman who attended the conference, Kiku Uno, emphasized that the presence of Asian female bodies enhanced the political message of the Indochinese delegates. She wrote, "Their physical presence had tremendous impact on the hundreds of Third World and white women. Here were six Asian women—physically small, sincere, friendly, often appearing extremely tired. Yet, whenever one spoke, it was with such clarity and with a background of personal involvement that the meaning of a people's revolution became a reality" (*Asian Women* 1971/1975, 82).

The 1971 Indochinese Women's Conferences politicized an entire generation of Asian American women and facilitated opportunities for their leadership. According to Uno, there were 120 Asian American women from the United States and Canada at the Vancouver gathering. They constituted roughly half of the approximately 200–250 Third World women in attendance and approximately one of every eight attendees overall (*Asian Women* 1971/1975, 82). Because Asian Americans resided predominantly in the US West, they likely attended in smaller numbers in Toronto, which was intended for residents of the East Coast and the Midwest. Yuri Kochiyama, a Japanese American activist best known for her work with the Black liberation movement and her political relationship with Malcolm X, did not attend the IWC. However, she learned about the conference through her political network, and she described the meetings in her keynote address to the East Asian Student Union's Asian Women's Conference in 1981, ten years after the IWC. Kochiyama shared, "For most North American women who attended [the IWC], it was the most moving event of that time" (Kochi-yama 1982, 13).

Asian American women did not just attend but also co-organized the conference. Pat Sumi was a Japanese American activist who traveled to North Korea, North Viet Nam, and Socialist China in the summer of 1970 with Black Panther leaders Eldridge Cleaver and Elaine Brown. Sumi worked with other Women of Color, which included African Americans, Chicanas, and American Indians, to demand separate time with the Indochinese female representatives, apart from white North American women. The white organizers had attempted to involve Women of Color individuals and organizations in planning the conference, but the latter felt marginalized by the planning process. Some Women of Color already had begun meeting to express political solidarity and to develop collective critiques, while others joined in these conversations through the organizing efforts of the IWC. They banded together collectively to issue a statement to the white organizers, stating that "since we have been denied an equal participation *with* white groups, we can only ask for equal but separate conferences. . . . The possibility of a confrontation between Third World and white women's groups at a joint conference would be disrespectful to the Indochinese women and would further reinforce the tensions that exist among North American women" ("We as Third World Women"). As a result of their efforts, the IWCs in both Toronto and Vancouver were subdivided into small conferences with one designated for Women of Color. The conferences not only presented an opportunity for Asian American women to engage with women from the Third World; Asian American women also exerted political leadership so that Women of Color in North America could bond politically.

Asian American women who could not travel to Canada read extensive coverage of the IWC in *Asian Women*, a widely circulated pioneering publication devoted to Asian American women's issues. Originally issued in 1971, the same year as the conferences, the journal was eventually reprinted three times. Asian American women based primarily in universities in California and/or engaged in community-based organizing wrote and published *Asian Women*. The journal prominently featured biographies of the Southeast Asian women who participated in the IWC as well as personal testimonies, poetry, and artwork by Asian American attendees. These materials appeared in a section titled "Third World Woman." Other writings in this part of the publication featured the lives and struggles of women in North Korea, Iran, and other Arab countries (*Asian Women* 1971/1975, 72–73,

87–88, 89–90).[2] The inclusion of writings about the Middle East indicates the expansive understanding of Asia in Asian American women's circles as early as the early 1970s.[3] The reporting on these activist encounters and critiques, which was circulated through *Asian Women* as well as in other movement publications, helped to create a common language, a shared sense of time, and an internationalist commitment to mutual responsibility (Anderson 1991).[4]

Asian American women turned to women in Asia for political role models and for political dialogue and theorization. Their mutual exchanges developed Third World feminist critiques of US empire and militarism, sexuality and reproduction, as well as capitalism and patriarchy. For example, Evelyn Yoshimura's essay "GI's and Racism" was frequently reproduced in Asian American and Asian American women's publications during the late 1960s and early 1970s. Yoshimura, a Japanese American activist, first published the article in the Los Angeles–based Asian American movement newspaper *Gidra*; it was then reprinted in *Asian Women* as well as *Roots*, a pioneering reader that helped establish Asian American studies as a discipline. Yoshimura emphasized the transnational circularity of US racial attitudes in the Viet Nam War and the importance of Asian women in reproducing this militarized racial socialization.

This and other Asian American critiques of the Viet Nam War pointed out that the US military relied upon and reproduced racial hatred toward Asians to motivate American soldiers to fight in Asia. By promoting the "view of Asian people as sub-human beings . . . the US military . . . can instill the values and mentality that is necessary to become effective killers" (*Asian Women* 1971/1975, 74). Cultivated during basic training on the US mainland and then on military tours in Southeast Asia, US soldiers carried and reproduced these racial attitudes back and forth across the Pacific. The evocation of Asian women played a central role in this racial education. As Yoshimura stated, US soldiers learned to regard "Asian women as a symbolic sexual object" (*Asian Women* 1971/1975, 74). Through the systematic creation of red light districts in Asian countries where US troops were stationed, the US military institutionalized the practice of American GIs frequenting Asian prostitutes in what sociologist Joane Nagel calls the "military sexual complex" (Nagel 2003, 191; also see Enloe 1990; Moon 1997; Stur 2011; Yuh 2002). Not limited to individual excursions, these practices became integral to military culture and discourse through ritualized retellings of these experiences. An Asian American Marine recalled of his boot-camp experience:

> We had these classes we had to go to taught by the drill instructors, and
> every instructor would tell a joke before he began class. It would always be
> a dirty joke usually having to do with prostitutes they had seen in Japan
> or in other parts of Asia while they were stationed overseas. The attitude
> of the Asian women being a doll, a useful toy, or something to play with
> usually came out in these jokes and how they were not quite as human as
> white women ... how Asian women's vaginas weren't like a white
> woman's, but rather they were slanted, like their eyes. (*Asian Women*
> 1971/1975, 74)

Such racialized and sexualized depictions of Asian women, used to foster
male bonding among US soldiers, shaped US military policies and practices
in Southeast Asia—in the brothels and in the general prosecution of war.

The Indochinese women who traveled thousands of miles to meet women
in North America bore witness to the US military sexual complex and the
gendered impact of militarism. Among the six female delegates from Southeast Asia, women who either had suffered traumatic abuse or could testify
to wartime atrocities tended to receive the most attention in activist publications.[5] Dinh Thi Hong, for example, made a powerful impact on conference attendees. A middle-aged housewife from South Viet Nam, Hong had
not been politically engaged in the movement for liberation before she was
imprisoned. Suspected of supporting the opposition to the South Vietnamese government, she was detained and tortured in some of the regime's
most notorious prisons. In her autobiographical narrative, she recalled having "pins [planted] in my fingertips," having "electrodes ... attached to my
ears and to my fingers, nipples and genitals ... and [being] tortured with
electricity until I was unconscious" (*Asian Women* 1971/1975, 83). In addition, her interrogators "forced water, lye and salt into my stomach and tram-
pled on my stomach until I vomited blood and was unconscious" (*Asian
Women* 1971/1975, 83). Illustrating the visceral and sexualized nature of torture, Hong's detailed account appeared in several publications produced
by organizations associated with the New Left, the Third World movements,
and women.

As the Vietnamese delegates explained how the US war in Viet Nam
depended on gendered and sexualized violence in Asia, Asian American
women emphasized the transnational nature of that violence. "We, as Asian
American women, cannot separate ourselves from our Asian counterparts,"
Evelyn Yoshimura argued. "Racism against them is too often racism against
us. ... The mentality that keeps Suzy Wong, Madame Butterfly and gookism

alive turns human beings into racist murdering soldiers and also keeps Asian Americans from being able to live and feel like human beings" (*Asian Women* 1971/1975, 76). Harkening back to decades of fictive representations of Asian women as available and vulnerable objects of Western military men and US military campaigns in Asia, Yoshimura invoked a longer history of colonial violence and racial subjection across the Pacific (J. Kim 2010; Kramer 2006; R. Lee 1999; Roediger 1992). As the appellation *Third World women* suggested, racialized women in the United States recognized that colonization and gender oppression operated in tandem both abroad and at home.

The political synergy between Asian American and Asian women also created an opportunity for Asian American women to form connections with Women of Color in the United States. Latina, Black, and Indigenous women also turned to women in socialist Asia for political inspiration. Maria Ramirez and Nina Genera, two Chicana activists based in the San Francisco Bay Area, recalled that attending the Indochinese Women's Conference in Vancouver marked their first opportunity to witness and interact with Third World women in the vanguard of an ongoing revolution (Ramirez and Genera 2007). Seeing Asian women as political leaders helped other Women of Color view Asian American women in the same light.

In addition, Asian American women articulated the political connections among their own experiences, those of Asian women, and the lives of other Women of Color in the United States and beyond. For example, in an article titled "Birth Control as Genocide," Marsha Takayanagi critiqued efforts to control the reproduction of Third World women in the United States and internationally. She connected Western concerns about the "population bomb" or over-reproduction in the Third World with the use of chemical weapons in Viet Nam, which has had long-term genetic effects; the forced sterilization of Black unwed women in the United States; the testing of reproduction technologies, such as the pill and IUD, on Puerto Rican and Mexican women; and the proposal to sterilize Japanese American women in incarceration camps during World War II (*Asian Women* 1971/1975, 99–102). Katheryn Fong, a Chinese American woman activist, extended the charge of racial genocide by critiquing the reproductive impact of immigration exclusion laws. Policies like the 1882 Chinese Exclusion Law engineered the racial and class makeup of the US polity. Designated "aliens ineligible for citizenship" through the 1790 Naturalization Act and subsequent court cases, almost all Asians were excluded from entry as well as citizenship rights. Those who arrived prior to enactment of this law or were able to navigate around these policies tended to be men. Consequently, the immigration policies, along with antimiscegenation laws that banned inter-racial marriage, deterred biological reproduction of those deemed racially undesirable (Bow 2013, 40). These gendered critiques of state racism and social reproduction did not necessarily result in pronatalist politics among Asian American women. The editors of *Asian Women* argued that they were "women who recognize birth control as a means of self-determination" (*Asian Women* 1971/1975, 128). However, these racialized and feminist critiques of both domestic and global forms of genocide helped Asian American women make political connections with Asian American men as well as Women of Color in the United States and globally.

This intersectional analysis of Third World women's oppression at the time was called "triple oppression." Women of color suffered from patriarchy, racism or imperialism, and capitalism. The economic component of racialized gender oppression was particularly important for radical Asian American women and Women of Color more broadly. Their interest in socialist Asian societies dovetailed with class critiques of capitalist exploitation in their communities. For example, *Getting Together*, a Chinese American activist newspaper based initially in New York and then in San Francisco's Chinatown, called for attention to the plight of low-income community residents. The newspaper and its sponsoring organization, I Wor Kuen—named after the Boxers, who challenged Western imperialism in China in the early twentieth century—advocated for low-income housing, supported higher wages and worker organizing, and criticized development strategies aimed at promoting tourism or investment capital. The organization's twelve-point platform, inspired by the Black Panthers' ten-point platform, called for "community control of our institutions and land," "decent housing and health and child care," and "a socialist society" (*Getting Together*, January 1971, 12). Gender was central to the organization's revolutionary agenda. With women central to the leadership of the group, I Wor Kuen also demanded "an end to male chauvinism and sexual exploitation" as part of its twelve-point platform (*Getting Together*, January 1971, 12).

Getting Together regularly featured stories about socialist Asia, particularly women in socialist Asia. The travels of Pat Sumi and her Chinese American co-delegate Alex Hing in North Korea, the People's Republic of China, and North Vietnam were highlighted in *Getting Together*. Sumi and Hing brought back eyewitness accounts of people's revolutions and the new societies being created under socialist Asian leadership. In a column titled

"Life in New Asia," Sumi commented on the importance of women's liberation as part of socialist liberation: "In every country we went to, everyone kept telling us that women are half the population, and if we all rose
up at once, the revolution would be over. So organizing women is very
important. The women of Asia have suffered under double and triple oppression before liberation. They were oppressed by imperialists, colonialists
(French, Japanese, etc.) and they were oppressed by the national bourgeoisie of each country which maintained capitalist oppression over them, and
they were also oppressed within their own families and cultures" (*Getting
Together*, November–December 1970, 16).

Because women in socialist Asia had already helped create their own liberation, Sumi, Hing, and the editors of *Getting Together* turned to them for
political inspiration. The newspaper regularly published stories and pictures
of Asian women as revolutionaries. One multiseries column traced the story
of Goldflower, a peasant Chinese woman, from victimization to participation in societal liberation. The unnamed narrator of this story explained the
motivation for publishing this story. While traveling in China, the narrator "discovered that the Communists' drive for power was touched at almost
every point by women, by their feelings, by their relationship to men, by
their social status, by their symbol as an object of property, religion and sex.
Because of this discovery, I decided that I would make use of the first available opportunity to talk with a Chinese farm woman about her life, her
innermost thoughts, her secret feelings" (*Getting Together*, August 1970, 8).

Various scholars have critiqued this desire to access the voice of the
subaltern (Bow 2013, 1–16; Spivak 1988, 1990). As Chandra Mohanty has
argued, feminist scholars in the West have tended to portray Third World
women as "ignorant, poor, uneducated, tradition-bound, religious, domes-
ticated, family-oriented, victimized, etc" (Mohanty 1988). This feminist
form of orientalism regards Women of Color as objects of rescue by their
Western sisters (Rupp 1997). In contrast, I have described the political inspiration provided by socialist Asian revolutionaries for US activists as a form
of *radical orientalism*. The activists who wanted to name US imperialism
tended to distance themselves from what they perceived as the militaristic
and racist values of mainstream American society. Consequently, these
individuals ironically followed in an orientalist tradition of reinforcing a
dichotomy between the East and the West, specifically between decolonizing Asia and imperial America (Said 1979). The radicalness of their orientalism stemmed from the way they inverted and subverted previous
hierarchies. Asian American feminist activists identified politically with

revolutionary Asian people, particularly women. As the ultimate symbols of oppression and antimodernity, Asian women could demonstrate how the most abject had the capability to enact and lead political revolutions. This political bond between Women of Color in the United States and those abroad was fundamental for the formation of a Woman of Color radical feminism.

ASIAN AMERICAN LIBERAL FEMINISM

Not all Asian American women who advocated for female liberation necessarily embraced socialist Asian women as political role models. In the concluding essay of *Asian Women*, titled "Politics of the Interior," members of the editorial team noted, "Asian-Americans have turned to Asia and to the traditional and revolutionary values of China and Vietnam. However, there are problems inherent in the uncritical adoption of the 'Asian' values for Asian-American women. . . . The liberation of our revolutionary sisters in China and Vietnam has taken place within socialist revolutions. Conditions are different from America and alien to the Asian-American experience" (*Asian Women* 1971/1975, 129).

Asian Women applauded the role of women in Asia in transforming their societies by combating US militarism and building socialism. However, the writers and publishers also point to the need for political ideologies and strategies that speak more directly to the conditions of Asian American women. In other words, they point to the limits of transnational analyses that posit commonalities between Asian and Asian American women. After all, Asian Americans, racialized as perpetually foreign, also strived to make rights-based claims and create legislative change in the United States. To explore a broader range of Asian American feminist activism, this section focuses on those who advocated for gender liberation but did so by seeking greater access and equality within the existing US political system. Asian American women participated in and provided leadership in women's organizations, previously understood as white-dominated spaces. Although a clear "minority" within these groups, Asian American women nevertheless shaped the politics and achievements of what might be described as mainstream feminism. I describe these political efforts as "liberal," but they also were deeply transformative.

Asian American women participated in and contributed to various "mainstream" or predominantly white women's organizations. For example, Patsy Mink, the first woman of color US legislator, played a central role in shaping feminist policies at the national level. She served in Congress from 1965 to 1977 and again from 1990 to 2002, when she passed away in office. She spearheaded key feminist legislation, like Title IX, renamed the Patsy T. Mink Equal Opportunity in Education Act after Mink's death. Title IX has had a profound impact on girls and women around the country by mandating gender equity for schools that receive federal funds. In Mink's case, it is perhaps fitting to characterize her as a liberal feminist, as someone who sought to create equal opportunities for women in American society. However, inclusion, which has its limits, also can be transformative. To better understand Mink's investment in liberal feminism as a woman of color, I analyze how Mink's politics of gender equity were shaped by her life experiences and understanding of intersectional oppression as well as the tensions and limits of a liberal politics of inclusion.

In 1967, Mink introduced a bill in the House of Representatives to provide federal funding for early childhood education. As she reflected in a 1975 speech, "That was the first time Congress focused on the need for publicly financed child care programs in America" (Patsy T. Mink Papers, Box 72, Folder 2, March 3, 1975). This is a bit of an overstatement. During World War II and the mid-1960s, there were previous federal efforts to support child care. During the war, providing child care was a temporary measure to recruit American women for defense work. During the War on Poverty in the mid-1960s, the federal government supported child care so that low-income parents might seek vocational training and employment. Also, programs like Head Start targeted disadvantaged children for comprehensive education as well as health and nutrition support. However, Mink's proposal, which she advocated for over the next decade or so, was unique in two ways. First, she argued for federal government responsibility to provide child care on a broader and more permanent basis. For Mink, child care should not to be an emergency measure, and it should be available to all families, regardless of the income of the parents. Second, Mink argued for the need for quality early childhood education. She wanted to advance the educational experiences of children beyond what she described as "custodial care." Her efforts to pass federal legislation to support ongoing, available quality child care held deep significance. As Mink argues, "The value of Federal legislation, as others before me have pointed out, is not only that it provides a specific program and specific amounts of money, but that it represents a national statement of purpose and support. It provides the inspiration for action and leadership at other levels of government, thus having an effect far beyond the simple provisions of law themselves" (Patsy T. Mink Papers, Box 72, Folder 2, March 3, 1975).

Patsy Mink's commitment to child care reflected her personal needs as a working mother as well as the collective needs of working women in Hawai'i. Mink, a third-generation Japanese American, grew up on a plantation on Maui in the 1920s and 1930s. The racialized and gendered economy of sugar plantations inspired demands for child care and maternity leave. Plantation owners and managers initially employed Native Hawaiians but began to recruit laborers from Asia as well as Portugal and the Caribbean during the late nineteenth and early twentieth centuries. These economic interests dovetailed with the political and personal investments of the Japanese empire and Japanese Americans. In the Gentlemen's Agreement of 1907, Japan agreed to US demands to restrict the entry of male laborers but mandated in return that immigrants already in the United States have the right to bring their wives. Women working in the cane fields of Hawai'i were paid less than the men. Equally important, women were perceived as having a calming influence on the larger community. Plantation owners believed that unattached men were too volatile and potentially too disruptive to plantation labor relations. Women and families were envisioned as stabilizing elements that encouraged dependence rather than radicalism. While plantation owners promoted an ideology of heteronormative domesticity for the purposes of pacifying laborers, working women who bore children received no special treatment. They worked until they gave birth and returned soon afterward. Few plantations provided child care. Instead, women often carried their children on their backs while they worked. Some organized among themselves to share childrearing duties. Older children also watched over younger ones. This informal system left much to be desired. Unsupervised children sometimes were injured or even died when the cane fields were burned for sugar production. Because of these difficult circumstances, the needs of women and families became integrated into the labor movement. The historic 1920 Labor Strike in Hawai'i included the demand for paid maternity leave (Okihiro 1991; Takaki 1983).

This history of labor exploitation of women as well as men, Japanese Americans, and other groups profoundly shaped Mink's political consciousness. Even though she eventually became a member of a professional class, she was a staunch advocate for labor interests as well as those of women. Mink helped launch a so-called Democratic Revolution in Hawai'i in the 1950s. Seeking to challenge the long-standing political power of

Republican plantation owners, the Democratic Party recruited the outsiders of Hawai'i (racial minorities, laborers and labor unions, political liberals and progressives) to engineer a series of political victories beginning in 1954. Mink initially served as a grassroots and behind-the-scenes organizer before she became a political candidate herself, first in the territorial congress, then the territorial and state senate, and eventually national office. Japanese American men were increasingly becoming involved in politics, but it was still rare for Japanese American women to be so publicly and politically engaged. And in fact, the leadership of the Hawai'i Democratic Party, an organization that Patsy devoted her efforts to build, prioritized Japanese American male candidates and obstructed her efforts to run for office (Bassford 2008).

Mink's experience with gender discrimination in both the political and professional realms was a constant reminder of the need for child care. She had graduated from the University of Chicago Law School in 1951. Like many other women in this era, no law firm would hire Mink, either on the mainland or in Hawai'i. Instead, she began a practice out of her parents' storefront in O'ahu, doing odd legal assignments. Her clients, often impoverished, sometimes bartered for her services. For her first case, Mink was paid with a fish. To establish her professional and eventually her political career, she and her husband had to find care for her daughter, Gwendolyn Mink, who was born in 1952. John Mink, a geologist whom Patsy met at the University of Chicago, was a flexible and supportive care provider. He cleaned and cooked and took care of Wendy. However, both parents worked, so they experimented with various forms of child care. When they registered Wendy with a church-based child-care center, Patsy and John were appalled that their daughter absorbed traditional gender stereotypes. When Wendy became a little older, she took the bus from school and spent afternoons with her mother and grandparents in their storefront. And when Patsy was elected to Congress in the mid-1960s after conducting a grassroots political campaign that succeeded despite hostility from her party, Wendy roamed the office buildings of the House of Representatives (Mink interview 2014; Wu and Mink).

These efforts to juggle work and family reflected broader trends in the United States. Despite the cultural emphasis on domesticity after World War II, American women, including mothers, were increasing their participation in the workforce. Women of color, who had a longer history and greater participation in the labor force, had ever-pressing needs for quality child care. According to Mary Dublin Keyserling, director of the Women's

Bureau, by 1967 there were "about 4 million working mothers with children under 6 years of age" in the United States. However, the "existing day care facilities are available for only 310,000 to 350,000 children" (Patsy T. Mink Papers, Box 68, folder 7, May 26, 1967). In response, a child-care movement emerged in the United States during the 1960s and 1970s.

To collectively lobby for federal legislation, Mink worked closely with various organizations, including mainstream feminist organizations at the national level like the National Organization for Women as well as locally based organizations serving working-class women and women of color. Rachel Pierce coined the phrase "Capitol Hill feminism" to capture how "women on the Hill adopted and adapted the rhetoric, ideological precepts, and policy goals of the women's movement" (Pierce 2014, 4). Also, Anastasia Curwood proposes the term *bridge feminism* to describe how Shirley Chisholm (Democrat of New York), the first African American woman to serve in the House of Representatives, helped to bridge the African American civil rights movement and the women's movement as well as the grassroots and the legislative arena (Curwood 2015). Mink's political coalitions included women's activist groups as well as other legislators, both male and female, who supported feminist legislation. In many of these initiatives, she worked with Chisholm, elected in 1969. They both served on the House Committee for Education and Labor, Mink since her election in 1965 and Chisholm for most of the 1970s.

Mink's advocacy for child care was part of her broader legislative agenda for gender equity. She advocated for equal opportunity for women in education, changes in the school curriculum and teacher training that would allow students to be exposed to nonsexist gender roles, and social welfare programs for the socially disadvantaged. She not only supported the Great Society programs of the 1960s but also vigorously defended welfare during the neoliberal reforms of the 1990s. In one sense, the programs she supported are "liberal"; she sought to create equal opportunity and government support for women in education and the economy. However, Mink's legislative agenda also reflected an understanding of the needs of various women: laboring, nonwaged, as well as professional women; women of color as well as white women.

Asian American women co-created Women of Color feminism in the 1960s and 1970s. During this era of decolonization, Asian American women turned to Asian women in socialist Asia as political role models and political interlocutors to formulate feminist critiques of US militarism, racialized sexuality, and capitalism. Asian American women also were members and leaders among mainstream feminists, working at the local and national levels to promote ideas, policies, and practices for gender equity.

There are tensions, however, between radical and liberal forms of feminism. The radical Asian American women activists who turned to socialist Asian women recognized a disconnect between Mink's political agenda and theirs. In an interview with Mink that appeared in *Asian Women*, the interviewer, Jean Quan, described their different attitudes toward electoral politics. The younger activist commented on "the irrelevancy of the electoral process—meaningless differences between political parties and candidates"; in response, Mink, whose political career was dedicated to building the Democratic Party and promoting a liberal legislative political agenda, asked, "What system is better?" (*Asian Women* 1971/1975, 105). The exchange led the interviewer to reflect, "Patsy Mink is 200% American. She has a deep faith in the American system and in this sense is not atypical of most of our parents. She sees racism and injustice, her response is to work harder in her attempts to make the American system work. This was the essence of our differences. . . . I have looked at the 'American way,' especially its systematic treatment of Third World peoples, and I question if the system was ever intended to work for Asians, nonwhite, or even the majority of working class Americans" (*Asian Women* 1971/1975, 106).

Quan was among those who felt fundamentally alienated from the United States in the early 1970s and sought political inspiration from decolonizing Asia. Mink, in contrast, believed that the United States could be reformed to achieve equality and justice. Ironically, Quan would go on in 2011 to become the first female mayor of Oakland and was widely criticized for authorizing violent crackdowns against the Occupy Movement.

In addition to this intra–Asian American tension, native Hawaiian feminists also have critiqued Asian American liberalism for maintaining settler colonialism (Fujikane and Okamura 2008; Saranillo 2010; Trask 1999). Even with unequal political and economic power compared to Haoles, or whites, Asians in Hawai'i nevertheless contributed to the impoverishment and disfranchisement of Native Hawaiians. In a poetic evocation, Haunani-Kay Trask criticizes white Americans and Asian Americans as equally complicit in colonizing Hawai'i:

Settlers, not immigrants,
from America, from Asia.
Come to settle, to take.
To take from the Native

That which is Native:
Land, water, women,
sovereignty
(Fujikane and Okamura 2008, vii–viii)

The fissures between Asian American liberal feminism and Pacific Islander sovereignty advocates reveal tensions in terms of political categories and strategies. Their differences highlight how a liberal politics of inclusion is at odds with a radical politics of national liberation. The charge of Asian settler colonialism also illuminates cracks within the Asian American and Pacific Islander categories. Both designations are pan-ethnic or perhaps more importantly pan-sovereign. Creating a common political agenda between such diverse peoples has been a challenging process, even through an emphasis on antiracism and anti-imperialism. As Trask and others point out, an antiracist agenda for Asian Americans may mean a bigger piece of the American pie, cooked from a recipe of native displacement and dispossession. The differences in political approach also reveal fissures in the Women of Color category. Although Indigenous peoples were evoked as part of the Third World in the 1960s and beyond, they also adopted the term *Fourth World* to indicate their historical and contemporary difference as the original inhabitants of lands around the world and their previous and once-again desired status as sovereign peoples. In an era in which self-determination and national liberation were key goals across the Third World and among Third World people in the United States, there was the potential for political mutuality between the "yellow, black, brown, red." However, if the goal for some Women of Color was not liberation but greater inclusion, then political coalitions become more difficult to form and maintain.

The political tensions between liberalism and radicalism among Asian American women activists and among Women of Color feminist activists reveal how strategies for gender, racial, and national liberation can conflict and contradict one another. Sandoval's formulation of "differential consciousness" among Women of Color emphasizes flexibility and mutuality between different political strategies and orientations. These differences nevertheless can harden into fundamental oppositions. Still, it is important to acknowledge the range of political strategies that Asian American women developed. Liberal and radical strands of feminism both emerged from political analyses of the lived experiences of Asian American women. Recognizing the impact of diverse forms of Asian American women's activism on their specific communities—Pacific Islander women, Women of Color feminists, and US women as a whole—provides a more accurate accounting of the history of women's activism.

NOTES

Acknowledgments: My deepest appreciation to Lynn Fujiwara and Shireen Roshanravan for conceiving the idea for this volume and for welcoming me into their effort. Thanks also for Kelly Fong, Dorothy Fujita-Rony, Jane Hong, Valerie Matsumoto, and Isabela Quintana for their helpful and supportive feedback at the inaugural meeting of our Asian American Women's History Writing Group. Finally, Noriko Ishii was the perfect host, asking her students to provide reflections about my talk at Sophia University in June 2016 based on this chapter.
Epigraph: The Mekong is a river, the world's twelfth longest, that crosses national borders in Southeast Asia. In the United States, the Mekong is primarily associated with Viet Nam and the Viet Nam War.

1   The individuals who became committed to a pan-ethnic Asian American identity and Third World liberation tended to be from certain Asian ethnic groups and particular generational backgrounds. Because of the history of Asian immigration and the legacy of US exclusion acts, approximately one million people of Asian Ancestry lived in the United States in 1965. From the mid-nineteenth through the mid-twentieth century, discriminatory laws either banned or severely limited Asian migration. In 1965, the United States passed the Hart-Celler Bill, which mandated equal quotas for every country in the world. As a result, Asian Americans, who had been predominantly American born, became predominantly foreign born (E. Lee 2015; Takaki 1998). In the late 1960s and early 1970s, the demographic shift was just occurring. Japanese Americans, Chinese Americans, and Filipinos constituted the three largest Asian ethnic groups. Within these groups, it was the generation of people who grew up in the aftermath of World War II who tended to become politically identified with the Asian American category. In addition to being exposed to the civil rights movement and other racial liberation movements, Asian Americans experienced racialization themselves. For example, Japanese Americans, who constituted half of the Asian American population, had been interned in camps during World War II out of suspicion of disloyalty. They faced numerous challenges in their attempts to reintegrate into American society after being designated the nation's enemy. Chinese Americans, long consigned to residential segregation, discovered economic and political opportunities when China was allied with the United States but again faced suspicion during the Cold War. Filipino Americans, whose home country had been colonized by the United States in the aftermath of the US-Philippine War, also lived in segregated communities and continued to engage in circulatory migration patterns to work in farming, fishing, as well as the US military. While all three groups worked together to create the Asian American movement, Japanese Americans seemed most inclined to identify as Asian American. They had already been singled out for being Japanese during World War II. Also, Japan was an imperial power that both colonized Asia and

served as a Cold War ally of the United States. Being Asian American and identifying with socialist Asia allowed Japanese Americans to critique racism and imperialism without claiming a troubling ethnic or national identification.

2   The fact that two of the authors requested anonymity reveals their concerns about
political persecution, either from Asian American communities in the United States
or from governments in Asia, as a result of their writings.

3   This project to include West Asia as part of the Asian American political imagination has become more urgent in the post-9/11 era of Islamophobia.

4   The role of activist media in fostering internationalism builds upon Anderson's
(1991) analysis of print media in fostering nationalism.

5   The delegation from Southeast Asia consisted of three teams of two female and one
male translator each for North Viet Nam, South Viet Nam, and Laos. A fourth delegation from Cambodia had intended to travel to Canada as well but was unable to do
so. Vo Thi The (age fifty), a professor of literature at the University of Hanoi and an
officer in the Viet Nam Women's Union, had visited Canada previously in 1969.
Given her seniority and experience, she served as an overall leader of the 1971
delegation. Nguyen Thi Xiem (forty), a gynecologist and obstetrician, was the vice
president of the VWU. Dinh Thi Hong (forty-six), a housewife, and Phan Min Hien
(thirty-one), a teacher, represented the Women's Union for the Liberation of South
Vietnam. Two additional teachers, Khampheng Boupha (forty-seven) and Khemphet
Pholsena (twenty-nine), represented the Laotian Patriotic Women's Association.
Each group was accompanied by a male translator: Nguyen Tri (forty-six), from
North Viet Nam; Trinh Van Anh (thirty-three), from the South; and Soukanh
Srithirath (thirty-four), from Laos ("The Indochinese Women's Conference" 1971, 3).

REFERENCES

ARCHIVAL AND MANUSCRIPT COLLECTIONS

Patsy T. Mink Papers. Library of Congress, Washington, DC.
"We as Third World Women . . . ," [n.d.]. Kathleen Hudson Women's Bookstore Collec-
tion, F-111, Subject Files, Folder "Indochinese Women Conference," Simon Fraser
University, Archives and Records Management Department, Vancouver, BC.

INTERVIEWS BY THE AUTHOR

Kotake, Donna. 2006. San Francisco, May 31.
Gwendolyn Mink. 2014. Washington, DC, March 18.
Ramirez, Maria, and Nina Genera. 2007. Hayward, CA, February 27.

OTHER SOURCES

Alexander, Michelle. 2012. *The New Jim Crow: Mass Incarceration in the Age of Color-
blindness*. New York: New Press.
Anderson, Benedict. 1991. *Imagined Communities: Reflections on the Origin and Spread
of Nationalism*. Rev. ed. New York: Verso.

Asian Women. 1971/1975. Berkeley: University of California, Asian American Studies Center.

Bassford, Kimberlee. 2008. *Patsy Mink: Ahead of the Majority.* DVD. Honolulu: Making Waves Films.

Bow, Leslie, ed. 2013. *Asian American Feminisms.* Vol. 1. London: Routledge.

Canaday, Margot. 2011. *The Straight State: Sexuality and Citizenship in Twentieth-Century America.* Princeton, NJ: Princeton University Press.

Curwood, Anastasia. 2015. "Black Feminism on Capitol Hill: Shirley Chisholm and Movement Politics, 1968–1984." *Meridians* 13 (1): 204–32.

Eng, David, and Alice Hom. 1988. *Q and A: Queer in Asian America.* Philadelphia: Temple University Press.

Enloe, Cynthia. 1990. *Bananas, Beaches, and Bases: Making Feminist Sense of International Politics.* Berkeley: University of California Press.

Espiritu, Yên Lê. 1993. *Asian American Panethnicity: Bridging Institutions and Identities.* Philadelphia: Temple University Press.

———. 1996. *Asian American Women and Men: Labor, Laws and Love.* Thousand Oaks, CA: Rowman and Littlefield.

Frazier, Robeson Taj. 2015. *The East Is Black: Cold War China in the Black Radical Imagination.* Durham, NC: Duke University Press.

Fujikane, Candace, and Jonathan Y. Okamura, eds. 2008. *Asian Settler Colonialism: From Local Governance to the Habits of Everyday Life in Hawaiʻi.* Honolulu: University of Hawaiʻi Press.

Gilmore, Stephanie, and Sara Evans. 2008. *Feminist Coalitions: Historical Perspectives on Second-Wave Feminism in the United States.* Urbana: University of Illinois Press.

Gore, Dayo F. 2016. "On Behalf of the Revolutionary Black People of the United States: African American Women Radicals in China and the Making of US Third World Solidarity Politics." Paper presented at Revisiting 1968 and the Global Sixties conference, New York University, Shanghai, China, March 14.

Hsu, Madeline Y. 2015. *The Good Immigrants: How the Yellow Peril Became the Model Minority.* Princeton, NJ: Princeton University Press.

"The Indochinese Women's Conference." 1971. Special issue of *Goodbye to All That,* April 20–May 4.

Itagaki, Lynn Mie. 2016. *Civil Racism: The 1992 Los Angeles Rebellion and the Crisis of Racial Burnout.* Minneapolis: University of Minnesota.

Kim, Claire Jean. 2000. *Bitter Fruit: The Politics of Black-Korean Conflict in New York City.* New Haven, CT: Yale University Press.

Kim, Jodi. 2010. *Ends of Empire: Asian American Critique and the Cold War.* Minneapolis: University of Minnesota Press.

Kochiyama, Yuri. 1982. "Asian Women: Past, Present and Future." *East Wind* 1 (1) (Spring/Summer): 12–15.

Kramer, Paul A. 2006. *The Blood of Government: Race, Empire, the United States, and the Philippines.* Chapel Hill: University of North Carolina Press.

Lee, Erika. 2015. *The Making of Asian America: A History.* New York: Simon and Schuster.

Lee, Robert G. 1999. *Orientals: Asian Americans in Popular Culture.* Philadelphia: Temple University Press.

Louie, Miriam Ching. 2001. *Sweatshop Warriors: Immigrant Women Workers Take on the Global Factory.* Boston: South End Press.

Luibhéid, Eithne. 2002. *Entry Denied: Controlling Sexuality at the Border.* Minneapolis: University of Minnesota Press.

Luibhéid, Eithne, and Lionel Cantu Jr., eds. 2005. *Queer Migrations: Sexuality, U.S. Citizenship, and Border Crossings.* Minneapolis: University of Minnesota Press.

Maeda, Daryl Joji. 2001. *Rethinking the Asian American Movement.* New York: Routledge.

———. 2009. *Chains of Babylon: The Rise of Asian America.* Minneapolis: University of Minnesota.

McDuffie, Erik S. 2011. *Sojourning for Freedom: Black Women, American Communism, and the Making of Black Left Feminism.* Durham, NC: Duke University Press.

Mohanty, Chandra Mohanty. 1988. "Under Western Eyes: Feminist Scholarship and Colonial Discourses." *Feminist Review* 30 (Autumn): 61–88.

Moon, Katharine H. S. 1997. *Sex among Allies: Military Prostitution in US-Korea Relations.* New York: Columbia University Press.

Moraga, Cherríe, and Gloria Anzaldúa, eds. 1983. *This Bridge Called My Back: Writings by Radical Women of Color.* 2d ed. New York: Kitchen Table Women of Color Press.

Nagel, Joane. 2003. *Race, Ethnicity, and Sexuality: Intimate Intersections, Forbidden Frontiers.* New York: Oxford University Press.

National Organization for Women. 2016. "Immigration as a Feminist Issue." Accessed April 23, 2016. https://now.org/resource/immigration-as-a-feministissue.

Okihiro, Gary Y. 1991. *Cane Fires: The Anti-Japanese Movement in Hawaii, 1865–1945.* Philadelphia: Temple University Press.

Pierce, Rachel Laura. 2014. "Capitol Feminism: Work, Politics, and Gender in Congress, 1960–1980." PhD diss., University of Virginia.

Roediger, David. 1992. "Gook: The Short History of an Americanism." *Monthly Review* 43 (March): 50–54.

Rupp, Leila J. 1997. *Worlds of Women: The Making of an International Women's Movement.* Princeton, NJ: Princeton University Press.

Said, Edward W. 1979. *Orientalism.* New York: Vintage Books.

Sandoval, Chela. 1991. "U.S. Third World Feminism: The Theory and Method of Oppositional Consciousness in the Postmodern World." *Genders,* no. 10 (Spring): 1–24.

Saranillo, Dean. 2010. "Colliding Histories: Hawai'i Statehood at the Intersection of Asians 'Ineligible to Citizenship' and Hawaiians 'Unfit for Self-Government.'" *Journal of Asian American Studies* 13 (3) (October): 283–309.

Scarlett, Zachary A. 2016. "The Chinese Sixties: Global Narratives and Maoist Politics after the Sino-Soviet Split." Paper presented at the Revisiting 1968 and the Global Sixties conference, New York University, Shanghai, China, March 15.

Shah, Nayan. 2001. *Contagious Divides: Epidemics and Race in San Francisco's Chinatown.* Berkeley: University of California Press.

———. 2012. *Stranger Intimacy: Contesting Race, Sexuality and the Law in the North American West.* Berkeley: University of California Press.

"South Asians for Black Power: On Anti-Blackness, Islamophobia, and Complicity." 2015. Queer South Asian National Network, September 11. https://queersouthasian

.wordpress.com/2015/09/11/south-asians-for-black-power-on-anti-blackness
-islamophobia-and-complicity.

Spivak, Gayatri Chakravorty. 1988. "Can the Subaltern Speak?" In *Marxism and the Interpretation of Culture*, edited by Cary Nelson and Lawrence Grossberg, 271–313. Basingstoke, UK: Macmillan Education.

———. 1990. "Poststructuralism, Marginality, Post-Coloniality and Value." In *Literary Theory Today*, edited by Peter Collier and Helga Geyer-Ryan, 219–44. Ithaca, NY: Cornell University Press.

Stur, Heather Marie. 2011. *Beyond Combat: Women and Gender in the Vietnam War Era*. Cambridge: Cambridge University Press.

"Success Story of One Minority Group in US." 1966/1971. *US News and World Report*, December 26. Reprinted in *Roots: An Asian American Reader*, edited by Amy Tachiki, Eddie Wong, Franklin Odo, and Buck Wong. Los Angeles: Asian American Studies Center, University of California.

Takaki, Ronald. 1983. *Pau Hana: Plantation Life and Labor in Hawaii, 1835–1920*. Manoa: University of Hawai'i Press.

———. 1998. *Strangers from a Different Shore: A History of Asian Americans*. Rev. ed. Boston: Little Brown.

Trask, Haunani-Kay. 1999. *From a Native Daughter: Colonialism and Sovereignty in Hawai'i*. Rev. ed. Honolulu: University of Hawai'i Press.

Wu, Ellen D. 2014. *The Color of Success: Asian Americans and the Origins of the Model Minority*. Princeton, NJ: Princeton University Press.

Wu, Judy Tzu-Chun. 2010. "Rethinking Global Sisterhood: Peace Activism and Women's Orientalism." In *No Permanent Waves: Recasting Histories of US Feminism*, edited by Nancy Hewitt, 193–220. New Brunswick, NJ: Rutgers University Press.

———. 2013. *Radicals on the Road: Internationalism, Orientalism, and Feminism during the Vietnam Era*. Ithaca, NY: Cornell University Press.

———. 2015. "Hypervisibility and Invisibility: The Indochinese Women's Conferences and Asian American Women." In *The Rising Tide of Color: Race, State Violence, and Radical Movements across the Pacific*, edited by Moon-ho Jung, 238–65. Seattle: University of Washington Press.

Wu, Judy, and Gwendolyn Mink. N.d. "Patsy Takemoto Mink: American Citizenship and Post–World War II Liberalism." In preparation.

Yamada, Mitsuye. 1981. "Invisibility Is an Unnatural Disaster: Reflections of an Asian American Woman." In Moraga and Anzaldúa, *This Bridge Called My Back*, 35–40.

Yuh, Ji-Yeon Yuh. 2002. *Beyond the Shadow of Camptown: Korean Military Brides in America*. New York: New York University Press.

PART TWO

EROTIC
(DIS)CONNECTIONS

Epistemologies of Asian American Sexual Politics

CHAPTER 3

WITHOUT ENHANCEMENTS

Sexual Violence in the Everyday Lives of
Asian American Women

ERIN KHUÊ NINH

IT IS HARD TO TAKE A NUANCED POSITION ON SEXUAL VIOLENCE, for reasons this essay will explain. It is additionally tricky to insist on nuances if one has not been a victim of rape, and I have not. Yet I do not feel like a stranger to this universe. As a woman who has lived alone, used to walk home alone, often at night—I am intimate with specters. As a college freshman whose first boyfriend ran a months-long campaign against my virginity, one he eventually won, I am familiar with ambiguity. As a kindergartner who managed to refuse her eight-year-old cousin's false choice between kissing him or his dick, I know it is possible to feel both proud and profoundly soiled, defective.

But there is also this, that in my senior year I felt honored beyond belief that my college professor on his way to the lecture hall had introduced himself to *me* and praised my work. That thereafter we met for lunches, and his approval watered my parched confidence. Then one day he drove me to dinner off campus, and afterward walking to the car took my hand. I berated myself for being naive—*so what if he had a wife and two sons?*—but at least if I did not wrench my hand away I must have shown the kind of fear that I was fortunate he wasn't the man to push past. Still, I needed his letter of recommendation for graduate school. The letter worked.

Something of this scene repeated itself at the end of grad school, with an adviser whose letter I needed as well. Even though I managed to deflect the advances actively this time, I can say without exaggeration that not until the day I received my notice of tenure and promotion—based on evaluations of my work by people I did not know and who knew me barely by name—was I able to pull the brackets from my achievements, excise the cancerous doubt that I did not deserve them.

There is the phone call one afternoon in my freshman dorm, when both my roommates were out. The male voice returned my friendly hello but did not identify himself. Believing this to be a game with some friend, I guessed. And guessed. And engaged in laughing banter. And realized much too inappropriately late that I had overshared with a stranger. When I announced intent to hang up, he threatened to call back, and to tell my roommates what I had done with him. I can't even imagine, much less recall, what leverage he could have made me give him by then, but I tearfully agreed to five more minutes in which I'd follow his instructions, after which (he promised) he'd never call again. I doubt I was convincing: a virgin who had never watched porn. But so crushing was the shame of my cooperation that until I began to write this essay, I had never mentioned the incident to anyone.

These plot points of my past surely explain why I teach not one but two courses on sexual violence. Called "Global Violence, Intimate Harm," the first course introduces rape as product of a patriarchal logic in which women are both nation and property: our function to bear patriarchy's community, our bodies its inheritance. Drawing from a wealth of Asian American feminist literature and criticism, these ten weeks frame sexual violence in the proportions of war, imperialism, and genocide, as indeed one of the fields on which such massive campaigns are waged. But alone, this classic Asian American feminist framework can also compartmentalize, allowing sexual violence to seem synonymous with World War II's comfort women, Vietnamese boat people's Thai pirates, the Third World child sold into sex trafficking, the uneducated immigrant whose husband beats her. Though important battlegrounds for scholarship and activism, these settings are also (conveniently) experientially distant, dangerously distancing.

In a self-reflexive critique of Korean American scholarship on comfort women, Kandice Chuh cautions against a number of investments that can shape the feminist construction of that violence and its victims: a US imperialist/nationalist ideology that finds in "battered, violated" women's bodies usable justification for war (Chuh 2003, 6); a self-serving objectification of another as powerless, such that the critic who takes up that cause as her own claims, "paradoxically, . . . a certain kind of academic power" (8). That is, Asian American feminism recognizes the pitfalls of a scholarship that "distances the observer from the practice and defines the observer as the antithesis of that practice, relies upon and perpetuates a failure to see subordinating practices in our own [First World, academic] culture" (Leti Volpp in Chuh 2003, 7). Yet, our body of work cannot be said to acknowledge sexual coercion of a sunny afternoon and Friday night, the conference room and couch, the anonymous and trusted of Asian American women's lives. Sift through the pages of Asian American feminist anthologies over the decades (much less through *Amerasia* or the *Journal of Asian American Studies*) and when the word *rape* occasionally appears it is usually one item in a list of other violences, not necessarily sexual, contained within a single paragraph of a long essay about something else. Rape as if a matter of fact, not a matter of study: not a problem requiring the attention of our best sociologists, cultural theorists, teachers. Sexual violence as if decades ago or countries away, or at least foreign to this classroom full of Asian American women who are learning to date.

My classrooms thus explain the writing of this essay, because term after term, some number of Asian American women in these courses make it known that there have been for them no safe distances from or provisional structures of heightened vulnerability; the rape they know is part of an everyday culture. "Dating in Rape Culture" has become the second course in my series, but for its syllabus I have been able to draw on nearly nothing by way of Asian American feminist literature or criticism.

Early biases, stemming at least in part from cultural nationalism, set Asian American feminism on a course to treat rape as epiphenomenal: its violence interesting only as illuminating a structural base, so to speak, of other violences. Its *victims* interesting mainly as forensic evidence, in the pursuit of a larger pattern of destruction. This model has grave limitations. *Making More Waves*, one of the definitive collections of Asian American feminist writing, includes a chapter titled "Violence in Our Communities." Written by Helen Zia, the essay is based on her work with a group "formed . . . to study the nexus of violence against Asian women and hate crimes" (Zia 1997, 207). It begins with five cases, presenting them as hate crimes that were not classified as such. Three of these figure rapes: a young girl raped and lynched, victims of a serial rapist, women gang-raped by fraternity brothers; all the victims Asian, all the perpetrators seemingly not. Addressing the exclusion of women from classifications of anti-Asian hate crime, the group responded by arguing for expansion of the definition of "hate violence" to mean any violence "used as a means of exerting power, control, and domination by one group over another" (Zia 1997, 209). Into this capacious category, they swept cases as varied as "the white man who claimed [a] 'phobia of Asians'" and pushed a stranger to her death on a subway platform; "the murder of an Asian woman by her [white] husband"; the shooting death "of an Asian woman by her [Asian] ex-husband"; even the shooting of a Chinese lesbian by her (battering?) Chinese lover: all "should be considered" hate crimes because in each is putatively "the ultimate exercise of power and control used by one to dominate the other" (Zia 1997, 210–11). Aside from diluting *hate* into a meaningless term, this argument also displayed a revealing disregard for the *nature* of the violent act: random or long-standing, intimate or stranger, sexual or not. Indeed, the essay granted rape no specificity as a type of crime; it is nonessential to the definition, little more than a stepping stone to arguing for the classification of violence against racially Asian women as racialized violence.

To be sure, there is a longtime debate among feminists over the more accurate/advantageous plotting of rape: onto a continuum of sexual coercions (from "an unwanted kiss" to verbal pressuring of a partner, including harassment [Gavey 1999, 60]), or, as Foucault along with early radical feminists would have had it, as a species of assault, an attack on the body comparable to any other (Haag 1996). But the "hate crime" essay above is not an example of that debate; it is instead an early and influential instance of the political priorities among Asian American feminists that have made rape uninteresting except as revealing of colonization, or military occupation, or genocide. Not *per se*. This is not to suggest that sexual violence ever happens in a gender-isolation chamber; it is to rail that within Asian American feminism, sexual violence should be deemed a thin charge without enhancements.

In making this point, I lean somewhat on arguments made by other feminists of color regarding the hierarchies that cast some rapes as political, others as derivative. Kimberlé Crenshaw, for instance, takes to task the "general tendency within antiracist discourse to regard the problem of violence against women of color as just another manifestation of racism" (Crenshaw 1991, 1257), including the interpretation of Black male violence against Black women as a subsidiary stage in a "cycle" of violence generated and initiated by white injuries against Black masculinity (1258). But as I see it, among women of color, even explicitly feminist (i.e., "antipatriarchal") discourse may treat sexual violence as derivative. That is, only for white women is it allowable that the most powerful lens through which to explain rape might sometimes be gender.

White feminist scholarship has had periodic sessions of vigorous theorizing about sexual violence, but it was last intensively debated well over ten years ago—arguably in the 1990s.[1] With the surge of national attention to rape and sexual harassment on college campuses in the past few years, however (as well as the #MeToo movement, which caught fire during the last editing stages of this collection), sexual violence is likely coming to the fore of mainstream feminist research once again. For Asian American scholars to weigh in this time would mean taking off some blinders. Because, of course, a gap in scholarship is more than a function of poor resource allocation; it is a function of (un)thinkable questions, (un)sanctioned politics.

Studies of domestic violence in Asian American communities (including but not specific to sexual abuse) are relatively common, especially in the social sciences (see, e.g., Rimonte 1989; Dasgupta 2007). But the "cultural" frameworks immediately invoked in such studies let on that—despite researchers' earnest mission to shine light into previously hidden corners of abuse—their range is set to recognize only a certain profile of victims: "immigrant battered women" who are likely subject to threats of deportation, "shame of failing to please one's husband, . . . and bringing dishonor to the natal family" (Dasgupta 2007, 3). Psychology highlights the "patriarchal aspects of Asian culture, in which women hold subordinate status to men," while balancing that eternal truism with the "Asian cultural emphases on self-control and interpersonal harmony [which] may serve as protective factors" (Okazaki 2002, 39); we learn that their inferior status along with "the value placed on harmony in interpersonal relationships" render "Asian women . . . generally less likely to openly challenge male behaviors, including sexual advances. As a result, Asian women may find it more difficult to 'say no' to unwanted sexual advances or tend to be silent about or tolerate the problems of sexual violence" (M. Lee 2001, 7).

Cultural essentialism aside, it is certainly gratifying to know that intimate partner violence primarily afflicts a quaint tribe of primitive ancestors, who bear no resemblance to the US-passport-bearing, Trinh Minh-ha–reading, interracial-dating Asian women on either side of our lecterns. Where I am going with this: we do not concern ourselves that the model minority can be raped, because the model minority does not exist. Yet sexual coercion takes place not only within the structural engines of war and punishment; it also takes place within the poststructural engines of productivity and reward. And on what grounds do we assume that Stanford rapist Brock Turner's victim is white?

In other words, what little Asian American feminist scholarship there is on sexual violence envisions its subject in Othering terms—*in the sense that* the prevailing concepts of "culture" it imagines victims to inhabit are so fossilized they might as well be stereotypes. "Domestic partner" is seemingly synonymous with "immigrant male enforcing home-country values"—even as, elsewhere in the field, it is a loudly known fact that straight Asian women often partner with white men. Whether these women are foreign-born or US-born, in 1980 or 2008, outmarriage to white men stands at about 40 percent (Qian and Lichter 2011, 1072). Moreover, second-, third-, and later-generation Asian Americans have increasingly begun to marry interethnically (and intergenerationally), such that even within intraracial pairings "cultural" assumptions are likely contested (Qian, Blair, and Ruf 2001). The current college population, meanwhile, may have a broad range of sexual encounters entirely unaccounted for by existing domestic violence paradigms: Asian women at Stanford in 2005, for example, were found to choose non-Asian partners for 47 percent of their long-term relationships, 59 percent of their dates, and 74 percent of their hookups (McClintock 2010, 56). If sexual coercion takes place within these couplings, the preset explanations cannot apply; whether sexual coercion takes place within these couplings, we have not bothered to look.

Splicing research on sexual violence with that on interracial gender dynamics seems in order, then, but even where the latter is concerned, care should be taken not to take stereotypes for social firmament. Long-standing common wisdom in Asian American studies says that "while today's Anglo-American women can be viewed as hard-working, tough, persistent, career-minded etc., Asian-American women are still seen today as sex toys, cute, subservient, man-serving" (Chen 1997, 55). But the "today" of that statement arguably better reflects the 1990s of its writing—or even the 1960s of the argument's first framing—than perceptions that greet young women thirty to sixty years later. As the model minority has become an increasingly dominant, *competitive* force in American educational and professional spheres (discursively, less a convenient foil to other minorities and more a threat to white preeminence), the racial gendering of Asian women has taken on new tones. For what Min Zhou and Jennifer Lee call Asian America's "new second generation," it may be that they are cast as neither "lotus blossom" nor "dragon lady": "American stereotypes of Asian women are becoming more masculine. . . . Asian American women are represented more in technical and business magazines than in women's and hobby magazines. Asian American female images occurred in work rather than in outdoor, social, or home settings. . . . [They are] presented as individuals who are more focused on their careers than on their families, *contradicting older stereotypes that portray Asian American women as domestic and submissive*" (Tsai, Przymus, and Best 2002, 204, emphasis added). What it is to present sexually as an Asian American woman "today"—in couplings across race, ethnicity, generation, and orientation—we cannot presume we know.

Perhaps the most perilous gap in scholarship on sexual violence, however, is not specific to Asian American feminism, and has to do not with areas of inquiry but with allowable degrees of nuance. Because even while sexual violence may take place along a continuum, agency is held to be binary: the violator is all agency, motivation, and action; the violated strictly acted upon, an effacing non-role. To suggest otherwise is to be taken as reversing entirely the charge of blame, because there is no permissible third option. In an important essay on this topic, Sharon Marcus cites the "gendered grammar of violence, where grammar means the rules and structure which assign people to positions within a script" and that script "induces men . . . to recognize their gendered selves in images and narratives of aggression," while it "encourages women to become subjects by imagining ourselves as objects" (Marcus 1992, 392, 393). Against her argument that men and women are *gendered* into roles as potential rapist and target—and that therefore women (no less than men) can act in greater or lesser accommodation to that patriarchal scripting—her critics have generally responded that this suggestion dangerously "ground[s rape] in the victim's behavioral or emotional dynamics *rather than* in the perpetrator's actions" (Mardorossian 2002, 756, emphasis added). Marcus's position is made equivalent to that of conservative antifeminists via a forceful flattening that, ironically, turns her critic's argument into caricature: we are told that when victims reflect upon ways they might have averted their assault "had they acted differently," this is a retroactive "coping mechanism in reaction to the rape . . . *and not a testimony of the victim's participation in gender socialization* before *the assault*" (Mardorossian 2002, 753, emphasis added). The first half of this claim is as surely true as the latter half is surely false: We are to believe that the woman in question did not participate in gender socialization until the moment of her rape? That until the fateful assault that transforms women into victims or survivors, they are not interpellated subjects or docile bodies of heterosexual norms? That men but *not* women are products of rape culture?

Asian American feminism's selective focus within sexual violence—on forms thoroughly couched in formal histories, in visible systems of economic exchange and military infrastructure—makes it even more inhospitable to suggestions of "participation in gender socialization before the assault." As defined by conditions of overwhelming power, a victim's agency is precisely what is vacated, and the very notion of her accountability, repugnant. But these are not the only conditions under which sexual coercion takes place, nor are they thus the only priorities that demand theorization. Moreover, the work of bringing the more "mundane" realities to knowledge ought not be delegated to psychology alone. To do so is, by default, to make the messy effects of rape culture a matter of measure, not of contention. That is, in addition to the descriptive work of incidences and prevalences, of incapacitated rape and sexual harassment, of attitudes endorsed by ethnicity and generation . . . we need the work that asks whether our rubrics—for culture, say, or consent—organize experience or obscure it. Marcus points to empathy ("a quality deemed feminine even when detached from female practitioners") as an example of gendering that makes women better prey: prodding victims to "identify" with would-be "rapists rather than to defend themselves from rapists' desire to destroy their targets" (Marcus 1992, 393). Hers is a highly controversial stance, where the orthodox feminist position is very clear: the victim is to be "innocent, blameless, and [most importantly] free of problems (before the abuse)" (Lamb 1999a, 108). Say otherwise and prepare to be trolled. But to posit an implicated "agency" in this context is not to imply simple self-determination; it is rather to take for our starting point its opposite: a subject trained to a certain habitus, disciplined to specific aspirations, tuned to particular needs. Such a subject, long before the moment of assault, has wishes—and they may well be problematic; has tendencies—and they likely do not serve her well. Such a subject can sign legally binding contracts—it is just that her consent is already compromised.

It is in *this* sense that I'd agree Asian American women's experiences of sexual coercion are "culturally" inflected:[2] sabotaged by the model minority paradigm *not as stereotype* but as *subject formation*. For Asian American women, the gendered grammar of violence joins with a scripting of the subject as the consummately obliging solution to social anxieties, workforce shortfalls, familial losses, communal dreams. What is consent for a subject whose algorithm for all things is to identify and meet the standards set by others? For whom the question of yes or no has been ontologically supplanted by the question of success or failure? When *what to do with one's life* is not a question for personal choice, why should *what to do with one's body* be any more than another occasion to make someone else happy?

However unwelcome, such a possibility follows a materialist feminist trajectory to its logical conclusion. If we grant that "social forces [may] represent a type of coercion similar to interpersonal coercion (although [distinct] from it)," then consent "becomes something broader than just a 'yes' to sex with a specific person, in a particular place, at a particular time. It becomes *a negotiation of social expectations, a way of expressing a social identity*, or of fitting in to a certain social world" (Beres 2007, 99, emphasis added). What my work on the psychic construction of the filial daughter compels me to see is the overdetermination of sexual compliance for a model-minority woman: young women operating within postfeminist ideals of selfhood may well engage "in undesired sex in order to make a man 'happy' in an encounter in which [they do] not want to disappoint him" (Burkett and Hamilton 2012, 822)—because to disappoint is to fail.

To be clear, this argument in no way implies that a woman's "no" should be disregarded, or her hesitation discounted. To the contrary. It is to argue that cultural scripts may so alienate a well-gendered subject from the validity of her own wishes that they can preempt violence: make coercion structural, not inflictive. That therefore any hesitation must be attended all the more scrupulously, and by all parties involved. That the indicative question is not necessarily the yes/no delineation of "affirmative consent"—extraction of agreement, legally binding. That the indicative question is instead "How do you feel?"

Subject formation is highly flammable talk when it comes to rape prevention, but for Asian Americans especially, who perpetually bemoan "perpetual foreigner" status, here is why it is necessary: the subject alienated from her own desires is not exotically tragic; she is uber-American. It is not Confucianism but Hollywood narrative cinema (Mulvey 1999) and Fifth Avenue billboards (Bartky 1997; Sobchack 1999) that train into women the relationship to their bodies as objects for male pleasure: "By re-enforcing that sex is about an image, that looking good is more important than feeling good, [Victoria's Secret] promotes rape culture" (Monroe 2012). "Postfeminist sexual agency" describes a potent cocktail of self-empowerment *qua* ability to be pleasing, such that a woman believes it to be a liberated, "individual choice to please her man" (Burkett and Hamilton 2012, 823). The term was coined to describe not geisha but contemporary sexual practices among young, Western women for whom Paris Hilton is a role model. To approach culture from this angle is to plot model-minority subject formation onto legitimately intersectional axes, and to theorize Asian American sexual violence along an American continuum, rather than as an invasive species.

Likewise, where Asian American men are perpetrators, "culture" must mean "rape culture" as much if not more than it means "pre-modern, non-Western inheritance." In this era after mixed-race campus shooter Elliot Rodger's murderous manifesto, it is imperative to think about sexual violence as a function of toxic masculinity:[3] where sexual conquests confer manhood, young men are raised to feel "entitled" to sex—and a woman's refusal (*denial*) does direct injury. This is a script in which Asian men may strive to play the leading role, or resent their typecasting, but it is unequivocally a homegrown, domestic genre.

Subject formation is not a professionally risky lens through which to study perpetrators, however—only victims. In this, there is a parallel to racialization: "An intellectual taboo surrounds the study of internalized racism. A major concern is that because internalized racism reveals dynamics by which oppression is reproduced, it will lead to blaming the victims and move attention away from . . . racist institutions and practices" (Pyke and Dang 2003, 151). Whatever threat internalized racism and sexism may pose to the clarity of political agendas, however, criticism that does not grapple with subject formation risks doing its subjects further injustice. Insofar as internalization means that subjects learn to facilitate their own harm, it is a theory of implicated agency. The young postfeminist, say, who has "actively decided to recompose her own sexuality in terms of the primacy of her partner's needs . . . has exerted agency by selecting to do so" and is "not trapped in a unidirectional system of power" (Burkett and Hamilton 2012, 829). To grant such a subject agency *even if implicated* holds open the possibility that she may come to discern her formation, her desires, her habitual ways of being, and having done so may alter them. Or, perhaps, to deny her implication is to foreclose for her a narrative rescripting. After all, what is a feminism that does not allow for consciousness-raising? A feminism that relieves the violated subject of a contributing role *of any kind* consigns her to a story of perennial victimhood, where she is as helpless to avert the next violation as she was the first. But if toxic femininity is learned, it can be unlearned. It is possible to love toxic masculinity, and it is possible to stop.

NOTES

1   To be fair, Asian American studies is not alone in handling the topic of sexual violence gingerly. In 2002, an article in the feminist journal *Signs* observed that "rape has become academia's undertheorized and apparently untheorizable issue. . . . [S]kim through the issues of feminist journals over the last ten years to see this puzzling scholarly neglect" (Mardorossian 2002, 743). Moreover, "when sexual violence is discussed in academic criticism, it is generally in terms of its cinematic representation" (746); add "literary representation" and this statement holds true in Asian American feminism as well, to this day.

2   . . . though they likely overlap more than they differ from other young women on the continuum of that violence.

3   Rodgers believed his superiority as a "beautiful Eurasian" entitled him to blond women, and he was enraged by what he felt to be his universal rejection as an Asian man. See Fang (2014), Shen (2016), and 18 Million Rising (2016).

REFERENCES

Bartky, Sandra Lee. 1997. "Foucault, Femininity and the Modernization of Patriarchal Power." In *Writing on the Body: Female Embodiment and Feminist Theory*, edited by Katie Conboy, Nadia Medina, and Sarah Stanburym, 129–54. New York: Columbia University Press.

Beres, Melanie. 2007. "'Spontaneous' Sexual Consent: An Analysis of Sexual Consent Literature." *Feminism and Psychology* 17 (1) (February): 93–108.

Burkett, Melissa, and Karine Hamilton. 2012. "Postfeminist Sexual Agency: Young Women's Negotiations of Sexual Consent." *Sexualities* 15 (7) (October): 815–33.

Chen, Edith Wen-Chu. 1997. "Sexual Harassment from the Perspective of Asian-American Women." In *Everyday Sexism in the Third Millennium*, edited by Carol R. Ronai and Barbara A. Zsem, 51–62. Abingdon: Routledge.

Chuh, Kandice. 2003. "Discomforting Knowledge: Or, Korean 'Comfort Women' and Asian Americanist Critical Practice." *Journal of Asian American Studies* 6 (1) (February): 5–23.

Crenshaw, Kimberlé. 1991. "Mapping the Margins: Intersectionality, Identity Politics, and Violence against Women of Color." *Stanford Law Review* 43 (6) (July): 1241–99.

Dasgupta, Shamita. 2007. *Body Evidence: Intimate Violence against South Asian Women in America*. New Brunswick, NJ: Rutgers University Press.

18 Million Rising. 2016. "#HyperMasculAZNs: Discussing Toxic Masculinity, Misogyny, and Patriarchy in the AAPI Community." Twitter chat, August 5. https://storify.com/Juliet_Shen/hypermasculazns.

Fang, Jenn. 2014. "Masculinity vs. 'Misogylinity': What Asian Americans Can Learn from #UCSB Shooting | #YesAllWomen," *Reappropriate*, May 28, http://reappropriate.co/2014/05/masculinity-vs-misogylinity-what-asian-americans-can-learn-from-ucsb-shooting-yesallwomen.

Gavey, Nicola. 1999. "'I Wasn't Raped, but . . . ': Revisiting Definitional Problems in Sexual Victimization." In *New Versions of Victims: Feminists Struggle with the Concept*, edited by Sharon Lamb, 57–81. New York: New York University Press.

Haag, Pamela. 1996. "'Putting Your Body on the Line': Theories of Violence and Feminist Politics of Rape, 1968–1975." *differences: A Journal of Feminist Cultural Studies* 8 (2) (Summer): 23–67.

Lamb, Sharon. 1999a. "Constructing the Victim." In *New Versions of Victims: Feminists Struggle with the Concept*, edited by Sharon Lamb, 108–38. New York: New York University Press.

———. 1999b. Introduction in *New Versions of Victims: Feminists Struggle with the Concept*, edited by Sharon Lamb, 1–12. New York: New York University Press.

Lee, Jennifer, and Min Zhou. 2015. *The Asian American Achievement Paradox*. New York: Russell Sage Foundation.

Lee, Mo Yee, and Phyllis F. M. Law. 2001. "Perception of Sexual Violence against Women in Asian American Communities." *Journal of Ethnic & Cultural Diversity in Social Work* 10 (2): 3–25.

Marcus, Sharon. 1992. "Fighting Bodies, Fighting Words: A Theory and Politics of Rape Prevention." In *Feminists Theorize the Political*, edited by Judith Butler and Joan Wallach Scott, 385–403. Abingdon: Routledge.

Mardorossian, Carine M. 2002. "Toward a New Feminist Theory of Rape." *Signs* 27 (3) (Spring): 743–77.

McClintock, Elizabeth. 2010. "When Does Race Matter? Race, Sex, and Dating at an Elite University." *Journal of Marriage and Family* 72 (1) (January): 45–72.

Monroe, Rachel. 2012. "Baltimore Feminists Prank Victoria's Secret—and Spark an Internet Revolution." *Baltimore Fishbowl*, December 10. www.baltimorefishbowl.com /stories/baltimore-feminists-prank-victorias-secret-and-spark-an-internet-revolution.

Mulvey, Laura. 1999. "Visual Pleasure and Narrative Cinema." In *Film Theory and Criticism: Introductory Readings*, edited by Leo Braudy and Marshall Cohen, 833–44. Oxford: Oxford University Press.

Okazaki, Sumie. 2002. "Influences of Culture on Asian Americans' Sexuality." *Journal of Sex Research* 39 (1): 34–41.

Pyke, Karen, and Tran Dang. 2003. "'FOB' and 'Whitewashed': Identity and Internalized Racism among Second Generation Asian Americans." *Qualitative Sociology* 26 (2) (Summer): 147–72.

Qian, Zhenchao, Sampson Lee Blair, and Stacey D. Ruf. 2001. "Asian American Interracial and Interethnic Marriages: Differences by Education and Nativity." *International Migration Review* 35 (2) (Summer): 557–86.

Qian, Zhenchao, and Daniel T. Lichter. 2011. "Changing Patterns of Interracial Marriage in a Multiracial Society." *Journal of Marriage and Family* 73 (October): 1065–84.

Rimonte, Nilda. 1989. "Domestic Violence among Pacific Asians." In *Making Waves: An Anthology of Writings by and about Asian American Women*, edited by Asian Women United of California, 327–37. Boston: Beacon Press.

Shen, Juliet. 2016. "Work in Progress: Emotional Abuse and Violence in Our Communities." AngryAsianMan.com, August 23. http://blog.angryasianman.com/2016/08 /work-in-progress-emotional-abuse-and.html?m=1.

Sobchack, Vivian. 1999. "'Is Anybody Home?' Embodied Imagination and Visible Evictions." In *Home, Exile, Homeland: Film, Media, and the Politics of Place*, edited by Hamid Naficy, 45–61. Abingdon: Routledge.

Tsai, Jeanne L., Diane E. Przymus, and Jennifer L. Best. 2002. "Toward an Understanding of Asian American Interracial Marriage and Dating." In *Inside the American Couple: New Thinking/New Challenges*, edited by Marilyn Yalom and Laura L Carstensen, 189–210. Berkeley: University of California Press.

Zia, Helen. 1997. "Violence in Our Communities: Where Are the Asian Women?" In *Making More Waves: New Writing by Asian American Women*, edited by Elaine H. Kim, Lilia V. Villanueva, and Asian Women United of California, 207–14. Boston: Beacon Press.

CHAPTER 4

PEMINIST AND QUEER AFFILIATION IN LITERATURE AS A BLUEPRINT FOR FILIPINX DECOLONIZATION AND LIBERATION

THOMAS XAVIER SARMIENTO

THE LITERARY IS A POWERFUL FORM OF ACTIVISM. IT CAN provide a blueprint for other worlds and other modes of living and being, inciting readers to enact change in their own worlds. Rather than presuppose the arts as simply aesthetic and removed from so-called on-the-ground organizing and mobilization, I see art as a valuable arm of political activism, building upon Filipinx studies scholars' "ongoing attempt to resurrect buried artistic and political models" found in Filipinx cultural production (Manalansan and Espiritu 2016, 5).[1] I developed this viewpoint in college as a gender studies major and student activist involved in one of the Filipinx campus organizations. These experiences introduced me to the power of cultural production to raise one's consciousness and engender action, whether grand or minute. As a young queer Pinoy (Filipino American male), my identification with Filipinx-ness was initially ambivalent at best (due to the seemingly heteronormative bent of dominant Filipinx American student activism on my campus), and it was through performance art and literature that featured gender- and sexually transgressive Filipinxs that I discovered a place for my intersectional subjectivity within the Filipinx struggle against colonial oppression and white supremacy.

In this chapter, I chart the productive possibilities that a peminist—or Filipinx American feminist—and queer political orientation offer to

Filipinx decolonization by tracing its manifestation in foundational, contemporary diasporic Filipinx literature. A peminist and queer Filipinx coalition engenders a more radical politics of liberation compared to an approach that centers race and coloniality alone. While some critics might cast feminist and queer concerns as secondary (or even tertiary) to antiracism and anti-imperialism, Women of Color feminisms remind us that all oppressions, and thus all struggles for liberation, are interlinked.[2] Filipinx feminist and queer scholars and activists who are in dialogue with the macropolitical project of Women of Color feminisms while focusing on the micropolitical context of the Philippines and its global diaspora share such a sentiment and argue that their investments in antisexism and antiheteronormativity are very much in line with antiracism and anti-imperialism.

Peminism centers Filipinx subjectivity. It is rooted in the Filipina/x standpoint and forwards a way of knowing and being that centers Filipina/x struggles for decolonization and sees gender and sexual liberation as key to those struggles. Although it has emerged from the unique positionality of Filipinas in the United States, it operates as an analytical lens that maps how racism and imperialism operate through gendered and sexualized bodies. Understanding peminism as an analytic avoids the trap of homogenizing, and thus essentializing, Filipina American experience. And while peminism accounts for queer sexualities, it is important to name queerness as a complementary analytic and subject position so as to avoid flattening the sociocultural differences between racialized genders and sexualities.

As Filipinx struggles against colonial oppression and white supremacy in the Philippines and its global diaspora over the past century and recent scholarship in Filipinx studies have demonstrated (see Cruz 2012; Diaz 2015; Fajardo 2011; Gonzalez 2013; Isaac 2006; Manalansan 2003; Mendoza 2015; Ponce 2012; R. Rodriguez 2010; and See 2009), gender and sexuality are central to Filipinx racialization and imperial subjugation. To privilege race as the primary lens through which to understand Filipinx experience forecloses critical engagement with the various systems of oppression that bear on the Filipinx body; such systems of oppression, besides racism, include but are not limited to classism, sexism, heterosexism, homophobia, transphobia, and ableism. While intersectional thinking has become the standard for contemporary progressive politics, how to put that theory into practice remains a challenge. To forward an intersectional and coalitional praxis as fundamental to Filipinx critique and political mobilization reshapes what might be deemed a Filipinx concern, transforming intra- and intergroup interactions and priorities for the better. Since "divide and conquer" is a tool of white supremacist capitalist heteropatriarchy, decolonization must replace such toxic tactics of domination with "define and empower" (Lorde 1983, 100). As Audre Lorde explains, to "define and empower" involves articulating the myriad ways power operates across a field of identities and embodied experiences and recognizing the force of collective action. It means seeing oneself as intimately connected with others. Such a relational way of knowing and being fosters mutuality.

For me, contemporary diasporic Filipinx literature is a fitting entry point to engage the productive entanglements of peminist and queer Filipinx critique for mapping out Filipinx decolonization and liberation. Through its fictive world making and re-membering, diasporic Filipinx literature blurs the lines between real and imaginary, between recorded History and speculative histories. In so doing, it opens up a space to see and feel differently. As Kandice Chuh (2003, 35–36) argues, Filipinx American literature directs Asian American studies to understand the field as not simply a discourse of race and ethnicity but a "discourse of sexuality" and postcoloniality. In its disloyalty to nation and its refusal to represent a singular identity formation, such cultural production aligns with intersectional feminisms' call to take seriously the mutually constitutive nature of oppression and queer theory's deconstruction of identity. As opposed to interpreting such texts exclusively as social history, I read them as aesthetic pedagogies that provide clues to how our world is and ought to be.

While contemporary diasporic Filipinx literature certainly encompasses multiple overlapping themes that concern racial-ethnic identity, gender and sexuality feature prominently, revealing a pattern that suggests these social formations are endemic, rather than simply ancillary, to diasporic Filipinx experience. However, rather than being overtly peminist and queer in its political orientations, diasporic Filipinx creative work is less prescriptive and more inviting. This invitational tone works to avoid reproducing a disciplinary impetus that outlines a singular pathway for decolonization and liberation.

Celebrated and criticized for its postmodern aesthetics, Filipina American author Jessica Hagedorn's writing exemplifies the relationalities among Filipinx decolonization, gender liberation, and queer unbecoming. Her best-known novel, *Dogeaters*, published in 1990, features an ensemble cast whose lives are intertwined by the forces of autocratic rule and neocolonial influence. Among its narrators are Rio Gonzaga, a Filipina mestiza whose family is financially and politically connected, and Joey Sands, a multiracial Filipino queer DJ who lives in the slums of Manila. As an assemblage of gendered, classed, sexualized, and racialized perspectives on postcolonial Philippines, the novel invites readers to develop a peminist and queer critique of nation and empire. Similarly, Hagedorn's second novel, *The Gangster of Love*, published in 1996, provides a complementary take on Filipinx material realities by shifting away from the Philippine nation/ homeland to the US diaspora. Narrated in part by Raquel "Rocky" Rivera, a Filipina migrant, the story follows her life in the United States from adolescence into adulthood as she unsuccessfully attempts to forget the life she, her mother, and her brother left behind in the Philippines. Whereas *Dogeaters* fictionalizes life in the Philippines under the US-backed Ferdinand Marcos fascist regime, *Gangster* fictionalizes the aftermath of the autocrat's fall from grace. Together, both novels illustrate the power of literature to account for political economic atrocities and thus to serve as a repository for subaltern collective memory; importantly, they also reveal the forms that might be taken by affective intimacies between gender and sexual dissent against hetero-masculine postcolonial nationalisms to usher in a more just society in the future present.

Dogeaters and *Gangster* are valuable pedagogical tools for speculating about what social justice might look like. Cultural production like Hagedorn's literature not only refracts society; it also creates society. Both novels eloquently speak to their sociohistorical contexts, responding to and creatively reimagining the complex world they inhabit. In their refusal to be representative of Filipinx America, both novels unsettle the myth of racial-ethnic authenticity. *Gangster* in particular centers on the protagonist's disavowal of her Filipina identity, not to reject her heritage but to suggest that she is much more than her ethnic identity. In other words, Hagedorn's novels showcase characters who embody complex personhood that loosely coheres around an imagined racial-ethnic community but is not exclusively defined by it.[3] Both novels' embrace of peminist and queer sensibilities depart from dominant Filipinx cultural nationalism, calling into question what it means to be Filipinx in the first place and proffering a more inclusive notion of Filipinx subjectivity.[4]

In fact, *Dogeaters* was the first novel I read by an author of Filipinx descent, and it reshaped my understanding of gender and ethnic studies and political resistance. Despite having been involved in Filipinx student organizing as an undergraduate, I often felt that my queer identity was at odds with the group. Hagedorn's novel, an assigned text in one of my undergraduate gender studies courses, taught me to regard my feminist, queer, and Pinoy identities as compatible and inextricably tied to one another.

Recognizing Hagedorn's fiction as part of the Women of Color feminist tradition of fusing creative writing and political consciousness (see Moraga and Anzaldúa 1983), years later as a university professor I assigned *Gangster* in my Women of Color feminism course (partly because I wanted to draw attention to Hagedorn's other work beyond *Dogeaters* and because it is set in the United States, which would be more familiar to my Kansas students) and invited my students to recognize how the literary can function not only as theory but also as a blueprint for political action.

Reading *Dogeaters* and *Gangster* as exemplary but not exhaustive of contemporary diasporic Filipinx literature that activates affiliation across different racialized genders and sexualities, I argue that a peminist and queer hermeneutic paves the way for decolonial Filipinx coalitional politics. In both novels, cisgender Filipina protagonists forge affective bonds with cisgender queer Filipino characters.[5] By foregrounding these heterosocial relationships, I highlight the peminist-queer coalitional politics Hagedorn's novels forward as an alternative to postcolonial Filipinx nationalism. While several scholars have analyzed the gender and sexual politics in *Dogeaters* (see Bascara 2006; Chang 2003; Isaac 2006; Lee 1999; Lowe 1996; Mendoza 2005; and Ponce 2012), and in *Gangster* to a lesser extent (see Balance 2016; and Ponce 2012), much of that scholarship does not explicitly articulate the p/feminist and queer relationalities Hagedorn's work traces. While some might argue that an attention to feminism presupposes that queerness is part of the conversation, or that an attention to queerness is necessarily feminist, as Gayatri Gopinath's (2005) work in diasporic South Asian public cultures argues, such is not always the case. As obvious as linking peminism and queerness might seem, especially given the roots of Women of Color feminist consciousness-raising as inclusive of queerness,[6] I argue that our contemporary moment must not take for granted the epistemic and political imperative to conceptualize the connections among antisexism, antiheteronormativity, antiracism, and anti-imperialism.[7] Paying attention to the peminist and queer Filipinx intimacies modeled by Hagedorn's characters works to remind and inspire us to continue forging intra- and intergroup solidarities across sociocultural difference if we are ever to live beyond our present.

FILIPINIZING FEMINISM

As I briefly outlined above, peminism aims to tease out the specificities of diasporic Filipina and Filipinx being. In her introduction to *Pinay Power*, the first published anthology on peminism, Melinda de Jesús (2005a, 5) defines peminism as "a specific form of feminist theory rooted in the *Filipina American* experience—an experience very different from the implicit (and thus explicit) subject of white liberal feminism . . . [that] describes Filipina American struggles against racism, sexism, imperialism, and homophobia and struggles for decolonization, consciousness, and liberation." Such a definition of peminism critiques hegemonic feminism's solipsistic tendency to center the experiences of white, cisgender, heterosexual, middle-class, US-based women. It also highlights peminism's commitment to an intersectional, decolonial politics. While peminism aligns with the broader project of Filipinx American critique as it seeks to remedy Filipinx American political and cultural invisibility and underrepresentation in the United States, it also calls attention to the particular "invisibility of Filipinas within Asian American and Filipino American studies" and "underrepresentation of Filipinas within the field of feminist studies" (de Jesús 2005a, 4). However, peminism is not simply a call for additive inclusion; rather, it provides a critique of the confluence of race, class, gender, sexuality, nation, and empire from the situated vantage point of Filipinas and demands a re-vision of political action.

Peminism also can be understood as Pinayism. Having coined the latter term, Allyson Tintiangco-Cubales (2005, 141) argues that Pinayism "aims to look at the complexity of the intersections where race/ethnicity, class, gender, sexuality, spirituality/religion, education, educational status, age, place of birth, Diasporic migration, citizenship, and love cross." For her, the particularity of Filipina American lives demands a unique brand of feminism that speaks to Filipina Americans. Rather than "finding a place for Pinays [Filipina American females] on the continuum of white feminism and black womanism," Pinayism aims "to create a place for [Pinays] outside [such a] continuum." In fact, "Pinayism is not just a Filipino version of feminism or womanism; Pinayism draws from a potpourri of theories and philosophies" (Tintiangco-Cubales 2005, 139). While she acknowledges the importance of Black feminisms in shaping her feminist consciousness, Tintiangco-Cubales also points to their limits in reifying a Black-white racial paradigm that fails to account for those who do not fit in either racial category and whose subjection under white supremacy is radically different from, though entwined with, African Americans. Thus, not unlike Chicana feminisms, Pinayism works to articulate the interstitial location of Filipina Americans navigating between and beyond a binaristic understanding of race in the United States as well as the fissures within their racial-ethnic community along the lines of gender and sexuality.

De Jesús's and Tintiangco-Cubales's articulations of Filipina American antisexist politics indicate that peminism/Pinayism shares in the intersectional, relational, and coalitional sensibilities of Women of Color feminisms from the unique vantage point of Pinays. And in alignment with Women of Color feminist politics, peminism/Pinayism is inherently antiracist and antihomophobic. Although it might be tempting to subordinate peminism/Pinayism as offshoots of Asian American feminisms, because of Filipinxs' particular histories of racial formation and coloniality as well as their vexed relationship to Asian America, peminism/Pinayism affiliates with but ultimately exceeds Asian American feminist formations. As Nerissa Balce (2016, 10) points out, "The history and culture of Filipino Americans cannot be understood as just another variant of the Asian American immigrant narrative, but as one that is uniquely scarred by colonization and codependence." Sarita See (2009, xxx) offers a similar observation of Filipinx American particularity that dissociates Filipinxs from Asian American panethnicity when she writes: "Filipino American difference . . . often is at odds with the deraced coalitional politics of Asian American studies, which has its own brand of color blindness to the detriment of racially heterogeneous Asian American communities like Filipino America with its explicit in-group vocabulary and coding for race mixture."[8] Moreover, Balce (2016, 10) and See (2009, xv) highlight how critiques of US imperialism in the Philippines align with postcolonial studies but radically depart from them in the blurring of colony and metropole. Such perspectives emphasize that Filipinx social formations must be studied in their own right. This is not a call for Filipinx exceptionalism; rather, as See (2009, xxx) puts it, "The so-called specificity of Filipino America can become the powerful basis for an altogether other kind of worldliness." Taking seriously Filipinx American critique respects Filipinx struggles for self-determination while also advocating for more specific analyses of how power operates on multiple scales.

In the context of Women of Color feminist discourse, de Jesús (2005a, 4) observes that while a body of Asian American women's writing exists, Filipina American voices have remained marginal due to "East Asian hegemony in Asian America, which has [led] to constructing and signifying Asian American women as of solely Chinese, Japanese, and/or Korean descent." She goes on to outline that "peminist theorizing shares many similarities with feminisms of color and Asian American feminisms—for example, the negotiation of the 'borderlands,' the emergence of mestiza consciousness, the simultaneous struggle to fight racism in the women's movement and sexism in our ethnic communities, as well as the pressure to 'pledge allegiance' to *either* culture *or* gender, but not both"; however, "what distinguishes [peminist discourse] is [its] gendered analysis of imperial trauma . . . and the articulation of Pinay resistance to imperialism's lingering effects" (6). Clearing a space for Filipinx and specifically Pinay perspectives on the effects of racism, sexism, homophobia, and imperialism, among other forms of oppression, works to decenter white hegemonic feminism as the primary interlocutor with which Women of Color feminisms engage.

Although peminism is rooted in the experiences and perspectives of Pinays, it more accurately indexes a way of knowing and being in the world. Accordingly, it is more useful to conceptualize it as an analytic. Such a move is not intended to decenter Filipina American voices; instead, understanding peminism as a politico-theoretical orientation resists the impetus to conflate racialized women's bodies with Women of Color feminist bodies of knowledge (Lee 2000). Tintiangco-Cubales (2005, 142) invites Pinoys "to engage in the conversation on Pinayism so that they may better understand a more complete rendition of the struggle of 'Filipinos in America.'" Such a provocation recognizes the structural relationalities between Filipinas and Filipinos as racial-colonial subjects in the United States. Frank Samson's contribution to *Pinay Power* responds to Tintiangco-Cubales's call, stating that Pinoys can participate in peminist discourse by "develop[ing] a Pinayist consciousness" (Samson 2005, 157), by recognizing "Pinayism as a way of life, a way of being in the world" (159). Developing a Pinayist consciousness encourages Pinoys to recognize that white supremacy manifests through heterosexist exploitation as a method to disempower men of color and subjugate communities of color (Tintiangco-Cubales 2005, 142; Samson 2005, 153). As de Jesús (2005a, 5) reminds us, "Far from being a slighting of Filipino American men or Filipino American culture in general, attention to Pinay voices and perspectives demonstrates our [peminist] commitment to the liberation of *all* Filipinos." Through the particular vantage point of Pinays and the prism of racialized gender and sexuality more broadly, peminism serves as a pathway for Filipinx decolonization and liberation. And yet, more than a decade after *Pinay Power*'s introduction of peminism into feminist and antiracist discourses, the term remains marginal. As a feminist queer Pinoy literary scholar, my response is to critically engage *Pinay Power*'s important contributions to Women of Color feminism and Filipinx critique and to continue exploring the power of peminism.

ENGAGING PEMINISM QUEERLY

Whereas de Jesús's definition of peminism and Tintiangco-Cubales's definition of Pinayism make clear that sexuality and antihomophobia are part
of the Filipina American feminist dialogue, the idea that p/feminism is
inherently queer or that queer is inherently p/feminist cannot be taken for
granted. Following queer of color and queer diaspora scholars (see Ferguson 2004; Gopinath 2005; Holland 2012; Manalansan 2003; and Muñoz
1999), my queer diasporic Filipinx theorizing develops from critical engagements with feminist and peminist epistemologies and ontologies. Such a
move refuses to silo critiques of racialized sexuality formations from gendered ones or to continue eclipsing the Women of Color feminist foundations of queer of color and queer diasporic critiques. Relatedly, Filipinx
studies scholars have cogently illustrated how antiracist and decolonial politics in Filipinx America also must be feminist and queer (see Cruz 2012; de
Jesús 2002; Isaac 2006; Mendoza 2005, 2015; Ponce 2012; and See 2009).

In line with this chapter's focus on the literary, de Jesús (2002), in her
rereading of arguably canonical Filipinx American literature, critiques the
heteronormative bias that subconsciously pervades literary interpretations
of Carlos Bulosan's novel *America Is in the Heart* and Bienvenido Santos's
collection of short stories *Scent of Apples*, a bias that also tarnishes ethno-
racial nationalist political activism in Asian America. Through her peminist optic, she brings to light the homophobia and heterosexism that often
circumscribe antiracist struggles and calls for an intersectional approach
to cultural politics. In centering the queer moments that occur in Bulosan's and Santos's work, she invites us to recognize that the foundations of
Filipinx American culture are queer, which has the effect of opening up
"different possibilities" that allow us to "imagine new vistas, new lives, and
new ways of being" (109). Once again building upon de Jesús, I gravitate
toward the feminist and queer moments of affiliation in Hagedorn's fiction
to underscore the intersectional foundations of contemporary Filipinx
critique.

My capitalizing on the intimacies among gender, sexuality, race, and
coloniality reflects a broader discussion in Women of Color feminisms and
queer of color and queer diasporic critiques that emphasizes the distinct yet
overlapping dialogic relations among these three epistemic formations. José
Esteban Muñoz's *Disidentifications* highlights an alternative genealogy
for queer theory—one that begins with the writings of radical feminists of
color collected in *This Bridge Called My Back*. For Muñoz (1999, 25), queer

of color critique is a disidentificatory strategy that ushers in a utopian world which makes the present more livable for minoritized subjects: "It is in [*This Bridge*'s] essays, rants, poems, and manifestos that we first glimpsed what a queer world might look like." Inspired by Muñoz's thinking, Roderick Ferguson (2004) arguably solidified queer of color critique as a mode of social and cultural analysis. Like Muñoz, Ferguson (2004, 111) is indebted to Women of Color feminisms, especially Black lesbian feminist theorizations, which have "marked the constitution of a heterogeneous labor force in diversified terms of ethnicity, nation, race, sexuality, and gender." However, given that Lisa Lowe's (1996) historical materialist Asian American feminist critique of capital bears on Ferguson's queer of color theorizing, it is worth recognizing Asian American feminisms' specific influence on queer of color critique. In connecting queer of color critique to Women of Color feminisms in general and to Asian American feminisms in particular, such work by Muñoz and Ferguson illustrates the necessity to think intersectionally and relationally in the fight for social justice and transformation.

While feminism and queer theory certainly share intellectual and political space, sustained engagement is necessary lest one become neglectful of the other. For Sharon Patricia Holland (2012), acknowledging queer of color critique's foundations in Women of Color feminisms is important; however, the disappearance of the female subject in much of contemporary queer theorizing is cause for concern. According to her, "Black.female.queer voices are foundational, but not generative, as there is little active engagement with the diversity of this relational voice." What she is saying here is that *black.female.queer* becomes a signifier for alterity, statically held in the past so as to clear space for contemporary queer (of color) theorizing. She instead wants us to think of the black.female.queer not as "singular" but as "relational" (81). Similarly, Gayatri Gopinath (2005) cautions against the (cisgender) male subjective bias of *queer* in her analysis of diasporic South Asian public cultures. Focusing specifically on the diasporic South Asian queer female subject, she argues that such a move works to "conceptualize diaspora in ways that do not invariably replicate heteronormative and patriarchal structures of kinship and community" (6). Moreover, reorienting toward the discursively constructed impossible subject and national and diasporic narratives brings queer and feminist thinking into productive conversation, thereby "challeng[ing] the notion that these fields of inquiry are necessarily distinct, separate, and incommensurate" (16). In aligning myself with Holland and Gopinath, not only do I situate queer as feminism's

interlocutor and vice versa, but I also foreground the feminine as mutual
with the sexually transgressive.[9]

Queer in Filipinx America not only nuances peminist investments in
racialized gender and sexual liberation but also unsettles white imperialist
notions of queer. A roundtable discussion by US-based Filipina lesbian and
bisexual women organizers included in Pinay Power reinforces the idea
that women's issues necessarily include queer women's issues. Moreover, echoing Gopinath's (2005) critique of queer as often conflated with men, the
roundtable discussants point out that queer Filipino men are largely visible
and provisionally accepted within the Filipinx community, whereas queer
Filipina women are rendered invisible and anomalous (Lipat et al. 2005, 195–
96). Complicating this tension between cisgender male and female queer
representation, Kale Fajardo (2008, 407) observes that Philippine and Filipina American feminists often misread trans Filipino men as lesbians, while
US notions of being trans fail to address the cultural specificities of trans
Filipinxs.[10] In Martin Manalansan's (2003, viii, 24) ethnography of diasporic
gay Filipino performative practices, he forwards bakla as a form of Filipino
queerness to signal the incommensurability of hegemonic white gay male
culture with that of diasporic queer Filipinos. Conversely, Victor Mendoza
(2015, 29) cautions against the ahistorical use of queer as a signifier for nonnormative Filipinx genders and sexualities given queer's racialized, imperialist connotative meanings during late nineteenth- and early twentieth-century
US overseas expansion. For him, queer is problematic not because it demar-
cates gender and sexual transgression, but rather because its racialized specificities often go unnoticed (Mendoza 2015, 29). The aforementioned queer
Filipinx perspectives underscore how an attention to the particularities of
Filipinx experience reworks queer's radical potential alongside peminist sensibilities. Building upon the epistemic politics of such scholars, this chapter
aims to position queerness and peminism as necessarily entwined modes of
living and being and turns to the literary as an entry point for reimagining a
more just society.

PEMINIST AND QUEER AFFILIATION IN *DOGEATERS*

The development of political consciousness—of becoming "woke," so to
speak—is one of the many thematic strands that weave together *Dogeaters*.
The novel opens with an excerpt on sleep from French physician Jean
Mallat's nineteenth-century travelogue *The Philippines*: "*They [Filipinxs]
have the greatest respect for sleeping persons*" (1). While such a colonial

observation seems anachronistic in Hagedorn's postcolonial narrative, the idea of "sleeping persons" stands as a metaphor of the uninitiated Filipinx masses who fail to recognize the systemic oppression rampant during the Spanish-colonized past and the novel's postwar/post-US-independence present. In fact, the novel's chapter introducing the character Daisy Avila, who particularly represents this transformation from sleep to consciousness, is titled "Sleeping Beauty." Here, Hagedorn plays with the literal and symbolic meaning of being asleep, as Daisy spends her time in a catatonic state after being crowned Young Miss Philippines, but also because she has not yet developed a political critique of the government like her father, Senator Domingo Avila, who "declares that our torrid green world is threatened by its legacy of colonialism and the desire for revenge" (100). Three chapters later, in "Breaking Spells," Daisy awakes from her catatonic state, "publicly denounce[s] the beauty queen pageant as a farce, a giant step backward for all women," and "accuses the First Lady of furthering the cause of female delusions in the Philippines" (109). By the novel's end, Daisy, who now goes by the alias Aurora, emerges as a leader of the resistance against the corrupt Philippine government.[11]

Like Daisy, Joey Sands transforms from living in a sheltered reality to occupying an unfiltered one when he accidentally witnesses the assassination of Senator Avila, Daisy's father. And like the beauty-queen-turned-guerrilla-fighter, he develops a political consciousness that is avowedly antinational and proto-p/feminist/queer. In the chapter "His Mother, the Whore," Hagedorn juxtaposes Joey's subjectivity with that of his deceased mother, Zenaida. At this early point in the novel, Joey distances himself from his mother, recounting only hearsay rather than direct memories of her. Narrated from his perspective, the chapter opens with "There are those who say my poor whore of a mother sold me to Uncle for fifty pesos. . . . They say she was still young and still beautiful, they shake their heads solemnly at the terrible waste. . . . They describe how she jumped in the river, a watery grave black with human shit. . . . They say Zenaida's ghost still haunts that section of the river. . . . She was a legendary whore, my mother. Disgraced and abandoned, just like in the movies" (42). After this vivid description of his mother's tragic life and death, Joey ends by saying, "I don't want to remember anything else about my sad whore of a mother" (43). A peminist sensibility would encourage Joey to recognize Zenaida's fate as indicative of the weight of US neocolonialism via militarism and capitalist exploitation of Filipina bodies following the Philippines' so-called independence from the United States in 1946 and would connect her struggles for survival to his own as a queer mestizo Filipino hustler. However, at this point in the novel, Joey, like Daisy, remains metaphorically asleep, which enables him to disconnect from similarly positioned subjects like his mother and the Filipinx underclass that inhabits the slums of Manila from which he hails.

The chapter then proceeds to reveal Joey's coming of age under the tutelage of Uncle, a man from the neighborhood slums who cares for him and other wayward boys. On one hand, Joey's abrupt refusal to say more about his "sad whore of a mother" may mask his shame and sadness at losing, at the young age of about five or six, a mother who was known by her line of work. On the other hand, it signals his attempt to show how he is different from her. Whereas the chapter's title ("His Mother, the Whore") suggests that Zenaida will be the focus, three pages of the four-page chapter are devoted to Joey. Supposedly unlike his tragic mother, who was at the mercy of her johns, Joey describes how he "take[s] advantage of the situation, run[s] men around, make[s] them give [him] money" (44). He even goes on to emphasize that *"I'm nobody's slave."* He closes the chapter by stating, "Right now I'm biding my time. I take good care of myself, I'm in control, my life is simple" (45). In framing his mother as more passive and presenting himself as more active in determining his lot in life, Joey disaffiliates with feminized subjection. Even though he engages in sex work like his mother, his efforts to show that he is the master of his destiny reveal his investment in masculinist notions of power and personhood.

It is only when Joey becomes a liability to the state that he realizes he is no different from his mother, the whore, and develops a proto-p/feminist consciousness. After accidentally witnessing the assassination of Senator Avila, an outspoken politician critical of the government's military human rights violations toward its people, Joey hopes to find a priest and confess what he has witnessed. In his mind, he imagines telling the priest, "Father, my name is Joey Sands. I'm a whore and the son of whore. I just saw Senator Avila murdered. How come I feel guilty?" (191). Whereas earlier in the novel Joey disidentifies with his status as a sex worker and the progeny of a Filipina sex worker and a Black American GI, in this moment, he accepts who he is. By avowing his mother, Joey re-centers the absented Filipina whose labor underwrites much of the Philippines' postcolonial economy.[12] This moment serves as a turning point in Joey's ontological consciousness, as he moves from living in a false reality where he believes he is singularly in charge of his destiny to realizing he is living in the nightmare that is postcolonial Philippines and must rely on the collective support of similarly positioned subjects for his survival: antinationalist Filipinas like Daisy/ Aurora and her cousin Lydia/Clarita and queer Filipinxs like Boy-Boy who occupy the fringes of Philippine society.

Joey's new affiliation with Filipina feminist guerrilla fighters at the novel's end carries the potential to instantiate other modes of being. In her reading of the novel, Rachel Lee (1999, 104) similarly points out how Filipina and queer Filipinx characters present an alternative to the hetero-masculinist postcolonial nation-state in order to emphasize that feminist and queer politics are not antithetical to nationalism and anti-imperialist critique. However, whereas she focuses primarily on the novel's array of female characters, positioning Joey as exceptional (74), I read the novel's entwinement of feminism and queerness as symptomatic of the fecund alliances necessary to uproot the legacies of multiple colonialisms. As Lee notes, "Because Hagedorn does not propose one way to save the world, the novel ultimately does not propose female or gay leadership as the only avenues of collective salvation. Rather, the novel highlights that leadership as legitimate as any other, while never endorsing this leadership as the final word, the one and only path toward liberation" (104). Here, Lee underscores how the novel opens up alternative realities, not to position them as ultimately better than the extant reality, but rather to illustrate the several possibilities for social justice when subaltern knowledges are taken seriously. Juliana Chang (2003) offers a similar reading of the power of the subaltern, again largely focusing on women. For Chang, subaltern femininity—"illegitimate, illicit, and illegible female labor" (652)—in the novel presents an alternative pathway for neocolonial modernity, and Zenaida is the quintessential embodiment of this disavowed femininity (658). However, in recognizing Joey's horizontal alignment with his mother and other trafficked women (e.g., the *bomba* [soft-core porn] star Lolita Luna, Daisy), the promise of subalternity rests on both feminization and queerness. Such an alliance points to the radical potential of affiliation based not on identity but on shared distance from power, as Cathy Cohen (1997) cogently argues.

By the novel's end, Joey has sought refuge in the mountains among guerrilla fighters with the help of his associate Boy-Boy, a queer shower dancer with ties to the anti-Philippine government resistance. Unexpectedly, he meets Aurora/Daisy and befriends her. In their shared exile, the omniscient narrator describes their budding friendship in the future tense:

> Weeks later, when she has grown to trust him, she will describe the
> absurd terms of her release from Camp Meditation. . . .

> They will get drunk together on cane liquor one night. She cries while
> Joey describes his mother.... They are together all the time. She teaches
> him how to use a gun. (Hagedorn 1991, 232–33)

Here, readers see a glimpse of the alternative world made possible through
p/feminist and queer affiliation; however, the narrative's open-endedness is
not prescriptive. By ending Daisy's and Joey's plot lines in this way, Hagedorn positions affective relationality and coalitional politics irrespective of
one's social identification as one antidote to autocratic corruption.

Whereas Daisy and Joey figure as the marriage of p/feminism and queerness, Rio, the novel's arguably primary narrator, embodies both at once.[13]
As a daughter of members of the privileged mestizx class, Rio seems like
an unlikely candidate for engendering subversive critique. However, her
refusal to align with either nationalist or antinationalist politics offers
another pathway for liberation. This inability to fully capture her political
alliance fittingly reveals her status as a guerrilla subject. Like the historical
guerrilla fighters who confounded the US military forces during the
Philippine-American War at the turn of the twentieth century through
seemingly erratic maneuvers that prolonged the war until the early 1910s,
and like the fictional guerrilla fighters in Dogeaters whose refusal to ignore
the atrocities committed by a fascist government offers hope through resistance, Rio's unreliable narration might seem benign and elusive but actually reveals the power of subaltern epistemology and ontology.

At the beginning of the novel, Rio recounts an afternoon outing with her
cousin Pucha circa 1956, during their adolescence. Sitting at the Cafe España
along with Lorenza, Rio's yaya (babysitter), Rio becomes "acutely aware of
the table of teenage boys next to [them], craning their necks and staring
lewdly at [her] cousin" (4). She goes on to narrate: "The loudest and largest
of the boys hisses lazily at my cousin, who makes a big show of pretending
not to hear.... Then he starts making kissing sounds with his fat lips. I am
disgusted by his obscene display and the giggling reaction of my flustered
cousin" (5). At the end of the novel, Pucha responds to Rio's recollection:
"Puwede ba [a Filipino/Tagalog idiom that loosely translates as 'really!?']?
1956, 1956! Rio, you've got it all wrong.... I may not remember all the details,
but I certainly should know WHO was making eyes at me in the Cafe
España" (248). She goes on to admonish Rio: "I just want you to get my damn
history straight ... you'd better wake up and accept it: 1959 was many years
ago" (249). Besides the queerness of Rio's storytelling, in her inability to "get
[Pucha's] damn history straight" (see Mendoza 2005, 820), Rio inhabits a

peminist-queer standpoint as an adult diasporic subject now living in the United States but who refuses to let go of the past, forgoes property femininity by remaining unmarried, and rejects the promise of crony capitalism for the Filipinx elite. And although Pucha charges that Rio is metaphorically asleep, Rio's subtle but no less effective critique of historical memory throughout the novel lays bare the force of counternarratives to so-called official Truth and indicates that she is in fact "woke."

PEMINIST-QUEER SOLIDARITY IN *THE GANGSTER OF LOVE*

While the previous section focused on queer affiliation with p/feminism primarily through the character Joey, and to a lesser extent Rio, in *Dogeaters*, this section focuses on peminist affiliation with queerness through Rocky, *Gangster*'s protagonist narrator. The novel's opening immediately, though implicitly, establishes Rocky's affiliation with her queer brother Voltaire, with the collective *we* symbolizing her refusal to disentangle her experience of immigration from that of her brother and her mother, Milagros. Though Rocky is the narrator for the novel, Hagedorn does not use the first two pages to establish who she is; instead, Rocky is introduced in relation to her brother: "Jimi Hendrix died the year the ship that brought *us* from Manila docked in San Francisco. My brother, Voltaire, and I wept when *we* read about it in the papers, but it was Voltaire who was truly devastated. Hendrix had been his idol" (5, emphases added). Rocky goes on to describe her brother's bold sartorial style, their parents' divorce, their journey to the United States, and Voltaire's political critiques of postcolonial Philippines. Of particular note is Rocky's mention that "my father once threatened to have Voltaire arrested for looking like an effeminate *bakla*" (5). This information immediately positions Voltaire as a queer subject, as *bakla* is a Filipino/Tagalog word that loosely translates as "gay." By devoting the novel's opening to Voltaire as narrated through Rocky's point of view, Hagedorn sets up Voltaire as a significant character, despite his relative absence through most of the novel. Voltaire's absent presence aptly illustrates how political orientations may not always foreground their multiple investments, but those investments nevertheless always inform them. As a proto-peminist coming-of-age tale, Rocky's affiliation with Voltaire enjoins readers to understand her racialized gender politics in relation to her queer adjacency.

Rocky's journey as a budding musician and into young womanhood reveals her distance from normative femininity and her alignment with dissident genders and sexualities, thus illustrating her deviation from so-called traditional Filipina-ness. While Rocky struggles to identify with her Filipina heritage, interpreting her disidentification with Filipinx-ness as an assimilatory move fails to recognize how she reworks the contours of diasporic Filipinx subjectivity. When she decides to leave San Francisco to pursue a music career in New York, she and her then-lover Elvis Chang stop in Los Angeles to visit her "kind of famous, very cool uncle Marlon," knowing "he'd take care of [them]" (67). Marlon, a former Broadway dancer who is queer and implied to be HIV-positive, serves as a father figure for Rocky. Reluctant yet ultimately supportive of her desire to become an artist, he also later connects her to more stable employment to make ends meet in between music gigs. This relationship between Rocky and Marlon is similar to her affiliation with Voltaire and presents readers with an alternative notion of family that is not based on a heteronormative nuclear structure.

Rocky's mother, Milagros, on the other hand, is less supportive of Rocky and is often critical of her daughter's actions. Rocky reflects: "On one of my visits back to San Francisco, my mother asks me why I try so hard to be a man. . . . She blames it all on coming to America" (127). While Milagros certainly loves her daughter, she views Rocky's independence as unconventional. Ambivalent about her mother, Rocky sees Milagros's tolerance of her father's marital unfaithfulness in the Philippines for longer than she would have as a weakness and thus "resolve[s] never to hand over that kind of power to any man or woman" (211). However, Milagros also exceeds the scripts of conventional femininity: "Rocky's mother was different, confronting her husband in public, making demands, issuing ultimatums" (211). In this way, Rocky may unconsciously derive her female power from her mother, who does in fact divorce her husband and becomes an entrepreneur in the United States by selling lumpia (eggrolls).

Keiko Van Heller, Rocky's best friend, dubbed "a 'rising feminist artist of color,'" further influences Rocky's proto-peminist/queer sensibilities (94). On tour, Rocky recounts, "I'm relieved to have any woman along for company. I've had to make do in the past with someone's hostile wife or druggie airhead girlfriend-of-the-moment, but I'm always grateful for their whiny female presence. (Rock 'n' roll's such a boys' club, and I'm sick of it. Whose guitar/dick/tongue is the longest and loudest?)" (128–29). Here, Rocky articulates the sexism she constantly faces as a rising rock-and-roll bandleader and the comfort she experiences in the company of other women, albeit ambivalently. Following this revelation, Rocky and Keiko spontaneously engage in a brief sexual encounter. Whereas the novel establishes Keiko as sexually fluid, it remains silent on Rocky's sexuality, much like Rio in *Dogeaters*. In fact, aside from this moment, the novel has Rocky romantically and sexually involved with cisgender men from different races and ethnicities. However, to interpret Rocky as heterosexual would be a misnomer. Rather, the novel's refusal to pin down her sexual identity works to counter the idea that Filipinx-ness is incommensurate with queerness. What's more, her affiliation with Keiko signals the promise of Women of Color solidarity.

In their respective readings of *Gangster*, Martin Joseph Ponce (2012) and Christine Balance (2016) focus on the novel's soundscapes to trace Rocky's, and by extension Hagedorn's, disidentificatory relationship to dominant Philippine and US cultures. Given the parallels between Rocky and Hagedorn in terms of their life trajectories from Manila to San Francisco to New York and their artistic endeavors as poets and rock bandleaders, Rocky can be read as a "literary rendition" of Hagedorn (Balance 2016, 117). For Balance, Hagedorn's "collaborative production and generative reception of US popular music within and beyond national borders," which Rocky models, ushers in alternative ways to conceptualize immigrant ethnic identity that refuse the demands of cultural authenticity (89). However, as Ponce (2012, 129) points out, "Hagedorn does not represent The Gangster of Love [Rocky's band] as a utopian form of sociality. . . . [T]he sexually charged relationships among the band members, and their disagreements over [artist expression and financial success], ultimately reveal that The Gangster of Love will not serve as some paragon of harmonious multiculturality."

Still, in holding out culturally hybrid aesthetics that do not "subordinate the significance of gender and sexual difference" vis-à-vis racial-colonial subjectivity, Ponce acknowledges *Gangster*'s queer potentiality to subvert the competing influences of US assimilation and Filipinx nationalism on diasporic Filipinxs (123). While Balance (2016, 121) does not couch Rocky's/Hagedorn's performative practices as explicitly peminist and/or queer, for me, such a rebellious spirit—as Balance puts it—aligns with peminist-queer politics. Indeed, the collaborative nature of Rocky's social and artistic practices (e.g., non-nuclear kinship with friends and lovers, the multiraciality of her band) exemplifies a peminist-queer sensibility that refuses the individualism of dominant US culture and the heteronormative mandates of ethnic nationalism. And although Ponce (2012) does read queerness into such acts, not seeing them as also explicitly peminist is a missed opportunity to acknowledge the coalitional politics inherent in Rocky's/Hagedorn's cultural production.

TOWARD A POLITICS OF REFUSAL AND
PEMINIST-QUEER WORLD MAKING

As I have argued throughout this chapter, Filipinx decolonialization and liberation not only rests on antiracist and anti-imperialist stances but also necessarily involves critical engagements with antisexism and antiheteronormativity. Filipinx nationalisms that excise their peminist and queer Filipinx affiliation and comrades unwittingly reproduce the (il)logics of coloniality and white supremacy. Relatedly, peminist struggles for gender liberation must be fundamentally queer, just as queer Filipinx struggles against heterosexism and homophobia must be decidedly peminist; to mobilize otherwise fails to engender solidarity across differences. And while peminism stands in solidarity with Asian American and Women of Color feminisms more broadly, to not make space for the particularities of diasporic Filipina/x experience reinforces structural inequality within subjugated populations, which of course is an extension of colonial domination. If Filipinx studies, Filipinx cultural production, and Filipinx movements for justice against colonial and neocolonial subjugation in the Philippines and its global diaspora have bequeathed us anything, it is the notion that power is complex and thus warrants multipronged approaches to reckoning with its effects. Such a robust genealogy of Filipinx decolonization and liberation reminds us that although more work remains, we have blueprints to guide us—which traffic in intersectional thinking and coalitional praxis.

By turning to contemporary diasporic Filipinx literature, I have charted the imaginative ways such work provides a template for enacting peminist and queer affiliation. Literature for marginalized communities often serves as an alternative archive to colonial knowledge. While literature certainly is not the only mode of re-membering and creating (as political action in the so-called real world similarly enacts justice), literature nevertheless instantiates a space to imagine differently the world in which we live. As Ernesto Martínez (2012, 3) posits, the literary taps into the affective dimension of sociality and "provid[es] an account of *what it feels like* to negotiate knowledge in oppressive contexts, rather than to simply tell people what to think." However, such a platform may be unintelligible to dominant society when subaltern subjects take center stage. In disarticulating the potentialities that diasporic Filipinx literature offers for Asian American and Women of Color feminist politics, though, my aim has been less prescriptive and more descriptive of extant ways of knowing and being that exist in tandem with their hegemonic counterparts. "Making sense" of the peminist and queer affiliations that already exist fictively and refract the so-called real world ultimately works to reckon with violent, systematic erasure of marginalized individuals and to account for the affiliations such individuals make across identities (Martínez 2012, 14, 16). With so much division in our current world, to affiliate may seem insignificant; however, affiliation creates the conditions of possibility to see beyond ourselves and to forge a robust front against *all* oppressions.

NOTES

1   Throughout this chapter, I use the nonbinary gendered term *Filipinx* when referring generally to people of Philippine descent and use the gendered terms *Filipina* (feminine) and *Filipino* (masculine) when the context warrants them.

2   Although Dylan Rodríguez (2010, 241n2) does not discount the important work of Filipinx feminist and queer scholars and activists, his polemical contribution to Filipinx studies could be interpreted as a reprioritization of race in studying Filipinx-ness: "The overarching argument of [*Suspended Apocalypse*] is that the production of the 'Filipino American' is defined—essentially and fundamentally—by a complex, largely disavowed, and almost entirely undertheorized relation to a nexus of profound racial and white supremacist violence" (11). Rather than center race as he suggests (192), I center an intersectional approach in disarticulating Filipinx racial formation.

3   For more on complex personhood, see Avery Gordon (1997).

4   Hanna (2017) turns to oral history to catalog the fissures of Filipinx queer identity in ethnic nationalist movements.

5   R. Zamora Linmark's *Rolling the R's* (1997) and Noël Alumit's *Letters to Montgomery Clift* (2003) are two notable examples of contemporary diasporic Filipinx literature that similarly showcase heterosocial intimacies. For more on the latter novel, see Sarmiento 2017.

6   See Combahee River Collective (1983) and Moraga and Anzaldúa (1983) as a whole.

7   The Black Lives Matter movement is an example of contemporary political organizing that necessarily affirms queer Black women and Black queer and trans people (Garza, Tometi, and Cullors n.d.).

8   See also Chuh (2003) and D. Rodríguez (2010) for more on the vexed relationship of Filipinx America to Asian America.

9   I realize that framing this dialogue between male scholars (Muñoz and Ferguson) and female scholars (Holland and Gopinath) may presuppose a gender divide; however, instead of reading them as oppositional, I see them as respectfully dialogic.

10   I use *trans* as an inclusive term for people who disidentify with the gender binary.

11   Incidentally, Aurora is the given name of Sleeping Beauty in Walt Disney's animated film *Sleeping Beauty* (1959).

12   See Guevarra (2009), Parreñas (2001), R. Rodriguez (2010), and Tadiar (2004) for more on the Philippines' reliance on feminized labor to support its economy.

13   See Lee (1999) and Mendoza (2005) for a more thorough reading of Rio's queerness.

REFERENCES

Alumit, Noël. 2003. *Letters to Montgomery Clift*. Los Angeles: Alyson.

Balance, Christine Bacareza. 2016. *Tropical Renditions: Making Musical Scenes in Filipino America*. Durham, NC: Duke University Press.

Balce, Nerissa S. 2016. *Body Parts of Empire: Visual Abjection, Filipino Images, and the American Archive*. Ann Arbor: University of Michigan Press.

Bascara, Victor. 2006. *Model-Minority Imperialism*. Minneapolis: University of Minnesota Press.

Chang, Juliana. 2003. "Masquerade, Hysteria, and Neocolonial Femininity in Hagedorn's *Dogeaters*." *Contemporary Literature* 44 (4): 637–63.

Chuh, Kandice. 2003. *Imagine Otherwise: On Asian Americanist Critique*. Durham, NC: Duke University Press.

Cohen, Cathy J. 1997. "Punks, Bulldaggers, and Welfare Queens: The Radical Potential of Queer Politics?" *GLQ: A Journal of Lesbian and Gay Studies* 3: 437–65.

Combahee River Collective. 1983. "A Black Feminist Statement." In Moraga and Anzaldúa 1983, 210–18.

Cruz, Denise. 2012. *Transpacific Femininities: The Making of the Modern Filipina*. Durham, NC: Duke University Press.

de Jesús, Melinda L. 2002. "Rereading History, Rewriting Desire: Reclaiming Queerness in Carlos Bulosan's *America Is in the Heart* and Bienvenido Santos' *Scent of Apples*." *Journal of Asian American Studies* 5 (2): 91–111.

———. 2005a. "Introduction: Toward a Peminist Theory, or Theorizing the Filipina/American Experience." In de Jesús 2005b, 1–15.

———, ed. 2005b. *Pinay Power: Peminist Critical Theory: Theorizing the Filipina/American Experience*. New York: Routledge.

Diaz, Robert. 2015. "The Limits of *Bakla* and Gay: Feminist Readings of *My Husband's Lover*, Vice Ganda, and Charice Pempengco." *Signs: Journal of Women in Culture and Society* 40 (3): 721–45.

Fajardo, Kale Bantigue. 2008. "Transportation: Translating Filipino and Filipino American Tomboy Masculinities through Global Migration and Seafaring." *GLQ: A Journal of Lesbian and Gay Studies* 14 (2–3): 403–24.

———. 2011. *Filipino Crosscurrents: Oceanographies of Seafaring, Masculinities, and Globalization*. Minneapolis: University of Minnesota Press.

Ferguson, Roderick A. 2004. *Aberrations in Black: Toward a Queer of Color Critique*. Minneapolis: University of Minnesota Press.

Garza, Alicia, Opal Tometi, and Patrisse Cullors. n.d. "A HerStory of the #BlackLivesMatter Movement." Black Lives Matter. Accessed April 30, 2016. http://blacklivesmatter.com/herstory/.

Gonzalez, Vernadette Vicuña. 2013. *Securing Paradise: Tourism and Militarism in Hawai'i and the Philippines*. Durham, NC: Duke University Press.

Gopinath, Gayatri. 2005. *Impossible Desires: Queer Diasporas and South Asian Public Cultures*. Durham, NC: Duke University Press.

Gordon, Avery F. 1997. *Ghostly Matters: Haunting and the Sociological Imagination*. Minneapolis: University of Minnesota Press.

Gueverra, Anna. 2009. *Marketing Dreams, Manufacturing Heroes: The Transnational Labor Brokering of Filipino Workers*. New Brunswick, NJ: Rutgers University Press.

Hagedorn, Jessica. 1991. *Dogeaters*. New York: Penguin.

———. 1997. *The Gangster of Love*. New York: Penguin.

Hanna, Karen. 2017. "Being Gay in the Filipina/o American Anti–Martial Law Movement: Revolutionary Politics, Nationalism, and Sexuality in the 1970s." Paper presented at the Association for Asian American Studies, Portland, OR, April 14.

Holland, Sharon Patricia. 2012. *The Erotic Life of Racism*. Durham, NC: Duke University Press.

Isaac, Allan Punzalan. 2006. *American Tropics: Articulating Filipino America*. Minneapolis: University of Minnesota Press.

Lee, Rachel C. 1999. *The Americas of Asian American Literature: Gendered Fictions of Nation and Transnation*. Princeton, NJ: Princeton University Press.

———. 2000. "Notes from the (non)Field: Teaching and Theorizing Women of Color." *Meridians: feminism, race, transnationalism* 1 (1): 85–109.

Linmark, R. Zamora. 1997. *Rolling the R's*. New York: Kaya.

Lipat, Christine T., Trinity A. Ordoña, Cianna Pamintuan Stewart, and Mary Ann Ubaldo. 2005. "Tomboy, Dyke, Lezzie, and Bi: Filipina Lesbian and Bisexual Women Speak Out." In de Jesús 2005b, 187–200.

Lorde, Audre. 1983. "The Master's Tools Will Never Dismantle the Master's House." In Moraga and Anzaldúa 1983, 98–101.

Lowe, Lisa. 1996. *Immigrant Acts: On Asian American Cultural Politics*. Durham, NC: Duke University Press.

Manalansan, Martin F., IV. 2003. *Global Divas: Filipino Gay Men in the Diaspora*. Durham, NC: Duke University Press.

Manalansan, Martin F., IV, and Augusto F. Espiritu. 2016. "The Field: Dialogues, Visions, Tensions, and Aspirations." In *Filipino Studies: Palimpsests of Nation and Diaspora*, edited by Martin F. Manalansan IV and Augusto F. Espiritu, 1–11. Minneapolis: University of Minnesota Press.

Martínez, Ernesto Javier. 2012. *On Making Sense: Queer Race Narratives of Intelligibility*. Stanford, CA: Stanford University Press.

Mendoza, Victor Román. 2005. "A Queer Nomadology of Jessica Hagedorn's *Dogeaters*." *American Literature* 77 (4): 815–45.

———. 2015. *Metroimperial Intimacies: Fantasy, Racial-Sexual Governance, and the Philippines in U.S. Imperialism, 1899–1913*. Durham, NC: Duke University Press.

Moraga, Cherríe, and Gloria Anzaldúa, eds. 1983. *This Bridge Called My Back: Writings by Radical Women of Color*. New York: Kitchen Table.

Muñoz, José Esteban. 1999. *Disidentifications: Queers of Color and the Performance of Politics*. Minneapolis: University of Minnesota Press.

Parreñas, Rhacel Salazar. 2001. *Servants of Globalization: Women, Migration, and Domestic Work*. Stanford, CA: Stanford University Press.

Ponce, Martin Joseph. 2012. *Beyond the Nation: Diasporic Filipino Literature and Queer Reading*. New York: New York University Press.

Rodríguez, Dylan. 2010. *Suspended Apocalypse: White Supremacy, Genocide, and the Filipino Condition.* Minneapolis: University of Minnesota Press.

Rodriguez, Robyn Magalit. 2010. *Migrants for Export: How the Philippine State Brokers Labor to the World.* Minneapolis: University of Minnesota Press.

Samson, Frank L. 2005. "Filipino American Men: Comrades in the Filipina/o American Feminism Movement." In de Jesús 2005b, 149–66.

Sarmiento, Thomas X. 2017. "Diasporic Filipinx Queerness, Female Affective Labor, and Queer Heterosocial Relationalities in *Letters to Montgomery Clift.*" *Women, Gender, and Families of Color* 5 (2): 105–28.

See, Sarita Echavez. 2009. *The Decolonized Eye: Filipino American Art and Performance.* Minneapolis: University of Minnesota Press.

Tadiar, Neferti Xina M. 2004. *Fantasy-Production: Sexual Economies and Other Philippine Consequences for the New World Order.* Hong Kong: Hong Kong University Press.

Tintiangco-Cubales, Allyson Goce. 2005. "Pinayism." In de Jesús 2005b, 137–48.

PART THREE

DECOLONIAL INVESTMENTS

Centering Indigeneity and Orienting
against Settler Complicities

CHAPTER 5

DECOLONIZING API

Centering Indigenous Pacific Islander Feminism

STEPHANIE NOHELANI TEVES AND MAILE ARVIN

> We Pacific Islanders are Indigenous people and we are NOT API. We
> are committed to creating political and spiritual solidarities with the
> Indigenous peoples of this land as a methodology for decolonization
> and for healing our communities.
>
> —FUIFUILUPE NIUMEITOLU

WE BEGIN WITH THIS QUOTE BY TONGAN ACTIVIST, SCHOLAR,
and community leader Fuifuilupe Niumeitolu, whom we both have had
the privilege of working with and learning so much from. Niumeitolu states
plainly: Pacific Islanders are not Asian / Pacific Islander (API). We write
this chapter as two Native Hawaiian[1] feminist scholars, and echoing Niumeitolu, we start by insisting that we are not Asian, and the acronym *API*
forecloses genuine possibilities for allyship by erasing differences between
and among Asian Americans and Pacific Islanders. This is a critique we
have been hearing for quite some time within Indigenous Pacific Islander
communities (Diaz 2004; Kauanui 2005; Hall 2005, 2015). Yet, as Pacific
Islanders, we never quite finish making this critique, in part because we
often find ourselves still scrambling for resources and space in Asian American political discourse because of how the federal government and other
institutions "count" us. This chapter asks: what kind of intellectual and
political work is necessary to dislodge the demographic grouping and supposed coalition between Pacific Islanders and Asian Americans so that we
can have conversations about the ongoing legacies of settler colonialism,
anti-Blackness, capitalist accumulation, and white supremacy that continue

to divide Indigenous peoples and communities of color? Specifically, what kinds of methodologies and strategies are necessary for Women of Color feminisms broadly and Asian American feminisms specifically to interrogate their own tendencies to gloss "the Pacific" (and its peoples) as an Asian American possession alongside their own liberal attempts to "include" our histories and cultures? What is necessary to change the current conversation (or lack thereof)?

CENTERING THE MOANA

The Pacific Ocean contains upward of 25,000 islands, extending from the Arctic to Antarctica and from the coasts of the Americas to the coasts of Asia. What are often referred to as the "Pacific Islands" number into 30,000, home to 2.3 million people and 1,500 languages, constituting a third of the earth's surface and nearly 50 percent of its water. Encompassed by a zone of volcanic and seismic activity known as the ring of fire, the region traverses the international date line and equator. All of the landmass on earth could fit into the Pacific Ocean. "Oceania" or the "Pacific Islands" are divided into three regions: Melanesia, Micronesia, and Polynesia, the colonial and anthropological product of a racialized set of European designations that Pacific Islanders now hold onto in empowering and problematic ways. "Oceania" is also sometimes a geopolitical grouping that includes Australia, New Zealand, the islands in Melanesia and Micronesia, Papua New Guinea, and sometimes the surrounding and insular islands of Southeast Asia. Oceania is distinct, however, as preeminently noted in the words of Tongan-Fijian scholar and poet Epeli Hau'ofa: "Oceania is us. We are the sea, we are the ocean. We must wake up to this ancient truth and together use it to overturn all hegemonic views that aim ultimately to confine us again, physically and psychologically, in the tiny spaces that we have resisted accepting as our sole appointed places and from which we have recently liberated ourselves. We must not allow anyone to belittle us again and take away our freedom" (Hau'ofa 2008).

Thus, Oceania is also a cultural and organizing force within Pacific Islander communities to reorient our perspective of the world as our ocean, as our homeland, a connectivity that transcends and traverses geopolitical formations, a knowledge that preceded Western cartographies and anthropological imaginaries of "the other" and will surely exceed it into the future. Hau'ofa is calling for the necessity of self-definition in the Pacific. While Oceania may have been the site of multiple and overlapping Spanish, British,

Dutch, German, French, Japanese, and of course, American colonialism, it remains an Indigenous Pacific space, mother to those who call her home. In essence, Oceania is more than a Magellanic space of transit, Enlightenment theater of tropical sensuality, or basin for military and capitalist struggle. For Pacific Islanders, Oceania is our mother and our home, wherever we are.

Representations of the Pacific Islands and Pacific Islanders have circulated globally through multiple discourses since the arrival of Europeans in the fifteenth century. Representations in sailor and missionary journals, artistic renderings, photographs, films, nonfictional or fictional literary works, and other formal performances contribute greatly to the ongoing perception of the region and its peoples. Imaginings of the exotic Pacific can be traced back to classic ideas about gender, sexuality, and nature. The influence of the Enlightenment and the emphasis on classical themes, Greece in particular, accompanied European travelers. As Patty O'Brien (2006) has argued, imperialist encounters in the Middle East, Asia, Africa, and the Americas and the cultural productions that resulted from them influenced sailors and missionaries when they arrived in the Pacific. Pacific women became conflated with mythologized women of antiquity, as they had an untamable and alluring sexuality derived from their close proximity to the ocean. Early European journals and travelogues characterized the Pacific as a sexual playground, noting that Pacific women were sexually available, existing in a kind of Garden of Eden with no mores or rationality. The Pacific and, by extension, its women were represented as "young, feminine, desirable and vulnerable" (Manderson and Jolly 1997, 103). Pacific women running wild (and unprotected) in turn reflected the powerlessness of Pacific men because they could not control women and society, thereby justifying the conquest of the Pacific and its women. As travelers traversed the Pacific, imperialist motivations and the Enlightenment pursuit of knowledge converged with nineteenth-century bourgeois sexuality on a landscape predicated upon differentiations from "others" that were demarcated by racial signifiers and sexual behavior (Stoler 1995).

Encounters in the Pacific were not, however, always about finding a heterosexual utopia. In fact, historians have discussed how early European accounts of islanders engaging in same-sex activities not only influenced European perceptions of islanders (as hypersexed, savage, and later "free"), but also helped define European sexuality. The early anthropological interest in the Pacific focused on sexuality especially, attempting to understand and codify the cultural significance of what anthropologists deemed nonnormative sexual identities and gender expressions (Wallace 2003; O'Brien 2006). The various identities and expressions that the West deems "nonnormative" existed then and now, not for the indices of anthro-porn, nor for the amusement of would-be gay tourists or a same-sex marriage agenda aspiring to forms of homonormativity that promise equal rights without accounting for Indigenous self-determination, but as representations of Indigenous Pacific epistemologies and values (Teves 2014; Goldberg-Hiller 2002). We push back against moves to look at the Pacific as a site of sexual freedom when such rhetoric is routed through primitivism and a pre-discursive indigeneity, rather than accounting for the ways Indigenous Pacific genders and sexualities are connected to an Indigenous alterity that represents other cultural forms of being and loving in the world, which hold significance beyond their value for the consumption of settlers. It's not that these expressions of gender and sexuality aren't useful to think through the constraints of heteropatriarchy and heteronormativity in multiple contexts, but we take issue with the ways such performances of Indigenous difference are taken up by non-Islanders in a manner that is divorced from a political and cultural context. For instance, many people might celebrate the existence of the *māhū*, the *fakaleiti*, the *takatapui*, or the *fa'afafine* but know absolutely nothing about the ongoing colonization of the Pacific or the cultural contexts from which these identities emerge.

There has always been an anthropological interest in the sexualities of Pacific Islanders. From the early staged documentary films of Robert Flaherty (*Moana*, 1926) to Margaret Mead (*Coming of Age in Samoa*, 1928), the Pacific is framed through an ever-present exoticization and a pervasive image as a tropical and sexual wonderland. As explained in *Bitter Sweet: Indigenous Women in the Pacific*, "The fantasy of the South Pacific has long represented for those of other places the possibilities of a pure space, outside the ambivalences of the 'developed' world. In particular, the manufactured images of the indigenous women of the Pacific embodied these imperial im/possibilities" (Jones, Herda, and Suaalii 2000, 12). As Moana feminists—feminists from the Moana (*Moana* is the Hawaiian, Sāmoan, and Tahitian word for ocean)—we take issue with this constant exoticization and trivialization of the power generated in our diverse expressions of gender, sexuality, and desire, which cannot be reduced to Western fantasy or frameworks (Silva 2007). It is imperative for us to underscore that the ongoing exoticization of the Pacific as a space of fantasy and freedom, as it was represented through European and American colonialism, is different than the ways Asian women are figured as representative of sexual excess rooted in Orientalism. Pacific Islanders are often linked with primitivist discourses and a perceived lack of civilization (Kauanui 2005, 130; Hall 2009, 24). This distinction encloses Pacific Islander women in the space of "the Native" and thus makes available our lands, oceans, and cultures, leaving them prone to dispossession, exploitation, and settlement.

In other words, Asian Americans (inside and outside academia) are represented differently in discourse than Pacific Islander women are; our issues differ considerably because Pacific Islander representations and identities are relegated to a perceived static and ahistorical space of fantasy. Thus, "API" or "Asia-Pacific" (women) is a categorization that should be approached critically and dispensed of when necessary, as we discuss later in this chapter. Further, we take issue with the ways this perceived solidarity or affinity in "API" allows Asian Americans to have some connection to Hawaiʻi. Asian Americans are not innocent when they claim Hawaiʻi as theirs because their great grandparents worked on Hawaiʻi plantations, or when they move to Hawaiʻi because they feel at home or connected to it after a vacation (because Asians are a political majority there, and they thus do not suffer anti-Asian racism in the same way they might in the continental United States). Desires for Hawaiʻi, the Pacific Islands, and the paradise they feign to represent is not just born out of colonial imaginaries; such desires are the underlying logic of settler colonialism, which actively fetishizes our cultures and marginalizes Pacific Islander struggles for self-determination. We say this not to be mean-spirited, but when Asian Americans lay claim to Hawaiʻi without a clear connection to Hawaiʻi as a real place (and note how Hawaiʻi stands in for the entire region), or when they dance hula, or use the term *hapa* to describe someone who is part-white and Asian without voicing solidarity with Native Hawaiians, they are participating in acts of erasure. As explained later in this chapter, *hapa* is a term that has been appropriated from Hawaiians by Asian Americans, who neglect to trace its origins as a Hawaiian concept that was used to delegitimize Hawaiian land claims through a rhetoric of biological racism and the vanishing Native (Hawaiian).

Far from being a pure space, Oceania is also a vexed space, and our people are heavily regulated by colonial governments. For instance, Pacific Islanders hold varying political and citizenship statuses, especially in the United States. Native Hawaiians have US citizenship, as do Chamorros and the inhabitants of Guam and the Commonwealth of the Northern Marianas, whereas American Sāmoans are nationals. While migrants from US Trust Territories of the Republic of the Marshall Islands, the Federated States of

Micronesia, and the Republic of Belau are allowed to move to and work freely in the United States, they do not have citizenship and often face difficulties acquiring crucial services such as healthcare, which many sorely need as a result of the ongoing health issues caused by the environmental degradation connected to radioactive contamination left by the US military, which dropped sixty-seven nuclear test bombs near their islands from 1946 to 1958. And finally, migrants from Tonga, Fiji, Aotearoa, or Papua New Guinea have no official historical or political relationship to the United States, yet they have been profoundly impacted by the ongoing colonization of the Pacific in which the United States and other Western nation-states play critical parts. As Vicente Diaz explains, we must remember too, although the entire Pacific has been affected by the presence of "Western powers," the Indigenous societies of the Pacific precede and will exceed American political and cultural presence (Diaz 2004, 185).

Such reminders of the powerful connections that have been and continue to be made among Indigenous Pacific Islanders are important particularly because our communities are at times in conflict. Though the designations Polynesia, Micronesia, and Melanesia were imposed by European explorers and by no means form the only mode of understanding Pacific regions and connections, many Polynesians in particular have internalized the European idea that Polynesians are the most "civilized" group of Indigenous Pacific peoples. As Maile Arvin writes elsewhere, Polynesians have been constructed in Western social scientific knowledge as being in close proximity to whiteness, in ways that naturalize not only the presence of white settlers in Polynesia but also the structure of white supremacy and its attendant anti-Blackness (Arvin 2013). Unfortunately, in Hawai'i today, there are recurrent bouts of anti-Micronesian sentiment on the part of Native Hawaiians who see Micronesians as undeserving of jobs and welfare because they are foreign (Lyons and Tengan 2015). In another vein, perhaps specifically because of the ways that anti-Blackness against Melanesians (who in European racial discourses have been constructed as "Black") has been naturalized, it has only been in the recent decade that we see stronger political organizing across the Indigenous Pacific to free West Papuans from a violent Indonesian occupation. Groups including Oceania Interrupted in Auckland have led inspiring actions to raise awareness and question Polynesian silence and complicity in regard to West Papua (Oceania Interrupted 2014). These kinds of complications, which focus on the real relationships and conflicts among Indigenous peoples in the Pacific, are too rarely considered because the scholarship and popular representation is so scarce, and what does exist largely focuses on relationships between Indigenous peoples and settlers. Yet it is clear that there is much work left to be done not only to decolonize each of our individual peoples' homelands but also to decolonize the ways we have all also internalized anti-Blackness, white supremacy, and other colonial ideologies.

In addition, as Pacific Islanders, our legitimacy as "scholars" in Western academia is extremely limited, although historically our cultures apparently had a great deal to teach the West about human behavior. There are not many Indigenous Pacific Islanders who are able to write and publish about ourselves and our communities. Academia can feel like a soul-crushing compromise that forces us into a market-driven publishing environment or encourages us to write in a style that isolates many of the communities that give us life. For many of us, the urgencies of daily life and political struggle are too great to ignore. Our presence in curriculums is thus scant, relegated to a day on most syllabi, and most commonly in the form of Haunani-Kay Trask's "Lovely Hula Hands." While that pioneering article itself remains an important critique of the tourism industry in Hawai'i and the broader Pacific—or in a sense, any space where fantasies of "the Native" and paradise maintain colonial imaginaries of "the other" and an "elsewhere" that provides freedom or at the very least respite—we encourage readers to look deeper, as we explain at the end of this chapter.

Actual Pacific Island people have a minor (yet growing) presence in academia as producers and subjects, but to be viewed as capable we must contend with Western grids of intelligibility. We encourage you to look to those voices and to listen to our critiques. We struggle to honor Indigenous and Western epistemes and ways of thinking simultaneously, learning to articulate our struggles through a Western frame, all the while trying to disrupt them (Jones, Herda, and Suaalii 2000, 11). We therefore advocate for an articulation (and expression) of Moana feminisms. Moana feminisms are preeminently a commitment to a decolonization of the entire Pacific that refuses to privilege recognition or inclusion through the nation-state, prioritizes culturally based solutions, yet can still be suspect of hypernationalisms within our own community, which can perpetuate exclusionary forms of belonging among ourselves.

This position may be at odds with Asian American feminist positions that do seek recognition from or greater inclusion in the state. However, as Grace Hong has shown, Women of Color feminisms have long fostered critiques of "the state as a site of violence, not resolution" (2006, xvi). Moana feminisms may resonate with Asian American feminists who are interested in critiquing US imperialism; yet it is also crucial that potential Asian American feminist allies to Moana feminists also acknowledge the differences and potential conflicts between these positions. As Hong (2006, xix) has argued through analysis of what she terms "coalition through difference" in Women of Color feminisms, coalition and community formation are dependent on the recognition of difference and conflict. For Asian American feminists, Moana feminisms may require a deeper reckoning with the ways the Pacific Islands are so often left out of "trans-Pacific" or "Asia-Pacific" analyses, or the common identification of Hawai'i with Asian Americans rather than Native Hawaiians. Overall, we are speaking from our specific positions as Kanaka Maoli women dedicated to a trans-Oceanic articulation of connectivity and a politic rooted/routed in our culture and political expressions. We write not to represent the monolith of Pacific voices, but instead to offer a series of recommendations for Asian American studies to integrate into its teaching and analysis.

1. ACKNOWLEDGE THAT YOU ARE ON INDIGENOUS LAND

Our first recommendation for Asian American feminisms is to acknowledge that you are on Indigenous lands, wherever you are. We reject the API label as a settler-colonial construct that subsumes Pacific Islander cultures and histories. Lumping in Pacific Islander with Asian erases our indigeneity. We hope that this chapter can forge a space of understanding and alliance between Pacific Islanders and Asian Americans. This alliance requires both groups to recognize indigeneity and accountability to the Native people in every place. Acknowledge that imperialism, war, capitalist expansion, and settler colonialism facilitated the transnational movement of Asians. The intention is not to erase these different motivations for migration, but to acknowledge how a system of white supremacy, heteropatriarchy, capitalist development, and ongoing colonialism and racism functions through a structure that rewards Asians for civic participation and cultural assimilation while ignoring the genocide and slavery upon which their aspirations for inclusion depend. We call for Asian Americans and Pacific Islanders to make a concerted effort to build alliances and solidarity with the Indigenous peoples of the lands on which you live. In the article "Decolonization Is Not a Metaphor," Eve Tuck and Wayne Yang explain that decolonization is often invoked in social justice circles and "progressive" curriculums to encourage a kind of critical consciousness, but it is actually a "settler move to innocence" because it also is a way to relieve the settler of "feelings of guilt or responsibility, and conceal the need to give up land or power or privilege" (2012, 21). You cannot invoke "decolonization" on stolen land that you have yet to acknowledge you are a settler on.

We push Asian American feminists to hear this call from Native studies to take seriously the critiques of settler colonialism and its implementation in the Americas and the Pacific. Use of the term *settler colonialism* rather than *colonialism* or *imperialism* has emerged to describe the ways settlers normalize their presence on Native lands, by eliminating the Native through a process that Patrick Wolfe (2006) calls "the logic of elimination." It is not a passing theoretical and activist trend; an understanding of settler colonialism is critical to the way we discuss life. Haunani-Kay Trask has long insisted on recognizing Hawai'i as a settler colony, writing that this means that "Hawai'i is a society in which the indigenous culture and people have been murdered, suppressed or marginalized for the benefit of settlers who now dominate our islands" (1999, 25). She argues that settler colonialism "has as one of its goals, the obliteration rather than the incorporation of indigenous peoples" (26). As a result, Indigenous peoples' daily struggles for sovereignty and decolonization must be understood "not as a struggle for civil rights but a struggle against our planned disappearance" (26). Wolfe similarly argues that settler colonialism requires the elimination of Natives, which should be understood as a structure that produces the conditions of settler presence on the land to replace Native peoples (Wolfe 2006, 402).

We recognize the vulnerability racialized migrants face, which Asian American studies has articulated, but we encourage a more in-depth theorization of our connections and differences, as a means to build broader solidarities among us. Iyko Day elaborates that you cannot use the same blanket of willful immigration as you do for white settlers or Asian migrants to the United States who faced restrictions until 1965. From "aliens ineligible for citizenship" to "enemy aliens" to the vulnerability undocumented and guest-worker populations face today, race certainly conditions status (Day 2015, 107). Asian Americans have been racialized and assimilated in a way that erases Indigenous claims, which has been critical to the settler project. By understanding how this process has impacted Natives as well as Asian Americans, we can, as Dean Saranillio (2013) discusses, assemble histories intersectionally, so that they can be understood and articulated without eclipsing each other's complexities.

The anthology *Asian Settler Colonialism in Hawai'i* (2008) makes an exceptional case for acknowledging the overlapping histories of displacement, dispossession, racism, and capitalist expansion that undergird the

forms of oppression we enact on one another in the name of aspiring to
Western forms of success. While this book focuses on the political context
of Hawai'i, it has wider applicability to the contiguous United States and
across the Pacific, where Asian settler populations are growing, particularly
on Guam, the Northern Marianas, and "American" Sāmoa. Settler colonialism in Hawai'i is enacted by a multiethnic population, a legacy of multiple
generations with roots in plantation labor immigration primarily from Asia,
which has given rise to a so-called local culture that overlaps with Kanaka
Maoli culture in precarious ways. The term *local* is used in Hawai'i to differentiate between Hawai'i-born residents and newcomers. This was and
continues to be a way for "local" Asian settlers and Kānaka Maoli to separate themselves from whiteness. Haole (i.e., white) people born and raised
in the islands are technically "local," but haole identification as such is
highly contextual. "Local" is politically linked most obviously to the legacy of land dispossession and ownership in the islands, where its history
was and continues to be most blatantly played out in plantation and tourist
economies. The discourse of "local" identity in Hawai'i is upset through
Asian settler-colonial critique, which contends that certain Asian settlers
have colluded with haole people and are also to blame for the disempower-
ment and displacement of the Kanaka Maoli people (Saranillio 2009; Fujikane and Okamura 2008).

Hawai'i's "local" political history is widely understood as a liberal
democratic revolution that involved working-class (primarily Asian) overthrow of a white political and business oligarchy in the mid- to late twentieth century. The Democratic Party came to power through an alliance
with labor, long associated with local descendants of Asian plantation
workers. Their victory is touted as inaugurating a litany of progressive
reform in Hawai'i and the United States. This was later heralded as proof
of Hawai'i's exceptionalism as a multicultural state, to form what Fujikane
and Okamura have described critically as "harmonious multiculturalism"
(2008). Asian settlers in Hawai'i achieved political and economic "success," ascending into local government positions, employment outside the
plantation system, educational success, and business. Hawai'i has historically been hailed as an international model of harmony, often invoking the
image of the melting pot, where the mixing of ethnicities and cultures
has produced a model of how the intermingling of peoples is not only
possible but successful (Okamura 2008). And yet, only some Asian settlers were able to "make it"—namely the Japanese in Hawai'i—while

Filipinos, alongside Kānaka Maoli and other Pacific Islanders, have not experienced similar success (Okamura 2008).

The suppression of Pacific Islanders is part and parcel of an Asian settler success story that obscures the differences in the cultural and political histories of Asian migrants and the material conditions of life in Hawai'i, particularly on the plantations. Asian diligence, however, is only possible because of the "spirit of aloha," which is crucial to any narrative of multiculturalism in Hawai'i, where Hawaiian culture is believed to naturally and happily incorporate all cultures. The political environment in Hawai'i obviously differs from the demographic context of the continental United States, where Asian Americans face racism and pressure to adhere to the model-minority myth. It is the responsibility of Asian Americans on the continent to question whether their longing for Hawai'i—as a tropical paradise or an Asian American space where they are free from racism—participates in the erasure of Native Hawaiians' historical and ongoing struggle against settler colonialism in their homeland. It is through the invocation of a supposedly welcoming Hawaiian culture that settler colonialism and its political apparatus can continue to be concealed.

Since the overthrow of the Hawaiian Kingdom in 1893, Native Hawaiians have actively resisted American colonialism and attempts at cultural genocide. Efforts to federally recognize the Kanaka Maoli people like a Native American tribe have been consistent since the early 1990s as a result of the "Apology Bill" in 1993 issued by President Bill Clinton, a bill that apologized for the United States' role in the illegal overthrow of the Hawaiian Kingdom, thus opening the door to a federal process to recognize Native Hawaiians as an Indigenous group with claims to self-determination. The "Apology Bill," however, is only a resolution, and resolutions are not laws. Thus, while it opened up a conversation about some form of redress for the injustices done to Native Hawaiians, it's just a statement that does not guarantee anything or give back one inch of land. Public apologies, like forms of reconciliation or recognition processes, operate as neoliberal efforts to "move forward" from the damage wrought by settler states (allegedly in the past), but do little to assist Indigenous peoples living in the present.

There are many opinions in the Hawaiian community about federal recognition versus independence. It is beyond the scope of this essay to detail the varying positions. Nonetheless, we urge Asian American feminists to learn more regarding the multiple ideas about what "sovereignty" means to Native Hawaiians, rather than, as we have sometimes observed, declaring that the sovereignty movement is a conflicted, divisive quagmire that Asian Americans will never be able to understand (one starting place is Goodyear-Kaʻōpua, Hussey, and Wright 2014). In brief, the "Akaka Bill," named after US senator Daniel Akaka, became a rallying point for many in the Kanaka Maoli community who view federal recognition or a "nation within a nation" structure as necessary to protect Hawaiian entitlement programs as well as a strategy to rebuild our communities and combat our ongoing colonization. Pro-Independence activists and scholars have warned that growing federal and state support for Hawaiian recognition are indicative of the settler-colonial forces that seek to further incorporate Hawaiian indigeneity, settle Hawaiian ceded land claims, and solidify military control of Hawaiʻi and the rest of the Pacific with a pivot toward Asia. While federal recognition would grant Kānaka Maoli specific rights as a domestic dependent nation under US federal jurisdiction, allowing us to form our own government as well as providing a number of other protections, it would simultaneously obfuscate Kanaka Maoli rights to self-determination under the International Declaration on the Rights of Indigenous Peoples. Over the past decade, many Kānaka Maoli have become critical of federal recognition, preferring to think of Hawaiʻi—as it is framed by legal scholars and activists—as illegally occupied by the US military. Extinguishing Hawaiian independence claims through the recognition process coincides with efforts to articulate certain forms of Hawaiian culture that do not challenge settler colonialism and can be easily accommodated.

American colonialism has had its tentacles in the Pacific since the early nineteenth century, which can most notably be observed in Hawaiʻi, Guam, the Northern Marianas, and American Sāmoa. Excluding Hawaiʻi, the latter all remain on the UN list of non-self-governing territories, which means that they have the possibility of undergoing a decolonization process. Votes on decolonization have been held in American Sāmoa, Guam, and the Northern Marianas. In the case of Hawaiʻi, the statehood vote in 1959, which was hailed as a moment of Asian American civic participation and political power (while many Native Hawaiians chose not to vote at all), has since been revealed as a moment when the actual process of the vote violated UN decolonization protocols by not listing independence or decolonization as an option on the ballot. Rather, the statehood ballot presented voters with the option to remain a territory or to "join the union" and become a state. The statehood vote is celebrated as a moment of Asian American political ascension, but it was made possible through a settler desire for inclusion in an American racial paradigm that marked Hawaiʻi and its largely Asiatic population as a threat and liability. This move to assert Asian American-ness occurred at the expense of Hawaiians.

In order for this not to extend in the future, we call for Asian Americans to interrogate their political positions and aspirations for inclusion. As scholars of settler colonialism have noted, for settler colonialism to be denaturalized, we must analyze how it operates not only in social or political spaces but in the very definitions and experiences of subjectivity (Morgensen 2011, 16). If settler colonialism is understood as a structure, to "unsettle" it, we must work on multiple levels of civic and private life to critique it and transform the way settlers and Natives interact with one another, within and across communities. It must be remembered that settler colonialism operates in such a way that cultural difference can be honored, even celebrated, all the while ignoring that indigeneity is not just a cultural difference but a political difference, because Indigenous peoples represent the prior and, in many cases, ongoing presence of an Indigenous nation. When you celebrate Indigenous culture but not Indigenous sovereignty, you are purposefully ignoring the active political claims that Indigenous people have under the UN Declaration on the Rights of Indigenous People and on their own terms. Beyond thinking about Asian American claims to the Pacific, we push for Asian Americans to look to the communities in which they are situated and to encourage active connection and solidarity with Indigenous peoples where they live. This requires partnering with, standing with, and supporting Indigenous nations, which are so often overlooked in American society and politics.

2. STOP USING TERMS LIKE "ASIAN PACIFIC WOMEN"

"Asia-Pacific" is most associated with the "Asia-Pacific Rim," a catchall that invokes the Pacific Islands, often without addressing them, and attaches its peoples to "Asia" or "Asian." Arif Dirlik cautioned using "Asia-Pacific" because it is rooted in the "overdeterminations in mutual histories of Oriental and Occidental colonial desires and anxieties, recharged by late global capital" (Diaz 2004, 186). When used in Asian American studies it presumes an affinity and connection among Asian American and Pacific Islander women, one that, in most instances, does not exist. Grouping us together does not serve a defined political goal because oftentimes islander women are a numerical minority in these spaces and our issues and would-be goals are not allowed space to develop or be discussed.

"Pacific Islander" and "Pacific Women" are diverse categories that also do not easily fit with "Asian Pacific Women" or within the "Women of Color" category often used in political organizing in the United States. Pacific women occupy varied political statuses across the Pacific and the terms of our identification as "American." We straddle immigrant and Indigenous statuses, depending on our story of migration or US occupation of our lands. Because of our small numbers, we are frequently unable to find a place in which we fit in a feminist narrative. Like other Native and Women of Color feminists, we face scrutiny from our community when we name ourselves "feminists," and we carry the burden of educating people about our varied histories and issues. One of the issues we most commonly confront as Pacific Islander women is that so much has been written about our islands, our cultures, our genders, and our sexualities that any expression we make individually or collectively must always respond to that imagery. Similarly, Sāmoans, Tongans, and Chamorros have to constantly explain that they are Pacific Islanders but not Native Hawaiian. Asian Americans from Hawai'i have to explain that they are not Native Hawaiian. Native Hawaiians have to explain that not all Pacific Islanders or Asian Americans are from Hawai'i or have a connection to it. The labor of undoing takes time, and it is exhausting to constantly have to educate Asian Americans about our struggles in an exchange that always feels one-sided. These exchanges usually put us in the position of sharing our culture to be included or to "create understanding" in an already crowded list of "Asian Pacific American" communities and concerns.

Lisa Kahale'ole Hall astutely argues in her essay "Which of These Things Is Not Like the Other: Hawaiians and Other Pacific Islanders Are Not Asian Americans, and All Pacific Islanders Are Not Hawaiian" (2015, 727–28) that "the pan-ethnic, pan-national category of 'Asian American' masks enormous cultural, historical, and demographic differences between different Asian groups in the United States in the service of creating a sociopolitical entity that is intelligible within the racial schema of the United States." We wonder, what was the utility of adding the P when the API was created for statistical purposes and there are no P there? If the P is there, how do we combat the idea that the P always feels like an add-on that has no political weight but is merely a gesture to be inclusive? Asian American scholars must do the work to engage Pacific Island studies as a reputable field of study if they are to include the P at all. Inclusion, as many have argued, is predicated on a capitalist and statist model of inclusion that incorporates communities and peoples through an additive logic that serves the politics of equity. The tokenism of including the *P* operates like an asterisk in the API category that loses our indigeneity in the pan-ethnic Asian American immigrant master narrative. Thus, API assimilates our Indigenous sovereignty and ways of knowing, and implies an imagined equal footing between Asian Americans and Pacific Islanders as immigrants, not Indigenous peoples (Tuck and Yang 2012, 23). As Kēhaulani Kauanui (2005, 129) has noted, there might be more commonality between Sāmoans and African Americans because of their similar racialization, or Hawaiians with American Indians because of the way that they are legislated by the federal government, or Chamorros with Chicanos because of the legacies of Spanish colonization.

More specifically, there is often an assumption that the *PI* is covered if Filipinos and/or Filipino Americans are included. This particular form of tokenism is unjust to both Pacific Islanders and Filipinos. Filipino Americans often suffer from specific forms of racism that place them in a hierarchy below other Asian American groups that seem to fit the model-minority stereotype. Further, some Filipinos are Indigenous, with strong ties to Indigenous cultures and politics. These are issues that deserve to be, and are being, addressed in Asian American studies, but they are not exactly the same as the issues faced by Pacific Islanders from Oceania. Both Filipino and Indigenous Pacific Islander issues deserve to be addressed in all their fullness and complexity, each in its own right, rather than collapsing them or only including them to prove that the PI in any API event or organization is covered. The histories and cultures of the Indigenous Pacific are vast, overlapping, and not reducible to the "Asia Pacific," so please delve deeper.

3. RECOGNIZE HULA AS REVERED KNOWLEDGE, NOT EXOTIC EXERCISE

Within Hawai'i, across the US continent, and indeed in parts of Asia, especially Japan, and even in Mexico, hula can be learned. Hula practitioners come from all backgrounds and with many different motivations. Depending on the context, this could mean that someone is interested in getting a workout (akin to a Zumba class), visited Hawai'i once and is interested in reconnecting to that experience, is drawn to what they believe hula represents, or is genuinely interested in becoming a hula practitioner. Often, it might be a combination of these motivations without much thought to the activity. On the US continent, hula practice is varied, especially beyond the West Coast, where hula easily transforms into colonial spectacle whereby the audiences have only colonial imaginaries to connect the dance to any kind of memory or experience.

In many cases, Asian Americans on the continent dance hula for the varying reasons cited above. We want to push Asian Americans (and ourselves) to acknowledge that hula practice is always subject to the colonial gaze, which continues to use its vision to justify the exoticization and belittlement of Hawaiian and by extension Pacific cultures. Everyone who dances hula must deeply examine their reasons for doing so. Seeking an exotic experience, or looking for some kind of paradisial, tropical magic to rub off on you, is not a justifiable reason. The pervasive image of the hula girl as known through popular culture and Hawai'i's tourism industry has long commodified and cheapened Hawaiian culture and made Native Hawaiians subject to the white, male, heterosexual gaze in particularly violent ways. You simply cannot be an ally to Native Hawaiian women if you seek to play that version of the hula girl.

We know these problems intimately because we both dance hula, in Oregon and California, respectively. We are relative beginners in hula. We dance with other Hawaiian women as well as white, Black, and Asian American women, and we genuinely enjoy their company. We also know that what brought us to hula and the difficulties we had in getting there are shaped in distinct ways by our identity as Hawaiians. For example, getting ourselves into the hula hālau required relinquishing guilt over not being "good Hawaiians" who already danced and spoke Hawaiian language. It required us to negotiate and resist the ways that the colonial image of the hula girl is always overlaid onto actual female hula dancers. We step into the hālau every week negotiating all of these complexities, and we do so because of a love for our ancestors and a desire to strengthen our knowledge. When people participate in hula, they should honor it as a practice that is rooted in a long-standing tradition that perpetuates Hawaiian culture and knowledge—whether in private or public performance—in whatever form the practice itself is taking. As Sharon Mahealani Rowe explains:

> Hula is a moving encyclopedia inscribed into the sinews and postures of dancers' bodies. It carries forward the social and natural history, the religious beliefs, the philosophy, the literature, and the scientific knowledge of the Hawaiian people. It is, therefore, more than the dance form of a particular Polynesian people, more than swaying hips and talking hands, more than competitions, vacation entertainment, or a weekly workout routine. Because the story of native Hawaiians is an ongoing one, hula is

important in the living present, and because that history and its politics are still very much evolving and revolving around unresolved questions, it is important to understand hula as a vital, creative art form and a lived experience that preserves a culture's values, continually forming and reforming identity in and through movement. (Rowe 2008, 31–32)

Hula is a site of knowledge. *Haumana* (students) of all backgrounds should approach it as a way of knowing, not just of movement, and acknowledge that it is an epistemology that has persisted and continues to transform because of Indigenous innovation. Hula *haumana*, like allies, should, in the words of Arvin, Tuck, and Morrill (2013, 21), "thoughtfully reflect on the specifics of why and what they are interested in" when becoming students of hula. People should look deeper into the motivations of why they dance hula. I have heard *haumana* of all levels explain that they find it beautiful and fulfilling, that they went to learn about Hawaiian culture, or that its "fun" and a way for them to connect with another culture. As Rowe explains above, hula extends beyond these seeming surface desires and represents an "idealized body of the Hawaiian people" and thus carries significant political weight for many Hawaiians whether they practice it or not. Hula performance is connected to the global movement of Hawaiian imagery that has been exploited in the name of colonialism and commerce. Rowe also theorizes that when people are drawn to the ancient hula, or hula *kahiko*, people are seeking a historical continuity with the past because they desire a connection with "authenticity," but the popularization of that desire is the very thing that has disconnected it from authenticity (Rowe 2008, 40).

We are not saying that only Native Hawaiians should be able to dance hula. As many independence advocates note today, the Hawaiian Kingdom was multiracial and will be in the future. We are pointing out that hula often means something different to Native Hawaiians, who have experienced generational losses of culture and knowledge due to ongoing colonialism. Hula does not have to mean the same thing to everyone who dances it, but there does need to be an acknowledgment of how dancers may be differently positioned and a commitment by all to honor hula as a rigorous and beloved form of Hawaiian knowledge, not simply a neutral dance form.

4. DO NOT JUST INVITE US TO DANCE

We encourage Asian Americans to think about how to do the work of addressing Pacific Islander concerns. Pacific Islanders are put in a bind when we seek inclusion—we have to reckon with "API" because that is often where the resources are—but this imagined affinity between us leaves Pacific Islanders in a position of constantly educating Asian Americans regarding our plight. We call for a more robust commitment from Asian American communities to educate themselves about our issues, beyond the political context of Hawai'i.

Asian Americans continue to hold onto their self-identification as API as a way to connect to Hawai'i, but the P (Pacific) often falls out, neglecting to create space for Fijian, Tongan, or Chamorros in their midst. In Oregon, Lani has had interactions with many Sāmoan, Chamorro, and Tongan college students who joined "Hawai'i Club" or attempted to take part in Asian American organizations to account for the P, only to be marginalized and feel out of place. Universities should hire Pacific Islander student specialists or academic advisers who work solely with Pacific Islander students and not with Asian American students. At some schools, we have both met Pacific Islander students who find more comfort in Native American spaces, because of a strong sense of a shared Indigenous experience. However, not all students know that there are multiple places they can go, and not all Native American student services staff are prepared to welcome Pacific Islander students too. Often, Pacific Islander student experience is one of not knowing where they fit in, so they choose not to engage.

This is something that goes largely unchecked because of the small numbers of Pacific Islanders in higher education as a result of lack of access. Also Native Hawaiian or Other Pacific Islander (NHOPI) students are often not disaggregated from API, making Pacific Islanders even harder to track. Still, they are increasingly entering college. Thirty-eight percent of Pacific Islander college-age youth are in college, but this is a statistic well below the national average (Empowering Pacific Islander Communities and Asian Americans Advancing Justice 2014, 5). The rise of Polynesian superstar football players (usually it is only Polynesians)—as proud as they make us—fails to tell the story of their kin who struggle working multiple jobs while going to school. The Polynesian football star is a stereotype that also produces opportunities. We know men of color in particular are exploited for their athletic talent, having their time monopolized by training rather than used for educational or social justice activities that might enhance awareness of their particular status on and off the field or court (Uperesa 2014).

There is a problematic ongoing conflation of Pacific Islander symbols within Asian American organizations who appropriate Hawaiian iconography to celebrate Asian Pacific Heritage Month. Normally it is Native

Hawaiians that they want to make space for. Pacific Islanders are always invited to dance at Asian American (Pacific Islander) events, to share our food, to tell our migration stories. Many universities and colleges feature an annual "Luʻau" often organized by a Hawaiʻi Club, which is usually a group of students from Hawaiʻi, a mixture of Asian American, Native Hawaiian, and sometimes a few Pacific Islander students who want to share and nurture their connections to home, most often Hawaiʻi. These events tend to involve some aspect of performance, usually hula, and food—lots of great wonderful food! Some Pacific Islander students on the continent have expressed comfort and belonging in Hawaiʻi Club. They talk about learning to dance hula as one of their few opportunities to connect to their indigeneity on the continent in a way that is celebrated by people at large. But, upon reflection, many have expressed sadness and frustration at not having their own space to discuss issues pertinent to their identities within and outside Pacific Islander communities. Lani has met these students at community events, where they explain how, in an attempt to make a Pacific-focused major, they took courses in anthropology where they learned a great deal about Pacific Islander archaeology and culture from Western perspectives but nothing about contemporary politics in the Pacific or the experiences of Pacific Islanders living in the diaspora in the United States and beyond.

Our intention is not to totally dismiss the efforts of Asian American studies or student groups and political organizations who are earnestly trying to "include" or "reach out" to Pacific Islanders. There are certainly many Asian American scholars and community members who want to create space for Pacific Islanders to make sure that they are being inclusive of our diverse cultures and history. This rarely turns into a discussion of the differences between Pacific Islanders and Asian Americans. We ask that people think more critically about these practices and spaces and find innovative ways to insert learning and cultural presentations. For example, through the mentorship of Kanaka Maoli scholar-activist Kehaulani Vaughn, last year the Pacific Islander Student Association at the University of California, Riverside put on a performance night that went beyond simply providing Pacific Islander dances for entertainment. The PISA students carefully framed each dance performed by themselves and other invited dance groups from Southern California, providing the audience with historical and political information about the various peoples to whom these dances belonged. The history and present of colonialism and imperialism in Guam, Hawaiʻi, Sāmoa, and other Pacific Island nations were centered and contextualized, so that the audience left thinking about what current political struggles Chamorros, Kānaka Maoli, Sāmoans, Tongans, and others (notably in West Papua) are facing. This is an excellent example of how to encourage responsible allyship in audiences who may come to a performance expecting only to be entertained with a hula. Vaughn's (in this case, volunteer) work reflects the success and necessity of Pacific Islander staffing and programming. We advocate for more hiring of Pacific Islander–focused staff and faculty to assist students and to support the growth of Pacific Island studies.

5. RECONSIDER YOUR USE OF *HAPA*

The use of *hapa* (or "Hapa," as some Asian American activists have hoped to distinguish it) as an identity by multiracial Asian Americans participates in the erasure of Native Hawaiians and the ongoing colonial expropriation of all things Hawaiian (Arvin 2013). *Hapa* is a Hawaiian language word literally meaning "part." As ku'ualoha ho'omanawanui has written, Kānaka Maoli began to use *hapa* in the late 1800s to signify Kānaka Maoli who also had genealogies linking them to haole (white), *pake* (Chinese), *kepani* (Japanese), and other immigrant groups to Hawai'i (ho'omanawanui 2012). Most often used in the phrase *hapa haole*, which often connoted a higher class status, ho'omanawanui persuasively argues that Kanaka Maoli usage of *hapa* was not pejorative but rather a way of expanding notions of Hawaiian-ness that were not dependent on Western ideas about race (ho'omanawanui 2012). *Hapa* was a way of making a space for and including as Kanaka Maoli the many Kānaka Maoli who had multiracial backgrounds, not about setting them apart (Ledward 2007).

Despite the fact that Kānaka Maoli continue to use *hapa* in this manner, Western racial ideas have crept in and shape how non-Hawaiians, and Asian Americans in particular, view *hapa*. Though *hapa* literally means "part," many people take *hapa* to mean "half," which indicates a more specific racial blood percentage. While *half* may be used in a colloquial sense to indicate biracial parentage among Asian Americans, being "half" Hawaiian is actually a distinct legal status for Native Hawaiians due to the Hawaiian Homes Commission Act of 1920. As Kauanui has detailed, this act sought to limit the number of Native Hawaiians eligible to lease homesteads, small plots of land deemed undesirable by plantations, by requiring eligible leaseholders to demonstrate that they were "of not less than one-half part blood" (Kauanui 2008). As with formations of blood quantum laws in other Indigenous contexts, the 50 percent blood requirement for

Hawaiian Homes was designed to be a kind of statistical genocide. Native Hawaiians with less than 50 percent blood were assumed to be already assimilating into American Territorial norms, and those with more than 50 percent would learn how to assimilate by paying rent on their homesteads and living in smaller nuclear family households (Kauanui 2008). Not far in the future, territorial officials and social scientists projected, there would be no Native Hawaiians who could meet the eligibility requirement because it was assumed that a new, racially mixed "neo-Hawaiian" race was forming in Hawai'i at this time (Arvin 2013). That new race would comprise multicultural American citizens, rather than a people associated with the former Hawaiian Kingdom.

Thus, it is not only that Asian Americans are appropriating a Hawaiian language term that has had a specific meaning for Native Hawaiians, but that the Asian American valorization of *hapa* (even if unwittingly) participates in constructing Hawai'i as a cheery, mixed-race, American melting pot. That melting pot ideal, propagated by sociologist Romanzo Adams and many popular representations of Hawai'i for a tourist audience, is a settler-colonial ideal (Arvin 2013). It has long covered up long-standing virulent racism—sometimes using the very language of anti-Black racism—that Native Hawaiians, Filipinos, Micronesians, and others face in Hawai'i. Asian American usage of *hapa* as a positive mixed-race identity thus erases the fact that Hawai'i and Native Hawaiians in particular are positioned quite differently in regard to discourses of racial mixture. Mainstream discourses of racial mixture have long helped structure a settler-colonial ideology that Native Hawaiians (through racial mixing with Asian and white settler populations) are destined to die out or assimilate.

Many Native Hawaiians have made such critiques, since at least the 1990s, when Asian Americans began identifying as *hapa*. Yet many Asian Americans see no problem in continuing to use the term. Throughout the 1990s and especially in the early 2000s, *Hyphen*, a magazine geared toward the Asian American community, had numerous stories and even special issues on *hapa* identity, often detached from any discussion of the political context of the use of the term or where it comes from. In 2007, there was a special "Hybrid" issue focused on the "contentious issue of hapa," where multiple articles detailed different perspectives on the use of the term. One article in particular described a longer history of *hapa* and advocated abandoning it. In the comments section many people came to the defense of using *hapa* because to dispense with it would continue to "divide" the Asian American and Pacific Islander communities. They argued further that the term *hapa* came out of Hawaiians intermarrying with Asians, so it is okay for Asians to use it (even if not in a Hawaiian context) and that *hapa* is not a pure traditional precolonial Hawaiian term (see, e.g., Mok 2007). Many people continue to feel a sort of pride in the use of *hapa* because it marks a mixed identity that can be validating to some, but again, is there a better way to honor one's heritage without appropriating another? The constant holding onto *hapa* represents yet another example of Asian American insistence on claiming Hawaiian (and Pacific) concepts because it represents a theoretical desired other that is exoticized in dominant American culture (but is not a threat). The ongoing use of *hapa* is a subtle tool of settler colonialism.

As Wei Ming Dariotis (2007) has written, "I hate to say this, but 'Hapa' has great mouth feel as a word, until the bad taste of Native Hawaiian oppression slips in." While many mixed-race Asian Americans continue to use *hapa* in problematic ways, several scholars and activists, including Dariotis, have publicly grappled with the problem and sought different ways to identify their communities. There is no easy answer, and we recognize that, as Dariotis notes, it is hard and even upsetting to consider giving up an identity that finally felt empowering. Yet, that empowerment should not come at the cost of furthering US amnesia about past and ongoing US settler colonization of Hawai'i. As Asian American mixed-race activist and scholar Sharon Chang has written, "We need to recognize that attempts to erase Native Hawaiians have been happening for a long time, that attempts persist today on purpose, and that using the word Hapa without (a) having any Native Hawaiian ancestry, or (b) any awareness of its history and significance, may make us complicit with white-dominant-colonial agendas which have maneuvered to wipe away and wipe out indigenous peoples for practically ever" (Chang 2014). Even if mixed-race Asian Americans continue to use *hapa*, we ask that they not rush to explain away this tension but continue to reflect on it and the possibilities of building real solidarity with Native Hawaiian people.

6. EXPAND NATIVE HAWAIIAN AND PACIFIC ISLANDER CURRICULA

In our experience, Asian American studies classes, when they address Hawai'i or the Pacific Islands at all, do so by assigning one of three texts: *Pau Hana* by Ronald Takaki, *Cane Fires* by Gary Okihiro, or Haunani-Kay Trask's essay "Lovely Hula Hands." The first two are about the Asian immigrant experience on Hawaiʻi's plantations, and each essentially erases the presence of Native Hawaiians by noting early on that Native Hawaiians did not really participate in the plantation economy. By contrast, Haunani-Kay Trask is a beloved, important Native Hawaiian scholar whose foundational writings and activism have inspired many to challenge settler colonialism in Hawaiʻi. Yet, her essay "Lovely Hula Hands" often becomes the token piece of writing assigned about Hawaiʻi in Asian American studies courses, and it is usually taught without placing it in the wider contexts of contemporary Native Hawaiian scholarship and activism and Pacific Islander issues more broadly. Today, there is no excuse for failing to assign more Native Hawaiian scholarship, given the richness of the growing number of works on Hawaiian history and politics. Below we note only a few of the expansive possibilities for readings focused on Hawaiʻi and the Pacific Islands that we hope Asian American studies and other ethnic studies courses may consider integrating into their curriculum.

In relation to Hawaiʻi, an important curricular shift is to begin not with the histories of Asian plantation labor in Hawaiʻi but with the history (and ongoing present) of settler colonialism, especially examining the overthrow of the Hawaiian Kingdom in 1893 and the region's subsequent annexation as a US territory in 1898. Noenoe Silva's writings in *Aloha Betrayed* explain how the overthrow of the Hawaiian Kingdom was actively contested by the Kanaka Maoli people and that the so-called natural American presence in Hawaiʻi is based on a pernicious myth that no one resisted the overthrow. In her analysis of the "Kūʻē Petitions" and the work of political groups in the late nineteenth century, she provides a detailed account of how power influences the way people think about Hawaiʻi, focusing on the willful denial of history by white historians who did not bother to consult Hawaiian language archives (Silva 2004). Read alongside "Lovely Hula Hands" or the entire book *From a Native Daughter*, Silva's work does more than make people think about the history of Hawaiian resistance; it also situates that history in a contemporary struggle that impacts Hawaiian women in particular ways, as we are often attacked by the settler community (and even our own) when we act in ways that defy the hula stereotype. We become subject to charges of being inauthentic or acting "against aloha," which is really a gloss for "Be quiet and get back in your place."[2]

Indeed, curricula should not limit the treatment of settler colonialism in Hawaiʻi and Kanaka Maoli resistance to the past, but rather should engage with contemporary scholarship and activism that describe the fullness and complexities of Kanaka Maoli lives today. One great text to start with is the recent anthology *A Nation Rising: Hawaiian Movements for Life, Land, and Sovereignty*, which showcases many of the multifaceted recent activist movements in Hawai'i, from efforts to protect land to revitalizing language and culture (Goodyear-Ka'ōpua, Hussey, and Wright 2014). Another significant work is ku'ualoha ho'omanawanui's *Voices of Fire: Reweaving the Literary Lei of Pele and Hi'iaka* (2014), which describes the robust history and present of what she theorizes as a Kanaka Maoli literary nationalism through in-depth readings of historical and contemporary *mo'olelo* (stories, histories, narratives) about the Kanaka Maoli goddesses/ancestors Pele and Hi'iaka. Another great resource is Kalaniopua Young's recent essay "From a Native Trans Daughter: Carceral Refusal, Settler Colonialism, Rerouting the Roots of an Indigenous Abolitionist Imaginary" (2015), which is easily taught alongside Haunani-Kay Trask's *From a Native Daughter*, which it takes off from. Sharing her own experience of incarceration and diaspora, Young powerfully addresses the specificities of how heteropatriarchy, transphobia, and settler colonialism intersect for transgender and/or *māhū* Native Hawaiians in the prison industrial complex, highlighting why prison abolition is essential to decolonization.[3]

Our expertise is rooted largely in Hawai'i, but we also find it important to make connections across Pacific contexts and, especially in US institutions, to not let Hawai'i stand in for the rest of the distinct, complex Pacific Islands and peoples. As Teresia Teaiwa (2016) has noted, in Pacific studies, it is "impossible to know everything about the 1200 distinct cultural groups among 7–10 million people living in and around the world's largest and oldest ocean, in some of the world's most vulnerable and precious ecosystems." Yet many recent works examine the intersections of Native Hawaiian and other Asian American and Pacific Islander communities in Hawai'i and the larger Pacific. Asian American studies curriculum should attempt to make similar connections and to frame Native Hawaiian and Pacific Islander issues within these broader contexts and structures that affect many communities, if in different ways, including settler colonialism, imperialism, the military-industrial complex, tourism, religion, and more. For example, Vernadette Vicuña Gonzalez's *Securing Paradise: Tourism and Militarism in Hawai'i and the Philippines* (2013) demonstrates how American settler-colonial and imperial structures of tourism and militarism have been deeply intertwined in similar ways in both Hawai'i and the Philippines. Rather than equating these two colonial experiences or identities, Gonzalez engages Asian settler colonialism as an important framework and demonstrates how the colonization of Indigenous people in Hawai'i and the Philippines has been linked through similar US policies and industries. Hokulani Aikau's *A Chosen People, a Promised Land: Mormonism and Race in Hawai'i* (2012) shows how Sāmoan, Tongan, Hawaiian, and other Pacific Islander communities have engaged with Mormonism as a way of making trans-Indigenous connections and pursuing decolonization in unlikely settings, such as the popular tourist destination the Polynesian Cultural Center.

We are building on a breadth of scholarship that came before us, and we are thrilled to be in such powerful company. Most recently *American Quarterly* had a special issue, "Pacific Currents," dedicated to interrogating the place of Pacific Island studies within American studies. The special issue featured scholars who are cited throughout this chapter, as well as newer voices—us, Tiara Naputi, Brandy Nālani McDougall, Craig Santos Perez, Joyce Pualani Warren, Kealani Cook, and others. Beyond this special issue, there are a growing number of Pacific Islander scholars; we encourage readers to seek them out and engage with them. Besides expanding Asian American studies curricula, we push departments and universities to dedicate entire courses to Pacific Islander studies that are not just anthropological in scope. A course on Pacific Islander studies will boost students' understanding of the role of colonialism in American history and its contemporary manifestations. These courses need permanent faculty and student support services.

We recognize that it may seem impractical to push for increased staffing and courses when academic labor and minoritarian critiques are increasingly under attack, but ethnic studies has emerged as a movement for social justice, and it will not go quietly even as administrators across the country attempt to suppress the legacy of its critiques. The recent protests at San Francisco State University against proposed budget cuts to the iconic College of Ethnic Studies have engaged a new crop of student activists who refuse to be silenced. In a statement posted online, the Pacific Islanders' Club demanded that the College of Ethnic Studies offer Pacific Islander studies courses and that faculty separate from Asian American studies. Despite being one of the fastest-growing ethnic groups in the country, Pacific Islanders continue to be an afterthought in curricula, and as we have discussed throughout this chapter, students often lack support on campus.

The Pacific Islanders' Club statement goes on to explain that Pacific Islander students are marginalized within ethnic studies, impacting the overall success of Pacific Islander students and the broader community (Pacific Islanders Club 2016). They astutely write, "We are more than a week in an Asian American studies course, and our histories are as rich and deep as the ocean from which we come from." Invoking the Moana, the students place themselves in a longer history of Pacific epistemologies and navigation. Rather than accept the status quo, they prioritize self-definition and self-determination, akin to the words of Hauʻofa (2008): "We must not allow anyone to belittle us again and take away our freedom." We continue to be inspired by these students; we end with their words because their protests allow scholars like us to do the work we do.

Despite our frustration with the API grouping, we are hopeful that these growing conversations will enhance our ability to listen and build with one another. A recent example evokes some hope as well as pointing to some work that remains to be done on the part of Asian Americans seeking to be substantially in coalition with Pacific Islanders. In 2015, the movie *Aloha* premiered, starring Emma Stone, a white actress, playing a mixed-race Chinese and Native Hawaiian character. Many Asian American writers circulated critiques of the film focused on how inappropriate it was to whitewash an Asian American character by casting Emma Stone instead of an Asian American actress. However, as we wrote with our collective Hinemoana of Turtle Island (2015) on the *muliwai* blog, very few of these critiques acknowledged that the character was supposed to be part Native Hawaiian, and that the movie overall rehashed long-standing cinematic tropes about Hawaiʻi as a romantic vacation paradise for white people, erasing the fact that Hawaiʻi continues to be an occupied settler colony of the United States. Shockingly, some critiques by Asian American writers did not even seem to understand that Native Hawaiians and Pacific Islanders are racially distinct from Asian Americans (e.g., Lee 2015).

Nonetheless, two pieces by Asian American feminist authors did acknowledge the erasure of Native Hawaiians as distinct from Asian Americans. In response to the overwhelming focus on non-Asian American casting, Sharon Chang (2015) noted in her blog *Multiracial Asian Families*, "I'm deeply invested in exploring the facets of a mixed-race Asian identity and looking at the many questions it raises in a raced/racist world. But I am *not* interested in a conversation about that identity which moves towards anti-indigeneity." Similarly, Julie Feng (2015), writing for the magazine *The Body Is Not an Apology*, squarely challenged Asian American critics for erasing earlier Native Hawaiian responses to the movie, urging them that even as she too desires better Asian American representation in Hollywood, "it can't happen at the expense of someone else's marginalization. Non-indigenous Asian Americans have to recognize complicity in our roles as settlers." Such responses are encouraging, and it is hard to imagine them existing in prior years, when Pacific Islanders were even more unseen and unheard of. They suggest what might be possible when Asian American feminists recognize that Asian Americans and Pacific Islanders are different in significant ways, and that Asian American moves to empower their own communities sometimes risk furthering the mainstream erasure of Pacific Islanders and our distinct concerns.

We have argued that for API to be more than simply a government-imposed reporting designation, there must be, as Hong has noted in her analysis of Women of Color feminisms, a coalition built through real recognition of the differences and conflicts between Asian American and Pacific Islander communities. There is much that Moana feminists and Asian American feminists have in common. We share simultaneous struggles against US imperialism and settler colonialism, white supremacy, and the expectations that our communities will simply "assimilate" into whiteness—all structures that are deeply gendered and thus wreak violence on Asian American and Pacific Islander women in particular ways. We also share analogous struggles within our own communities to decenter heteropatriarchy and anti-Blackness in the many ways that we have internalized such ideals. But the call we have put out in this essay is clear. To advance our important common work, Asian American feminists must recognize and change the ways they participate in Pacific Islander erasure and cultural appropriation, and commit to being our allies in decolonization. We look forward to the possibilities such change will enable for all of us.

NOTES

1   Throughout this chapter, we alternate between *Native Hawaiian* and *Kanaka Maoli* to refer to any person descended from the Indigenous people inhabiting the Hawaiian Islands before 1778. *Kānaka Maoli* with the macron over the *a* is the plural of *Kanaka Maoli*.

2   Other important works that examine the history of settler colonialism in Hawai'i and Kanaka Maoli agency and/or resistance include (this is by no means a comprehensive list, only a starting point) David Chang's *The World and All the Things upon It: Native Hawaiian Geographies of Exploration* (2016), Marie Alohalani Brown's *Facing the Spears of Change: The Life and Legacy of John Papa ʻĪʻī* (2016),

Kamanamaikalani Beamer's *No Mākou Ka Mana: Liberating the Nation* (2014),
Keanu Sai's *Ua Mau Ke Ea: Sovereignty Endures: An Overview of the Political and
Legal History of the Hawaiian Islands* (2013), Sydney Iaukea's *The Queen and I: A
Story of Dispossessions and Reconnections in Hawai'i* (2011), Jonathan Osorio's *Dis-
membering Lāhui: A History of the Hawaiian Nation to 1887* (2002), Kanalu Terry
Young's *Rethinking the Native Hawaiian Past* (1998), and Lilikalā Kame'eleihiwa's
*Native Land and Foreign Desires: A History of Land Tenure Change in Hawai'i from
Traditional Times until the 1848 Māhele* (1992).

3   Other works focusing on contemporary Native Hawaiian issues include (but are not
limited to) Brandy Nālani McDougall's *Finding Meaning: Kaona and Contemporary
Hawaiian Literature* (2016), *The Value of Hawai'i, Vol. 2: Ancestral Roots, Oceanic
Visions* (2014), Noelani Goodyear-Kā'opua's *The Seeds We Planted: Portraits of a
Native Hawaiian Charter School* (2013), and Ty Tengan's *Native Men Remade: Gender
and Nation in Contemporary Hawai'i* (2008).

REFERENCES

Aikau, Hokulani K. 2012. *A Chosen People, a Promised Land: Mormonism and Race in
Hawai'i*. Minneapolis: University of Minnesota Press.
Arvin, Maile. 2013. "Pacifically Possessed: Scientific Production and Native Hawaiian
Critique of the 'Almost White' Polynesian Race." PhD diss., University of California,
San Diego.
Arvin, Maile, Eve Tuck, and Angie Morrill. 2013. "Decolonizing Feminism: Challenging
Connections between Settler Colonialism and Heteropatriarchy." *Feminist Forma-
tions* 25 (1): 8–34.
Chang, Sharon. 2014. "Say Hapa, with Care." *AAPI Voices*. http://aapivoices.com/hapa
-with-care.
———. 2015. "Yea, *Aloha* Is Super White, but What's Up with the Way We're Talking
about It?" *Multiracial Asian Families*, June 2. http://multiasianfamilies.blogspot.com
/2015/06/yea-aloha-is-super-white-but-whats-up.html.
Dariotis, Wei Ming. 2007. "Hapa: The Word of Power." *Mixed Heritage Center*. www
.mixedheritagecenter.org/index.php?option=com_content&task=view&id
=1259&Itemid=34.
Day, Iyko. 2015. "Being or Nothingness: Indigeneity, Antiblackness, and Settler Colonial
Critique." *Critical Ethnic Studies* 1 (2): 102–21.
Diaz, Vicente M. 2004. "'To "P" or Not to "P"?': Marking the Territory between Pacific
Islander and Asian American Studies." *Journal of Asian American Studies* 7 (3):
183–208.
Empowering Pacific Islander Communities and Asian Americans Advancing Justice.
2014. "A Community of Contrasts: Native Hawaiians and Pacific Islanders in the
United States." https://advancingjustice-la.org/sites/default/files/A_Community_Of
_Contrasts_NHPI_CA_2014.pdf.
Feng, Julie. 2015. "The Problem with *Aloha* Is Not the Lack of 'Asian' Faces: On Asian
American Complicity in the Erasure of Indigeneity." *The Body Is Not an Apology*,
June 13. http://thebodyisnotanapology.com/magazine/the-problem-with-aloha-is

-not-the-lack-of-asian-faces-on-asian-american-complicity-in-the-erasure-of -indigeneity.

Fujikane, Candace, and Jonathan Y. Okamura. 2008. *Asian Settler Colonialism: From Local Governance to the Habits of Everyday Life in Hawai'i*. Honolulu: University of Hawai'i Press.

Goldberg-Hiller, Jonathan. 2002. *The Limits to Union: Same-Sex Marriage and the Politics of Civil Rights, Law, Meaning, and Violence*. Ann Arbor: University of Michigan Press.

Gonzalez, Vernadette Vicuña. 2013. *Securing Paradise: Tourism and Militarism in Hawai'i and the Philippines*. Durham, NC: Duke University Press.

Goodyear-Ka'ōpua, Noelani, Ikaika Hussey, and Erin Kahunawaika'ala Wright. 2014. *A Nation Rising: Hawaiian Movements for Life, Land, and Sovereignty, Narrating Native Histories*. Durham, NC: Duke University Press.

Hall, Lisa Kahale'ole. 2005. "'Hawaiian at Heart' and Other Fictions." *Contemporary Pacific* 17 (2): 404–13.

———. 2009. "Navigating Our Own Sea of Islands." *Wicazo Sa Review* 24 (2): 15–38.

———. 2015. "Which of These Things Is Not Like the Other: Hawaiians and Other Pacific Islanders Are Not Asian Americans, and All Pacific Islanders Are Not Hawaiian." *American Quarterly* 67 (3): 727–47.

Hau'ofa, Epeli. 2008. *We Are the Ocean: Selected Works*. Honolulu: University of Hawai'i Press.

Hinemoana of Turtle Island. 2015. "On Cameron Crowe's *Aloha* and Indigenous Pacific Films We Actually Recommend." *Muliwai*, June 16. https://morethantwominutes .wordpress.com/2015/06/16/on-cameron-crowes-aloha-and-indigenous-pacific-films -we-actually-recommend.

Hong, Grace Kyungwon. 2006. *The Ruptures of American Capital: Women of Color Feminism and the Culture of Immigrant Labor*. Minneapolis: University of Minnesota Press.

ho'omanawanui, ku'ualoha. 2012. "From Captain Cook to Captain Kirk, or, From Colonial Exploration to Indigenous Exploitation: Issues of Hawaiian Land, Identity, and Nationhood in a 'Postethnic' World." In *Transnational Crossroads: Remapping the Americas and the Pacific*, edited by Camilla Fojas and Rudy P. Guevarra Jr., 229–68. Lincoln: University of Nebraska Press.

———. 2014. *Voices of Fire: Reweaving the Literary Lei of Pele and Hi'iaka*. Minneapolis: University of Minnesota Press.

Jones, Alison, Phyllis Herda, and Tamasaillau Suaalii. 2000. *Bitter Sweet: Indigenous Women in the Pacific*. Dunedin, NZ: University of Otago Press.

Kauanui, J. Kēhaulani. 2005. "Asian American Studies and the 'Pacific Question.'" In *Asian American Studies after Critical Mass*, edited by Kent Ono, 123–43. Malden, MA: Blackwell.

———. 2008. *Hawaiian Blood: Colonialism and the Politics of Sovereignty and Indigeneity*. Durham, NC: Duke University Press.

Ledward, B. C. 2007. "On Being Hawaiian Enough: Contesting American Racialization and Native Hybridity." *Hulili: Multidisciplinary Research on Hawaiian Well-Being* 4 (1): 107–43.

Lee, Chris. 2015. "I'm Not Buying Emma Stone as an Asian American in *Aloha*." *Entertainment Weekly*, May 29.

Lyons, Paul, and Ty Tengan. 2015. "COFA Complex: A Conversation with Joakim 'Jojo' Peter." *American Quarterly* 67 (3): 663–79.

Manderson, Lenore, and Margaret Jolly. 1997. *Sites of Desire, Economies of Pleasure: Sexualities in Asia and the Pacific*. Chicago: University of Chicago Press.

Mok, Harry. 2007. "Hapa Featured in Hyphen Hybrid Issue." *Hyphen*, December 19. http://hyphenmagazine.com/blog/2007/12/19/hapa-featured-hyphen-hybrid-issue.

Morgensen, Scott Lauria. 2011. *Spaces between Us: Queer Settler Colonialism and Indigenous Decolonization*. Minneapolis: University of Minnesota Press.

O'Brien, Patty. 2006. *The Pacific Muse: Exotic Femininity and the Colonial Pacific*. Seattle: University of Washington Press.

Oceania Interrupted. 2014. "Oceania Interrupted." https://oceaniainterrupted.com.

Okamura, Jonathan. 2008. *Ethnicity and Inequality in Hawai'i*. Philadelphia: Temple University Press.

Pacific Islanders Club. 2016. "The Stake Pacific Islanders Have in Ethnic Studies." *Medium*, February 29. https://medium.com/@picsfsu/the-stake-pacific-islanders -have-in-ethnic-studies-133e1bf0a196.

Rowe, Sharon Mahealani. 2008. "We Dance for Knowledge." *Dance Research Journal* 40 (1): 31–44.

Saranillio, Dean Itsuji. 2009. "Seeing Conquest: Colliding Histories and the Cultural Politics of Hawai'i Statehood." PhD diss., University of Michigan.

———. 2013. "Why Asian Settler Colonialism Matters: A Thought Piece on Critiques, Debates and Indigenous Difference." *Settler Colonial Studies* 3 (3–4): 280–94.

Silva, Noenoe. 2004. *Aloha Betrayed: Native Hawaiian Resistance to American Colonialism*. Durham, NC: Duke University Press.

———. 2007. "Pele, Hi'iaka, and Haumea: Women and Power in Two Hawaiian Mo'olelo." *Pacific Studies* 300 (March/June): 159–81.

Stoler, Ann Laura. 1995. *Race and the Education of Desire: Foucault's History of Sexuality and the Colonial Order of Things*. Durham, NC: Duke University Press.

Teaiwa, Teresia. 2016. "The Classroom as a Metaphorical Canoe: Co-operative Learning in Pacific Studies." Accessed March 22, 2016. https://www.academia.edu/23069100 /The_classroom_as_a_metaphorical_canoe_Co-operative_learning_in_Pacific _Studies.

Teves, Stephanie Nohelani. 2014. "A Critical Reading of Aloha and Visual Sovereignty in *Ke Kulana He Māhū*." *International Journal of Critical Indigenous Studies* 7 (1).

Trask, Haunani-Kay. 1999. *From a Native Daughter: Colonialism and Sovereignty in Hawai'i*. 2d ed. Honolulu: University of Hawai'i Press.

Tuck, Eve, and K. Wayne Yang. 2012. "Decolonization Is Not a Metaphor." *Decolonization: Indigeneity, Education & Society* 1 (1): 1–40.

Uperesa, Fa'anofo Lisaclaire. 2014. "Fabled Futures: Migration and Mobility for Samoans in American Football." *Contemporary Pacific* 26 (2): 281–301.

Wallace, Lee. 2003. *Sexual Encounters: Pacific Texts, Modern Sexualities*. Ithaca, NY: Cornell University Press.

Wolfe, Patrick. 2006. "Settler Colonialism and the Elimination of the Native." *Journal of Genocide Research* 8 (4): 387–409.

Young, Kalaniopua. 2015. "From a Native Trans Daughter: Carceral Refusal, Settler Colonialism, Re-routing the Roots of an Indigenous Abolitionist Imaginary." In *Captive Genders: Trans Embodiment and the Prison Industrial Complex*, 2d ed., edited by Eric Stanley and Nat Smith, 83–96. Oakland: AK Press.

CHAPTER 6

BECOMING RESTIVE

Orientations in Asian American
Feminist Theory and Praxis

TAMSIN KIMOTO

LIKE MANY PEOPLE LIVING IN THE UNITED STATES, I HAVE LIVED
my entire life on Indigenous land and have rarely thought seriously about
what it means to make a home on stolen land. When asked where home is
for me, I respond that my home is Honolulu, regardless of where I happen
to live at the time. Indeed, I often remark to friends that Hawai'i is one of
the few places where I feel totally comfortable in my skin. While I have
always refused the term when people refer to me as Hawaiian, I have frequently used Hawaiian words to describe myself and my racial identity in
particular: *hapa*, as a term often used by multiracial and mixed-race people
with some Asian descent, felt right for many years of my life as a way of
naming my racial identity. However, J. Kēhaulani Kauanui (2008) prob-
lematizes such a use by placing the term in its historical context as having
specifically emerged to name persons of mixed *Hawaiian*, or Kanaka Maoli,
descent rather than anyone of mixed Asian or Pacific Islander descent.
While words can and do change over time, Indigenous languages have
often been transformed or even eliminated as part of settler-colonial projects of displacement and erasure (cf. Zepeda and Hill 1991). In the case of
Hawai'i, Noenoe Silva (2004) traces how colonizers deployed the Hawaiian language to erase Kanaka Maoli ways of life even as it was used to resist
these efforts. Learning these histories required a shift in how I understood

myself in relation to the sense of home that Hawai'i has always evoked. This is an ongoing process.

This chapter begins from these moments of recognizing ways in which we contribute to ongoing settler-colonial projects. I want, in particular, to think about how we, as Asian American feminist theorists, might develop theories that do not elide our role in the theft of Indigenous land, the erasure of Indigenous cultures, or the outright genocide of Indigenous peoples. This requires a way of thinking that allows us to be restive in our orientation.[1] As a word, *restive* has two contradictory meanings. On the one hand, it means a willful desire to move from where one is. On the other hand, it is a stubborn insistence on remaining where one is. A restive orientation to our theory and praxis allows Asian American feminists to theorize our own liberation in ways that also attend to our investments in settler-colonial projects. To develop this orientation, I begin by elaborating the notion of being oriented and how our specific orientations as Asian Americans in and toward white heteropatriarchy[2] allow for unique possibilities of disorienting and reorienting ourselves. From there, I consider restiveness as a refusal to move by thinking through the dynamics of silence and solidarity. The final part of this chapter takes up restiveness as a refusal to stay in place by problematizing the language of home. In the latter two sections especially, I contextualize my account specifically within Hawai'i because of its high Asian American population, the struggles of the Kānaka Maoli, and the potential therein for Asian American feminists to work for liberation alongside Indigenous peoples.

TOWARD A RESTIVE ORIENTATION

In this section, I begin to develop the notion of a restive orientation to think through how Asian American feminist theory might approach coalitional praxis with other Women of Color feminists. While I explicitly try in other sections of this chapter to think Asian American feminist theory in relation to Indigenous feminisms, my discussion in this section is more general. Audre Lorde writes of the need for coalitional thinking among Women of Color feminists in terms of a reciprocal respect for differences and recognition of how we might contribute to one another's oppressions: "The threat of difference has been no less blinding to people of Color. . . . The need for unity is often misnamed as a need for homogeneity" (Lorde 1984, 119). Further, she notes that we have much to learn from one another's anger and "the truths between us" (127–28). This orientation to differences and to the overlaps and divergences between us informs the attention to coalition that one finds in the work of Women of Color feminists.

Similarly, Andrea Smith (2006) has argued that addressing white supremacy requires recognizing and challenging three pillars that produce various racializations of people of color in the United States: Genocide, Slavery, and Orientalism.[3] The final of these pillars, which she also defines in terms of war, holds that one of the enduring features of how Asian Americans, Arab Americans, and Latin Americans are positioned in the United States is as always having ties to other nations.

While there might be some truth to this type of grouping under a singular pillar, careful parsing of these ethnic and racial groupings demonstrates the tenuousness of these connections. For example, tracing Arab American histories requires grappling with a presumed relation to Islam, and the parsing of "good" and "bad" Muslims, through the turning point of 9/11 in tracing a shift from the relative invisibility of Arab Americans to their hypervisibility in light of the "War on Terror" (Naber 2008, 4).[4] No singular event similarly dominates the discourse on Asian Americans, and the specific histories evoked in the deployment of *terrorism* as a concept in the contemporary racializations of Arab Americans are crucial because of the way they shape the visibility of those they name. Similarly, the specific histories of Latinx people in the United States, which include the movement of borders across people as well as people across borders and, with the exception of Brazilian people, an assumed relation to a single language, Spanish, even as local dialects transform it, demonstrate a very different kind of presumed foreignness between Latin Americans and Asian Americans in the United States. Furthermore, the language of the "illegal" has come to dominate current discussions of Latinx people in political discourse in the United States, and there does not seem to be such a singular term that circulates around Asian Americans. Wars on drugs or "illegals," the "bad hombres" of the current political moment, organize much of the US political discourse around Latinx people.

There is, then, a multiplicity implicitly at work in the specific and plural racializations of Asian Americans. This is not to deny the multiplicities involved in actual Arab American and Latin American racial formations, but it is to point to the failure of either white heteropatriarchal politics or Asian American activists to coalesce around a particular issue as a vital lesson for Asian American feminist theory. This lack of coherence is precisely because of the various racial histories embedded in Asian America. We can trace this back through the history of Asian America, marked by a variety of legislative and executive actions and the blatant notions of yellow peril that undergird much of our cultural histories (cf. Tchen and Yeats 2014). However, yellow peril is an effective concept precisely because of its epistemic weakness; it names nothing other than a vague threat of invasion or cultural domination. Yellow peril, at most, names a kind of unruliness, and it does so through only partial inclusion of who we might think of as counting under the umbrella of Asian American.

Falguni Sheth (2009, 69) describes the unruly by drawing on the notion of strangeness and argues that "strangeness implies a certain primordial fear, which for centuries has appeared to require that certain 'housecleaning' strategies must be employed to eliminate or manage the strangeness." While the category of Asian American has its origins in activist movements as a way of generating solidarity among Asian Americans and with other people of color, the term now often serves to reduce complexity and elide entire histories and differences within the category itself. Indeed, viewed in this way, the entire category of Asian American is somewhat arbitrary, intended in some way to capture the multiplicity of peoples with ancestors originating in Asia and certain parts of the Pacific who seem united, other than by this geographical genealogy, only by our affinity with strangeness.[5] "Asian American," then, has become a way to contain an unruly population and designate the potential for social threat or failure to assimilate properly. In part because we are perceived as necessarily possessing foreign ties or as in some way entrenched in Eastern traditions, Asian Americans experience incredible pressures to assimilate into US (read: white) cultural norms (Lowe 1996; Zhou and Xiong 2005).

We might argue that the model minority myth organizes Asian America into a coherent racial formation. The model minority myth names the pervasive cultural belief that Asian Americans become "successful" in the United States by performing well on educational and socioeconomic axes and not making trouble. Due to the prevalence and pervasiveness of the model minority myth, Asian Americans are often made invisible or silenced as a genuine racial minority group in the United States; this myth continues to make it difficult for Asian American students and scholars to articulate the specific nature of oppression in educational institutions and fails to note the wide disparity, on average, between members of various subgroups, such as Hmong or Filipino Americans, within the umbrella of Asian American (Wing 2007). The economic valence of the model-minority myth is especially important for understanding how Asian America is positioned relative to whiteness. Cheryl Harris (1993) traces the history of whiteness in relation to property law to show how whiteness doubles as a right to ownership and as something that is owned. This economic vision of racial privilege and personhood is implicit in the narratives of bootstrapping that undergird the model-minority myth: through hard work at school and at a job, one can integrate into US society and move up the social ladder to positions that effectively mirror those of one's white counterparts. Indeed, the myth of Asian and Asian American success is so prevalent that white nationalists often overestimate our representation among the ranks of economic elites; in a November 2016 article for *Vanity Fair* aptly titled "Steve Bannon's Racist Comments about Silicon Valley Are also Wildly Inaccurate," Maya Kosof discusses Bannon's claim that most tech companies, between two-thirds and three-quarters, are led by an Asian or Asian American CEO.

The model-minority myth, then, has quite a bit of reach, and it certainly affects how one is perceived as an Asian American in the United States, but this does not seem to be quite the same as how antiterrorism and anti-immigration rhetoric and policies materially impact Arab American and Latin American communities in the United States. Flattening these material realities into a single pillar curtails the political and critical force of our various resistances by homogenizing them. Homogenization of difference can make our differing, even competing, goals and investments unclear and makes coalition building all the more difficult. If, as Lorde insists, coalition depends on recognizing the truths between us, then coalition is only possible insofar as we develop and retain clear understandings of how it is that we are oriented toward one another under conditions of white heteropatriarchy. Smith's pillar of Orientalism, then, risks distortion by assuming too readily that a single term is adequate to the various histories and politics that she hopes to name.

We need, therefore, to attend to the ways we are informed by living under white heteropatriarchy. Being informed means, of course, what kinds of truths we learn about ourselves and others, but it also means the ways we are formed as a matter of thinking how it is that we are constituted as subjects. These dual meanings point to how we are turned away from our own histories and the histories of others through political and epistemic practices of distortion. Returning to the framing of Orientalism, with critical attention to the risk of distortion, can provide a helpful starting point for thinking about restiveness as an orientation to theory and politics. Sara Ahmed (2006, 120–21) reads the notion of orientation through the lens of Orientalism as a kind of world-facing through which whiteness comes to be a starting point: "Whiteness becomes what is 'here,' a line from which the world unfolds." This means that whiteness as concept rather than a bodily feature shapes how it is that objects are arranged in space relative to one another and how they are turned toward or away from one another; we can think here of Audre Lorde and the anger of Women of Color feminism as a response to this orientation. If *orientation* literally refers to a way of being turned in space, then part of what an orientation does is call our attention to how the space and the objects occupying that space are positioned relative to one another and to ourselves. Certain objects appear more or less in reach, and the way they, or we, are turned can cause our apprehension of them to be warped or incomplete. Attending to the phenomenon of experiencing others or ourselves as "out of place"—as in the experience of being called to account for where we are *really* from—allows us to understand how it is that objects come to occupy the positions they do as an effect of settling into a space.

If whiteness is a here in the sense of arranging racialized subjects, then it must also be understood as a there in the sense of being an implicit and coercive goal toward which nonwhite, racialized others must strive. Whiteness is that toward which we are oriented and the barometer by which we measure our own successes. In the white-black binary that often frames US understandings of race, this has often meant that Asian Americans are pitted against Black Americans, such that Frank Chin (1974) writes that the regard many whites have for Asian Americans is due in large part to the fact that we are not Black. As Allison Roh Park (2016) argues, Asian Americans often seem like a fickle placeholder between poles of black and white because we are both near to and held at a distance from whiteness. Indeed, depending on whom we happen to be talking about, one's relative proximity to or distance from whiteness shifts dramatically. An investment in or an orientation to whiteness necessarily involves an assimilation into it, but this assimilation is always tacit and partial for Asian Americans (Kim 1999). For example, white nationalists might have romantic or friendly social relations with us, demonstrating a proximity to whiteness that other racialized groups lack, but we remain "slant eye imports" and therefore are held at a distance from whiteness.[6] There is, then, a complexity involved in understanding the racialization of Asian Americans that is not quite captured in these binary models, even as it remains vitally important to understand how relatively privileged we tend to be in US race relations.

As a result of how Asian Americans are positioned, as simultaneously proximate to and distant from whiteness, we might then be particularly well situated to be disoriented and to disorient dominant racial hegemonies. By *disorientation*, I refer to those kinds of experiences that "make it difficult to know how to go on" (Harbin 2016, 13). These involve the "uprooting of whole systems of belief" in ways that challenge even the basic assumptions or implicit norms that organize our daily lives (Harbin 2016, 79). The experience with which I opened this chapter might be one example of such a disorientation; by relearning *hapa*, a term I had used to make sense of my relation to whiteness, I was confronted, through its specifically Kanaka Maoli history, with the need to let the word go as something that helped me move through the world. Disorientation involves letting go of certain guideposts we have used to orient ourselves in relation to whiteness, but, as Harbin demonstrates, disorientations rarely tell us how to reorient ourselves to go on in a world that has suddenly become unfamiliar to us. This is precisely the point at which restiveness or a restive orientation becomes helpful for thinking through how Asian American feminist theory might orient itself. Because *restiveness* as a term involves both the desire to move from one's place and to remain in that place, restiveness entails an examination and unsettling of the place one is in: Where is it that one desires to stay? What works against one's movement from that place? What demands that one move?

A restive *orientation*, then, is one that allows us to think in two directions simultaneously: to unsettle the place one is in while also remaining on the move toward another place, and to remain in a certain place while unsettling that toward which one is oriented. This might take a number of forms. Restiveness in orientation might entail acknowledging without eliding the relative racial privilege of Asian Americans in the United States while simultaneously addressing the ways white heteropatriarchy specifically disadvantages Asian Americans. Restiveness might look like rearticulating the there of white heteropatriarchy so that we are oriented toward Blackness rather than whiteness and asking seriously what it might mean to orient ourselves in this way without appropriating, assimilating, or overwriting the lives and experiences of Black Americans. The restive orientation I elaborate in the remaining sections of this chapter grapples with what it means to insist on the place of Asian Americans in the United States and in coalition with other Women of Color feminists if we refigure our relations to that place in relation to Indigenous peoples—that is, an orientation to simultaneously thinking about ourselves as perpetual foreigners and as settler-colonizers. Whatever the case, restiveness in orientation involves an inhabitation of failure—the failure to fit neatly into either side of a white heteropatriarchal binary or to assimilate fully into white heteropatriarchy or to do adequate justice to other people of color—and an insistence on unruliness as a kind of being out of sync with hegemonic logics. This has the potential to subvert the model-minority myth by shifting our investments and the parameters by which we judge ourselves as successful or not; such a shift requires an entire reconfiguration of the ways white heteropatriarchy currently orients our epistemic, economic, and political frameworks.[7]

RESTIVENESS AS STAYING IN PLACE

As an insistence on staying where one is, restiveness necessarily forces the question of where it is that one finds oneself. Shireen Roshanravan (2012) describes a practice of staying home as a way of addressing the whitewashing thrust of globalizing feminisms; the move to the transnational is often a way of eliding the real politics and differences of Women of Color feminists in the United States, and staying at home would require US feminists to take these seriously. Restiveness as an orientation for Asian American feminist theory might require a similar demand to stay at home as a way of refusing to move. This is not a refusal to move in the sense of remaining invested in the orientations of white heteropatriarchy. Instead, this is a refusal to make the move from unruliness to order involved in the assimilation to white heteropatriarchal norms; put another way, the refusal to recede into the background is a way of staying at home. Invisibility is a common theme in Asian American studies (Yamada 1979; Sue et al. 2007; Wing 2007). As a kind of invisibility, silence has played a crucial role in Asian American racial formations and histories. Patti Duncan (2004) traces multiple ways silence has been used to oppress Asian Americans and how Asian American women writers, in particular, have been able to rework that silence for productive ends. However, the push to stay silent, to not make trouble, is also part of how Asian Americans have oriented themselves over generations to be positioned in ways that are relatively privileged in US racial dynamics. Staying at home, in the sense of challenging our epistemic frameworks as described by Roshanravan, might require staying with the particular forms of silence and invisibility in Asian America.

One way this might work is through an attentiveness to the memory and history that silence shapes. Sara Ahmed (2006, 44) notes the spectral nature of histories that shape the surfaces of what appear even as they are concealed in this shaping. This invocation of the "specter" calls to mind Maxine Hong Kingston's *The Woman Warrior* and the multiple ghost stories that appear throughout the text and frame Hong Kingston's narrative. Jane Wong (2016) argues that ghost stories and themes of haunting recur throughout Asian American literature and figures her own work as a poet in this way. As a figure, the ghost calls the past to the present and suggests that the past continues to materialize even as we move beyond it temporally. The ghost in the case of Asian American histories might be any number of things: legacies of Western colonialism and imperialism that displace entire populations, histories of policies of exclusion and internment, individual family dramas and traumas, the rise and fall of geopolitical entities, and so on. The past continues to affect the present and how we orient ourselves within it, and staying with silence would require thinking through what silence hides in our histories.

However, the ghost might also refer to the ways our silence has ill served our interests in the United States as well as the interests of Indigenous peoples and other people of color. In an interview describing her experiences in professional philosophy, Emily Lee describes how prevailing understandings of Asian Americans as silent, invisible, and passive affect how others encounter her: "At times, it appears if I speak at all, people immediately assume I'm aggressive" (Lee and Yancy 2015). The push to stay silent and to avoid making trouble leads, as Lee describes, to the expectation of silence, such that any speech outside the expected places—and especially dissenting speech—appears as an aggressive or violent act. This expectation of silence and invisibility is precisely what Mitsuye Yamada (1979) refers to in her call to recognize invisibility as unnatural and unnecessary and as something that we might end. As a strategy of resisting racism, invisibility has not worked precisely because of the ways in which we are unable or not allowed to articulate how white heteropatriarchy affects Asian American communities. In this case, silence might also refer to the ways our speech, when we do speak, is often used to uphold white heteropatriarchy, as in the "tiger mom" narrative of how to raise successful children.

Given that these forms of silence have both isolated Asian Americans from other people of color and allowed for particular Asian American experiences to stand in for the whole, staying home as part of a restive orientation necessitates amplifying unruliness and speaking in those ways that appear at odds with the hegemonic arrangements of racial capital. If silence refers to both the refusal to speak up against white heteropatriarchal norms and speech that maintains those norms, then Yamada's call to end invisibility might also be understood in terms of speaking in ways that confound these norms and draw on different conceptual registers—a kind of restiveness in the sense of unsettling the place one is in. Of the many memes to emerge from the 2016 presidential elections and the subsequent inauguration of Donald Trump, perhaps one of the most poignant images was of an Asian American woman at the inauguration wearing purple and raising both her hands into the air with middle fingers extended. Resistance Auntie, as she was quickly dubbed, is powerful because Asian American people, especially women, are typically absent or absented from depictions of political actions in the United States. Resistance Auntie is a powerful image for restiveness as staying in place precisely because she demonstrates a clear refusal to get over the transparently violent realities of white heteropatriarchy or assimilate into them. Part of the reason staying in place while unsettling that place is a vital component of a restive orientation is because it calls attention to what has been left unsaid or what kinds of histories might continue to haunt and orient us in the present.

At the same time, staying in place requires attending to how it is that we come to occupy the physical spaces we do. In the United States, this necessarily means confronting the realities of settler colonialism and our participation in it. In the case of Hawai'i, this means acknowledging the displacement of the Kānaka Maoli and the ongoing exploitation of Hawaiian land, and working to resist these in solidarity with Native Hawaiian activists. In an article for the *Honolulu Civil Beat* titled "The Heart of a Hawaiian: We Are Mauna Kea," Lani Cupchoy describes the history of development on the slopes of Mauna Kea, a volcano and Kanaka Maoli sacred site on the Big Island, and the movement to protect Mauna Kea from further development by outside interests. On social media, the hashtag #WeAreMaunaKea has been used to express solidarity with those engaged in on-the-ground efforts defending Mauna Kea. The defenders and their supporters remain largely Kānaka Maoli, as Asian American residents of Hawai'i have so often failed to support the efforts of the people we helped displace (LaDuke 1999; Trask 1999). Asian Americans constitute the single largest racial group in Hawai'i, and it is not difficult to believe that Asian American civic leaders and activists in Hawai'i supporting We Are Mauna Kea would have a significant impact on efforts to protect the volcano. Support for these efforts must be understood not only as support for another oppressed group under white heteropatriarchy and capitalist exploitation, but also as unsettling the places in which Asian Americans find themselves in the racial landscape of the United States. Restiveness about place means placing Asian American concerns in concert with the resistant actions of Indigenous peoples. This requires both an unsettling of place and a reconfiguration of orientations away from whiteness.

RESTIVENESS AS STAYING ON THE MOVE

In the previous section, I described restiveness as the refusal to move, in terms of a kind of staying home that entailed grappling with the particular histories of Asian America and, in particular, the trajectories of silence in our communities. As a way of unsettling that place, a restive orientation requires both resisting the specific ways white heteropatriarchy affects Asian American communities and acknowledging how our relative racial privilege under white heteropatriarchy has often been to the detriment of Indigenous peoples. This latter concern brings to the fore especially a concern with our orientation under conditions of white heteropatriarchy and capitalism, so I want to turn now to considering restiveness as a refusal to stay in place and an unsettling of where we are oriented. A refusal to stay in place is especially important given the need to do justice to Indigenous peoples. Kyle Powys Whyte (2016) describes the present as his ancestors' dystopia, a description that is jarring both because of its obvious truth and because it contrasts with how our own ancestors might have viewed immigrating to the United States. Indeed, the incorporation of Hawai'i into the United States as a state, along with attendant rights that have undoubtedly served Asian American interests, has been quite costly for Native Hawaiians: "Full American citizenship, that is, full American 'rights,' thus accelerated the de-Hawaiianization begun with the theft of [their] government, lands, and language in the 1890s" (Trask 1999, 89). Unsettling our orientation toward whiteness as Americanness begins with working against the destruction of Indigenous lands and cultures and acknowledging the present as dystopia.

It is important to acknowledge that Hawai'i is a very particular place in the United States. It is one of the few places where people of color outnumber white people, and the influence of these various peoples remains present in the architecture, in cultural and social norms, and in various homes, though at a rapidly diminishing level. In college, I remember learning that students who wanted to do an exchange program between my university in Arizona and a university in Hawai'i were required to attend study abroad orientations because students on these exchanges tended to experience Hawai'i as a foreign space. Popular depictions of Hawai'i rarely prepare white students for the reality that, as white people in Hawai'i, they are not in the majority. Sara Ahmed (2006) reminds us of the importance for any project in orientation to think about how those spaces in which we orient ourselves come to be and how objects within them are arranged. In the case of Hawai'i, there is a complex history to be told.[8] With specific regard to it as a site of colonial occupation, the sugar industry plays a vital role; the early industry was defined by the development of plantations that put Native Hawaiians and Chinese immigrants into the fields for the profit of white men (Takaki 2009). Industrialization in Hawai'i, then, has always been oriented toward whiteness. Over time, Asian Americans have come to occupy more prominent roles in Hawai'i's political and social landscape, but this has been largely possible through the displacement of Native Hawaiians (Trask 1999; Kana'iaupuni and Malone 2006). Asian American interests in Hawai'i are oriented in ways that align with whiteness and against those of Native Hawaiians. This is precisely the sort of there that Asian American feminists ought to put under pressure through a refusal to stay in that alignment.

This orientation toward whiteness is clear in the movement to preserve Mauna Kea and in the silence of Asian Americans in Hawai'i regarding the volcano and other Kanaka Maoli struggles. Recall that silence is both the absence of speech and speech in the service of white heteropatriarchy. A consistent theme in Native American studies is critical discussion of the construction of Indigenous peoples as not present, frozen in time, or living somewhere else that is not *here*; Haunani-Kay Trask (1999, 126) draws our attention to the way these constructions are part of the colonial projects of erasing and exploiting Native peoples: "It is not merely that Hawaiians are institutionally powerless to decide how and whether their people and their cultural remains should be studied *at all*. It is that a whole way of life, of being in and with the world, has been obliterated. The destiny that is left to Native people then becomes an imposed life of never ending struggle in a losing war." One of the key sites of these battles is the ongoing fight to preserve land. Winona LaDuke (2005) traces the histories of Indigenous cultural movements and demonstrates how Native peoples are actively engaged in projects of ongoing cultural transformation; the recovery of tradition is not a way of returning to a past but a way of moving toward a different future than the one promised by colonialism. Reworking our understandings of how things are arranged—whiteness as future and indigeneity as past— requires shifting our investments in white heteropatriarchy by refusing to stay in the places of relative privilege that we might be afforded. Restiveness as an orientation to theorizing and political action for Asian

American feminists, then, means remaining on the move and evaluating our success or failure in struggles for liberation by rearticulating the guiding posts.

Returning to Shireen Roshanravan's (2012) adaptation of Haunani-Kay Trask's insistence that we stay home, I want to add here that when we do stay home, in the sense of critically examining our epistemic assumptions and the gaps that elide Women of Color feminists, we find the demand that we do not stay at home or in place. Staying at home entails also a refusal to remain where it is that one finds oneself at home. Home, as a space where we have spread out and find ourselves easily (Ahmed 2006), is also where we cannot stay because life under conditions of white heteropatriarchy orients us in the world in ways that we do not necessarily always fully comprehend. A project of unsettling place requires, as any theory articulating a demand for justice ought to, a dual orientation to staying in that place and moving away from it. As Trask's demand shows, solidarity with Indigenous peoples also requires recognizing that one may not be wanted there or is unwelcome. In the case of Hawai'i, not staying at home might literally mean leaving.

RESTIVE COALITIONS

My goal in this chapter, rather than to advocate any specific political actions, has been to describe how Asian American feminist theory might orient itself in relation to Indigenous political resistance. As an orientation to theory, restiveness entails unruliness by embracing those things that are strange or unfamiliar to us and shifting our epistemic and political foundations. Restiveness begins in an acknowledgment that we can neither remain where we are nor move toward where we are headed, while also insisting that we stay right where we are and keep on the move. Restiveness is an approach to the unity without homogeneity that Audre Lorde (1984) insists is vital to liberate all of us. This is clear in the case of Asian American feminist theory when we consider ourselves in relation to Indigenous peoples, especially in the case of Hawai'i. The demand to end Asian American invisibility (Yamada 1979) or silence, a desire to move from where one is while insisting on the specificity of where we are, must be articulated in conjunction with a radical shift in how we orient ourselves and our projects in relation to justice for Indigenous peoples. This is the hard work of coalition building that is key for both our theoretical and political projects.

NOTES

1 I use the term *restive* largely as a result of listening to C. Riley Snorton elaborate the contradictory meanings of the term in talks drawn from his forthcoming book, *Black on Both Sides: A Racial History of Trans Identity* (Minneapolis: University of Minnesota Press, 2017). At this time, it is difficult to say how my conceptual use of restiveness is related to Snorton's, but I remain indebted to him for drawing the term to my attention.

2 Throughout this chapter, I use the phrase *white heteropatriarchy* as synonymous with *white supremacy*. I do so following the work of scholars who have argued that racism and heteropatriarchy work through logics and mechanisms that are mutually reinforcing and often identical. See Collins (2004), McWhorter (2009).

3 My reference to Smith here, especially in the context of a chapter articulating the need to listen and respond to the demands of Indigenous peoples, is fraught. A number of op-eds on *Indian Country Today* have addressed claims that she has perpetrated a kind of fraud by claiming Cherokee ancestry when there is no clear or consistent basis for that claim. If true, these sorts of misleading claims reproduce and maintain logics of colonialism that have displaced, dispossessed, and disenfranchised Indigenous peoples in the United States. My citation of her, then, should not be understood as an endorsement of her as a Woman of Color feminist; rather, my interest in citing her is that she demonstrates a commonplace understanding of race that simultaneously acknowledges and flattens racial complexity by acknowledging different mechanisms of racialization while still maintaining a homogenizing space for racial others. In Smith's case, I argue that she has flattened very real and important differences in the racialization of Asian Americans, Arab Americans, and Latin Americans in the United States.

4 What I mean to say here is not that only Arab Americans are Muslims; rather, what is at stake in the politics of Islamophobia is the racialization of Muslims as Arab such that Arab American communities are often disproportionately affected by Islamophobic policies and attitudes.

5 Importantly, this category ought not include all people originating in the many islands in the Pacific Ocean. Pacific Islanders and Pacific Americans, while often lumped into a single demographic with Asians and Asian Americans, face significantly different challenges and navigate very different histories and oppressions. For a discussion of the specificity of Pacific experiences and the need to avoid integrating them into the category of Asian American, see Kauanui 2005. Understanding Pacific Islanders and Pacific Americans as a distinct racial group, however, does not entail inattention to their specific histories and the role of Asians and Asian Americans in perpetuating oppression. See Lani Teves and Maile Arvin's chapter, "Decolonizing API: Centering Indigenous Pacific Islander Feminism," in this collection for an in-depth elaboration of why and how Asian American feminisms must account for Asian American settler-colonial erasures of Indigenous Pacific Islander peoples, resources, experiences, and histories.

6 The "slant eye imports" reference comes from an article reporting on Jeffrey Dillon, who disrupted a protest in San Francisco. According to a Facebook comment by

Dillon, he is obviously not racist because his wife is one of these "imports" (cf. Fiona Lee, "Motorcyclist in Custody after Allegedly Attempting to Run Over Trumpcare Protestors," *Hoodline*, June 21, http://hoodline.com/2017/06/motorcyclist-in-custody -after-allegedly-attempting-to-run-over-trumpcare-protestors).

7   Two key concerns emerge here. First, despite my criticisms of Andrea Smith and my worries that the phrase *Asian American* obfuscates intra-Asian difference, I use *Asian American* throughout this chapter as though it named a singular or homogenous racial experience. I want to be clear that I understand the term as one that is fraught and necessarily fails to capture the heterogeneity of Asian Americans even as it provides indexical utility by allowing us to quickly refer to a number of heterogeneous groups. Of course, its indexical use value is also precisely why we have to attend to how it is used and what its use obfuscates. Second, one might worry that I am proposing some version of a "middleman minority thesis" (Bonacich 1973) in my use of orientation in thinking about Asian American feminisms. This thesis addresses the economic phenomenon of ethnic minorities who occupy a middle-class position rather than the low-class positions one might expect of an ethnic minority and who are often, as might seem to be the case for Asian Americans, used as ways of legitimating unjust racial hierarchies such as white/Black disparities in the United States. My own use of a seeming "middleman" position, however, is not based in an account of economic class disparities. While economics and class are certainly relevant for a discussion of Asian Americans, my interest is in thinking about how we are specifically racialized as not fully in one place or another. Restiveness, as I develop it here, depends on occupying an unstable position in racial hierarchies. Another way of putting this is that I am thinking of Asian Americans as occupying a more dynamic and ambiguous position than the intermediate positioning implied by the middleman thesis. Intermediacy implies a kind of stable and reliable positioning between two poles.

8   Such a history is beyond the purposes of this chapter, but several of the sources I cite here provide helpful starting points for an understanding of Hawaiian history. See especially Trask (1999), Silva (2004), Kauanui (2008).

REFERENCES

Ahmed, Sara. 2006. *Queer Phenomenology: Orientations, Objects, Others*. Durham, NC: Duke University Press.

Bonacich, Edna. 1973. "A Theory of Middleman Minorities." *American Sociological Review* 38 (5): 583–94.

Chin, Frank. 1974. *Aiiieeeee: An Anthology of Asian-American Writers*. Washington, DC: Howard University Press.

Collins, Patricia Hill. 2004. *Black Sexual Politics: African Americans, Gender, and the New Racism*. New York: Routledge.

Duncan, Patti. 2004. *Tell This Silence: Asian American Women Writers and the Politics of Speech*. Iowa City: University of Iowa Press.

Harbin, Ami. 2016. *Disorientation and Moral Life*. Oxford: Oxford University Press.

Harris, Cheryl I. 1993. "Whiteness as Property." *Harvard Law Review* 106 (8): 1707–91.

Kanaʻiaupuni, Shawn Malia, and Nolan Malone. 2006. "This Land Is My Land: The Role of Place in Native Hawaiian Identity." *Hūlili* 3 (1): 281–307.

Kauanui, J. Kēhaulani. 2005. "Asian American Studies and the 'Pacific Question.'" In *Asian American Studies after Critical Mass*, edited by Kent A. Ono, 121–43. Malden, MA: Wiley-Blackwell.

———. 2008. *Hawaiian Blood: Colonialism and the Politics of Sovereignty and Indigeneity*. Durham, NC: Duke University Press.

Kim, Claire Jean. 1999. "The Racial Triangulation of Asian Americans." *Politics and Society* 27 (1): 105–38.

LaDuke, Winona. 1999. *All Our Relations: Native Struggles for Land and Life*. Cambridge, MA: South End Press.

———. 2005. *Recovering the Sacred: The Power of Naming and Claiming*. Cambridge, MA: South End Press.

Lee, Emily, and George Yancy. 2015. "Asian, American, Woman, Philosopher." *New York Times Opinionator* blog, April 6. https://opinionator.blogs.nytimes.com/2015/04/06/asian-american-woman-philosopher/?_r=0.

Lorde, Audre. 1984. *Sister Outsider*. Berkeley, CA: Crossing Press.

Lowe, Lisa. 1996. *Immigrant Acts: On Asian American Cultural Politics*. Durham, NC: Duke University Press.

McWhorter, Ladelle. 2009. *Racism and Sexual Oppression in Anglo-America: A Genealogy*. Bloomington: Indiana University Press.

Naber, Nadine. 2008. "Introduction: Arab Americans and U.S. Racial Formations." In *Race and Arab Americans Before and After 9/11: From Invisible Citizens to Visible Subjects*, edited by Amaney Jamal and Nadine Naber, 1–45. Syracuse, NY: Syracuse University Press.

Park, Allison Roh. 2016. "A Reflection on my Non/Asian American Life." *Race Files*, May 16. www.racefiles.com/2016/05/16/a-reflection-on-my-nonasian-american-life.

Roshanravan, Shireen. 2012. "Staying Home while Studying Abroad: Anti-Imperial Praxis for Globalizing Feminist Visions." *Journal of Feminist Scholarship* 2: 1–23.

Sheth, Falguni. 2009. *Toward a Political Philosophy of Race*. Albany: SUNY Press.

Silva, Noenoe K. 2004. *Aloha Betrayed: Native Hawaiian Resistance to American Colonialism*. Durham, NC: Duke University Press.

Smith, Andrea. 2006. "Heteropatriarchy and the Three Pillars of White Supremacy: Rethinking Women of Color Organizing." In *Color of Violence: The INCITE! Anthology*, edited by INCITE! Women of Color Against Violence, 66–73. Cambridge, MA: South End Press.

Sue, Derald Wing, Jennifer Bucceri, Annie I. Lin, Kevin L. Nadal, and Gina C. Torino. 2007. "Racial Microaggressions and the Asian American Experience." *Cultural Diversity and Ethnic Minority Psychology* 13 (1): 72–81.

Takaki, Ronald. 2009. "The Sugar Kingdom: the Making of Plantation Hawaiʻi." In *Asian American Studies: A Reader*, edited by Jean Yu-Wen Shen Wu and Min Song, 21–34. New Brunswick, NJ: Rutgers University Press.

Tchen, John Kuo Wei, and Dylan Yeats. 2014. *Yellow Peril: An Archive of Anti-Asian Fear*. New York: Verso.

Trask, Haunani-Kay. 1999. *From a Native Daughter: Colonialism and Sovereignty in Hawai'i*. Honolulu: University of Hawai'i Press.

Whyte, Kyle Powys. 2016. "Our Ancestors' Dystopia Now: Indigenous Conservation and the Anthropocene." In *The Routledge Companion to the Environmental Humanities*, edited by Ursula K. Heise, Jon Christensen, and Michelle Niermann, 206–15. New York: Routledge.

Wing, Jean Yonemura. 2007. "Beyond Black and White: The Model Minority Myth and the Invisibility of Asian American Students." *Urban Review* 39 (4): 455–87.

Wong, Jane. 2016. "Going toward the Ghost: The Poetics of Haunting in Contemporary Asian American Poetry." PhD diss., University of Washington.

Yamada, Mitsuye. 1979. "Invisibility Is an Unnatural Disaster: Reflections of an Asian American Woman." *Bridge: An Asian American Perspective* 7 (1): 11–13.

Zepeda, Ofelia, and Jane H. Hill. 1991. "The Condition of Native American Languages in the United States." *Diogenes* 39 (153): 45–65.

Zhou, Min, and Yang Sao Xiong. 2005. "The Multifaceted American Experiences of the Children of Asian Immigrants: Lessons for Segmented Assimilation." *Ethnic and Racial Studies* 28 (6): 1119–52.

CHAPTER 7

NAVIGATING COLONIAL PITFALLS

Race, Citizenship, and the Politics of
"South Asian Canadian" Feminism

SUNERA THOBANI

FOLLOWING THE DEATHS OF TWO ELDERLY SOUTH ASIAN
Canadian women at the hands of their spouses in Surrey, British Columbia, a local newspaper interviewed a prominent feminist activist in the
community. Having worked in the antiviolence movement for a number of
decades, she offered the following observation: "Our men somehow or the
other have never really learned to control their anger and they haven't
stopped thinking that a wife is something they own—a 'thing' they own
and not even a human being." She then went on to state, "So every time
anything happens, they get angry and it goes to this extent, which is really
surprising. I was also very surprised—two cases in our community about
our seniors" (Mall 2014, 1–2).

Notable for their generalizations, the above comments also point to a self-
depiction of what is now known as the "South Asian Canadian" community that is informed by, and conforms to, the multicultural discourse that
prevails in the country. Since the 1971 adoption of multiculturalism as state
policy, state classificatory systems encapsulate diasporic South Asian communities, like other communities of color in Canada, as "immigrant," "visible minority," and "newcomer"; as such, these communities have been
constructed in the national imaginary as identifiable by the peculiarity and
the confines of their "cultural" identity. Critics of multiculturalism have

pointed to the racial and gender politics organized by this discourse, which, they argue, implicitly centers the whiteness of the nation to map the difference of the nation's Others. Firmly associated with peoples of color, multiculturalism sustains their designation as perpetual cultural outsiders to the nation regardless of the actual status of their citizenship. In contrast, the Euro-Canadian subject comes to embody the nation's values and its identity.[1] The interview with which I begin this chapter provides a glimpse into how deeply this official language of cultural difference permeates the contemporary politics of South Asian Canadian-ness and the dominant forms of feminist activism that have emerged within the communities thus defined.

It is notable that although the feminist activist quoted above expresses her surprise at the violent deaths of the two elderly women, this does not deter her from reaching the conclusions she does about "our men," "their" treatment of "their wives" as "things," and "their" murderous "anger." Even when her own experience and knowledge of the community ("I was amazed") ruptures the culturalist paradigm she draws upon, the narrative of a culturally sanctioned gendered misogyny is nevertheless invoked to suture the incongruence that she herself cannot overlook. Predictably enough, she goes on to advocate for more state funding for immigrant women's organizations to fight violence against women in their communities. It is also notable that the potential to undermine the culturalist narrative is to be found in the media report itself. After quoting the feminist, the reporter goes on to delineate a number of issues other than "culture" that are seen as relevant to the experiences of elderly women within the community, which include social isolation, increased household responsibilities, financial abuse, and depression. Yet these issues—which would help historicize and contextualize the material conditions that may have contributed to the violence they suffered—were mentioned in passing; they did not shape the analytical frame. These issues thus proved ineffectual in displacing the readily circulated—and accepted—culturalizing discourse as articulated by the South Asian feminist.

In this chapter, I unpack the complexities of the politics associated with the category *South Asian Canadian/American*, a project made all the more urgent by the feminist politics that are grounded in this term. Having acquired considerable currency in the present moment, *Asian Canadian*, like the related category *immigrant*, is a contested term. The same, of course, can be said of *South Asian Canadian*, along with its nomenclature, which includes among its historical antecedents *East Indian*, *Indo Canadian*, *visible minority, people of color,* et cetera. As critical feminist scholars have noted, these terms render invisible—albeit in different ways—the internal hierarchies and dynamics of power within the communities thus designated as they conflate and homogenize these as discrete, neatly bounded entities.[2] The gendered politics signaled by these classifications render simultaneously invisible and hypervisible vital aspects of those whose lives they claim to define. So, for example, the term *South Asian Canadian woman* constructs a particular racialized subject position that is highly visible in the national imaginary; colonial ideologies of passive victimhood and patriarchal cultures characterized by misogynist violence become inscribed onto this subject/object, which renders invisible her struggles against the social, economic, and political forces that shape, and are shaped by, her structural location.

The feminist politics arising from the designations *immigrant* and *visible minority* range from active embrace of these classifications and their associated multicultural politics to the expressions of the more critical and self-reflexive self-designations *Women of Color* and *South Asian Canadians*, which seek to build broader antiracist solidarities, gesture to the national/regional politics within South Asia, and contest the culturalist paradigm that is so pervasive within Canada. Clearly, whether these designations are forged from above or below, so to speak, becomes a crucial matter. What is equally significant, I believe, is how the politics of self-designation from below engage and negotiate the politics of classification from above, that is, from within state practices. In what follows, I demonstrate that the political terrain inhabited by the paradigm *South Asian Canadian* is fraught with peril, for it is infused with the colonial logics that shape Canadian, and Western, governmentality within a global field.

The discursive practices that culturalize South Asian Canadians, however, are not static. Indeed, these practices are presently undergoing a profound shift as they are informed by the global war on terror that is reshaping the not only global politics but also the state's machinery for managing immigration and citizenship. So, for example, the official immigration guide, *Welcome to Canada*, which is provided to incoming immigrants, warns the immigrant—while simultaneously reassuring the national— that "Canada's openness and generosity do not extend to barbaric cultural practices that tolerate spousal abuse, honor killings, female genital mutilation, forced marriage or other gender based violence" (Citizenship and Immigration Canada 2013, 36). This association of violence against women with immigrants, and more precisely, with their cultural difference as a form of innate "barbarism," thus shapes the lives not only of newly arriving immigrants but of the South Asian diasporas constructed as "immigrant"; such constitution of difference engulfs Canadian citizens of South Asian descent and organizes their everyday reception within the national cultural space. Drawing on older histories, the national/racial/gender politics deployed by these constructs are thus always already at play; they shape the ideological terrain for the making of the national subject as both above and beyond such gendered barbarism, and for the containment of "immigrants," particularly the women, in the stifling grip of racializing cultures.

In the following sections, I think through the complexities and challenges presented by the formulation *Asian American* as a politico-epistemological—not to mention ontological—paradigm by way of examining one of its variants, *South Asian Canadian*. Three main questions organize this inquiry: How does the formulation *South Asian Canadian*, including the feminisms associated with this, take up the actual terms that define it, that is, *South Asian* and *Canadian*? How does this formulation negotiate the processes of state and nation formation in the specific site of its articulation, namely, settler colonialism in North America? And finally, how does this formulation engage the contemporary conditions remaking the national and global politics that enmesh South Asian Canadians in the war on terror and its Islamophobic ideology?

Although these questions are taken up at a theoretical level, I draw upon the empirical research on, and media representations of, South Asian Canadians, along with my activism in antiracist, anticolonial, and antiwar feminist movements in Canada. Further, I situate these questions within the histories of Canadian nation formation and immigration to interrogate their present and to contextualize them within the volatile racial politics of white resentment in the global war on terror that are remaking the sociocultural landscape in North America. Here, I am particularly interested in what the "new" invasions and occupations of the global war reveal about the changing nature and forms of the coloniality that have shaped both Canada and South Asia. Given that Islamophobia—a discourse constituting the figure of the Muslim, including Muslims from South Asia, as the source of the most lethal threat to national and global security—is the dominant ideology of the contemporary political moment, I attend to how this is reshaping the meanings attached to nation (Canadian) and diaspora (South Asia-Canadian).

My analysis of South Asian Canadian as a political and epistemological construct leads me to make three main arguments. First, the definition of *South Asian* and *Canadian* that grounds this construct is made more on the basis of geography than politics, such that its analytic frame does not center the settler-colonial nature of North America nor the colonial histories of the making of South Asia. Instead, this construct privileges migration and resettlement, globalization and citizenship, at the cost of attending to the foundational logics of Western colonialism, sovereignty, and subjectivity. By this, I mean that the settler-colonial nature of the Canadian nation-state and the coloniality that structures migration flows from South Asia are normalized such that the reproduction of coloniality—settler colonialism in North America and the neocolonial/imperialist domination of South Asia—is treated as inevitable. This approach limits the horizon of possibilities for the future in the collective imaginary of South Asian Canadian politics, curtailing the radical contestation of power relations in contemporary national and/or global politics.

Second, the singular focus on immigration as the originary issue grounds South Asian Canadian political projects in the rights-based framework that privileges citizenship, that is, inclusion in the regime of rights and entitlements of the nation-state, above anticolonial politics and practices. As such, the violence entailed in the institution of citizenship itself goes largely un/under-interrogated. The expansion of the institution of citizenship to incorporate South Asian Canadians more fully simultaneously deepens the practices that organize the destruction of Indigenous sovereignty. Moreover, this treatment of citizenship as the sole horizon of political struggle overlooks the role of this institution in organizing the juridical dehumanization of particular communities, as is presently evident in the racialization and demonization of the figure of the Muslim, including the South Asian Muslim. If anything, the war on terror demonstrates how swiftly the rights of citizenship can be eroded—even rescinded—by the state's construction of racialized Others as existential enemy and hence a threat to the existence of the national community. The post-9/11 erasure of the rights of Muslims reveals how this institution functions to produce them as objects deserving of state and vigilante violence.

Third, as a construct that privileges geography, migration, and inclusion, the political project of South Asian Canadians has been unable to contest the dehumanization of Muslims that is presently underway in North America and South Asia. Instead, as the Islamophobic discourse becomes ever more deeply institutionalized into the governance practices of the nation-state, non-Muslim South Asian Canadians have acquired greater proximity to Canadian nationals by distancing themselves from, and furthering the social and political isolation of, Muslims, including those from South Asia. In supporting and/or legitimizing—passively or otherwise— the violence directed toward Muslims, non-Muslim South Asian Canadians have become more fully integrated in North American projects of nation and state formation, thereby legitimizing the colonial wars waged by the United States and Canada in their "new" occupations in the Middle East. Consequently, I argue, this political construct remains oriented toward coloniality in general and Westernity in particular. Whether "South Asian Canadian" can be a political project of transformation—that is, a viable project in contemporary struggles for justice—is an open question. For, as I demonstrate throughout this chapter, the radical potential of this formulation is undercut by the politics of containment that are structured into its very constitution by its neglect of the actualities of settler colonialism in North America and Western coloniality in South Asia.

INTERROGATING LOCATIONS

If the annals of Canadian history are replete with echoes of sentiments such as those in the following quotation, dated to the 1920s,[3] the second quotation, from a contemporary news account, indicates that these sentiments are worth a revisit. The racial/colonial tropes foundational to Canadian nation-state formation clearly remain in place, irrespective of the shifts that have taken place in definitions of national identity.

> British Columbia is one of the last frontiers of the white race against the yellow and the brown. It is a land where a hoary civilization meets a modern one, and where the swarming millions of ancient peoples, strung into restless life by modern events, are constantly impinging on an attractive land held by sparse thousands of whites. And here, the alarmed British Columbian, clamorous for Asiatic exclusion, feels that he is taking the long view. . . . [British Columbia is] a community of half a million souls which stands in the sea gate of the northwest Pacific, and holds it for Saxon civilization. (Buchignani, Indra, and Srivastava 1985, 5)

> The town council of Herouxville, a sleepy community dominated by a towering Roman Catholic Church, has adopted a declaration of "norms"

that it says would-be immigrants should be aware of before they
settle here.

Among them, it is forbidden to stone women or burn them with acid.
Children cannot carry weapons to school. That includes ceremonial religious daggers such as kirpans even though the Supreme Court of Canada
has ruled that Sikhs can carry kirpans in schools.

However, children can swim in a pool with boys and girls alike,
because they can't be segregated.

And for the record, female police officers in Herouxville, 165 kilometres
northwest of Montreal, can arrest male suspects. Also part of the declaration is to allow women to drive, dance and make decisions on their own.

"We're telling people who we are," said Andre Drouin, one of six town
councillors and the driving force behind the declaration passed earlier
this month. (Moore 2007)

Sentiments such as those expressed above are regularly found in contemporary representations of South Asian Canadians in mainstream media
and political discourses; they also underpin contemporary constructs of the
"terrorist" threat seen to emanate from Muslims, often in far more color-
ful tones.

I have discussed in my earlier work how Canada is produced as a triangulated colonial/racial formation (Thobani 2007). The genocidal practices
that led to the dispossession of Indigenous peoples from their territories
produced them as "Indians," constitutively bound to the Canadian national
subject defined as British and French (Thobani 2007). Gender and sexuality were central to Indigenous dispossession, for it was through sexual
violence, gendered disenfranchisement, and the imposition of Western
heteropatriarchal and capitalist class relations that the land was appropriated and made available to European settlers (Lawrence 2004; Monture-
Angus 1995). Canadian sovereignty is hence grounded in an originary
violence that became codified as the rule of law to underpin what the nation
presently experiences as a liberal-democratic system of rights and entitlements. These relations of indigenous dispossession, however, do not feature among the major concerns taken up in contemporary South Asian
Canadian—including feminist—politics. Instead, the prevailing political
objective is full inclusion in the social, economic, and political edifice
erected through the institution of citizenship on this colonial foundation.

If the categories *Canadian* and *Indian* are not legible outside settler colonial logics, the same is true of the appellation *South Asian Canadian*,

which cannot be understood outside the context of the these logics and those of the various migrations that tied the colonization of North America to that of South Asia. European settlement of Indigenous territories and their enslavement of Africans into this "new" world were tied to the migrations from Asia that were to provide the labor required for economic expansion demanded by global capitalism. During the nineteenth and early twentieth centuries, this development required not only the migration of European settlers, particularly women, but also increased migrations from China, Japan, and India. As Dua (2007) has demonstrated in her study of Canadian immigration policies of this period, the settler state considered the restriction of female migration from South Asia to be crucial to its production of the nation. While male migration from Asia was organized to ensure the provision of labor, the sexuality and reproductive capacity of Chinese and South Asian women were considered a threat to the production of Canada as a "white man's country." The imposition of exclusionary policies reduced the Chinese and South Asian presence in the country, as male migration was organized to be transient in nature.

While the fear of miscegenation soon sparked support for female migration from Asia, as Dua finds in her study, this inclusion of women from South Asia (known as "Hindoos") nevertheless refined the larger exclusion of Asians from the body politic. Allowed into the country as wives, mothers, and daughters, the women's presence aided the production of ethnic/racial enclaves that reproduced the racial cohesion of the nation as white.[4] This racial/gender construction of South Asian women plays out in contemporary immigration policies that organize their migration under the family sponsorship class, which constructs the women as dependent family members.[5] It is notable that these historical processes and policies are the context for the production of the identity presently named "South Asian Canadian." The conditions shaping this earlier migration from a colonized South Asia into a settler-colonial Canada are thus central to the constitution of this identity, in the past as in the present, and to its productive forms of subjectivity.

There is another significant aspect of Canadian state and nation formation that continues to escape the attention of a good number of activists and scholars working with the construct of South Asian Canadian. This is the role of migration from South Asia in shaping the structure of sovereignty developed by the Canadian state during the mid-nineteenth and early twentieth centuries. In her study of this early period of migration from British India into the Dominion of Canada, Mongia (2007, 397) shifts the analytical lens from immigration policy to the form of "sovereignty, security and mobility" shaped by such migration. In so doing, she argues that the measures adopted by the Canadian state to control this migration were constitutive of state sovereignty as including the control of mobility across its borders, and hence, the policing of these borders.

This control of borders, Mongia (2007) explains, brought into being a form of sovereignty that extended state regulation over the mobility of subjects. Previously, such control was not an aspect of state sovereignty. Mongia shows how it was by instituting racially discriminatory immigration policies to regulate the entry of migrants from India—who had the legal status of British subjects at the time—that the Canadian state constructed its authority over its "national" borders. Eschewing the idea that migration "throws askew the distinctness of nation-states," Mongia's study leads her to conclude that "migration is implicated in *producing* the distinctness of nation-states through the category of state sovereignty" (388). This border control is being refortified yet again by the antiterrorism measures that are now part and parcel of the securitization of the nation itself, even as the reach of the sovereignty of the Canadian state was extended internationally by its participation in the occupation of Afghanistan.

The sovereignty of the Canadian nation-state can thus be defined as rooted in the acquisition and control of Indigenous territories as well as the assertion of border control over migration and settlement, such that immigration is linked internally to Indigenous dispossession. These entangled processes have led to highly asymmetrical relationships between, and among, the various populations under the control of this state: dispossession and physical-cultural extinction for Indigenous peoples and conditional racial/cultural inclusion of South Asian Canadians into a national project that integrates them into various projects of state violence. These practices also construct the "immigrant" as an interloper who threatens to overwhelm the nation's resources, a construct that leaves South Asian Canadians on the defensive despite their citizenship, required to prove their worth and loyalty to the nation-state as supplicants. Where the economic contribution of South Asian immigrants enabled them to advance their access to citizenship during the last third of the twentieth century, this extension of rights did little to dislodge the settler-colonial logics of violent dispossession that ground the nation-state. Indeed, this logic only becomes more deeply entrenched in the remaking of the nation-state as tolerant and plural-minded through the presence of multicultural Others.

HORIZONS OF WESTERNITY

In 2008, the *Vancouver Sun* profiled one hundred "Indo-Canadians" whom the newspaper defined as "making a difference" in British Columbia.[6] Although eighteen of these individuals were born in Canada and the rest had lived in the country for periods ranging from six to eighty-four years, their photographs were superimposed on a map of South Asia on the newspaper's front page.[7] The message of this representation is not difficult to decipher. These individuals may be important personages, socially and economically influential in the province of British Columbia and hence in Canada. They may all be Canadian citizens. Indeed, they may even be Canadian born. They all, nevertheless, "belong" to South Asia. A few days later, Statistics Canada reported that visible minorities account for 16.2 percent of the country's population, with South Asians the largest group among them, at 25 percent (Gandhi 2008, A1, A9). In the century since the first migrants from South Asia arrived in British Columbia, they had become the largest nonwhite racial minority in the country. In the national/racial imaginary, however, they really "belong" back there.

The politics of constituting South Asian Canadians as Other than "real" Canadians are complex and have shifted over time and space. These politics thus require careful unpacking. *South Asian Canadian* is, of course, constitutively linked to the term *immigrant*, a homogenizing term that reveals more about the enduring power of racial nation formation than about the peoples it claims to define.

As mentioned in the previous section, numerous terms have evolved to classify peoples of South Asian origin in Canada, beginning with the names *Hindoos*, *Orientals*, *East Indian*, and *non-preferred races*, which were terms in widespread use until the mid-twentieth century, when they expanded to include *immigrants*, *Visible Minorities*, and *newcomers* in the latter half of the century. These designations were accompanied by the self-defined categories *Indo-Canadian* and *people of color*. The increased migration from countries including Pakistan, Bangladesh, and Sri Lanka in the late twentieth and early twenty-first centuries has made the category *South-Asian Canadian*—considered more inclusive of this heterogeneity—more pronounced. The term was considered more desirable, including by feminists, as part of a strategy to transcend the narrower and more exclusionary ossification of identity within the nationalist politics in the region. Yet such broadening of identity in a period when the category *South Asia* was being incorporated into area studies and US and Canadian foreign policy as a matter of geostrategic interest in the US-led neoliberal globalization that pushed for opening up national borders in the Global South to the flow of capital, trade, and investment surely cannot be ignored.

The terms referencing/producing South Asian Canadian identity were thus steeped in the particular politics and social dynamics of the distinct political juncture in which they were articulated, whether from "above" or "below," so to speak. These terms express the imperatives driving the push-and-pull factors of inter/national migration, as well as the shifting colonial/ racial logics of nation formation. In the case of Canada, the categories *immigrants*, *visible minorities*, et cetera, as they referred to "Indo-Canadians," reflected not only the liberalization of the Canadian nation-state, and its adoption of multiculturalism, this also spoke to the post-independence moment of the Indian nation-state. Moreover, these designations were articulated in relation to the modernity of the national subject and the impossibility of Indigenous futurity in these different sites, culminating in the now-dominant category *South Asian-Canadian* as organizer of a modernizing identity and collective social consciousness.

The paradoxical impact of the (non)citizen status incorporated into the term *immigrant*—simultaneously integrationist and ejectionist— aligned the immigrant political horizon with that of the nation/al. Seeking political recognition and parity with the white national, the subject position inhabited by the immigrant imbibes the nation's racial construct of itself and sparks the ambition of striving toward the same status as that of the national. This process leads to integration into the co-constitutive relation of the *national* to the *immigrant*, and of both to the *Indigenous* within a colonial-liberal order. The mutuality of such practices of national self-making in relation to the South Asian Other can be seen at work in the media profile of the outstanding *Indo-Canadians* referred to earlier; the same process is mirrored in the *immigrant*'s making of herself as Other, as evidenced in the South Asian feminist activist's commentary on gendered violence cited above.

South Asian Canadian feminist formulations of their political projects have been ambiguous, ranging from treating their constituencies as excluded "immigrant" subjects who desire inclusion, that is, as ethnically and/or racially marginalized subjects engaged in struggles for equality, or as subjects whose cultural distinctness in ancestry, language, and heritage requires the nation to respond with a sensitivity to their cultural difference.[8] Often, these projects are not exclusive and do overlap. With few exceptions, much of these politics have been connected to community-based activism linked to providing social services, advocacy for equitable immigration and employment policies, contesting racism and racialized constructs of the nation, and struggling for equal citizenship. However, the cost of this focus on state and nationalist practices and discourses includes their internalization in processes of identity formation and the normalization of the ongoing politics of "old" and "new" colonialism and occupations, whether in North America or South Asia. These become an organizing feature of "immigrant" politics and consciousness if they are not contested through an anticolonial political praxis. In the absence of such a praxis, the official language of multiculturalism functions to internally disaggregate identities along ethnic, linguistic, and national lines, wherein these distinctions are attributed to particular forms of cultural essentialisms in a relation of tension with the overarching category *South Asian Canadian*, which sutures over—albeit to different effect—these internal hierarchies. The obfuscation of the ongoing coloniality of these processes, essentialisms, and omissions enable the subject produced as South Asian Canadian to be treated as a transparent and self-evident form of subjectivity and identity, oppressed and exploited from "outside" but stable on the "inside." Such an assumption of the category's self-evident form of identification is based on the ideological erasure of the racial and colonial histories of violence that have produced Canada, Indigenous nations, and South Asia within a globally interconnected system of Western coloniality.

The forms of consciousness and identities thus constituted in engagement with state classifications, policies, and practices further the notion of a transparent and autonomous subject position with a (mostly) secured status as sovereign—that is, a juridical subject—as is implicitly suggested by the appellation *South Asian Canadian*, even when articulated from below. State support for forms of identity that eschew recognition of their coloniality becomes an onslaught on the radical anticolonial traditions within these communities, as evidenced in the Canadian state's funding for multicultural organizations that elevate conservative and reactionary forms of "culture." Imbibing the discourse of cultural essentialism—made legible to and rewarded by the state—underwrites access to a measure of services and entitlements, yet this comes at the cost of a tenuous official recognition that reproduces the incommensurability between the "immigrant," the "indigenous," and the "national" subject.

Seeking a relation of conviviality with the Canadian nation-state, a key assumption shaping the political paradigm of South Asian Canadian politics is that its subject has already acquired access to the status of the autonomous, self-determining, liberal Subject, even if this remains yet to be fully realized. The aspirations of this immigrant Subject-in-the-making as liberal and oriented toward futurity emerged within the racial framework of a colonial order that denied this status to the colonized populations in North America; the status of this "subject" is now taken as universally accessible in the South Asian Canadian political paradigm, despite the persistence of coloniality in the international order, including the settler colonialism of the Canadian nation-state. This basic assumption of South Asian Canadian politics posits its subject as now well on its way to garnering the sovereign status of the national subject in a transnational framework. This assumption, as I show below, remains unwarranted in light of the new forms of coloniality and dehumanization that are revealed in the treatment of particular communities of South Asians, namely Muslims. When the present condition of these communities is taken into consideration, the conceit that South Asian Canadians have secured for themselves the status of the sovereign subject becomes difficult to sustain.

RETHINKING POLITICAL HORIZONS

Following the mass shootings in a mosque in Quebec City that left six Muslim men dead and nineteen others injured (Stevenson and Gordon 2017), Liberal member of parliament Iqra Khalid introduced a motion in the House of Parliament calling for the government to condemn Islamophobia and other forms of racial and religious discrimination and to take action to "quell the rising public climate of hate and fear" (Elghawaby 2017). Soon after introducing the motion, which did nothing to change existing Canadian laws, she was reported to have been inundated with hate messages, including the following: "Real Canadians will rise up and get rid of the [blank] Muzzie stench in Ottawa"; "Kill her and be done with it"; "She is sick, she is here to kill us and she needs to be deported"; "We will burn down your mosques"; "Why did Canadians let her in? Ship her back"; "Why don't you get out of my country, you are a disgusting piece of trash, and you are definitely not wanted here by the majority of actual Canadians," and so on.[9] The public response and threats of violence directed toward a member of parliament who is a Muslim of South Asian origin only served to underscore the point of the parliamentary motion: the growing intensity and visibility of Islamophobia in Canadian politics and public life.

The recent construction of Muslims, including those of South Asian origin, as "terrorists" reveals the fallacy of the assumption that the juridical status of "citizen" has been secured for South Asian Canadians, or indeed, I would argue, for other Asian Canadians. As a good number of studies have demonstrated, the US Patriot Act and the antiterror legislation in Canada have redefined the meaning of law, citizenship, immigration, and border control in the name of national security (Thobani 2007; Maira 2004; Olwan 2013). The global war thus rendered tenuous the status of the Muslim as the rights-bearing subject that grounds the liberal democratic political structure. These measures have become entrenched in state policy and social institutions over the course of the war. In other words, the normalization of what were initially presented as emergency measures demonstrates how closely the remaking of Canadian sovereignty and subjectivity relies on the remaking of the Other, the Muslim in this case, as an existential threat to the nation. This remaking, I argue in this section, enables non-Muslim South Asians to claim greater proximity to the Canadian national subject by participating in and advancing the Islamophobic discourse that now grounds the remaking of this subject.

Numerous studies of the antiterror measures directed toward Muslim communities have found that the figure of the Muslim has been constructed in US and Canadian national imaginaries as an enemy of the values and cultures of these nation-states (Maira 2004; Razack 2008; Thobani 2007; Jiwani 2011). As such, the Muslim is constructed as the embodiment of this threat of terror and, as such, has been stripped of the rights of citizenship and the protection of the state. Muslims of South Asian origin in Canada, not to mention those in South Asia and other parts of Asia (including the "Near" and "Middle" East) are caught up in this dragnet. Security certificates, racial profiling, deportation, rendition, torture, assassination, bombing, entrapment, and collective punishment are among the practices that have become instituted and are now publicly supported in the governance of Muslims at the national and global level.

In this climate, South Asian Canadians, offered the possibility to enhance their cultural capital through support for the international realignment of the Canadian nation-state in the global war, have acquired new avenues for political and social advancement. Here, I discuss one notable example, that of the new Canadian minister of defence, the Honorable Harjit Sajjan. Appointed minister upon the election of the Trudeau government, Mr. Sajjan, a Sikh of South Asian origin, had served with the police for eleven years and then in the Afghan war with the Canadian military. In the latter capacity, he was awarded the Meritorius Service Medal "for reducing the Taliban's influence" in the region of Kandahar (Baluja 2015). Described as the "best single Canadian asset in theatre" (Baluja 2015), Mr. Sajjan was reported to have been picked for specific duties in Afghanistan "because of his experience in dealing with gangs because the Taliban were nothing more than bunch of thugs and gangs," according to then commander of the Multinational Brigade (AFP 2015). That Sajjan wore a turban, that young Sikh men have been constructed as particularly prone to gang membership and criminality, that Sikhs and the Muslim Taliban are seen to be the same, and that Sajjan's insider knowledge was considered the significant factor in his successful career in the Canadian occupation of Afghanistan speak to the racial/cultural politics of the military, state, and nation.

The impact of the global war on the citizenship rights and social integration of South Asian Canadian communities demonstrates the fraught nature of this institution. Rather than proceeding along an incremental and cumulative trajectory toward greater inclusion—or instead of the ideological borders of the Canadian and US nations that construct them as Other having become more porous—the war demonstrates that the policing of American and Canadian identity has become more fortified in the relation of enmity to the figure of the Muslim. This construction of the Muslim enables those South Asian Canadians who are seen to uphold the security of the nation, as well as its values and culture, to claim their share in this restructuring of the national identity. The post-9/11 configuration of alliances in the nation-state allows for the collective national consciousness to crystalize along cultural-religio-racial lines, creating new points of alignment for the national subject with other previously excluded subjects, including those immigrants working toward integration into the nation-state. The resulting fortification of the relation between state and nation/al, and between these and the aspiring South Asian Canadian immigrant, helps to confirm the exalted status of the national at the domestic level and of Canada at the international level.

More examples that illustrate this ideological cordoning off of Muslims of South Asian origin include construction of the singularity of the "honour crime"; the attacks on Muslim women wearing hijab; the lack of organized political protest within the South Asian Canadian community against the introduction of the Barbaric Cultural Practices Act; the lack of political connection between the construction of the Sikh male as "terrorist" in the 1990s (when the politics of Sikh separatism dominated the dynamics of intracommunity engagement) and the contemporary construct of the Muslim as "terrorist"; and the silence in non-Muslim South Asian communities regarding the Ontario proposal to allow Muslims to draw upon Shar'ia in family dispute resolution. The distancing of non-Muslim South Asians from Muslim South Asians on these issues was indicative of the split among these communities, and of their shifting affiliations and allegiances.

Nowhere was this change more evident than in the antiviolence feminist coalitions that had previously existed in these communities, gestured to by the comments of the feminist activist cited at the beginning of this chapter. During the 1990s, these feminist coalitions—bringing together "immigrant" women's politics with those of the Women of Color antiracist politics that had critiqued the construction of immigrant communities, including South Asians, as culturally backward and patriarchal by pointing to the male violence that is a feature of Canadian society; Women of Color politics had also challenged the effects of immigration policies that made immigrant women vulnerable to increased male domination and control. With the advent of the war on terror, no such feminist analysis was forthcoming from Women of Color with regard to the construction of Islam and Muslim cultures as innately misogynist and violent. Certainly this situation has begun to shift somewhat as the occupations of Afghanistan and Iraq failed to lead to quick victories for the US alliance, as had been anticipated; the rightward shift in the political culture of the United States and other Western societies that highlights the racisms fueled by the global war on terror is also having an effect in reshaping relations among feminists of color and Muslim feminists.

If the extent of the reconstitution of race, colonial, and gender politics in the global war is evident in the spectacular rise of Donald Trump, in Canada it is evident in the incorporation of South Asian Canadians, through the discourse of multiculturalism, into the upper echelons of the settler state. That this discourse does not contest the Islamophobia that is the ideological bedrock of the global war is not accidental, for multiculturalism has helped consolidate the cultural construction of Muslims as adherents of a barbaric and misogynist culture associated with Islam, isolating them from the other immigrant communities in a manner that helps crystallize the remaking of Canadian national identity as endangered and innocent of implication in the new occupations of the early twentieth century.

The inability of the larger South Asian Canadian communities, including the feminists among them, to confront the present religio-racial targeting of Muslims, I argue, can be read as a political consequence of the narrowly construed definition of sovereignty—access to citizenship—that is embedded in the South Asian Canadian political imaginary. The post-9/11 articulation of the sovereignty of the North American settler states, the

United States and Canada, is remaking the two vital aspects of sovereignty discussed in the above sections. The first is the territorial aspect of this sovereignty, which is as central to settler-colonial politics in North America as this is to the Western domination of the Middle East and the South and Central Asian regions. The invasion of Afghanistan demonstrated that imperialist domination maintains its ability to transform itself into colonial occupation. The second is the recasting of the forms of identity and subjectivity of "South Asian Canadians" in a moment when their "cultural" essence can be harnessed to advance the Western nation-state's geostrategic interests. These reinvigorated aspects of sovereignty were linked in the occupation of Afghanistan, which drew upon the settler-colonial nature of the Canadian nation-state and rearticulated this to its redefined role as an occupation force in Central Asia. Likewise, the global war reveals that the political activism associated with the paradigm of *South Asian Canadian* was unable to respond to either the anticolonial politics of Indigenous peoples fighting for sovereignty over their lands or the anticolonial and antiracist struggles of Muslims against the Islamophobia that now shapes the geopolitical field.

Further, leaving uninterrogated the relation between sovereignty and the antiterrorism measures enacted at the nation's borders, South Asian Canadians have, with few exceptions, acquiesced in the erosion of the citizenship of Muslims in Canada and in the destruction of the post-independence states in the Middle East and Central Asia. Given that mere suspicion of links to "terrorist" activity can be used to detain, deport, torture, incarcerate, or even murder Muslims, non-Muslim South Asian Canadians have an incentive to disassociate themselves from the Muslims among them and, in the process, assert their religio-cultural "difference" from these Muslims. The immense public support among Canadian and US nationals for fighting "terrorists" wherever they are found, for racial profiling wherever the state deems this necessary, and for delivering Muslim women from the "imprisoning" hijab extends Islamophobia into the homes, schools, courts, workplaces, cinemas, shopping malls, and social service agencies that organize the daily lives of Canadian nationals. This Islamophobia is shared by non-Muslim South Asian Canadians, with remarkably few exceptions.

Yet, it should be remembered that the present treatment of Muslims by the colonial/imperial state also reveals that the juridical status of the South Asian Canadian also remains tenuous. If the governing ideology of the war on terror targets Muslims as a threat to the survival of the nation's values, the racial/culturalizing practices encoded in the reproduction of this nation also reveals it to be an inherently exclusionary project.

REPRODUCING COLONIALITY?

This chapter began with the recognition that the processes set in motion by the colonial/racial practices in the founding moment of Canadian nation and state making continue to be reiterated in the relations among the populations subsequently constituted as "Indians," "immigrants," and "Canadians." The uneven and asymmetrical processes through which South Asian Canadians are constituted as such in this web of relations are thus organized not only with regard to the status and subjectivity of nationals but also with regard to Indigenous and the other communities located within this terrain. I have argued that the political construct of *South Asian Canadian* leaves uninterrogated the triangulated relations that constitutively bind these populations, relations that were forged in and reproduced by ongoing coloniality and raciality. Consequently, the struggle for access to citizenship and integration into democratic institutions, which remain key objectives of South Asian Canadian feminisms, reproduces the ongoing dispossession of Indigenous peoples and the colonial violence of the nation-state at home and abroad, so to speak.

Moreover, taking the post-independence moment as evidence of the transcendence of coloniality in South Asia, the politics arising from the present construction of the South Asian Canadian paradigm privileges immigration, resettlement, assimilation, and citizenship as among the most salient factors shaping the experiences of these communities. Consequently, historical and emergent forms of coloniality are rendered invisible in this paradigm, and the positionality of South Asian Canadians is taken up primarily in relation to the politics of the nation-state rather than in engagement with Indigenous histories, understandings, or critiques of settler colonialism. The collective imaginary of peoples of South Asian origin in North American communities remains fixated on acquiring proximity to the forms of whiteness that inform the hegemonic US and Canadian national frames. Rethinking the structural location of these South Asian communities in relation to Indigenous communities, as well as other people of color, in North America would open up the possibilities for transformative political alliances. My argument, however, is that neglect of the actual temporal and spatial forms assumed by coloniality, its forms of sovereignty and subjectivity in North America as in South Asia, derails the radical potential of the politics of opposition within the South Asian immigrant community in Canada. A shift away from the immigrant-oriented

politics of these communities and toward a historicized and contextualized anticolonial understanding of the forms of sovereignty that are presently remaking North American nation-states as well as those in South
Asia, would be a necessary step in the realization of this potential.

NOTES

1   See Bannerji (2000), Ahmed (2000), and Thobani (2007) for critical perspectives on
    multiculturalism in specific national and international contexts.
2   For more on the intersections of race, gender, nation, and class in Canada, see Ban-
    nerji (1995), Thobani (2007), and Jiwani (2011).
3   In addition to Buchignani, Indra, and Srivastava (1985), see also Bolaria and Li (1988).
4   These futuristic anxieties permeated the early nineteenth-century national debate
    on whether it was prudent to exclude the undesired women altogether (thus encour-
    aging "their" men to remain transient) or allow their limited presence (and avert the
    harm of interracial sexual relations between male migrants and white women). See
    Dua (2007, 445–66).
5   See Thobani (2007) for a discussion of the family sponsorship program.
6   The front page of the newspaper's weekend edition ran the feature under the title
    "100 Influential Indo-Canadians in B.C." (Shore and Bolan 2008).
7   The other eighty-two individuals were reported to have their "origin" in South Asia
    as well as other parts of Asia, Africa, Europe, the Middle East, the Caribbean, and
    Fiji (Randy and Bolan 2008).
8   These ambiguities can be found in the essays published in various collections on
    "South Asian" women in the diaspora. See, for example, the collection of essays in
    Puwar and Raghuram (2003) and Women of South Asian Descent Collective (1993).
9   While the opposition party introduced its own countermotion to remove the focus
    on Islamophobia, one opposition MP running for the leadership of the Conservative
    Party sent out a press release in support of the motion as introduced by Iqra Khalid.
    See Lum (2017).

REFERENCES

AFP. 2015. "Decorated Sikh Soldier Takes Command of Canada's Military." *Hindustan
    Times*, November 7. www.hindustantimes.com/world/decorated-sikh-soldier-takes
    -command-of-canada-s-military/story-g520QfSvQ5wVYrocTgdWoJ.html.
Ahmed, Sara. 2000. *Strange Encounters: Embodied Others in Post-Coloniality*. New
    York: Routledge.
Baluja, Tamara. 2015. "Harjit Sajjan: Meet Canada's New 'Badass' Defence Minister."
    Canadian Broadcasting Corporation, November 4. www.cbc.ca/news/canada/british
    -columbia/harjit-sajjan-badass-canada-defence-minister-1.3304931.
Bannerji, Himani. 1995. *Thinking Through: Essays on Feminism, Marxism and Anti-
    racism*. Toronto: Women's Press.

———. 2000. *The Dark Side of the Nation: Essays on Multiculturalism, Nationalism and Gender.* Toronto: Canadian Scholars Press.

Bolaria, B. Singh, and Peter S. Li. 1988. *Racial Oppression in Canada.* Toronto: Garamond Press.

Buchignani, Norman, Doreen M. Indra, with Ram Srivastava. 1985. *Continuous Journey: A Social History of South Asians in Canada.* Toronto: McLelland and Stewart.

Citizenship and Immigration Canada. 2013. *Welcome to Canada: What You Should Know.* Her Majesty the Queen in Right of Canada.

Dua, Enakshi. 2007. "Exclusion through Inclusion: Female Asian Migration in the Making of Canada as a White Settler Nation." *Gender, Place and Culture* 14 (4): 445–66.

Elghawaby. Amira. 2017. "Anti-Islamophobia Motion Offers a Chance to Take Stand against Hatred: Why Quibble over Semantics?" *CBC News*, February 19. www.cbc.ca /beta/news/opinion/m103-stand-against-hatred-1.3988771.

Gandhi, Unnati. 2008. "Facing Up to a New Identity." *Globe and Mail*, April 3, A1, A9.

Jiwani, Yasmin. 2011. *Discourses of Denial.* Vancouver: University of British Columbia Press.

Lawrence, Bonita. 2004. *"Real" Indians and Others: Mixed-Blood Urban Native Peoples and Indigenous Nationhood.* Lincoln: University of Nebraska Press.

Lum, Zi-Ann. 2017. "Iqra Khalid, Liberal MP, Reads Threats Received over Anti-Islamophobia Motion." *Huffington Post*, February 16. www.huffingtonpost.ca/2017 /02/16/iqra-khalid-threats-islamophobia_n_14803770.html.

Maira, Sunaina. 2004. "Youth Culture, Citizenship and Globalization: South Asian Muslim Youth in the United States after 9/11." *Comparative Studies of South Asia, Africa and the Middle East* 24 (1): 221–25.

Mall, Rattan. 2014. "Violence among Seniors Exposed by Two Murders: Government Funding of Programs Is a Must." *Indo-Canadian Voice*, 1–2.

Mongia, Radhika V. 2007. "Historicizing State Sovereignty: Inequality and the Form of Equivalence." *Comparative Studies in Society and History* 49 (2): 384–411.

Monture-Angus. Patricia. 1995. *Thunder in My Soul: A Mohawk Woman Speaks.* Halifax: Fernwood Publishing.

Moore, Dene. 2007. "Quebec Town Bans Kirpans, Stoning Women." *Globe and Mail*, January 20. www.theglobeandmail.com/news/national/quebec-town-bans-kirpans -stoning-women/article678227.

Olwan, Dana. 2013. "Gendered Violence, Cultural Otherness, and Honour Crimes in Canadian National Logics." *Canadian Journal of Sociology* 38 (4): 533–55.

Puwar, Nirmal, and Parvati Raghuram. 2003. *South Asian Women in the Diaspora.* Oxford: Bloomsbury Academic.

Razack, Sherene. 2008. *Casting Out: The Eviction of Muslims from Western Law and Politics.* Toronto: University of Toronto Press.

Shore, Randy, and Kim Bolan. 2008. "100 Influential Indo-Canadians in B.C." *Vancouver Sun*, March 29, A1, A6, D1, D6, D7, D8, D9.

Stevenson, Verity, and Sean Gordon. 2017. "'This Can't Be Real': Witnesses Recount Night of Quebec City Mosque Shooting." *Globe and Mail*, January 31. www.theglobe andmail.com/news/national/this-cant-be-real-witnesses-recount-night-of-quebec -city-shooting/article33854638.

Thobani, Sunera. 2007. *Exalted Subjects: Studies in the Making of Race and Nation in Canada*. Toronto: University of Toronto Press.

Women of South Asian Descent Collective. 1993. *Women of the South Asian Diaspora: Our Feet Walk the Sky*. San Francisco: Aunt Lute Books.

PART FOUR

BEYOND "CULTURE CLASH" REDUCTIONS

Organizing against State and Interpersonal Violence

CHAPTER 8

THE LANGUAGE OF CARE

Hmong Refugee Activism and
a Feminist Refugee Epistemology

MA VANG

ON MARCH 22, 2016, I SAT IN ON ONE OF THE SEVEN WEEKLY
three-hour Partners in Healing shaman training workshops in the board-
room at Mercy Medical Center Merced. These workshops, scheduled on
Tuesday evenings from six to nine, were led by the program's co-developer,
Palee Moua. Those present at the workshop included thirteen shaman participants from all over California's Central Valley; Moua, a Mercy medical
staff member; a social worker from the Merced County Human Services
Agency; and me. Of the thirteen shamans, about five are men and the rest
women. The shamans range in age from their thirties to their sixties. The
evening's workshop focused on chronic diseases, cancer, and hospice care.
The first hour of the workshop focused on chronic diseases, of which diabetes and high blood pressure have the highest incidence in the Hmong
community. The nurse explained in English the causes, symptoms, and
treatments for the diseases while Moua interpreted in Hmong for the shamans. Moua explained to the shaman participants that chronic disease is
a bodily, rather than spiritual, affliction so they should encourage their
patients to see a doctor for proper treatment and management of their
blood sugar or blood pressure levels. In addition, because the chronic diseases are long-term illnesses, shamans should explain to their patients to

continue their diet and exercise regimens to maintain favorable levels of blood sugar and blood pressure.

Although a couple of the shamans asked clarifying questions about whether having gestational diabetes means a person will develop diabetes later in life and about the levels of cholesterol needed to stay healthy, a few others asked questions that were more personal. One woman shaman asked why she developed diabetes after her car accident. Another shaman asked if the nurse would look at her feet during the break because she had a concern with them (she seemed to suggest that she had diabetes). This exchange was important because it revealed that the shaman participants not only gained information to help their patients but also learned about ailments they might be personally struggling with. The shaman participants' questions also showed how their roles as spiritual healers were informed by social experiences and their own health concerns, which made them relatable to their patients. Training workshops like this one demonstrate how the Partners in Healing program is premised on this lateral relationship between shamans and members of the community, and it develops a connection between communities and medical and social service institutions.

Such lateral relationships and connections, which contribute to the value of programs like Partners in Healing, emerged from dedicated refugee activists like Moua who advocate for refugee communities' access to care through interpreting and cultural mediation. Partners in Healing is a nationally known program created for shamans to learn about biomedical procedures and to expand biomedicine's knowledge of the work of shamans (Helsel, Mochel, and Bauer 2004, 934–35). It developed a partnership between healthcare organizations and Hmong communities by implementing an orientation program for Hmong shamans. The project began in 2000 through Healthy House Within a MATCH Coalition, a nonprofit organization.[1] The program is a model for developing similar programs with traditional healers from other racial/ethnic groups. The project has a dual curriculum: one program to train shamans and the other to train physicians as part of their three-year residency at the hospital (Moua 2016). Although the program began around 2000, Mercy Hospital did not implement its Hmong Shaman Spiritual Healer policy to allow shamans to practice at patients' bedside until 2009.[2] This policy allowed a shaman to conduct nine different ceremonies unsupervised by doctors and hospital staff. Moua is its anchor because she brokers and bridges relationships among shamans, doctors, and hospital administrators to operationalize the curriculum.

Moua is an activist who mediates refugees' relationships with local institutions and their agents, including healthcare professionals, social service providers, and organizational leaders. As she facilitates the training session for the shamans, she also interprets for them, shifting between speaking in the first person as if she were asking the question and using the third person. Moua explained to the group that as an interpreter for Hmong, she carries a burden because she cannot be direct with patients and families. She has to be gentle and explain that they need to spend time with each other rather than telling them that death is imminent. As an interpreter she must maintain a professional demeanor to mediate communication between healthcare providers and Hmong patients. She says, "You hope with the families," but it is only after the appointment that "you [can] cry and laugh with patients and families" (Moua 2016). Moua's approach to interpreting emphasizes care for refugees and the importance of language and social relationships to refugee advocacy.

Moua's role as an interpreter bridges the language gap to create change in the integrated areas of social and cultural mediation and program development. Therefore, her work to maintain Hmong language, build an archive of terminology, and create programs like Partners in Healing expands our understanding of feminist refugee epistemologies that center local knowledge.[3] In their essay on cultural organizing in California's Central Valley as critical praxis, Erica Kohl-Arenas, Myrna Martinez Nateras, and Johanna Taylor (2014, 9) explain that "the process of recognizing, celebrating, and activating immigrants' cultural rights counters systems of patronage and policing, and recognizes immigrants as productive agents of social change." Arts and culture already exist as a social change strategy that programs harness as a "human right" to challenge "histories of invisibility, marginalization, and inequality" (10). Therefore, cultural acts such as claiming one's indigenous name or language are deeply political acts (20). Indeed, refugee activism around what I will explain as a *language of care* rather than "language as social barrier" activates refugee cultural capital.[4]

Care in humanitarian relief has been a primary site of regulation for the management of refugee populations worldwide. Although humanitarian care purports to rescue refugees from military and other state-perpetuated forms of violence, refugees often encounter the human rights regime and states' racist violence during and after resettlement. Relatedly, state and private systems of care have served to manage immigrant women's and Women of Color labor and bodies. Health is one site of care that highlights the intersections of experiences of Asian refugee and immigrant women with those of Women of Color in the United States. I argue that refugee activism around care activates a feminist refugee praxis to decenter state and Western ideas of care as gendered racial management, and instead privileges refugee epistemologies and practices of well-being. In other words, refugee activists work to prevent deaths in their communities by employing a language of care that involves Hmong/refugee worldviews in the social and institutional translation of care.

This chapter employs what I call an ethnography of care and well-being to examine how refugee activists, most of whom are women, engage with US social welfare and health institutions to address gaps in care for their communities. An ethnography of care and well-being emphasizes the affective labor of refugee activists that plots what M. Jacqui Alexander (2005, 7–8) describes in her conceptualization of the "crossing" as a "move away from living alterity premised in difference to living intersubjectivity premised in relationality and solidarity." My approach draws from feminist ethnography that asserts a feminist epistemology to examine how knowledge is produced and informed by a politics of social justice (Davis and Craven 2016, 9). This methodological approach also emphasizes praxis—the bridging of theory and practice (10). An ethnography of care and well-being underscores the intersections of feminist epistemology and praxis. It enacts as well as theorizes ways of centering non-Western knowledges and languages. Refugee activists, I suggest, engage in feminist epistemologies that assert the refugee as a knowing subject whose displaced condition *teaches* us about various forms of state management, as well as one who *produces* knowledge about care. As such, feminist refugee epistemologies reveal the refugee as a figure who emerged from the overlapping context of colonialism and militarism yet has also been subjected to the simultaneous oppressions of humanitarian and state management en route to and upon arrival in the United States.

This chapter's analysis of refugee community negotiations of health, race, and gender expands the convergences of Asian American feminisms and Women of Color politics with decolonial feminisms to foreground the antiracist and anticolonial trajectories of a Hmong feminist praxis and a feminist refugee epistemology (FRE) that underscores refugee "practices of life making" (Espiritu and Duong 2018, 588). Yên Lê Espiritu and Lan Duong conceptualize a feminist refugee epistemology (FRE) through their reading of displacement in Vietnamese and Syrian refugee art as a method of analysis that conceptualizes "refugee artwork as a crucial site of new forms of knowledge that would otherwise not be produced or shared" (589). FRE calls attention to refugees' complicated and rich daily existences in the collaborative acts and intimate spaces.[5] I engage with a feminist refugee analysis alongside a Hmong feminist approach that emphasizes a praxis of care around language making, sociocultural revitalization, and community well-being. These feminist convergences encapsulate the cross-currents of different feminisms—what Alexander calls the crossroads of migrancy under empire "and the genealogies of feminist, neocolonial, and 'queer' politics" (8–9). Alexander's reminder that rather than being born a Woman of Color, one becomes a Woman of Color (9) highlights the importance of Chandra Mohanty's (2003, 7) assertions of a feminist solidarity across borders that seeks to decolonize knowledge and practice anticapitalist critique. Together, decolonial feminism's project of theorizing alternative epistemologies to disrupt the totalizing force of colonialism and Women of Color feminism's coalition to reformulate culture and agency to counter the simultaneous oppressions of capitalism, Western nationalism, and national liberation (Ferguson 2004, 116) chart a fruitful intersection to theorize a Hmong feminist approach. A Hmong feminist approach to taking care of each other is not an additive to the existing forms of feminist theorizations, but rather shifts the frame of reference to emphasize non-Western and noninstitutional practices and epistemologies.

REFUGEE ACTIVISM AND FEMINIST REFUGEE EPISTEMOLOGY OF CARE

Refugee activism defines the intricate ways in which refugees advocating for their communities must face and address the overlapping institutions of oppression they encounter in remaking their lives in the United States. The term does not refer to activists working on behalf of refugees, but to the refugees who have experienced violence and displacement. These activists received an education in their home countries and, while in the camps or after resettlement, in/voluntarily become advocates for their people. Their advocacy involves more than just interpreting services. They utilize trained medical and language skills as well as reinforcing their communities' subjecthood and knowledge. As a refugee activist, Moua works to address multiple issues rather than a particular health or social welfare concern. As interpreters and advocates, Moua and others like her broker relationships between physicians or social workers and patients/clients. They help transform the relations between communities and institutions. In *Buddha Is Hiding*, Aihwa Ong (2003, 6) examines how the technologies of government determine a different mode of being human and valuing life. Ong's study explores how each domain of government "teaches" Cambodian refugees to be citizen-subjects and how Cambodian Americans pursue their own values. Refugee activists must navigate the ways government domains such as social services, healthcare, employment, and child welfare services work together to shape refugees into proper subjects.

Moua's refugee activism exercises critical feminist epistemologies and praxis in connecting community issues to women's issues, thus working against institutional oppression. As feminist scholars have argued, for Women of Color, health cannot be separated from community health, in the sense that "women's and reproductive health care could only be understood within a broad context of health care needs that improved the life quality of the entire community" (Nelson 2005, 100). These community concerns include access to food, housing, and education. Indeed, a feminist refugee epistemology centers refugee knowledge and stories, the secrets and silences produced by state violence, and critical cultural forms to advance refugee survival and life.

Shamans hold spiritual and political leadership roles in health and well-being. Because about half the shamans in the Hmong community are women, centering the important role of shamans disrupts the patriarchal structure of care and leadership. Whereas existing scholarship on Hmong and contemporary Hmong practices prioritize a patrilineal clan social system in which male clan leaders make decisions about the spiritual and social well-being of the extended clan families, the Partners in Healing project found that Hmong shamans and traditional healers have always had positions of spiritual, religious, and political leadership (Hmong Shaman Spiritual Healer Manual). Rather than the clan leaders holding positions of influence, the shamans are often the first choice among Hmong to seek consultation and care to treat illnesses (Spiritual Healer Manual). Other community health projects encountered the same trend in their efforts to advocate and educate on health issues.[6]

The shaman program served a dual purpose: to highlight the important role shamans serve in Hmong communities, as the primary defense concerning health and well-being, and to empower shamans to promote well-being.[7] Reinforcing the role of shamans, then, disrupts the heteropatriarchal structure of power and Western paradigms of care and knowledge. In this way, a Hmong feminist epistemology that emphasizes care has a significant social and political impact on the Hmong patriarchal structure, as well as being an antiracist and anticolonial approach. It centers Hmong geographic knowledge and migratory patterns or strategies of storytelling. This perspective views stories as mobile and histories as moveable pasts. The approach is "informed by the scholarship on transnational and Native feminist theories in which they interrogate colonialism, racism, US liberal empire, and (hetero)patriarchy as ongoing structures of power through the lens of gender and sexuality. In addition, I borrow from the work of feminist anthropologists who suggest 'ethnographic refusal' and critical-listening practices to articulate Hmong women's narrative strategies" (Vang 2016, 30–31).

Feminist epistemology constitutes ways of knowing that push the boundaries of presumed knowledge about women, showing that feminist politics are about asserting women's knowledge. Citing Trinh T. Minh-ha's caution that the label "feminism tends to become an occupied territory," Basuli Deb (2016, 183) explains that "occupied territory refers to epistemological violence: the proclamation of authority over feminist knowledge by the global North." While the label of feminism can reproduce inequalities across racial and geopolitical boundaries, "pushing the limits of feminist epistemology" can enable "new knowledge about the other and new definitions of transnational feminist solidarity politics" (Deb 2016, 183). And as Alexander notes, summoning "subordinated knowledges that are produced in the context of the practices of marginalization" might help to "destabilize existing practices of knowing and thus cross the fictive boundaries of exclusion and marginalization" (7). Hence, rethinking what is considered acceptable knowledge and practices of care has the potential to not only shape institutional standards but bridge different feminist formations.

"HELP PEOPLE NOT TO DIE": PALEE MOUA

During one of our first meetings, Moua explained that she became a community health equity and cultural advocate because Hmong people had died enough in Laos during and after the war, and she wanted to "help people not die" here in the United States due to lack of access to resources and institutional policies and practices. She also wanted to help women access proper healthcare. When she arrived in the United States in 1976, she felt embarrassed talking about family planning and women's health issues through her husband and a male interpreter, and she knew that other Hmong women felt the same way. She wanted to interpret for these women so that they did not have to discuss women's health issues through a male interpreter with a healthcare provider (Moua 2015). The contexts of war, genocide, and migration combined with racialized experiences in the United States situate refugee concerns at the intersection of Women of Color politics and Asian American issues.

Health became a way to measure the strain refugees and immigrants put on communities and institutions, as well as an indicator of their integration into their new society writ large. In a *Los Angeles Times* story on the resettlement of seven thousand Southeast Asian refugees in the Linda Vista community of San Diego, Robert Montemayor focused on how the influx of refugees displaced the community's white, Black, and Mexican American residents from housing and social services, especially healthcare at the Linda Vista Health Care Center. The clinic became a measure of the impact of the refugees on the community, especially when it reported an estimated 1,300 encounters with patients each month. Facing rising tensions among Linda Vista's existing communities, clinic director Roberta Feinberg explained that "the refugees had so many health problems when they came in that we had to give them acute care." The clinic's director of the psychosocial division, Jean Nidorf, further elaborated that these refugee health problems included inactive tuberculosis, chronic intestinal parasites, anemia, skin conditions, dental issues, acute depression, and anxiety (Montemayor 1980). This story reveals not only the burden of refugees but also their neediness, because they arrive with chronic diseases and acute psychological issues. The refugee is already marked as an unhealthy body needing medical care. Immigration scholars have noted how such health screenings at the US borders and within communities racially defined immigrants' entry and communities of color fit for citizenship.[8]

However, this medicalization of refugees did not begin upon their arrival in the United States. In fact, a significant element of refugee processing involved health screenings for chronic diseases such as tuberculosis and sexually transmitted diseases, as well as drug use. For Hmong refugees who practice polygamy, refugee processing also involved forcing them to choose one wife, which brought the management of sexuality into the realm of health regulations. Whereas such health screenings impacted both men and women, forced sterilization of refugee women in addition to the violence and death caused by war links refugee women's concerns with those of Women of Color. Forced sterilizations of refugee women, mostly Vietnamese, occurred in Refugee Relocation Centers at US military bases throughout the United States. A memorandum, dated September 2, 1975, from Interagency Task Force for Indochina director Julia Vadala Taft to the senior civilian coordinators at these relocation centers communicated the

Department of State's policy to postpone all nontherapeutic sterilizations of refugees until families had been resettled "into a more normal living situation." The policy also reinforced the secretary of state's "moratorium on nontherapeutic sterilizations of minors and legally incompetent individuals" (Taft 1975b). That such a memo existed in the refugee resettlement task force files revealed the prevalence of nontherapeutic sterilizations, which were done not to maintain the health and well-being of the individual but to forcibly reduce the number of refugee children. Even more disconcerting, relocation center volunteers and staff took it upon themselves to make these decisions in the refugees' supposed best interest. These forced sterilizations often occurred with insufficient medical care (Taft 1975c).

Refugees were subjected to the logic of genocide both in wartime and in the resettlement process. By December 22, 1975, the Task Force records showed three abortions at Eglin Air Force Base, Florida, and fifty-seven at Camp Pendleton, while the US Public Health Service performed twenty-one abortions at Fort Indiantown Gap, Pennsylvania (Taft 1975a).[9] No funds were earmarked for abortions or forced sterilizations, and only medical costs for the termination of pregnancies were reported in the expenditures. Hence, there was no record of these medical procedures, and it was easy for Task Force officials as well as House Representatives to justify the abortions that did happen. These sterilization practices show how the state and its apparatuses predominate in refugee rescue and care. More poignantly, these sterilizations of refugee women revealed the connection among race, gender, and reproduction control as a larger issue of racist violence perpetuated against Women of Color.[10]

The management of refugee bodies necessitated that refugee activists' work, like that of Moua, mediate the impact of medicalization on refugee women. Moua has spent the forty years since her arrival in the United States helping the Hmong refugee community navigate US institutions, working especially with women and their access to healthcare. She arrived at the age of twenty with her husband, Dan Moua, and three children, landing in Richmond, Virginia, in 1976, and moving to Merced in 1977. Moua was born in Xieng Khouang province and attended primary school in Vientiane, Laos, learning Lao and French. Like many Southeast Asian refugee families in the late 1970s and 1980s, Moua's family moved a second time to Planada, California, a farming community outside Merced, to reunite with extended family and pursue farming. She was part of the first wave of Hmong families to relocate to California's Central Valley in search of better opportunities. These Hmong families lived in migrant camps with

Mexican farmworkers and worked alongside them. In Planada, Moua got her first job as a child-care provider at a daycare for children of migrant workers, Hmong and Mexican.

After the farm labor season ended, the Hmong families relocated to Merced, where Moua took English classes at Merced College and started working at the local health clinic in its Women, Infants, and Children (WIC) program. In this capacity, Moua became an interpreter for Hmong families, especially for Hmong women accessing family planning and prenatal care. Because there were few Hmong who knew English, Moua and her husband, then a young couple in their midtwenties, stepped up to help: "I went to help in the hospital and the social service agency while my husband helped at the social service agency and at the court." She explains: "The more you help, the more you saw the problems so you learned that . . . it will not work if I say it this way, I should say it like this. So I slowly learned to fix and change phrases" (Moua 2016). Here, Moua explains how she changed language phrasing to convey the social context of care rather than interpret words directly.

Between 2000 to 2013, Moua created institutional change in her work for Healthy House as the director of case management, director of cultural brokerage, director of cultural services, the community liaison for the Shaman Project, and an interpreter. She is currently the director of Southeast Asian community engagement for the Building Healthy Communities Health Equity Project and a special project coordinator for the Human Services Agency of Merced County. Through her work, Moua has developed a Hmong glossary for health-related terminology, led the chronic disease community health education, developed the shaman training curriculum, and trained interpreter trainers. As the curriculum developer and trainer for both the interpreter training and Partners in Healing programs, Moua advocated for the centralization of Hmong knowledge and social context to effectively bridge communities and institutions.

THE LANGUAGE OF CARE: TRANSLATING KNOWLEDGE AND WORLDVIEWS

The first hour of the workshop I observed was devoted to discussing chronic diseases; the second hour focused on cancer. According to research on Asian Americans, Hmong have the highest incidence of cancers, including nasopharynx, stomach, liver, larynx, non-Hodgkin lymphoma, cervical, and leukemia. Again, shamans are encouraged to refer their patients for cancer screenings and visits to their doctors. The shamans can reassure their patients that they will perform shaman rituals at home or at the hospital once the doctors have prescribed a treatment plan. Moua estimates that trained shamans refer 80 percent of their patients to doctors. In fact, a shaman who completed the program revealed to Moua that once he started referring his patients to the doctor, "eighty percent of my patients never come back to see me" (quoted by Moua 2016). The shaman is the first person that Hmong individuals see—for those who still practice shamanism. S/he encounters the patient first and determines a diagnosis or treatment plan and whether or not that plan should involve a doctor. "It is not [only] the shaman who should refer a patient," Moua said. "The doctor must also refer." As an example, patients suffering from tuberculosis and soul loss both experience night sweating. If a doctor has conducted X-rays and other tests but cannot make a conclusive diagnosis, s/he should refer the patient to a shaman, because this patient may be suffering from soul loss. In this way, sickness from dab/spirit and chronic disease is "very close" (Moua 2016).

Moua's integral and interrelated work with interpreting and shaman training programs demonstrates a "bottom-up" feminist refugee approach that centers Hmong refugee language and knowledge. Although not a shaman, Moua has a deep understanding of shaman practices so that she is able to "place the words together" to interpret their meanings in language, both Hmong and English (Moua 2016). One shaman ascertained that Moua is a shaman ambassador. A shaman ambassador does not perform shaman rituals per se but is there to "balance things so they exist in harmony/*sib haum xeeb*" (Moua 2016). Moua's translation of Hmong knowledge and worldview establishes a *language of care* that focuses not on how language and terminology can accurately and directly convey meaning from one language to another but on how to communicate one's worldview about care. The language of care is a feminist refugee epistemology that focuses on refugee well-being as a politics of hope and survival rather than on the refugee as a social and political problem.

Language (and terminology) has been a noted barrier to Hmong patient/refugee access to healthcare in two ways: it limits communication between doctors and patients, and even if they can communicate through an interpreter, the unequal English and Hmong terminology means that there is insufficient language to convey ailments Hmong patients experience. Due to this language issue, healthcare and social service professionals assume that Hmong do not have words for English medical terms. According to Moua, a colleague who helped develop the Partners in Healing program often remarks to the professionals: "Oh, Hmong don't have the word, Hmong don't have the terminology, no, Hmong don't have any word." This ingrained belief about a Hmong lack of language informs interactions not only between patients and doctors but also between refugee activists and their white colleagues. Part of the refugee activist's advocacy for the language of care occurs in the context of program building and teachable moments with colleagues.

Language barriers have direct consequences for patients because they compound doctors' dislike of Hmong. Since a standard Hmong healthcare terminology has yet to be developed and the doctor already has a negative perception of Hmong patients, "when you go interpret for a Hmong patient, the doctor is usually upset at us because each Hmong person interprets differently" (Moua 2016). As such, popular and academic representations of "cultural clashes" that highlight the conflict between a backward Hmong medicine and epistemology and a progressive Western/US medical regime[11] actually point to the unequal gendered racial context of refugee and immigrant health.

Language, often viewed from an institutional perspective as a barrier to refugee and immigrant health, also fails to convey these groups' ways of knowing, their sources of knowledge, or their worldviews. An exchange between Moua and her colleague regarding the shaman program revealed that the lack of language and terminology worked both ways:

> When I started developing the shaman program, I would ask her for the English word for Hmong words that I described to her.
>
> She said, "Oh no, Americans don't have those words" [*laughing*].
>
> I said, "Okay, now we balance out." I said frankly, "Now you know, huh?" They think that we have few words and the language is not equivalent to English. So when we developed the shaman program . . . I noted the difference as I translated the curriculum.
>
> She said, "Now I know that *the world is not the same one as I thought I knew*" [*laughing*]. (Moua 2016, emphasis added).

This colleague's statement that the world is not how she thought reveals how translating shaman practices for the development of the shaman program exposes the privileging of Western/US concepts of health and care as fundamental to traditional interpreting methods. While interpreting practices showed a lack of Hmong equivalents for English and medical terminology, the development of the shaman program revealed that English often lacks equivalents for Hmong terminology, because the program asserts a Hmong epistemology about how care involves the well-meaning language of relationships and refugee knowledge.

A language of care emphasizes the importance of social relationships to counter individualized notions of care. In training doctors to work with interpreters, Moua explained, "Look, we Hmong build a set of relationship titles. When I see a younger or older uncle, I don't say 'you, you, me, me,' right? I say, 'Uncle, the doctor asks you to do this.'" These relationship titles establish a communal and kinship connection that disrupts the "you" and "I" individualized relation and decenters the doctor as the source of knowledge. "First person doesn't work for Hmong," Moua exclaims. "For example, if I say, *you* go get your blood drawn, *your* stool shows that you have a health problem so *I* will have you go take an X-ray . . . so if I say 'I, I' or 'you, you,' it doesn't make sense, right?" (emphasis added). She elaborates on the need to switch between the first and third person: "You must be the doctor to say to the patient, 'I can see that this will be an issue of concern later on, so you must go [get an X-ray], Uncle [*txiv hlob*], you must go.'" Moua affirms to the Hmong patient that the doctor did indeed call him uncle even though she is the one who used the term. She understands her role as translating social contexts and building relationships between the doctor and patient in the interest of helping Hmong patients (Moua 2016).

The importance of social relationships in providing care draws from Hmong social and kinship systems. The interpreter must switch between the first and third person and address Hmong patients by their titles as uncle, auntie, grandma, or grandpa because s/he has a relationship with the patient, whether it is formal or not. The patient will address the interpreter as daughter, son, or daughter-in-law, so it is important to build upon established Hmong knowledge and social relationships. Moua (2016) explains: "When you go interpret, they [Hmong patients] call you daughter-in-law, right? So you must use *mother-in-law* or *older/younger aunt* [to address them], right? When they arrive [at the doctor's office], they address you directly, 'Daughter-in-law, come help me!' Ma, you know that it's very difficult. It's up to me, right? If I don't know how to build their relationship and communication, they're not going to have a good relationship."

To establish trust, the interpreter builds and maintains a relationship between the doctor and patient. Sometimes when the patient asks Moua why the doctor is upset with her/him, she explains in an honest and "nice way" but never directly: "The doctor is upset at you because the doctor is very worried about you. S/he is very worried about you because s/he worries about your illness, but you have not taken the medication that s/he prescribed" (Moua 2016).

The language of care Moua developed affirms the value of social connections in providing care and mediates different practices of healing and care across institutional, belief, and language barriers. The shaman curriculum trains shamans and doctors that their care should complement each other, not take away the other's effectiveness and value. The distinct but complementary roles of shamans and doctors mean that shamans heal the spirit and soul whereas doctors heal the physical body. Like doctors who specialize in different parts of the body, shamans have different expertise. The shaman's expertise depends on her/his energy's ability to flow and connect with that of the patient. As an example, Moua makes clear to the doctors to not presume gender preference in referring Hmong patients to shamans. Although gender inequality exists, shaman healing does not operate along gender lines: "Do not think that a male shaman will be able to better heal a male patient, no. Maybe calling upon a man shaman will not work, but a woman shaman may be better able to heal the male patient" (Moua 2016). In turn, doctors at Mercy Hospital have made an effort to explain to their residents, since adoption of the shaman policy, that once a shaman has arrived to treat a patient, the doctors and nurses should allow the shaman to do her/his work before they continue with medical procedures. In this complementary practice, it is believed that the shaman's work to call the patient's soul back to be with the body will make medications more effective, and patients will heal faster from surgeries (Moua 2016).

CONCLUSION

Care for refugees involves more than just survival from violence and displacement. It means attending to the health and well-being of a community in a way that incorporates its knowledge and understanding of self and community. Though refugees escaped military violence, they are often subjected to state and institutional violence during and after the resettlement process. Rather than excavate the institutional side of care, this chapter has focused on the refugee perspective and one refugee activist's efforts to help her community "not die" anymore after war and displacement by creating programmatic changes that incorporate refugee epistemology. By theorizing and enacting an ethnography of care and well-being, my research and analysis of refugee activism conjoins critical feminist epistemologies with feminist refugee praxis to center alternative ways of knowing and being.

I have argued that refugee activism helps "people not die" by employing a language of care. The language of care is the refugee activist's assertion of her expertise to create accessible care that focuses not only on the individual but on a community's well-being. It is a feminist refugee epistemology and a decolonial praxis of building an archive of terminology that centers community relations and Hmong refugee knowledge. As a refugee activist, Moua advocated for the Partners in Healing program: "I'm so proud of myself for what I have done since there is no other program, there is only this program in the nation. . . . I see how we have helped our Hmong people and help Hmong to have face and value" (Moua 2016). The program and hospital policy, along with the interpreting programs, have created tremendous changes in how Hmong view Western medicine and US institutions, as well as how doctors view their Hmong patients.

It is important to note the precarious position of programs that address the concerns of communities of color. For instance, the Partners in Healing program is only partially institutionalized, even though it has received institutional and national recognition. It always faces the risk of losing grant funding and institutional or organizational stability. Even though the hospital has adopted the shaman policy, it minimally funds the training program. Only a portion of Moua's time is funded. The policy's existence can also reinforce ideas about racial difference. Moua explained that the program was adopted because "others view Hmong and their shamans as stupid people who do not know anything so they need to learn to open their minds, right?" This exceptionalizing of Hmong racial backwardness is coterminous with the success of the program. Furthermore, the policy's existence overshadows other attempts at spiritual healing by Native American communities in the region. Rather than rely on institutional support, such programs may benefit from concerted feminist solidarity efforts that affirm the activism of Women of Color and refugee/immigrant women to insist on community health and knowledge as a part of women's care. It is more crucial than ever to continue to center local knowledges and non-Western languages to understand what care and well-being looks like for those who were never meant to survive under US/European empire.[12]

NOTES

Acknowledgments: I thank Palee Moua for sharing her knowledge and time with me. She spent many hours explaining her extensive work to bridge the Hmong community and local institutions in Merced. She also made time to carefully read through drafts of this chapter to clarify information. Any mistakes, however, are my own.

1   Healthy House was founded in 1998 by Marilyn Mochel, a registered nurse. Its goal was to improve the health of people throughout Merced by providing interpretive services at medical facilities and trying to close the gap between Hmong beliefs and Western medicine. Its top funders as of 2012 included Mercy Medical Center, the California Endowment, and the California Wellness Foundation. For more about Healthy House, see Amaro 2012. Moua, through her various roles for Healthy House as the director of case management, cultural brokerage, and cultural services, as well as an interpreter, co-created the program with Marilyn Mochel. The program is focused on sharing knowledge and skills and respecting shamans as healers to bridge the gap in healthcare access for Hmong patients.

2   Janice Wilkerson, the hospital's director of mission integration co-wrote this sha-man policy, for which the hospital gained national attention for its innovative approach to incorporating patients' beliefs. For information about the hospital pol-icy, see "Hospital's Shaman Program a Success" (2010).

3   The published scholarship about the Partners in Healing program and Hmong healthcare in Merced take a biomedical and institutional approach that misses the opportunity to address how community activists and interpreters help Hmong patients access healthcare. See Helsel, Mochel, and Bauer (2004) and Warner and Mochel (1998). This chapter centers the role of the key community/refugee activist involved in the everyday work of developing the program, training shamans and doctors, and interacting with patients and hospital staff—all to ensure the health and well-being of Hmong who encounter healthcare institutions and providers.

4   For more on race and community cultural wealth, see Yosso (2005).

5   Theorizing feminist refugee epistemology is, as Espiritu and Duong (2018, 610) note, itself a feminist collaboration in the "formation of ideas and arguments." FRE is a critical concept of the Critical Refugee Studies Collective, of which Espiritu, Duong, and myself, with Mohamed Abumaye, Victor Bascera, Nigel Hatton, Lila Sharif, and Khatharya Um, are founding members. I further collaborate with Moua as a refugee activist to engage with a feminist refugee analysis of refugee "social reproduction and innovation" in the everyday (588).

6   A Hmong American health advocate and activist remarked that when she started her community-based Project Prevention to promote awareness around hepatitis B and encourage Hmong to seek screenings and treatment, her group initially approached the clan leaders to inform families about the disease and the activities of the group. Because hepatitis B significantly impacts Hmong communities but is rarely discussed, and clan leaders, who are all men, were assumed to have authority and influence over their respective clans (extended families), this activist and her group thought they could capitalize on this existing social structure to promote health and well-being in the Hmong community. However, they learned that clan leaders do not talk to the families they represent about health and well-being, focus-ing instead on issues such as cultural practices, economic mobility, and education. It is actually the shamans, the traditional spiritual healers, who exert influence in health and well-being because Hmong who still practice shamanism seek advice

from shamans over the clan leaders. Although it is known that shamans have this influence, the emphasis on clan politics has obscured this practice.

7   The shaman program and hospital policy had significant legal and social impacts for shamans. Hmong shamans and Hmong families practicing shaman rituals faced social stigmatization and legal consequences for violating city ordinances against having live animals within city limits and for noise complaints. Residents viewed the practice as backward and premodern, calling for Hmong refugees to "return to Laos if they couldn't adhere to the American way" (Arax 1995). Authorities in Fresno, Merced, and Stockton renewed enforcement of city ordinances that prohibited raising and slaughtering pigs and chickens to curtail Hmong religious practices (Arax 1995). These religious practices were blamed for Hmong "cultural clashes" with the US health system and led to enactment of a law further disparaging shaman practices. The program and policy have allowed participants to help in court proceedings regarding citations of animal cruelty. In addition, shamans receive social and institutional recognition for their work. Shamans who completed the training program received certificates of recognition from the hospital, the mayor, the city council, the county board of supervisors, and other local organizations. They also received a badge that they carry with them when treating patients in the hospital. These documents offer shamans social acknowledgment of their important roles in improving the lives of Hmong communities and institutional recognition for their work as healers.

8   See Luibhéid (2002), Shah (2001), Molina (2006), and Park (2011).

9   These military bases as temporary relocation centers mostly housed Vietnamese refugees. For more on how refugees are routed through military bases, see Espiritu (2014).

10 For more on state control of Women of Color reproductive rights, see Roberts (1997, 2000), Nelson (2003), and Ross et al. (2016).

11 For popular representations, see Fadiman (1997) and episodes from the television shows *Doogie Howser, M.D.* (season 3, episode 4), *Grey's Anatomy* (season 2, episode 5), and *House* (season 8, episode 18).

12 I thank Shireen Roshanravan for underscoring this important point in my work.

REFERENCES

Alexander, M. Jacqui. 2005. *Pedagogies of Crossing: Meditations on Feminism, Sexual Politics, Memory, and the Sacred.* Durham, NC: Duke University Press.

Amaro, Ysenia. 2012. "Health House an Unhealthy Work Environment? Workplace Allegations Surface." *Merced Sun-Star,* July 28.

Arax, Mark. 1995. "Hmong Sacrifice of Puppy Reopens Cultural Wounds: Traditions: Immigrant Shaman's Act Stirs Outrage in Fresno, but He Believes It Was Only to Cure His Ill Wife." *Los Angeles Times,* December 16.

Davis, Dána-Ain, and Christa Craven. 2016. *Feminist Ethnography: Thinking through Methodologies, Challenges, and Possibilities.* Lanham, MD: Rowman and Littlefield.

Deb, Basuli. 2016. "Cutting across Imperial Feminisms toward Transnational Feminist Solidarities." *Meridians* 13 (2): 164–88.

Espiritu, Yên Lê. 2014. *Body Counts: The Vietnam War and Militarized Refuge(es)*. Berkeley: University of California Press.

Espiritu, Yên Lê, and Lan Duong. 2018. "Feminist Refugee Epistemology: Reading Displacement in Vietnamese and Syrian Refugee Art." *Signs: Journal of Women in Culture and Society* 43 (3): 587–615.

Fadiman, Anne. 1997. *The Spirit Catches You and You Fall Down: A Hmong Child, Her American Doctors, and the Collision of Two Cultures*. New York: Farrar, Straus and Giroux.

Ferguson, Roderick A. 2004. *Aberrations in Black: Toward a Queer of Color Critique*. Minneapolis: University of Minnesota Press.

Helsel, Deborah, Marilyn Mochel, and Robert Bauer. 2004. "Shamans in a Hmong American Community." *Journal of Alternative and Complementary Medicine* 10 (6): 933–38.

"Hospital's Shaman Program a Success—One Year Later Headliners Revisited." 2010. *Fresno Bee*, October 15.

Kohl-Arenas, Erica, Myrna Martinez Nateras, and Johanna Taylor. 2014. "Cultural Organizing as Critical Praxis: Tamejavi Builds Immigrant Voice, Belonging, and Power." *Journal of Poverty* 18 (1): 5–24.

Luibhéid, Eithne. 2002. *Entry Denied: Controlling Sexuality at the Border*. Minneapolis: University of Minnesota Press.

Mochel, Marilyn, with Palee Moua. 2000. "Hmong Shaman Spiritual Healer Manual." Hmong Shaman Spiritual Healer Policy. Unpublished.

Mohanty, Chandra Talpade. 2003. *Feminism without Borders: Decolonizing Theory, Practicing Solidarity*. Durham, NC: Duke University Press.

Molina, Natalia. 2006. *Fit to Be Citizens? Public Health and Race in Los Angeles, 1879–1939*. Berkeley: University of California Press.

Montemayor, Robert. 1980. "Indochinese Influx Puts Added Strain on Health Clinic in Linda Vista." *Los Angeles Times*, December 1.

Moua, Palee. Interview by Ma Vang, Merced, CA, October 2015 and March 11, 2016.

Nelson, Jennifer. 2003. *Women of Color and the Reproductive Rights Movement*. New York: New York University Press.

———. 2005. "'Hold Your Head and Stick out Your Chin': Community Health and Women's Health in Mound Bayou, Mississippi." *NWSA Journal* 17 (1): 99–118.

Ong, Aihwa. 2003. *Buddha Is Hiding: Refugees, Citizenship, the New America*. Berkeley: University of California Press.

Park, Lisa Sun-Hee. 2011. *Entitled to Nothing: The Struggle for Immigrant Health Care in the Age of Welfare Reform*. New York: New York University Press.

Roberts, Dorothy. 1997. *Killing the Black Body: Race, Reproduction, and the Meaning of Liberty*. New York: Pantheon Books.

———. 2000. "Black Women and the Pill." *Family Planning Perspectives* 32 (2): 92–93.

Ross, Loretta, Elena Gutierrez, Marlene Gerber, and Jael Silliman. 2016. *Undivided Rights: Women of Color Organizing for Reproductive Justice*. Chicago: Haymarket Books.

Shah, Nayan. 2001. *Contagious Divides: Epidemics and Race in San Francisco's Chinatown*. Berkeley: University of California Press.

Taft, Julia Vadala. 1975a. Letter to the Honorable Joshua Eilberg, House of Representations. December 22. In Interagency Task Force for Indochina, Department of State, Center for Hmong Studies Archives, Concordia University, Saint Paul, MN.

———. 1975b. "Memorandum for Senior Civilian Coordinators on Policy Statement on Nontherapeutic Sterilizations in Refugee Relocation Centers." September 2. In Interagency Task Force for Indochina, Department of State, Center for Hmong Studies Archives, Concordia University, Saint Paul, MN.

———. 1975c. "Requests for Abortions by Indochinese Refugees." June 12. Interagency Task Force for Indochina, Department of State, Center for Hmong Studies Archives, Concordia University, Saint Paul, MN.

Vang, Ma. 2016. "Rechronicling Histories: Toward a Hmong Feminist Perspective." In *Claiming Place: On the Agency of Hmong Women*, edited by Chia Youyee Vang, Faith Nibbs, and Ma Vang, 28–55. Minneapolis: University of Minnesota Press.

Warner, Miriam E., and Marilyn Mochel. 1998. "The Hmong and Health Care in Merced, California." *Hmong Studies Journal* 2 (2): 1–30.

Yosso, Tara J. 2005. "Whose Culture Has Capital? A Critical Race Theory Discussion of Community Cultural Wealth." *Race Ethnicity and Education* 8 (1): 69–91.

CHAPTER 9

NEGOTIATING LEGACIES

The "Traffic in Women" and the Politics of
Filipina/o American Feminist Solidarity

GINA VELASCO

I WAIT IN THE AUDIENCE AS *NATIONAL HEROES*, A DRAMATIC
vignette presented at the 2006 Pilipino Cultural Night (PCN) performance,
[Re]creation, at the University of California at Berkeley, begins with a
completely silent, dark stage. I am surrounded by hundreds of expectant
Filipina/o American students and their families, eager to witness this annual
performance of Filipina/o American culture, which is repeated on college
and high school campuses across the West Coast.[1] As I wait in the dark, the
figures on stage are lit sequentially. One by one, the characters' tear-streaked
faces become visible. The main character, a Filipina migrant domestic
worker named Baby, cries out, "This is not my country. This is not my
home. This is not my family. This is not my daughter. My daughter is far
away, sick, dreaming of me holding her in my arms. Yet I hold someone else's
child. It does not matter how much my bones ache, or that I am so tired. I will
work as hard as I can to pay for her school, and her medicine, and her clothes"
(Pilipino American Alliance 2006).

This emotional monologue implicitly references the broader discourse
of the "traffic in women," through which Filipina/o gendered labor migration is figured in Filipina/o diasporic culture. As the characters on stage,
Baby and Flor, tearfully describe the pain of family separation, the young
Filipina/o Americans in the audience are introduced to the contemporary

crisis of the Philippine nation: outward labor migration, in the form of maids, nannies, nurses, and sex workers who provide devalued labor for a global economy. Vignettes such as *National Heroes* teach young Filipina/o Americans about the Philippine nation's reliance on overseas labor migration. *National Heroes* describes the lives of two Filipina domestic helpers working abroad, Flor and Baby. The themes of familial separation and sacrifice structure the narrative of *National Heroes*. Flor must work to support her sick mother and son in the Philippines, and Baby must pay for medicine and healthcare for her sick daughter. While Baby takes care of her employer's child, her interaction with her own daughter is limited to transnational phone calls. The figure of the exploited migrant worker, often represented through the discourse of the "traffic in women," is central to the diasporic imagination offered in *National Heroes*. Through *National Heroes*, the primarily Filipina/o American audience members are introduced to the material reality of the Philippine nation under capitalist globalization, in which migrant workers provide flexible, gendered labor for the Global North.[2]

Filipina/o diasporic cultural production, such as the *National Heroes* vignette, reflects the broader discourses through which Filipina/o diasporic solidarity is imagined. The figure of the Filipina "trafficked woman" is essential to the emergence of Filipina/o American feminism. I argue that two key characteristics of Filipina/o American feminisms are the struggle against the hyperexploitation of gendered Filipina/o labor under capitalist globalization; and an explicitly anti-imperialist framework that foregrounds the violence of US imperialism as the key historical condition of possibility for Filipinas/os in the United States. I consider Filipina/o American feminisms within a transnational frame, as one node in the broader constellation of Filipina/o diasporic feminisms.[3] Galvanized around transnational political campaigns against "sex-trafficking," as well as labor abuses of Filipina migrant workers, Filipina diasporic feminisms critique the gendered effects of globalization and the afterlives of US empire.[4]

From scholarship on gendered labor migration to the work of Filipina/o American feminist organizations, such as GABRIELA USA and Af3irm, the "traffic in women" discourse is central to Filipina/o diasporic feminisms. Feminist scholars in Philippine studies, such as Neferti Tadiar (2004), argue that the figure of the Filipina migrant worker stands in for the subordination of the Philippine nation in the global capitalist order. Feminist social scientists in Filipina/o American studies, such as Robyn Rodriguez (2010) and Ana Guevarra (2010), detail the ways the Philippine nation acts as a labor-brokerage state, exporting the gendered labor of Filipina maids, nannies, nurses, and sex workers. In both scholarly and activist articulations of Filipina/o diasporic feminisms, the figure of the Filipina migrant worker is often collapsed with the figure of the trafficked woman. Many Filipina/o American activists use the discourse of trafficking to refer to the coercive and exploitative labor conditions that Filipina/o migrants experience more broadly, not necessarily within sex work. From the former Gabriela Network's (now Af3irm) long-standing Purple Rose Campaign against sex trafficking to Filipina/o American organizations, such as Damayan, that focus on the rights of migrant domestic workers, the discourse of trafficking is a central rhetorical and analytical framework through which transnational Filipina/o feminist solidarity is articulated.[5]

Focused on the figure of the Filipina "trafficked woman" in both scholarly and popular feminisms, this essay examines the politics of Filipina/o American diasporic feminist solidarity. I ask how Filipina/o American feminists can participate in transnational movements against the exploitation of gendered Philippine labor under capitalist globalization without reproducing problematic state discourses of the "traffic in women," such as the US Trafficking Victims Protection Act (TVPA), which has had negative material effects on the lives of migrant workers.[6] To do so, I put into conversation transnational feminist and Women of Color feminist critiques of the representation of the Third World woman worker with a consideration of the politics of diasporic solidarity.[7] I consider the distinctions and convergences between transnational feminisms and Women of Color feminisms, exploring how each theoretical framework allows for an analysis of the politics of Filipina/o diasporic feminist solidarity, given the pervasive discourse of the "traffic in women," as well as the implications for a broader notion of Asian American feminisms. I ground my analysis in Women of Color feminisms' emphasis on a coalitional politics based on shared political goals rather than an essentializing notion of sameness (Moraga and Anzaldúa 2002; Lorde 2010).

In particular, I emphasize the dual positionality of Filipina/o Americans, often perceived as inheritors of US capital, as well as interlocutors between the feminized Philippines and the masculine power of US imperialism and militarism.[8] Situated between US empire and Philippine revolutionary nationalisms, the Filipina/o American feminist is located in the belly of the beast, even as she is an important actor in transnational political movements against US imperialism and capitalist globalization. I write from the position of a queer, Filipina American scholar-activist who is both deeply committed to and implicated in Filipina/o diasporic feminist social movements, as well as attentive to the risky politics of representation in the traffic in women discourse. I thus situate my scholarly voice within, not apart from, the following debates.

The traffic in women discourse has been a thorny subject of debate in transnational feminist theory for some time. Within the broader sex wars of feminism, along with debates on pornography, the traffic in women discourse has galvanized fierce debates about the legitimacy of sex work versus the forced labor of trafficking. Transnational feminist scholars have critiqued the representation of "trafficked women" as victims, contesting the broader representation of the Third World woman worker in Western feminism as lacking agency and in need of rescue.[9] Indeed, the figure of the "trafficked woman" has been essential to broader transnational feminist organizing, and to Filipina/o American solidarity organizing in particular. As Mina Roces has noted in the context of women's movements in the Philippines, the Filipina trafficked woman is an important figure in feminist narratives that critique the prostitution of Filipina women in the global sex trade.[10] Roces (2012, 66) notes that "the dominant narrative is that prostitution is identified as VAW [violence against women] and not sex work."

Although many Filipina/o American feminist groups have organizational and material ties to women's movements in the Philippines, Filipina/o American feminists must also contend with the effects of the traffic in women discourse deployed by the US state, given the passage of the Trafficking Victims Protection Act in 2000. The US state discourse of sex trafficking bolsters distinctions between US citizens and nonnationals, drawing on implicitly racialized and gendered notions of citizenship. Filipina/o American feminists' use of the traffic in women discourse must be situated within the broader US discursive landscape of popular and state discourses about trafficking, which feminist scholar Julietta Hua (2011, xix) argues are constituted by "government documents, media coverage, academic studies, and nonprofit, nongovernmental literatures." She describes the way images of sex workers construct racialized and gendered notions of US national belonging (7). As Hua notes, US "state documents disproportionately represent trafficking victims as immigrants—nonnationals who are outside the normative parameters of national citizenship" (72). While passage of the Trafficking Victims Protection Act (TVPA) has discursively constructed the "trafficked woman" as a racialized Other within US racial formations, it has also had negative material effects on the lives of Filipina/o migrant workers in other national sites of Filipina/o transnational migration, such as Japan.

While legislation like the TVPA promises to protect victims, state antitrafficking discourses often limit the transnational mobility of migrants. The material effects of antitrafficking legislation are a key context for situating Filipina/o diasporic feminists' use of the traffic in women discourse. Sociologist Rhacel Salazar Parreñas (2008, 137) notes that antitrafficking laws have led to increased migration restrictions specifically for women, often resulting in increased vulnerability and exploitation for Filipina migrant workers. Filipina entertainers in Japan have specifically been targeted as "trafficked persons." In her ethnography of Filipina entertainers / bar workers in Japan, Parreñas argues that the TVPA has led to increased requirements for professional training of Filipina entertainers by the Philippine state and necessitated working with middlemen brokers in the Philippines (137). According to Parreñas, the debt incurred by Filipina entertainers required to undergo expensive "professional" training by Philippine middleman brokers constitutes a form of debt bondage that amounts to coerced labor (157). Thus, the very laws that attempt to prevent trafficking of Filipina/os may actually lead to conditions of forced labor.

State and nongovernmental discourses of trafficking that focus almost exclusively on sex trafficking, equating all forms of sex work with sex trafficking, have negative material effects on the lives of migrant workers more broadly. In contrast to the dominant discourse of sex trafficking, feminist sociologist Kamala Kempadoo (2005, xvii) argues that the majority of trafficking occurs in the hospitality, manufacturing, and service industries, not in the sex industry. However, in the dominant discourse of sex trafficking, voluntary prostitution is linked to sex trafficking, which is framed within a moralizing discourse that Denise Brennan (2010, 143) calls a "sex panic." Brennan argues that the overemphasis on sex trafficking in antitrafficking efforts has resulted in less effort focused on other forms of forced labor (141). For example, in 2004, all but one of the fifty-nine prosecutions brought against traffickers involved sexual exploitation (142). In addition, the TVPA Reauthorization Acts of 2003 and 2005 incorporated an antiprostitution gag rule, which prohibited international NGOs from receiving US funding unless they have a policy explicitly opposing sex work (Chang and Kim 2007, 3). This has alienated sex workers from anti-AIDS/HIV efforts and prevented sex workers from protecting their sexual health, as healthcare workers and social service providers are required to denounce sex work to receive US funding (Chang and Kim 2007, 15).

In addition, US law enforcement's "raid and rescue" approach to trafficking has led to increased criminalization and detention of immigrants. For example, Grace Chang and Kathleen Kim (2007, 11) note that a 2005 "raid and rescue" case, dubbed Operation Gilded Cage, involved raiding ten brothels in San Francisco, leading to the "rescue" of 120 migrant women. However, after questioning the women and finding out that they were voluntary participants in sex work, and thus not legal victims of trafficking, federal officials placed them in immigration detention. Migrants who identify themselves as voluntary or consenting participants in their migration or employment at any point are deemed ineligible for benefits under T-visas as legal victims of trafficking. US law enforcement's "prosecutorial focus of sex trafficking alienates migrant rights advocates, who fear that antitrafficking work invites excessive prosecution in immigrant communities while ignoring the harm these communities face as exploited workers in domestic work, agricultural work, and in industrial and factory work" (Chang and Kim 2007, 5).

This overemphasis on sex trafficking is characteristic of some Filipina/o American feminist political campaigns as well. For example, Af3irm's Purple Rose Campaign uses a discursive framework that equates trafficking with sexual violence. As one of the oldest Filipina/o American feminist organizations, Af3irm (previously GabNet) has played a significant historical role in the development of Filipina/o American feminisms.[11] Af3irm's website describes the Purple Rose Campaign: "We renew our resolve and push forward as the Purple Rose Campaign evolves to encompass sex trafficking and mail order brides into a nationally-coordinated campaign against sexual violence towards and commodification of transnational/women of color" (Af3irm 2014).

Although Mina Roces (2012, 66) has noted that the discourse of sex work as a form of sexual violence—often equated with migration practices such as correspondence marriage ("mail order brides")—is a dominant narrative in women's movements in the Philippines, this discourse has been critiqued by some transnational feminist and Filipina/o American feminist scholars as moralistic and implicitly anti–sex worker (Kempadoo 2001; Boris, Gilmore, and Parreñas 2010; Brennan 2010). Given the broader debates on trafficking and sex work among both Philippine feminists and Filipina/o feminists in the diaspora, my intention is not to malign the efforts of Af3irm, or other organizations concerned with the welfare of Filipina sex workers, but to emphasize how, as Filipina/o American feminist activists and scholars, our use of the discourse of sex trafficking may buttress US state policies that result in increased detention, deportation, and harm to migrant workers.

In contrast to a moralistic framework that equates all forms of gendered labor with sexual labor and thus sexual violence, a discursive and material shift is necessary to safeguard migrant workers' rights. Damayan, a New York City–based workers' rights organization, focuses on domestic labor exploitation, not prostitution, in its antitrafficking campaign, Baklas: Break Free from Labor Trafficking and Modern Day Slavery, which is co-organized by the feminist organization Women Organized to Resist and Defend (WORD). Rather than focus exclusively on sexual labor or prostitution, Damayan looks at cases such as that of Dema Ramos, "a domestic worker, who was trafficked to the US by a Kuwaiti diplomat, and labored as a domestic worker in the household, where she was forced to work at least 18 hours a day, seven days a week with no days off, for approximately 69 cents per hour" (Damayan 2016). Although not explicitly framed in feminist terms, campaigns such as Damayan's Baklas antitrafficking campaign are implicitly feminist in that they struggle against the coercive working conditions of forms of gendered labor—domestic labor—that can rightly be considered human trafficking. Indeed, Brennan (2010, 144) argues that migrants' rights organizations are better situated than antiprostitution organizations to "find trafficked individuals and to facilitate migrant activists in taking leadership roles in the fight for better working conditions."[12] Thus, it is crucial to foreground migrant worker activism as an integral component of Filipina/o American feminist activism.

As feminist scholars and activists, we must work toward combating the conditions of exploited and coerced racialized and gendered migrant labor, while remaining skeptical of moralistic frameworks of trafficking that focus almost exclusively on sexual labor as violence against women. Thus, we need to reframe the traffic in women discourse to address the reality of trafficked migrant labor today. As such, it is crucial that Filipina/o American and Filipina/o diasporic feminists think critically about how to avoid the reification of state and nongovernmental discourses of trafficking that focus almost exclusively on sexual labor—to the detriment of other forms of gendered and racialized labor that are trafficked in a global economy—which also increase the risk of detention and deportation for migrant workers who are targeted by the "raid and rescue" practices of US law enforcement. Emphasizing the politics of representation in the kinds of language and images we use to discuss gendered labor and antitrafficking campaigns is vital to avoid reproducing an antitrafficking discourse that actually contributes to the increased exploitation and precarity of gendered migrant workers, whether they perform sexual labor or domestic labor. Indeed, Parreñas (2008, 166) argues that feminists must reclaim the discourse of trafficking, unburdening this term of the moralistic, anti–sex work framework that characterizes the dominant form of this discourse and remobilizing it to attend to the actual conditions of coerced labor, both gendered and otherwise, that accompany neoliberal capitalism. Parreñas contends, "'Trafficking' is a term that feminists need to reclaim. We need to recognize that the multiple forms of trafficking in existence in the twenty-first century require multiple solutions. Not all trafficked persons are in need of rescue, rehabilitation, and reintegration. Antitrafficking campaigns should advocate for improved conditions of labor and migration. . . . But, rather than facing restrictions that discourage and make difficult their labor migration to Japan, trafficked persons such as the talents whom I met in Japan need greater control over their migration and labor" (166).

Instead of enacting laws and policies that make migrants even more vulnerable to trafficking, such as the criminalization of sex work or increased requirements for training for entertainers, feminists—and Filipina/o diasporic feminists in particular—must carefully consider how our participation in antitrafficking, anti–sex work discourse may actually contribute to greater precarity for migrants performing gendered labor. To do so, it is essential to differentiate dominant state and popular discourses of trafficking from the ways this discourse can be used productively, and accurately, in grassroots political campaigns.

The dominant discourse of sex trafficking as the primary form of trafficking relies on what Galusca (2012, 3) terms a "regime of truth," citing Michel Foucault's work on discourse and power. Although Galusca refers specifically to US investigative journalism's sensationalist covering of sex trafficking in the popular media, this "regime of truth" regarding sex trafficking characterizes state and nongovernmental discourses as well. The figure of the victimized trafficked woman also characterizes the work of international feminist NGOs such as the Coalition Against Trafficking in Women (CATW), presenting US journalists and feminist activists as Western saviors of trafficked women from the Global South (Galusca 2012, 2). In investigative journalism and popular media in particular, the "regime of truth" about trafficking is constituted through the production of truth claims, "a complex process whereby empirical claims, based on journalistic investigations and witnessing, draw on emotionally charged imagery of sexual exploitation and commodification" (Galusca 2012, 5). However, this regime of truth is not limited to popular media; it is reproduced in Filipina/o diasporic and Filipina/o American political discourse as well. The risk of representing migrant workers from the Global South as victims in need of saving by feminists in the Global North haunts Filipina/o diasporic and Filipina/o American popular discourse.[13] How, then, can Filipina/o American and Filipina/o diasporic feminists organize against the extreme exploitation of coerced—indeed, trafficked—forms of gendered labor, without reproducing a regime of truth that relies on a static figure of the Filipina victim of sex trafficking? What politics of representation are necessary to avoid the political pitfalls of diasporic feminist solidarity?

NEGOTIATING LEGACIES, FORGING FUTURES: ARTICULATING A COALITIONAL ASIAN AMERICAN FEMINISM

The legacy of Women of Color feminisms and transnational feminisms provides theoretical and political inspiration for future articulations of both Filipina/o American feminisms and Asian American feminisms. While much of the critique of the traffic in women discourse emerges within more recent transnational feminist scholarship, I find it useful to return to Chandra Mohanty's (1997, 7) earlier conceptualization of the Third World woman worker as a subject position from which to imagine and enact transnational feminist politics and solidarity. Mohanty argues that a focus on the Third World woman worker "is not an argument for just recognizing the 'common experiences' of Third-World women workers, it *is* an argument for recognizing (concrete, not abstract) 'common interests' and the potential bases of cross-national solidarity—a common context of struggle." This focus on the Third World woman worker shifts the emphasis from the "victimhood" of trafficked women to an analysis of how the specific social location of the Third World woman worker "illuminates and explains crucial features of the capitalist processes of exploitation and domination" (7). Although Mohanty wrote this article more than twenty years ago, it is worthwhile to revisit the significance of the politics of representation of the Third World woman worker to Filipina/o diasporic feminist solidarity. A focus on the systematic exploitation of racialized and gendered labor, embodied in the figure of the Third World woman worker, encourages us to envision a pro–migrant worker, pro–sex worker approach to ending labor trafficking. In contrast, the dominant discourse of the sexual traffic in

women positions sex workers as victims within a moralistic, heteronormative logic that is often implicitly anti–sex worker.

Thus, Filipina/o American and Filipina/o diasporic feminist solidarity
can be imagined and enacted in struggle against the "regime of truth" of
sex trafficking, in order to reconceptualize "Third-World women as agents
rather than victims" (Mohanty 1997, 7). An emphasis on gendered labor, or
"women's work," rather than sexual exploitation and violence, returns us
to Mohanty's notion of the Third World woman worker as a key subject
position from which to imagine transnational solidarity. Mohanty describes
"women's work," or gendered labor, as a key framework of analysis: "I argue
for a notion of *political solidarity* and *common interests*, defined as a community or collectivity among women workers across class, race, and national
boundaries which is based on shared material interests and identity and
common ways of reading the world" (8, emphasis mine). While it may seem
that Mohanty is arguing for solidarity based on a common cultural identity or experience, the common interests she speaks of draw on a shared
social location in relation to the exploitation of neoliberal capitalism.

Women of Color feminisms provide a generative framework for considering Mohanty's call for a transnational "common context of struggle." Sandra Soto's (2005) germinal article, "Where in the Transnational World Are
US Women of Color?," elucidates the distinctions and convergences between
transnational feminisms and US Women of Color feminisms. Soto argues
that, despite attempts by some transnational feminists to distance themselves from Women of Color feminisms, "it is *at best* premature to position
women of color (as an area of study and/or political collective) in contra-
distinction to transnational feminist studies and practices" (117). In response
to the argument that the figure of the woman of color functions as a homogenized figure of racial and gender difference, Soto reminds the reader of
the original charge of Women of Color feminisms, which, rather than eliding difference—whether racial, national, sexual, gender, or class—has been
to emphasize the impossibility of reducing women of color to a unitary,
uncomplicated collective (119). Indeed, as the original name of one of the
oldest academic feminist of color collectives, the Research Cluster for the
Study of Women of Color in Collaboration and Conflict (advised by Angela
Davis), demonstrates, the coalitional political project of Women of Color
feminisms has never been an easy or "natural" project.[14] Chela Sandoval
articulates the risk of homogenization in efforts toward a Women of Color
feminist coalitional politics in her critique of the 1981 National Women's
Studies Association Conference:

Though empowered as a unity of women of color, the cost is that we find it easy to objectify the occupants of every other category. The dangers in creating a new heroine, a political "unity" of third world women who together take the power to create new kinds of "others" is that our unity becomes forged at the cost of nurturing a world of "enemies." And in the enthusiasm of our empowered sisterhood, perhaps a greater cost lies in the erasure of our many differences. However, if one attribute of power is its mobile nature, there can be no simple way of identifying our enemies or our friends. (1990, 65)

Sandoval's recognition of the uneasy notion of Women of Color feminisms as a collective project, her emphasis that the "greater cost lies in the erasure of our many differences," reiterates a key tenet of Women of Color feminisms. We are not necessarily "natural" allies. Indeed, these differences are key to identifying what forms of coalitional political work can happen under the banner of Women of Color feminisms. In her reflection on the legacy of *This Bridge Called My Back*, M. Jacqui Alexander (2002, 88) cites Paolo Freire: "To wrestle with these questions we must adopt, as daily practice, ways of being and relating, modes of analyzing, strategies of organizing in which we constantly mobilize identification and solidarity, across all borders, as key elements in the repertoire of risks necessary to see ourselves as part of one another, even in the context of difference." Alexander points to the legacy of Women of Color feminisms in not only building intentional coalition across difference among US women of color, but in recognizing the transnational dimensions of solidarity.

Thus, the legacy of key texts such as *This Bridge Called My Back* is not an essentialist view of women of color as a homogenized collective, but rather one that paves the path for forms of transnational feminist solidarity. Alexander's call to "constantly mobilize identification and solidarity, across all borders" is generative for envisioning forms of Filipina/o American participation in Filipina/o diasporic feminist solidarity. Given our social location in the imperial center, the United States, Filipina/o American feminists' use of the discourse of sex trafficking is especially fraught. Within a broader material context in which US law enforcement targets migrant workers through "raid and rescue" tactics, while the effect of the US TVPA in the Philippines leads to greater debt bondage for Filipina entertainers in Japan, we must be careful in the ways we mobilize a discourse of trafficking. The location of Filipina/o Americans in the United States and the increased criminalization of migrants in the

current US political context make it especially crucial to resist US state policies (such as the TVPA) and practices of antitrafficking that lead to greater
detention and deportation of migrants while limiting funds for international
NGOs that refuse to take a stance against sex work. A radically different
discourse of trafficking that focuses on the rights of all migrant workers—
including sex workers—is necessary to enact transnational and diasporic
Filipina/o feminist solidarity in the face of neoliberal capitalism.

While Women of Color feminisms, and their intellectual descendants,
transnational feminisms, are generative models for envisioning Filipina/o
diasporic solidarity, Women of Color feminisms' recognition of intentional
coalitional politics across differently racialized and gendered social locations is also a key framework for theorizing the relationship of Filipina/o
American feminisms to Asian American feminisms. Echoing both Soto's
(2005, 119) and Sandoval's (1990, 65) critiques of uncomplicated notions of
unity among Women of Color, we must similarly interrogate the inclusion
of Filipina/o American feminisms in the project of Asian American feminisms, if we are to avoid the simplistic notions of unity or inclusion that
Soto and Sandoval resist. To do so, it is first necessary to consider the broader
relationship between Filipina/o American studies and Asian American
studies.

As many Filipina/o American studies scholars have noted, the inclusion
of Filipina/o Americans into the project of Asian America is an uneasy one
at best, due to the enduring presence of US imperialism as the constitutive
condition of possibility for Filipinas/os in the United States (Campomanes
1995, 8; Espiritu 2003, 25; Rodriguez 2006, 148; San Juan 1998, 20). E. San
Juan (1998, 20) argues that "the chief distinction of Filipinos from other
Asians domiciled here is that their country of origin was the object of violent colonization by US finance capital. It is this foundational event, not the
fabled presence in Louisiana of Filipino fugitives from the Spanish galle-
ons, that establishes the limit and potential of the Filipino lifeworld." Asian
American studies' tendency to focus on notions of inclusion and exclusion
through immigration often obscures US empire as the founding historical
event for the presence of Filipinas/os in the United States (Chuh 2003, 34).
Thus, the incorporation of Filipina/o American feminisms into Asian
American feminisms is not an easy or uncomplicated theoretical and political move.

If Women of Color feminisms have taught us to avoid demographic or
categorical uses of the term *women of color*, forcing us to think through the
intentional use of the term as a form of political coalitional work, can we

use a similar approach to theorize the concept of Asian American feminisms? Filipina/o American feminisms are not categorized within the concept of Asian American feminisms simply due to demographic reasons. Instead, political and intellectual labor must be put into articulating what kinds of coalitional possibility make this a useful and necessary endeavor. What defines the "coalitional moment" of Filipina/o American feminisms as a form of Asian American feminism? A "coalitional moment," according to Karma Chavez (2013, 8), is a moment in which "political issues coincide or merge in the public sphere in ways that create space to reenvision or potentially reconstruct rhetorical imaginaries." From this frame, what kinds of coalitional politics would make the broader rubric of Asian American feminisms key to the goals of Filipina/o American feminisms?

The centrality of anti-imperialist struggle that situates Filipina/o American feminisms within the legacy of Women of Color feminist anti-imperialist critique is also key to envisioning Filipina/o American participation within a broader notion of Asian American feminism. Within the genealogy of Women of Color feminisms, there is a long history of anti-imperialist thought and solidarity with the Global South. From the use of the term *US Third World feminism*, which implies solidarity between US Women of Color and the Global South, to the critiques of US imperialism in *This Bridge Called My Back*, to the more recent political and scholarly work of Incite! Women of Color Against Violence, Women of Color feminisms have long emphasized an analysis of US imperialism as a key tenet of their political critique (Moraga and Anzaldúa 2002, xvii; Incite! 2006). Cherríe Moraga (2002, xvi) wrote, in the foreword to the 2002 edition of *This Bridge Called My Back*, "A generation ago, our definition of a US feminism of color was shaped by a late 1970s understanding of colonialism and neocolonialism in the United States, as well as our intra-cultural critique of the sexism and heterosexism in race-based liberation movements." The politics of Third World solidarity that animated earlier iterations of Women of Color feminisms and the explicitly anti-imperialist analysis offered by later iterations—particularly after the start of the war on terror in 2001—are also key elements of contemporary Filipina/o American feminisms, given their focus on the gendered effects of US imperialism in the Philippines and their strong connections with Philippines-based women's organizations.

Likewise, a shift to an explicitly anti-imperialist analytical framework in Asian American feminisms offers a coalitional moment for articulating a common context of struggle with Filipina/o American feminisms, beyond a simple demographic inclusion of Filipina/o Americans into Asian America. Much like the ways Women of Color feminists identified struggle against US colonialism and imperialism as a coalitional political goal in the 1970s, Asian American feminisms can articulate a similar politics of solidarity with Filipina/o American feminisms, grounded in a shared critique of US empire. Expanding on the foundation of earlier Asian American feminist texts that articulated critiques of transnational gendered Asian and Asian American labor in relation to the US nation-state and global capitalism, Asian American feminisms must foreground US empire, and its relationship to exploited Filipina migrant labor, as key sites of coalitional political struggle with Filipina/o American feminisms.[15]

A CRITICAL LOVE: VISIONS FOR ASIAN AMERICAN AND FILIPINA/O AMERICAN FEMINIST SOLIDARITY

As I argued earlier in this chapter, Filipina/o American feminist participation in Filipina/o diasporic political movements hinges on the central figure of the trafficked woman, a sign of the transnational labor upon which the Philippine economy relies in the context of neoliberal capitalism. As such, Filipina/o American feminisms can take political and intellectual inspiration from the legacy of both Women of Color feminisms and transnational feminisms in negotiating the politics of representation in the traffic in women discourse. From transnational feminisms, Filipina/o Americans can return to Mohanty's (1997, 7) consideration of the politics of representing the Third World woman worker. In doing so, we must emphasize the material effects of state and nongovernmental discourses of the traffic in women, taking into consideration the increased exploitation and vulnerability of migrant workers caused by US state laws such as Trafficking Victims Protection Act (TVPA). Parreñas (2008, 157) argues that the TVPA actually leads to conditions of debt bondage for Filipina bar workers / entertainers in Japan, who are forced to go into debt to finance the increased Philippine state requirements for "professional" training. Similarly, the overemphasis on the moralistic discourse of sex trafficking occludes the actual cases of coerced, trafficked labor, which primarily occur in the hospitality, manufacturing, and service industries (Kempadoo 2005, xvii). By foregrounding the material effects of the discursive construction of trafficking as a "regime of truth," Filipina/o American feminists can interrogate how our political campaigns may contribute to increasing precarity for Filipina/o migrant workers (Galusca 2012, 3). Indeed, a shift to emphasizing migrant workers' rights,

rather than a moralizing discourse of sex trafficking, is often more effective in combating the hyperexploitation of gendered Filipina/o labor
(Brennan 2010, 144). Ultimately, Filipina/o American feminist participation
in Filipina/o diasporic feminist solidarity means recognizing both our differences—in particular, our specific social location in the United States,
given the negative effects of US state antitrafficking policies on migrants
both here and abroad—as well as our commonalities with comrades across
the Filipina/o diaspora.

A return to the vision and legacy of Women of Color feminisms, in its
emphasis on an intentional coalitional politics that recognizes—instead of
eliding—difference, is crucial for Filipina/o American feminisms, as well as
a broader notion of Asian American feminisms. Filipina/o American feminisms can draw inspiration from Women of Color feminisms' emphasis on
recognizing difference, as opposed to simplified notions of sameness within
collectivity, in theorizing our participation in both Filipina/o diasporic feminisms and Asian American feminisms. As Filipina/o Americans, we are
positioned as the supposed inheritors of US capital, as well as racialized
minorities in a white supremacist US state. Similarly, Women of Color feminisms' recognition of distinct social locations within political coalitions and
their enduring emphasis on anti-imperialist solidarity provide a theoretical
and political blueprint for enacting a vision of Asian American feminisms that can encompass the struggle against US empire fundamental
to Filipina/o American feminisms.

Avoiding a simple demographic inclusion model, which would posit
sameness based on a notion of similar racialization compared to Asians in
the United States, a coalitional politics would require Asian American feminists to articulate an investment in struggles against US empire, an essential element of Filipina/o American feminisms. Similarly, it is crucial to
distinguish the social locations of various Asian American groups, as the
racialization, access to higher education, income levels, and so on, in
Filipina/o American communities can vary greatly from other Asian American groups. Lastly, a return to the Women of Color feminist legacy of
internal critique and loving disagreement—the "conflict" in the name
Women of Color in Collaboration and Conflict—is crucial for both
Filipina/o American and Asian American feminisms. Here, I take inspiration from feminist activist-scholars such as Nadine Naber (2012), who critiques Arab and Arab American national liberation movements using a
feminist and queer analysis even as she remains committed to and imbri-
cated within these movements. Building on the legacies of transnational and

Women of Color feminisms, our movements must be able to sustain these forms of loving internal critique and debate. There is no moving forward without it.

NOTES

1   Pilipino Cultural Nights (PCNs) or Pilipino Cultural Celebrations (PCC) are annual performances organized by Filipina/o American students at universities across the US West Coast. With budgets in the tens of thousands of dollars, these events bring together hundreds of Filipina/o Americans for a night of traditional Philippine dance, hip hop dance, and theater. See Gonzalvez (2009).

2   This analysis of *National Heroes* draws on my discussion of this vignette in my forthcoming book, under contract with the University of Illinois Press.

3   I use the term *Filipina/o American feminisms* to refer to feminist movements made up primarily of Filipina/o Americans and based in the United States. I include Filipina/o American feminisms within the broader notion of Filipina/o diasporic feminisms, which is not limited to the United States. The organizations that make up Filipina/o American feminist movements often emphasize their connection to the Philippines, focusing on the exploitation of gendered Filipina/o labor and the lasting effects of US imperialism. For example, Filipina/o diasporic feminist organizations have emerged in Canada and throughout the multiple sites of the global labor diaspora of Filipinas/os.

4   There is a wide breadth of scholarship in both transnational feminisms and Women of Color feminisms on the gendered and racialized international division of labor. See Chang (2000), Parreñas (2008), R. Rodriguez (2010), and Guevarra (2010).

5   For a description of the Purple Rose Campaign organized by Af3irm, see the #Not YourFetish campaign (Af3irm 2014). See the antitrafficking campaign of Damayan, based in New York City (Damayan 2016). While Af3irm includes both domestic workers and sexual labor under the rubric of trafficking, Damayan focuses on labor abuses of migrant domestic workers.

6   The Trafficking Victims Protection Act (TVPA) was passed in 2000, packaged with the Violence Against Women Act (HR 3355), intended in part to provide protection for noncitizen dependents surviving abuse. According to Hua (2011, xvii–xix), the TVPA defined the context of trafficking in terms that emphasized the sexual exploitation of women and children, including "prostitution, pornography, sex tourism, and other commercial sexual services." With the TVPA came the establishment of the US state infrastructure, bureaucracy, and resources to address trafficking, including the Office to Monitor and Combat Trafficking. Hua notes that between 2001 and 2005, an estimated $375 million was allocated to antitrafficking efforts.

7   See Kempadoo and Doezema (1998) for a critique of the traffic in women discourse.

8   I discuss the position of the figure of the Filipina/o American *balikbayan* (the expatriate who returns to the Philippines) in my forthcoming book from University of Illinois Press. I also discuss Vicente Rafael's analysis of the figure of the Filipina/o American *balikbayan* within the Philippine popular imaginary. Vicente Rafael (2000, 208) distinguishes between overseas contract workers and *balikbayans*:

"Whereas overseas contract workers (OCWs) are seen to return from conditions of near abjection, *balikbayans* are frequently viewed to be steeped in their own sense of superiority, serving only to fill others with a sense of envy."

9   While transnational feminists Kamala Kempadoo and Jo Doezema (1998) argue that migrant sex work, which is often collapsed under the traffic in women discourse, is a legitimate form of labor that should come with rights and protections, feminists such as Kathleen Barry (1995) argue that all forms of sex work constitute violence against women. Kathleen Barry founded the Coalition Against Trafficking in Women (CATW).

10 Mina Roces (2012) describes the broader narrative of Filipina prostitutes as victims, arguing that this has been a powerful narrative for Filipina feminist organizing in the Philippines. Roces notes that, simultaneously, Filipina women's organizations seek to transform prostitutes into political agents, as "feminist women's organizations have been proactive in forging alliances with the former prostitutes and giving them a feminist education through participation in gender workshops and by co-opting them in some activist campaigns" (64). Roces intentionally uses the term *prostitution*, as this is the discourse used in the Philippines, as opposed to the term *sex work*, which has been taken up by many feminists who argue that sex work is a legitimate form of labor (Kempadoo and Doezema 1998). I choose to use the term *sex work* to align myself with the latter position.

11 My intention is not to focus my critique exclusively on Af3irm as an organization. As stated in the previous note, Mina Roces (2012) describes how the discourse of sex trafficking, in which sex workers are presented as victims (whether they are voluntarily participating in the sex trade or not), is a rhetorical and political strategy used by many women's organizations in the Philippines as well. Thus Af3irm is not unique in its emphasis on sex work as a form of violence. Despite my critique of the Purple Rose Campaign's framing of sex trafficking as a form of violence, I recognize Af3irm's (and previously GabNet's) significant contributions to Filipina/o American feminisms, such as its campaigns against the negative effects of economic globalization and forms of US imperialism such as the Visiting Forces Agreement (Enrile and Levid 2009, 102). For a history of GabNet, see Enrile and Levid (2009).

12 Other Filipina diasporic political organizations in the United States, such as Filipinas for Rights and Empowerment (FIRE), based in New York City, organize explicitly around women's issues, while also focusing on migrant labor issues. See FIRE's website, https://firenyc.wordpress.com/about-us.

13 In my forthcoming book, I discuss the politics of representing Filipina sex workers in the Filipina American film *Sin City Diary*, directed by Rachel Rivera (1992).

14 Established in 1991 by graduate students and faculty at the University of California, Santa Cruz, the Research Cluster for the Study of Women of Color in Collaboration and Conflict (WOC Research Cluster) was supported by funds provided by Professor Angela Y. Davis, UC Presidential Chair from 1995 to 1998, and the Center for Cultural Studies. The WOC Research Cluster held conferences, organized one of the longest-running Women of Color film festivals, and developed and co-taught curricula. Members of the WOC Research Cluster went on to found the activist-scholar

organization Incite! Women of Color Against Violence. As a member of this group from 2001 to 2008, I co-curated the annual Women of Color film festival, coordinated a research symposium, participated in a dissertation writing group, and co-taught a course, "Women of Color: Genders and Sexualities," with Elisa Diana Huerta. See the Research Cluster's website, http://www2.ucsc.edu/woc/, accessed on August 23, 2016.

15 Here, I recognize the history of foundational Asian American feminist scholars who have focused on critiques of transnational gendered labor under global capitalism. See Lowe (1996) and Kang (1997).

REFERENCES

Af3irm. 2014. "Af3irm Marks Milestone 15 Years of the Purple Rose Campaign, Renews Resolve for Justice with Launch of Transnational Work Here and Abroad." Press release, February 14. www.af3irm.org/af3irm/2014/02/af3irm-marks-milestone-15-years-of-the-purple-rose-campaign-renews-resolve-for-justice-with-launch-of-transnational-work-here-and-abroad.

Alexander, M. Jacqui. 2002. "Remembering This Bridge, Remembering Ourselves: Yearning, Memory, and Desire." In *This Bridge We Call Home*, edited by Gloria E. Anzaldúa and Analouise Keating, 81–103. New York: Routledge.

Barry, Kathleen. 1995. *The Prostitution of Sexuality*. New York: New York University Press.

Boris, Eileen, Stephanie Gilmore, and Rhacel Parreñas. 2010. "Sexual Labors: Interdisciplinary Perspectives toward Sex as Work." *Sexualities* 13 (2): 131–37.

Brennan, Denise. 2010. "Thoughts on Finding and Assisting Individuals in Forced Labor in the USA." *Sexualities* 13 (2): 139–52.

Campomanes, Oscar. 1995. "The New Nation's Forgotten and Forgetful Citizens: Unrepresentability and Unassimiliability in Filipino American Postcolonials." *Hitting Critical Mass, a Journal of Asian American Cultural Criticism* 2 (2): 145–200.

Chang, Grace. 2000. *Disposable Domestics: Immigrant Women Workers in the Global Economy*. Cambridge, MA: South End Press.

Chang, Grace, and Kathleen Kim. 2007. "Reconceptualizing Approaches to Human Trafficking: New Directions and Perspectives from the Field(s)." *Stanford Journal of Civil Rights and Civil Liberties* 3 (2): 317–44; Loyola-LA Legal Studies Paper No. 2007-47. Available at SSRN: https://ssrn.com/abstract=1051601.

Chavez, Karma. 2013. *Queer Migration Politics: Activist Rhetoric and Coalitional Possibilities*. Urbana: University of Illinois Press.

Chuh, Kandace. 2003. *Imagine Otherwise: On Asian Americanist Critique*. Durham, NC: Duke University Press.

Damayan. 2016. "Baklas: End Labor Trafficking and Modern Day Slavery." Accessed August 23. https://www.damayanmigrants.org/campaigns/baklas.

Enrile, Annalise V., and Jollene Levid. 2009. "GAB Net: A Case Study of Transnational Sisterhood and Organizing." *Amerasia Journal* 35 (1): 92–107.

Espiritu, Yên Lê. 2003. *Home Bound: Filipino American Lives across Cultures, Communities, and Countries*. Berkeley: University of California Press.

Galusca, Roxana. 2012. "Slave Hunters, Brothel Busters, and Feminist Interventions: Investigative Journalists as Anti-Sex-Trafficking Humanitarians." *Feminist Formations* 24 (2): 1–24.

Gonzalvez, Theodore. 2009. *The Day the Dancers Stayed: Performing in the Filipino/American Diaspora*. Philadelphia: Temple University Press.

Guevarra, Anna Romina. 2010. *Marketing Dreams, Manufacturing Heroes: The Transnational Labor Brokering of Filipino Workers*. New Brunswick, NJ: Rutgers University Press.

Hua, Julietta. 2011. *Trafficking Women's Human Rights*. Minneapolis: University of Minnesota Press.

Incite! Women of Color against Violence. 2006. *The Color of Violence: The Incite! Anthology*. Boston: South End Press.

Kang, Laura Hyun Yi. 1997. "Si(gh)ting Asian/American Women as Transnational Labor." *positions* 5 (2): 403–37.

Kempadoo, Kamala. 2001. "Women of Color and the Global Sex Trade: Transnational Feminist Perspectives." *Meridians* 1 (2): 28–51.

———. 2005. "Introduction: From Moral Panic to Global Justice: Changing Perspectives on Trafficking." In *Trafficking and Prostitution Reconsidered: New Perspectives on Migration, Sex Work, and Human Rights*, edited by Kamala Kempadoo, Jyoti Sanghera, and Bandana Pattanaik, vii–xxxiv. Boulder, CO: Paradigm.

Kempadoo, Kamala, and Jo Doezema, eds. 1998. *Global Sex Workers: Rights, Resistance, and Redefinition*. New York: Routledge.

Lorde, Audre. 2010. "The Master's Tools Will Never Dismantle the Master's House." In *Feminist Theory: A Reader*, edited by Wendy Kolmar and Frances Bartkowski, 15–17. New York: McGraw Hill.

Lowe, Lisa. 1996. *Immigrant Acts: On Asian American Cultural Politics*. Durham, NC: Duke University Press.

Mohanty, Chandra. 1997. "Women Workers and Capitalist Scripts: Ideologies of Domination, Common Interests, and the Politics of Solidarity." In *Feminist Genealogies, Colonial Legacies, Democratic Futures*, edited by Jacqui M. Alexander and Chandra Mohanty, 3–29. New York: Routledge.

Moraga, Cherríe, and Gloria Anzaldúa. 2002. *This Bridge Called My Back: Writings by Radical Women of Color*. New York: Women of Color Press.

Naber, Nadine. 2012. *Arab America: Gender, Cultural Politics, and Activism*. New York: New York University Press.

Parreñas, Rhacel Salazar. 2008. *The Force of Domesticity: Filipina Migrants and Globalization*. New York: New York University Press.

Rafael, Vicente. 2000. *White Love and Other Events in Filipino History*. Durham, NC: Duke University Press.

Roces, Mina. 2012. *Women's Movements and the Filipina: 1986–2008*. Honolulu: University of Hawai'i Press.

Rodriguez, Dylan. 2006. "'A Million Deaths?' Genocide and the 'Filipino American' Condition of Possibility." In *Positively No Filipinos Allowed: Building Communities and Discourse*, edited by Antonio T. Tiongson Jr., Edgardo V. Gutierrez, and Ricardo V. Gutierrez, 145–161. Philadelphia: Temple University Press.

Rodriguez, Robyn Magalit. 2010. *Migrants for Export: How the Philippine State Brokers Labor to the World*. Minneapolis: University of Minnesota Press.

Sandoval, Chela. 1990. "Feminism and Racism: A Report on the 1981 National Women's Studies Association Conference." In *Making Face, Making Soul / Haciendo Caras: Creative and Critical Perspectives by Feminists of Color*, edited by Gloria Anzaldúa, 55–71. San Francisco: Aunt Lute Books.

San Juan, E., Jr. 1998. *Filipino Bodies: From the Philippines to the United States and Around the World*. Boulder, CO: West View Press.

Soto, Sandra. 2005. "Where in the Transnational World Are US Women of Color?" In *Women's Studies for the Future: Foundations, Interrogations, Politics*, edited by Elizabeth Lapovsky Kennedy and Agatha Beins, 111–24. New Brunswick, NJ: Rutgers University Press.

Tadiar, Neferti. 2004. *Fantasy-Production: Sexual Economies and Other Philippine Consequences for the New World Order*. Hong Kong: Hong Kong University Press.

CHAPTER 10

RACE, REPRODUCTIVE JUSTICE, AND THE CRIMINALIZATION OF PURVI PATEL

PRIYA KANDASWAMY

IN MARCH OF 2015, AN INDIANA COURT SENTENCED PURVI PATEL, a thirty-three-year-old Indian American woman, to twenty years in prison after having convicted her of feticide and neglect of a dependent. Almost two years prior, Patel had gone to the emergency room at Saint Joseph Regional Medical Center in Mishawaka with heavy vaginal bleeding. While she initially denied being pregnant, after repeated interrogations from doctors, Patel revealed that she had suffered a miscarriage in her bathroom at home and, believing the fetus to be dead, had left the remains in a dumpster outside her family's restaurant. Suspicious of her story, hospital staff quickly contacted the police. A search of the dumpster ensued, and the police recovered the fetus in question. When Patel awoke from surgery in the hospital, she was met with a police interrogation. A month later, the district attorney brought criminal charges against her, and what had begun as a trip to the emergency room was transformed into a long legal nightmare and the possibility of spending decades in prison.

Patel endured a lengthy and highly publicized trial on the feticide and neglect charges, in which the prosecution alleged that Patel had induced an abortion with pills she had obtained illegally on the internet. While legal abortions are exempted from Indiana's feticide law, the prosecution argued that Patel's supposed abortion was not exempt because it was self-induced illegally with no medical supervision. At the same time, the prosecution maintained that Patel had had a live birth and that because she left the body in the dumpster rather than seeking medical help on the baby's behalf, she was also guilty of neglect of a dependent.

Citing Patel's arrest and conviction as a shocking and outrageous example of the threat a Republican war on women poses to fundamental reproductive rights, mainstream feminist activists have drawn attention to the contradictory nature of the simultaneous convictions for feticide and neglect as well as the lack of substantial evidence in the case. For example, there was no medical evidence that Patel actually took abortifacient drugs. The prosecution built its case almost entirely on text messages between Patel and her closest friend. Similarly, the evidence that Patel had given birth to a live baby was questionable at best, consisting primarily of one forensic pathologist's testimony that a lung float test—a technique from the seventeenth century—confirmed that the fetus had taken a breath.[1]

As the first woman to be convicted of feticide for termination of her own pregnancy, Purvi Patel's case set a dangerous precedent for criminalization of self-induced abortion, behaviors during pregnancy that might potentially harm a fetus, and even miscarriage. Given these implications, advocates for pregnant women, pro-choice activists, and Asian American feminist organizations mobilized strongly in defense of Patel. Largely due to the support of these groups, Patel was able to appeal her conviction with partial success. In July of 2016, an Indiana appeals court ruled that the "legislature did not intend for the feticide statute to apply to illegal abortions or to be used to prosecute women for their own abortions," thereby vacating the feticide conviction. The appeals court reduced Patel's neglect of a dependent conviction from a class A felony to a class D felony, arguing that while Patel was guilty of neglect, the prosecution failed to demonstrate that her failure to provide medical care was the primary cause of the infant's death. At her resentencing hearing in August of 2016, Patel's prison sentence was decreased to eighteen months, and she was released with time served. While her release was a significant victory that speaks to the power of the organizing on her behalf, Patel was still forced to endure the trauma of an arrest and high-profile trial, a felony conviction, and substantial time in prison for the circumstances under which she ended her pregnancy.

The ruling that feticide statutes do not apply to abortions set an important legal precedent for pro-choice activists and dealt a significant blow to one pro-life strategy for criminalizing abortion. However, Purvi Patel's case is still cause for alarm among Asian American and Women of Color feminists. While the stakes in this case are frequently understood as protecting women's right to choose, Purvi Patel's circumstances powerfully demonstrate how the reduction of reproductive justice to pro-life versus pro-choice positions necessarily marginalizes the more complex experiences of women of color. On the one hand, the pro-life position falsely equates protecting life with the criminalization of abortion in ways that disproportionately impact women of color. On the other hand, however, the emphasis on choice as the alternative to criminalization often ignores racial and class disparities in how choices are distributed. Choice in itself is an individualizing framework that mirrors the values of consumer capitalism and privileges those who have more choices (Smith 2005). The right to choose has generally meant the right to choose among existing options rather than the power to shape the choices one has or the resources to actualize one's desires. Put a different way, Purvi Patel's choices certainly should not be criminalized. However, the best choices available to Patel were to hide her pregnancy from everyone except her best friend, covertly obtain abortifacient drugs, endure the loss of her pregnancy alone in her own bathroom, discard the remains from her abortion in a dumpster to maintain her secret, and when she felt her health was in danger, seek medical help on her own from providers that she rightly feared would harshly judge her actions. Even if Patel had not been arrested, these choices certainly do not constitute reproductive justice. Rather, they demand that Asian American feminists ask why Patel's choices were so limited to begin with and how the significant barriers she faced could become the basis for her own criminalization.

In this chapter, I explore these questions by drawing attention to the historical processes that constitute the political, cultural, and economic landscape in which Patel's criminality becomes possible. Taking both innocence and guilt as contextually specific constructs rather than fixed truths rooted in evidence, I am interested in exploring the more mundane but often hidden institutional forces that form the backdrop for understanding Patel's circumstances and actions. In particular, I highlight the role that immigration control and the criminal justice system have played in controlling women of color's reproduction. Consideration of these institutional forces demonstrates that Patel's case is neither exceptional nor extreme but rather an extension of a long history of racialized and gendered state violence. My hope is that by shifting attention toward these institutions we might make them central sites in the struggle for reproductive justice and recognize the role the US state plays in structuring hierarchies within and between communities of color as we develop strategies of resistance.

While Patel's conviction has primarily been framed in terms of its implications for women's rights, my analysis begins from a reproductive justice framework, which recognizes that historically the regulation of reproduction has been shaped as much by race, class, immigration status, and ability as by gender. Reproductive justice as a concept emerges out of and has been a central site for the development of Women of Color feminist theory and practice. In moving beyond pro-choice frameworks, Women of Color have articulated a reproductive justice politics that connects a broad range of issues as part of an expansive claim to bodily, familial, and community autonomy. Reproductive justice refuses to conflate its goals with abortion rights, recognizing the many obstacles women of color have confronted in having and raising children. At the same time, reproductive justice also moves away from centering individual decisions about childbearing and instead focuses on the economic, political, and cultural forces that shape those decisions and how their outcomes are experienced. Constitutive of new kinds of political identities, reproductive justice connects Women of Color with specific and different experiences in a shared coalitional struggle against the common forces that produce those different experiences (Ross 2006; Silliman et al. 2004). In this spirit, this chapter seeks to both locate Patel's conviction within the specificity of her experience as an Asian American woman and, building upon a Women of Color feminist politics, examine how that specific experience is constituted in relation to the regulation of other Women of Color. Rather than define Asian American women's experiences in terms of their difference from or similarity to white women's experiences, this essay strives to make visible the "common differences" (Mohanty 2003, 523) in the ways the state seeks to control the reproduction of differently situated women of color.

TARGETING ASIAN WOMEN: RACE, CULTURE, AND IMMIGRATION LAW

Though only 2 percent of Indiana's population is Asian, the only two women to be charged under their feticide law for the loss of their own pregnancies have been of Asian descent. Patel's arrest followed on the heels of a failed attempt to convict Bei Bei Shuai of both feticide and murder. An immigrant from China, Bei Bei Shuai attempted suicide in the last trimester of her pregnancy. She survived the attempt, and doctors performed an emergency Caesarean section in an effort to save her baby, who passed away just a few days later. Shuai spent more than a year in jail before the felony charges against her were eventually dropped in exchange for a plea to a lesser misdemeanor charge of criminal recklessness. Prosecutors clearly sought to make examples of both Shuai and Patel, pursuing harsh punishments against them in an effort to expand the reach of feticide statutes. Taken together, these cases raise questions about why pregnant Asian women are being specifically targeted and what role racialized and gendered constructions of Asian women's potential criminality played in prosecutors' belief that a jury would convict these women. In this section, I look specifically at the role these constructions played in Patel's prosecution as well as the structural forms of racialized heteropatriarchy that these constructions often work to obscure.

The prosecution's case against Purvi Patel relied heavily on racist stereotypes of Asian women as deceptive, manipulative, and inconceivably foreign in their actions. In the trial itself, prosecutors argued that Patel's behavior and affect were evidence of her guilt. Hospital nurses testified that Patel displayed a surprising lack of emotion at the hospital and instead spent most of the time on her phone. The prosecution emphasized the way that Patel had disposed of the fetus, painting a picture of a callous and treacherous woman who left a live baby to die in a dumpster. Even the judge described Patel as having "treated the child, literally, as a piece of trash" (Dasgupta 2015). While race was not specifically named in these representations, the depiction of Patel as a cold, robotic monster who lacked maternal instinct and compassion certainly played on stereotypes about Asian women and Asian culture more generally. These stereotypes were mirrored in media coverage of the trial. The vast majority of articles published about Patel highlighted her Indian heritage and included either a police photograph of her or a photograph of her being brought into the courtroom in handcuffs as she tried to hide her face from the camera. The only images that circulated of Patel, these dehumanizing photographs portrayed her as guilty even before a verdict had been determined.

Several critics have pointed out that the decision to prosecute both Shuai and Patel had less to do with their own actions and more to do with widespread stereotypes that China's One Child Policy and high rates of female infanticide in India reflect a cultural disregard for fetal life that carries into the diaspora. Ashwini Tambe (2015) argues that "China and India serve as poster children in global evangelical crusades against abortion," and that this perception makes women like Shuai and Patel easy targets for prosecutors looking to expand the policing of pregnant women. Similarly,

Miriam Yeung (2015), executive director of the National Asian Pacific American Women's Forum (NAPAWF), notes that "Asian women have been singled out when it comes to criminalized reproduction because of ugly stereotypes that claim we have a disregard for life. Pointing to India and China, anti-choice advocates argue that Asian cultures are prone to child neglect and abortion." Organizations like NAPAWF have drawn parallels between the Shuai and Patel cases and the recent proliferation of bans on sex-selective abortions that also specifically target Asian women. As of 2014, eight states have passed laws that ban abortion on the basis of the sex of the fetus, and since 2009 twenty-one states and the federal government have considered similar legislation. These bans deploy racist depictions of Asian communities as inherently patriarchal and holding a traditional preference for sons to further limit access to abortion (Kalantry and Yeung 2014). Notably, these bans masquerade as protecting future Asian girls from their own communities as they curtail Asian women's reproductive freedom more generally. As NAPAWF points out, they rely on the idea that Asian women are incapable of making sound reproductive choices and actually pose a danger to their future daughters, which needs to be policed with state intervention (Jorawar 2015). Sensationalized representations of traditional Asian patriarchy simultaneously pose idealized innocent girls as victims and their mothers, families, and larger communities as foreign, criminal, backward threats from which they need to be liberated.

In Purvi Patel's trial, prosecutors, those who would defend her, and the media all suggested that Patel's actions were motivated by a desire to hide her sexual activity from her "traditional," patriarchal Hindu family, who disapproved of premarital sex. Whether used to provide a motive for Patel's actions or to garner sympathy for her circumstances, these explanations reduce a complicated situation to a clash created by a traditional, patriarchal Hindu culture that is fundamentally incompatible with progressive American values. Whether Patel is a victim or an agent of Hindu patriarchy, the culprit is a backward, foreign culture that poses a threat to unborn children and ultimately does not belong in this country.

This narrative resonates strongly with other criminal cases in which Asian cultural difference is deployed to reduce complex circumstances to simplistic narratives about tradition and modernity. Leti Volpp (2010, 2011) has shown that, in these narratives, the West is figured as modern, democratic, progressive, and feminist while the East is characterized as tradition-bound, authoritarian, backward, and patriarchal. Volpp notes that white people who commit criminal acts are seen as individuals who either made poor choices or have particular character flaws while Asians who commit similar acts tend to be seen as driven by their culture. Importantly, these constructions rely upon a misconception of Asian culture as a static artifact and Asian people as simply products of their culture who are incapable of making individualized choices (Volpp 2010, 2011). In a context in which reproductive rights are framed as the right to choose, this denial of Asian women's individual agency becomes the basis for denying their reproductive autonomy. Because Asian women are seen as driven by their culture, they cannot be trusted to make good choices, and therefore, those choices should be taken away from them either through sex-selective abortion bans or, in Patel's case, the criminalization of self-induced abortions. At the same time, the focus on Hindu cultural patriarchy works to constitute US culture as neutral and irrelevant to Patel's actions. US patriarchy and racism are rarely seen as motivating Patel's actions though she lives in a state where abortion is difficult if not impossible to access for most women[2] and there is a well-documented history of medical abuses against communities of color in the United States, ranging from coercive sterilization to pharmaceutical testing.

The invocation of Hindu culture in this context works to obscure the political and economic forces that shape immigrant communities and experiences. For example, blaming Patel's patriarchal family makes invisible the structural barriers she encountered to actualizing her reproductive choices and also obscures the complexity of gender relations within her family and community. In addition, the hegemonic tendency to blame Asian cultures puts Asian American feminists in the position of always having to defend their communities against the racist representation that they are inherently patriarchal. This can have the effect of silencing Asian American feminist critique, making it difficult to grapple with the very real problems gender hierarchies pose in Asian American communities.

Rather than see culture as ossified and unchanging, it is important to understand how economic structures and legal regimes shape immigrant cultures. My point is not to suggest that Patel did not experience patriarchy in the home or that culture is irrelevant to understanding her experience. Rather, I want to challenge the idea that a "traditional Hindu culture" exists in the abstract and instead point to the ways power relations in communities are also shaped by the practices of the US state. This approach moves away from either demonizing or defending Asian immigrant cultures and instead asks how those cultures are constituted as such in the US context.

Rather than see the US state as an outside force that might intervene in Asian American communities to protect women and girls from patriarchy, I argue that the US state is already very much a presence in these communities, one that works to produce or at least exacerbate heteropatriarchal social relations.

This phenomenon can most clearly be seen in immigration policy. Historically, immigration law has been an important tool for regulating Asian reproduction and shaping Asian immigrant cultures and kinship formations in the United States. The United States' very first restrictive immigration law, the Page Law, curtailed the migration of Chinese women under the pretense that they were prostitutes. Enforcement of the Page Law reproduced the idea that Asian women were deceptive, manipulative, and a sexual threat, and these efforts were central to the emergence of new technologies for policing identity at the border (Luibhéid 2002, 31–54; Yung 1995, 15–51). More generally, state efforts to cultivate exclusively male labor migrations from Asia were rooted in a desire to limit family formation, settlement, and reproduction of those populations in the United States. These efforts worked to maintain Asians as a highly exploitable labor force whose cost of reproduction was borne elsewhere (Glenn 1983). In addition, these regulations shaped the kinds of early Asian immigrant cultures that developed in the United States, leading to the formation of "bachelor" societies and an array of alternative family forms (N. Shah 2001, 77–104).

Changes to immigration law in 1965 enabled increased migration from Asia but still shaped the Asian immigrant communities formed in the United States in very specific ways. First, employment preferences privileged individuals who were highly educated in technical fields in the migration process. This contributed to the perception that Asians as a group (particularly East Asians and South Asians) were high-achieving "model minorities." While immigration law selected for those who were likely to be economically successful in the United States, this success was often attributed to Asian culture and used to suggest that communities of color which remained economically marginalized were culturally deficient. Not only did the model-minority myth pit Asian communities against other communities of color, but it also fostered hierarchy in those communities, which came to be dominated by a diasporic bourgeoisie, which defines its particular values as the values of an entire culture. For Indian immigrant communities, this has exacerbated existing hierarchies based on gender, sexuality, class, caste, religion, and national or regional origin. Because what counts as Indian culture is frequently defined by those with the most power in the diaspora, challenges to these hierarchies are often reframed as attacks on traditional Indian culture and as enabling racism against Indian communities in the United States by publicly airing that community's internal problems (Bhattacharjee 1998; Shah 1997).

Second, the privileging of family reunification in immigration law adds to these dynamics. In critiquing representations of immigrant communities as homophobic, Chandan Reddy has argued that the privileging of family reunification (in which the family is defined as a heteropatriarchal unit) in immigration law works to produce and exacerbate homophobia in immigrant communities. Much like the construct of the model minority erases the fact that immigration law selects for highly educated, economically advantaged Asian immigrants, ideas about Asian cultural heteropatriarchy erase the way immigration law fosters communities organized through heteropatriarchally defined families. In addition, as Reddy (2005) points out, neoliberal privatization of welfare responsibilities has made immigrants more reliant on the family as a vehicle for economic survival, as there are fewer public sources of support. Notably, this privatization makes immigrant families much more reliant on women's work, often positioning immigrant women as subordinated by patriarchal practices within the home though they are primary economic sustainers of their families. As Grace Chang (2000, 125) notes, these forms of economic restructuring have been "founded on the tacit assumption that women of color can make do with less and work more."

Viewed this way, we might refrain from thinking about Purvi Patel as a victim of immigrant culture and rather see her situation as reflecting the complexities produced by the legal regimes and economic demands that structure immigrant communities. Patel's family owns and operates a restaurant in South Bend. On the one hand, this places her family in a privileged position in relation to members of immigrant communities who primarily work for others in the food service industry and an African American community that has experienced high rates of unemployment due to deindustrialization and structural exclusion from business ownership. On the other hand, the small family-owned business is a site of great economic precarity for many immigrants. In particular, family businesses rely heavily on the exploitation of familial labor and produce a structure in which individual well-being is closely tied to the success of the family business.

Media coverage of Patel's case indicates that Purvi Patel was in fact the primary source of economic support for her family and that she also did the work of caring for her parents and elderly grandparents. This suggests that, as is the case for many in immigrant communities, Patel's economic context in the United States actually ties her very closely to the needs, demands, and expectations of her family in ways that are about economic survival and not just "traditional" culture. Attention to these details opens up the possibility for a much more nuanced understanding of why Patel might have chosen to hide her pregnancy from her family, one that does not fall back on trite representations of traditional Hindu culture. Patel's situation also reflects the complex web of people that women of color are responsible for caring for in a context in which there are fewer social supports for individuals and families in general. Patel's criminalization (framed as protection of her fetus) is then a violence done not just to her but also to all of the people who depended upon her, whose lives are also made much more precarious by her incarceration. Rather than seeing her community as simply the source of the problem, it is important to instead recognize the important role Patel played in her community and the way that community is harmed by her criminalization.

PROTECTING THE FETUS: PREGNANCY AND THE PRISON INDUSTRIAL COMPLEX

Purvi Patel's arrest and prosecution reflect a changing legal landscape in which the fetus is increasingly recognized as a distinct subject and potential victim of crime. While it has received more attention than most, Patel's case is actually one of many in which a pregnant woman has been arrested for harm to her own fetus, and her story should be placed in this context. Paltrow and Flavin's (2013) study of over four hundred such cases found that the vast majority of women arrested were low income, 59 percent were women of color, and 52 percent were African American. In most of the cases studied, if the woman had not been pregnant, the arrest would not have occurred, and the majority of arrests relied upon interpretations of laws that were not originally intended to be applied to women in relation to their own pregnancies, such as child abuse, neglect, and homicide. While the increasing recognition of the fetus as a victim warrants particular attention, these findings also mirror the broader patterns of an expanding prison industrial complex, suggesting that the specific problem of the criminalization of pregnant women needs to be understood as linked to the growth of the carceral state more generally.

Since the 1980s, incarceration rates in the United States have grown exponentially even though crime rates have consistently decreased. This growth has disproportionately impacted communities of color, especially Black communities. Bureau of Justice statistics show that people of color make up more than 60 percent of the prison population and that 35.8 percent of the prison population is Black. Specifically among women, the incarceration rates of Black women are more than twice that of white women (Sentencing Project 2016). The growing number of incarcerated people and the racial disparities in incarceration rates reflect a historical shift in the role that prisons play in US state-building projects. As Ruth Wilson Gilmore (2007) demonstrates, the expanding prison industrial complex emerges as a way the state reinvents itself in the context of multiple converging economic, political, and cultural crises. Increasingly, the state's legitimacy is defined by its capacity to punish crime, and prisons become a means of resolving crises in capitalism through the warehousing of surplus populations. While a more complete discussion of the historical forces behind the development of a prison industrial complex is beyond the scope of this chapter, I focus on the significance of the proliferation of racialized constructions of crime for understanding the treatment of pregnant women in the law, the constitution of fetal victimhood, and the relationship between Asian American and Women of Color feminisms.

Prison expansion requires the invention of more and more crimes to be punished in harsher and harsher ways. As more prisons are built, they are filled through the criminalization of a broader range of activities and more stringent sentencing practices. Crime itself is an ideological construction that locates the source of social problems within individuals and obscures the social structures that shape and constrain an individual's actions. For example, constructing Purvi Patel as a criminal suggests that she is the problem that needs to be dealt with rather than addressing the racial, gender, and class inequalities that shape her experiences and the experiences of others like her. While crimes against fetuses certainly represent a very small portion of new crimes, the construction of pregnancy as a site of crime should be understood within the larger historical context of the increasing criminalization of more and more aspects of everyday life. Currently, the federal government and thirty-eight states have feticide laws, unborn victims of violence acts, or amended homicide statutes that explicitly include fetuses as potential victims. While the specific terms of these laws vary from jurisdiction to jurisdiction, in general, they recognize the fetus as a distinct person and thereby enable prosecutors to charge perpetrators of violence with a separate crime for harm done to the fetus (National Conference of State Legislatures 2015).

Historically, these laws have emerged as a response to violence against pregnant women. For example, the federal Unborn Victims of Violence Act became law in 2004 in the aftermath of the highly publicized murder of Laci Peterson. Peterson was eight months pregnant at the time of her death, and under California law her husband, Scott Peterson, was convicted of two separate counts of homicide, one for his wife's murder and one for the murder of Conner, his unborn child. In the aftermath of the case, Laci Peterson's family campaigned hard for a federal law that would recognize the fetus as a separate victim of crime in cases where a pregnant woman is harmed, arguing that their family had suffered not one but two great losses. The Unborn Victims of Violence Act, which is also known as Laci and Conner's Law, did exactly this. Including specific language that defined an unborn child as "a member of the species homo sapiens, at any stage of development, who is carried in the womb," it essentially establishes crimes against the fetus as a new category of federal crime.

Most feminists have opposed the Unborn Victims of Violence Act and similar state laws because of the dangers that the legal recognition of fetal personhood might pose to pregnant women's rights. However, these laws mirror the strategies of mainstream feminist antiviolence activists, who redefined violence against women in the 1990s as a crime that should be addressed through enhanced policing and stiffer penalties. While these feminists were largely successful in getting legislation like the Violence Against Women Act passed, their successes were built upon a shift from viewing domestic violence as a symptom of structural patriarchy to redefining it as an individual crime that should be addressed by punishing an individual perpetrator (Bumiller 2008; Ferraro 1996). Women of Color feminists have highlighted the limitations of this approach, emphasizing the way it actually harms many women of color who are more likely to be seen as perpetrators than victims, and the ways it legitimizes a criminal justice system that does tremendous harm to communities of color by casting itself as a protector of vulnerable women (Richie 2000; Incite! 2006).

In many respects, the limitations of legislation that humanizes the fetus for the purpose of prosecuting crimes are similar. While these laws ostensibly protect pregnant women, they are frequently used against those same women. Although the federal law and some (but not all) of the state laws pertaining to fetal victims do explicitly exclude legal abortions and harm done by a pregnant woman to her own fetus, these laws establish a precedent of fetal personhood that has been the basis for the arrest and prosecution of hundreds of pregnant women, including Purvi Patel. As Paltrow and

Flavin (2013, 323) demonstrate, "Even when women are not charged directly under feticide laws, such laws are used to support the argument that generally worded murder statutes, child endangerment laws, drug delivery laws, and other laws should be interpreted to permit the arrest and prosecution of pregnant women in relationship to the embryos or fetuses they carry." It is important to note that the legal basis for recognizing fetal personhood has been the capacity to be a victim of a crime and that other aspects of legal personhood such as agency, culpability, or rights beyond the right to state protection are largely irrelevant. This has the effect of constituting the fetus as fundamentally innocent and thereby an idealized subject of protection. However, while producing a legal separation between pregnant people and their fetuses legitimizes the criminal justice system as a protector of unborn children and enables the prosecution of pregnant people for harms done to fetuses, it does not promote fetal health or well-being in the long run because this is intrinsically dependent on the health and well-being of the person carrying the fetus. To frame the interests of the fetus and the pregnant person in antagonistic terms, as fetal personhood statutes do, locates potential harm to the fetus in individual pregnant people (or other individuals) rather than in the array of structural forces that produce negative outcomes for pregnancies and for children.

Race and anti-Black racism in particular play a central role in how victims and perpetrators of crime are constructed. For example, while assaults against white (or, in the case of Laci Peterson, white-passing) women have garnered a great deal of attention and been the impetus for new feticide legislation, violence against pregnant women of color remains largely ignored. The year before Peterson's murder, Evelyn Hernandez's body was found in the San Francisco Bay under remarkably similar circumstances. An immigrant single mother from El Salvador, Hernandez was also eight months pregnant. However, her murder received little media or police attention and to this day remains unsolved (St. John 2003). Historically, pregnancy has not afforded Black women the protections that it has afforded white women. Under slavery, Black women were denied all rights of motherhood. While their reproductive capacity was central to the slavery economy, pregnant Black women were not spared harsh labor conditions or the violent forms of punishment to which enslaved people were frequently subjected (Davis 1981, 8–11). After emancipation, Black women's reproduction was increasingly associated with degeneracy, and Black women became the targets of a range of eugenic projects from coercive sterilization to punitive welfare policies that situated their bodies as threats to be controlled rather than sites of protection (Roberts 1997). In addition, the widespread construction of the Black female body as threat has made it difficult to recognize Black women as potential victims of violence. This is evident in a plethora of contemporary examples, ranging from the failure to acknowledge Black women as victims of sexual assault to the criminalization of Black women's self-defense to pervasive police violence against Black women.

While pregnant women of color and pregnant Black women specifically are less likely to be seen as victims of crime, they are significantly more likely to have fetal personhood statutes used against them. A striking example of this has been the arrest of pregnant women who use crack cocaine on charges such as child abuse and endangerment. Beginning in the 1990s, these arrests were some of the earliest examples of the systemic criminalization of pregnant women, paving the way for other kinds of cases. As Dorothy Roberts demonstrates, these arrests drew specifically on a long history of representations of Black women as bad mothers. Though no medical evidence substantiated the claims that proliferated about "crack babies," and there was significant evidence that legal substances like alcohol and tobacco have more substantial effects on a fetus than cocaine, the "crack mother," imagined as a Black woman, became a specific target of the criminal justice system. In much the same way as in the criminalization of Patel, healthcare providers played a driving role in the criminalization of "crack mothers." As Roberts (1997, 175) documents, despite comparable rates of substance abuse between white and Black pregnant women, healthcare providers were ten times more likely to report Black women to the authorities.[3]

Building on racist perceptions and a long history of medicalized racism, the criminalization of substance-using pregnant women elaborated linkages between the health care and criminal justice systems that made women seeking necessary medical care vulnerable to surveillance and policing. Roberts (1997) notes that the primary objective of this targeting was the punishment of Black women rather than the protection of future Black children. This is evidenced both in the negative impact that incarceration has on pregnancy outcomes and in the lack of investment or interest in providing these women with treatment for their addictions even when the women themselves sought out this option. Rather, the figure of the "crack mother" came to be seen as both a symbol and source of the structural violence wrought by racial inequality. Rather than address an array of factors, including economic inequality, unequal access to healthcare, inadequate food and housing, and environmental racism, which lead to significantly increased infant mortality for Black babies, the public blamed Black mothers and employed the criminal justice system to punish them.

While, in Purvi Patel's case, it is the choice not to have a baby that is criminalized, in the case of substance-using mothers the choice to have a child is criminalized. However, at the heart of both cases is the idea that women of color's reproduction needs to be monitored and controlled by the state and that women of color should be punished for being "bad mothers." While fetal personhood statutes theoretically protect pregnant women and their fetuses as innocent victims of violence, in actuality they produced practices of criminalization that are bifurcated by race. In the case of idealized white subjects, the fetus emerges as a subject alongside the innocent pregnant woman, as an additional victim whose death enhances the tragedy of violence against women. In the case of women of color and other subjects who are not easily recognized as ideal victims, these statutes position pregnant women in an antagonistic relationship with their fetuses, and the fetuses become the basis for criminalizing women of color for being pregnant at all or for the actions that they take in relation to their pregnancies. Although these statutes are ostensibly designed to protect the fetus, they reflect little actual concern for the health or future of children in communities of color. By divorcing the interests of the fetus from those of pregnant people and the communities they are embedded in, the law turns the fetus into an abstraction that legitimates the state's power to punish.

While Patel's case is usually not placed in the context of the criminalization of "crack mothers," the resonances between these cases highlight the implications that an infrastructure of criminalization built through anti-Black racism has for other communities of color. In the United States, discourses about crime are shaped first and foremost by anti-Black racism, and the practice of policing crime derives from efforts to police and control Black communities dating back to slavery. However, just as anti-Black racism fuels the expansion of carceral institutions, the prison industrial complex casts a wide net that entangles many other communities. For example, while anti-Black racism has been mobilized to construct the infrastructure for incarcerating pregnant women for harm done to their fetuses, that infrastructure can readily be used against a broad range of other people, including Asian American women like Purvi Patel or Bei Bei Shuai. In many ways, Patel's case has been easier to take up within mainstream feminist discourse because she is more easily seen as innocent, and her situation is easily assimilated to a pro-choice narrative. However, it is important that Asian American feminists resist the tendency to cast Purvi Patel as a sympathetic victim and instead contest the ways that innocence and guilt are themselves racialized constructions. This requires making connections among the ways the criminalization of pregnancy affects differently situated women of color.

COALITIONAL POSSIBILITIES

The mobilizations by Asian American feminists in defense of Purvi Patel were both powerful and effective in securing her release from prison. These efforts also provide an important opportunity for building coalitions among Women of Color feminists to challenge the systemic forces that make the criminalization of pregnant women of color possible at all. By moving beyond a pro-choice politics and locating immigration control and the criminal justice system as key sites in a coalitional struggle for reproductive justice, Asian American feminist engagements with individual cases like Patel's can become the basis for a larger movement for social transformation. While I hesitate to offer prescriptive solutions that might simplify the complexity inherent in coalitional politics, I want to conclude by highlighting three key questions that this analysis raises for the future direction of reproductive justice organizing in Asian American communities.

First, in addition to continuing to challenge stereotypes of Asian cultures as inherently patriarchal, it is important that Asian American feminists grapple with how the US state actively produces and exacerbates gender hierarchies in Asian American communities. How do we draw attention to and challenge the ways immigration law and a neoliberal economic context shape gender and sexual relations in our communities and families? It is important not to simply address the state as an intervening force but also to see the role that state power plays in constituting Asian American subjectivities and internal community relations. This, I think, enables us to see the struggles against hierarchical power relations within communities as connected to rather than distinct from or a detriment to struggles against racialized and gendered state violence.

Second, challenging the criminalization of pregnant people requires making concrete connections between reproductive justice and dismantling of the prison industrial complex. While criminalization as a framework rests upon blaming individuals for structural problems, reproductive justice shifts the focus away from individual decision making and toward the structural inequalities that shape and curtail those decisions. While the pro-choice versus pro-life framework has centered the question of whether or not the fetus should be recognized as a subject, politically, for Women of Color, it seems more relevant to contest the idea that criminalization is ever an appropriate response to structural inequalities (Roberts 1997; Smith 2005). For example, some of the most frequent crimes that pregnant women are charged with include child abuse, neglect, and endangerment. While pro-choice activists have contested these charges on the grounds that a fetus is not actually a child, Black feminist and antiprison activists might point out that these kinds of charges are also regularly used to criminalize Black mothers for the effects of racialized poverty and have become a tool for state removal of Black children from their communities (Roberts 2002). Therefore, from the perspective of Black women and others who are vulnerable to criminalization, it makes sense to challenge the use of these charges more generally rather than simply arguing that they do not apply when the victim is a fetus.

Finally, much of the debate about reproductive rights has focused on the question of fetal personhood. While making the fetus into a legal person has been a significant and effective conservative strategy for curtailing abortion rights, I would like to suggest that the question of whether the fetus should legally constitute a person is the wrong question. I would argue that the problem with fetal personhood statutes is not that they recognize the potential humanity of the fetus but rather the way they constitute that humanity as independent from and in an antagonistic relationship with the pregnant person. As such, these statutes are embedded more broadly in a liberal construction of personhood in which individual well-being is divorced from community well-being. This model of independent personhood enables the punishment of pregnant women but does not actually reflect a concern for fetal health, which cannot be separated from the health of the pregnant person and the communities they are embedded in.

Similarly, Purvi Patel's conviction also rests upon a conception of her as individually responsible for the structural inequalities that marginalize her and her community. While a woman's right to abortion has been secured within the legal framework of privacy and individual choice, in truth meaningful reproductive autonomy also rests upon community self-determination.[4] If Patel had not been structurally marginalized on multiple fronts, her story might look very different. In addition to not being criminalized, perhaps she could have gotten an abortion in a safe and supportive environment in which she did not feel that her sexual and reproductive decisions put her at odds with her community. While it may seem risky to abandon the language of individual choice in a moment in which basic reproductive rights are under assault, a reproductive justice politics requires the development of more complicated ways of thinking about situated personhood that are grounded in a recognition of interdependency and complexity. The idea that political liberation requires the recognition and cultivation of new kinds of subjectivity has been central to Women of Color politics and offers a useful place from which to begin this project.

To conclude, the criminalization of Purvi Patel was made possible at the conjuncture of racist representations of Asian cultures as inherently patriarchal, the regulation of Asian immigrant families and labor through immigration policy, and an infrastructure for incarceration that was constructed primarily through the mobilization of anti-Black racism. The treatment of Patel's pregnancy and abortion cannot be abstracted from this context, as a political lens that focuses exclusively on reproductive rights attempts to do. Asian American feminisms in their specific relationship to Asian feminisms, Women of Color feminisms, and Asian American communities are uniquely positioned to challenge the conditions that underpin assaults like the one on Patel. The insights of Women of Color feminisms, in particular, suggest that Asian American feminisms must remain critical of the framework of individual rights and appeals for state protection. We might instead ask, how might the Asian American feminist mobilizations that successfully worked to free Purvi Patel from prison become the basis for building deeper connections between a movement for reproductive justice and a movement for prison abolition? At the heart of a project like this would be the recognition that the transformation of state structures, internal community dynamics, and individual subjectivities are intimately connected and that collective action within and between communities of color has the potential to work at all of these scales simultaneously.

NOTES

1   Purvi Patel's arrest and trial were highly sensationalized in the media. Because Patel and her family refused to speak to the press, it is difficult to know what actually happened the night she lost her pregnancy. The details compiled here and referenced later in the chapter represent the basic facts that most media reports agree on and the facts of the case that are outlined in the appeal verdict. At the appeal, Patel's legal counsel effectively conceded that Patel had aborted her fetus. For this reason, throughout this chapter, I refer to the loss of her pregnancy as a self-induced abortion. For more details, see Purvi Patel v. State of Indiana, 2016, Court of Appeals of Indiana, available at www.in.gov/judiciary/opinions/pdf/07221601tac.pdf.

2   In the state of Indiana, to have an abortion, a pregnant individual must first receive state-directed counseling that discourages abortion and then endure an eighteen-hour waiting period. Abortions are not covered by health insurance except in cases of rape, incest, or when the pregnancy poses a danger to the parent's life. Even individuals with private insurance must purchase additional insurance to cover elective abortions. On top of this, there are only twelve abortion providers in the entire state, and 61 percent of women live in a county where there are no abortion providers (Guttmacher Institute 2015).

3   Similarly, Paltrow and Flavin (2013) found in their survey of all cases in which pregnant women were arrested for harm to their fetus that health care providers played a more significant role in reporting African American women than white women. In nearly half of the cases involving African American women, arrest stemmed directly from a report by a healthcare professional. The same was true of less than a third of cases involving white women.

4   For one excellent example of what this might look like, see Jennifer Nelson's (2003) discussion of the Young Lords Party's demand for "abortion under community control."

REFERENCES

Bhattacharjee, Anannya. 1998. "The Habit of Ex-Nomination: Nation, Woman, and the Indian Immigrant Bourgeoisie." In *A Patchwork Shawl: Chronicles of South Asian Women in America*, edited by Shamita Das Dasgupta, 163–85. New Brunswick, NJ: Rutgers University Press.

Bumiller, Kristin. 2008. *In an Abusive State: How Neoliberalism Appropriated the Feminist Movement against Sexual Violence*. Durham, NC: Duke University Press.

Chang, Grace. 2000. *Disposable Domestics: Immigrant Women Workers in the Global Economy*. Cambridge, MA: South End Press.

Dasgupta, Sayantani. 2015. "Pregnant Women Are Now Targets: The Tragedy of Purvi Patel." *Salon*, April 26. www.salon.com/2015/04/26/a_terrifying_floodgate_for _prosecuting_women_why_purvi_patel_is_not_a_terrorist_partner.

Davis, Angela Y. 1981. *Women, Race and Class*. New York: Random House.

Ferraro, Kathleen. 1996. "The Dance of Dependency: A Genealogy of Domestic Violence Discourse." *Hypatia* 11 (4): 77–91.

Gilmore, Ruth Wilson. 2007. *Golden Gulag: Prisons, Surplus, Crisis, and Opposition in Globalizing California*. Berkeley: University of California Press.

Glenn, Evelyn Nakano. 1983. "Split Household, Small Producer and Dual Wage Earner: An Analysis of Chinese-American Family Strategies." *Journal of Marriage and the Family* 45 (1): 35–46.

Guttmacher Institute. 2015. "State Facts about Abortion: Indiana." www.guttmacher.org /fact-sheet/state-facts-about-abortion-indiana.

Incite! Women of Color Against Violence. 2006. *Color of Violence: The Incite! Anthology*. Cambridge, MA: South End Press.

Jorawar, Shivana. 2015. "Miscarriage of Justice: Asian-American Women Targeted and All Women Threatened by Feticide Laws like Indiana's." *NAPAWF News*, April 7.

https://napawf.org/2015/04/miscarriage-of-justice-asian-american-women-targeted
-and-all-women-threatened-by-feticide-laws-like-indianas.

Kalantry, Sital, and Miriam Yeung. 2014. "Replacing Myths with Facts: Sex-Selective
Abortion Laws in the United States." University of Chicago International Human
Rights Clinic. https://napawf.org/wp-content/uploads/2014/06/Replacing-Myths
-with-Facts-final.pdf.

Luibhéid, Eithne. 2002. *Entry Denied: Controlling Sexuality at the Border*. Minneapolis:
University of Minnesota Press.

Mohanty, C. T. 2003. "'Under Western Eyes' Revisited: Feminist Solidarity through
Anticapitalist Struggles." *Signs* 28 (2): 499–535.

National Conference of State Legislatures. 2015. "Fetal Homicide State Laws." www.ncsl
.org/research/health/fetal-homicide-state-laws.aspx.

Nelson, Jennifer. 2003. *Women of Color and the Reproductive Rights Movement*. New
York: New York University Press.

Paltrow, Lynn M., and Jeanne Flavin. 2013. "Arrests of and Forced Interventions on
Pregnant Women in the United States, 1973–2005: Implications for Women's Legal
Status and Public Health." *Journal of Health Politics, Policy and Law* 38 (2): 299–343.
doi:10.1215/03616878-1966324.

Reddy, Chandan. 2005. "Asian Diasporas, Neoliberalism, and Family: Reviewing the Case
for Homosexual Asylum in the Context of Family Rights." *Social Text* 23 (3–4): 101–19.

Richie, Beth E. 2000. "A Black Feminist Reflection on the Antiviolence Movement."
Signs: Journal of Women in Culture and Society 25 (4): 1133–37. doi:10.1086/495533.

Roberts, Dorothy. 1997. *Killing the Black Body: Race, Reproduction, and the Meaning of
Liberty*. New York: Pantheon Books.

———. 2002. *Shattered Bonds: The Color of Child Welfare*. New York: Basic Civitas.

Ross, Loretta. 2006. "Understanding Reproductive Justice: Transforming the Pro-choice
Movement." *Off Our Backs* 36 (4): 14–19.

Sentencing Project. 2016. "Trends in U.S. Corrections." http://sentencingproject.org/wp
-content/uploads/2016/01/Trends-in-US-Corrections.pdf.

Shah, Nayan. 2001. *Contagious Divides: Epidemics and Race in San Francisco's Chinatown*. Berkeley: University of California Press.

Shah, Purvi. 1997. "Redefining the Home: How Community Elites Silence Feminist
Activism." In *Dragon Ladies: Asian American Feminists Breathe Fire*, edited by Sonia
Shah, 46–56. Cambridge, MA: South End Press.

Silliman, Jael Miriam, Marlene Gerber Fried, Loretta Ross, and Elena Gutiérrez. 2004.
Undivided Rights: Women of Color Organize for Reproductive Justice. Cambridge,
MA: South End Press.

Smith, Andrea. 2005. "Beyond Pro-choice versus Pro-life: Women of Color and Reproductive Justice." *NWSA Journal* 27 (2): 119–40.

St. John, Kelly. 2003. "Eerily Similar Case Languishes in Obscurity / Torso of Missing
Pregnant Mom Was Found in S.F. Bay Last Year." *SFGate*, April 21. www.sfgate.com
/news/article/Eerily-similar-case-languishes-in-obscurity-2621215.php.

Tambe, Ashwini. 2015. "The Indiana Foeticide Case: Why Purvi Patel's Indianness
Matters." *Scroll.in*, April 3. http://scroll.in/article/718081/the-indiana-foeticide-case
-why-purvi-patels-indianness-matters.

Volpp, Leti. 2010. "Excesses of Culture: On Asian American Citizenship and Identity." *Asian American Law Journal* 17 (1): 63–81.

———. 2011. "Framing Cultural Difference: Immigrant Women and Discourses of Tradition." *Differences* 22 (1): 90–110.

Yeung, Miriam. 2015. "How Asian American Women Became the Target of Anti-abortion Activism." *Washington Post*, November 4. www.washingtonpost.com /posteverything/wp/2015/11/04/how-asian-american-women-became-the-target-of -anti-abortion-activism.

Yung, Judy. 1995. *Unbound Feet: A Social History of Chinese Women in San Francisco*. Berkeley: University of California Press.

PART FIVE

INCOMMENSURABILITY AND (IN)VISIBILITY

Theorizing an Asian American Feminist Praxis

CHAPTER 11

MULTIPLICITY, WOMEN OF COLOR POLITICS, AND AN ASIAN AMERICAN FEMINIST PRAXIS

Lynn Fujiwara

IN 2008 I PUBLISHED *MOTHERS WITHOUT CITIZENSHIP, ASIAN Immigrant Women and the Consequences of Welfare Reform* (University of Minnesota Press). My book was based upon several years of field research with community-based organizations and advocacy efforts in the San Francisco Bay Area in the wake of President Clinton's welfare and immigration reform. The connection between the demonization of single mothers and the move to "end welfare as we know it," presented an opportunity to examine how race, gender, and poverty could work to dismantle a program that (though fraught with problems) at least attempted to keep women and children out of destitution.

Noncitizens were to suffer massively from welfare and immigrant provisions that worked collaboratively to dismantle all sorts of immigrant rights. Most immediate was the devastating impact on elderly and disabled immigrants receiving assistance under the Supplemental Security Income program, as well as all immigrants receiving food stamps. My field research commenced with a forum conducted by several Bay Area immigrant coalition groups. As the speakers began to explain the new rules, the folks in the audience began to express fears about how they were going to survive or how they would care for their ailing parents. I learned about the suicide hotlines that community organizations implemented because distraught immigrants were so fearful of what was going to happen to them.

When I began to think about studying welfare and immigration from the perspective of immigrant welfare participants, I knew that I wanted to understand the day-to-day experiences based upon their social locations, racial and gendered experiences, and community involvement. I planned to conduct interviews with immigrant welfare participants. I started with a very idealistic notion of feminist research as a way to give women's voices agency and self-empowerment. In my book I speak about the difficulties and unexpected challenges I encountered, which led to a more feminist activist (formally known as participatory activist research) approach, but I do not convey fully the level of complexity that I navigated as a US-born Woman of Color facing multiple levels of difference as I set out to understand the structural and experiential consequences of welfare and immigration reform.

I began by volunteering at citizenship drives organized by community organizations throughout the Bay Area. Although one of the citizenship program directors encouraged me to make phone calls to set up interviews with women who were current recipients, I soon realized that the power differential, along with my language limitations, would be devastating. I assumed that there would be some way that I could communicate my identity as a single mother from a working-class background and my intentions to make welfare more accessible for women facing poverty. Instead, my immediate introduction (in English) as someone doing research on the consequences of welfare reform was enough to evoke fear in those I sought to interview. Usually the first question they asked was whether they "had" to talk to me, and when they found out that they didn't, they quickly hung up. But in one instance a woman became very worried that I was calling because she was in trouble. She put her young daughter on the phone to translate. I could hear her anxiously proposing questions for her daughter to ask me, which her daughter would then translate. The daughter was clearly uncomfortable, as she sighed often and asked her questions hesitatingly. Once her mother was convinced that I was not a state agent prying into her affairs, she told her daughter to hang up.

I felt so horrible. I could not believe that I had put these women in the very position I was trying to critique. I quickly realized that I myself (with no research budget) could not conduct interviews with this group of women. I spent a lot of time after those phone calls feeling terrible for invading the lives of these women and the daughter as well, and for causing them so much discomfort. I asked myself how I had failed to foresee the harmful consequences of this communication approach. I recognized that I had inflicted violence through language, power, and my seeming appearance as a representative of the state. I abandoned my plan to conduct interviews and shifted my approach to a participant activist/advocacy research model by volunteering in advocacy efforts, demonstrations, citizenship drives, and citizenship classes.

Before the book was published, I wrote an article for a special edition on feminist methodologies in a prominent feminist journal. Given the complex nature of my research, I utilized the article as a way to work through my positionality, limitations, and negotiations as I strove to conduct feminist research. The multiple levels of difference demonstrated a precarious positionality that would significantly impact the course of my research project. Here, though I and my subjects all fit within the category Asian / Asian American, we could not have been farther apart in terms of power, resources, language, and citizenship.

In the article, I utilized feminist theorists like Aihwa Ong, Kamala Visweswaran, Pierrette Hondagneu-Sotelo, and Patricia Zavella as a way to critique the complexity and incommensurability I found while trying to engage in interviews and explain how my project transformed into a feminist activist research methodology through community mobilization efforts. Although the heart of my article was a critique of my attempt to conduct interviews, one reviewer's criticism haunted me years after: "I could not believe you tried to conduct your interviews in English, this was unforgivable. . . . From a transnational feminist approach, those interviews never would have been conducted in English." At the core of this reader's critique was my lack of engagement with transnational feminist studies, and my foundational framework from the perspective of a US-born citizen. I abandoned that article, and it wasn't until many years later that I reworked it for a talk in Asian American Studies at UCLA. It was there that fellow scholars and audience members heard my self-denigration and shame and in their insightful feedback challenged me to rethink my own positionality as a US woman of color navigating an intellectual system where transnationality often takes primacy in feminist studies and where understandings of racial and class difference are reduced or even erased in the context of neoliberal global studies.[1] In the end, my reworking of *multiplicity* gave me the tools and language to better critique the multivalent and incommensurable levels of power at play in my research experience.

As I write this chapter in 2016, it marks the twentieth anniversary of the passing of the 1996 immigration and welfare reform laws under Bill

Clinton. Unfortunately this anniversary has met with little public or scholarly commentary; it could be that our current battles under the Trump administration have dispersed activist efforts to defending what social democracy we have left, with nearly every avenue of civil, human, indigenous, and global rights at stake. Making sense of this twenty years later is a long time coming, and perhaps even a much-needed resolution to an emotionally haunting experience that started with scathing reviews of a methods piece I had written over ten years ago. I revisit these issues in my work to critically reflect on the way I understand the multiple layers of difference at play between myself as a researcher and the community whose histories and experiences compound their political vulnerability. Looking back, I can see with clarity that what is at stake is much more than a scholarly bruising, but rather, a women of color racial/class politics that is in tension with at once transnational feminist assumptions of commonality and the invisibility of Asian American women as embedded in historical and contemporary neoliberal projects of racialized violence.

This regrappling gives me the opportunity to reengage with Lisa Lowe's conceptualization of multiplicity in Asian America. Lowe's iconic article, "Heterogeneity, Hybridity, and Multiplicity: Marking Asian American Differences," was first published in *Diaspora: A Journal of Transnational Studies* in 1991. At the time, this article gave scholars in Asian American studies an important conceptual tool to contend with the complexity, tensions, contradictions, and incommensurabilities within Asian America. Lowe's chapter challenges Asian America as a monolithic or homogeneous identity against a context of whiteness, racial formation, neoliberalism, US imperialism, and transnationalism. She pushes scholars and researchers to take on the thorny issues of intraethnic privilege and power, the reproduction of oppressions, and a consciousness for solidarity and coalition. Utilizing the notion of valences, Lowe notes the incommensurabilities within the heterogeneous group constituting Asian America and considers the possibilities of future solidarities through multivalent points of political commonality. Lowe's formulation of heterogeneity, hybridity, and multiplicity gave feminist scholars like myself the theoretical language to engage the complexities of difference and to insert Asian American issues into intersectional dialogues.

Because intersectionality exposes the inability of the state's top-down logic to make intelligible the complexity of Asian American struggles, it also exposes the need for a coalitional praxis in Asian American feminist research. Accordingly, a coalitional praxis that presumes the multiple inter-dependent heterogeneous subjectivities of Asian Americans requires us to utilize the lens of multiplicity, a lens that foregrounds racialized neoco-lonial systems of neoliberalism and globalization to illuminate incom-mensurabilities within and across Asian America as sites of coalitional consciousness-raising; in turn, the lens of multiplicity gives us the tools to read and engage otherwise conflicted moments as generating knowledge that fuels a coalitional praxis committed to Asian American feminist change on the ground. Examining the point of contention by the feminist journal's reviewer, I emphasize the increasing significance of multiplicity as a con-ceptual framework to unpack the complex differences within a racial minoritized group that is majority foreign born.

In this chapter, I expand on Lowe's conceptual usefulness of multiplic-ity to critically interrogate the interdependent heterogeneous subjects pro-duced through multiple valences of power toward an Asian American feminist praxis that carries forward feminist of color calls for intersection-ality. Legal scholar Kimberlé Crenshaw is noted for coining the term inter-sectionality to address the failure of antidiscrimination law to see Black women as litigants based simultaneously on race and gender. Crenshaw's analysis exposed the ways Black women are rendered invisible through single-axis modalities of understanding oppression such as race, gender, and class. Her theory of intersectionality complicates relative positionalities by embedding intersecting locations within power structures that are shaped simultaneously by race, gender, and class.

As intersectionality took epistemological primacy, feminist scholars put this theoretical framework into methodological and political action. While intersectionality has become a commonplace concept among millennials, putting this framework into praxis continues to be challenging. On Sep-tember 24, 2015, after the tragic death of Sandra Bland in a Texas jail cell, Crenshaw published an article in the *Washington Post* titled "Why Intersectionality Can't Wait." Crenshaw (2015) says, "Today, nearly three decades after I first put a name to the concept, the term seems to be every-where. But if women and girls of color continue to be left in the shadows, something vital to the understanding of intersectionality has been lost." Her point here is to highlight the persistent invisibility of Black women and girls, who also face injustice and death at the hands of the police. In a simi-lar vein, Latoya Peterson (2015), the editor at Racialicious.com, insists that intersectionality must be more than an academic term utilized to theorize identity or social position: "It becomes too easy to allow some feminists to recite the pillars of an intersectional feminism while still finding a thousand ways to marginalize people out of the framework."

I begin with this cursory reflection on feminist of color conceptualizations of intersectionality, positionality, and social location, as a way to guide my use of multiplicity as a conceptual tool that complicates what can be an oversimplification of intersecting identity locations. In particular, I think about how the development of US Third World and multiracial feminist perspectives moved epistemological frameworks to engage in complex examinations of women of color in the United States, whose experiences are shaped by colonial processes of racial and gendered domination. At the heart of this connection I strive for an Asian American feminist praxis grounded in difference and heterogeneity while engaging Women of Color politics that situate Asian Americans within broader racial gendered discussions. The understanding that *difference* plays out in power relations is not new, but how we go about examining difference can obscure or illuminate the power relations and the varying impacts of social policies that shape people's circumstances differently. In the following sections I use the Women of Color feminist methodology of *theorizing in the flesh* to illustrate the incommensurabilities within Asian America that pushed me to rethink the conceptualization of multiplicity as a format for an Asian American feminist praxis that aligns with the coalitional politics of Women of Color.

MULTIPLICITY: POSITIONALITY AND INCOMMENSURABILITY

In Lowe's iconic 1991 article she points to a discussion in a short story between two Chinese American women, each harboring a fear that the other does not see her as authentically Chinese. The idea of racial authenticity is multifaceted and complex, but in this context the women held onto markers of language, time in China (homeland), and family practices. Lowe's timely intervention reflects on the multiplicity and heterogeneity in Asian America as post-1965 Asians in America have forged new communities and presence in the United States, in relation to third-, fourth-, and fifth-generation Asian Americans whose ancestors primarily migrated to America before the 1924 immigration bar to most of Asia. Often referred to as two separate waves of immigration, the descendants of first-wave immigrants have vastly different experiences from transnationals, migrants, refugees, and their children since 1965. Lowe states, "As with other diasporas in the United States, the Asian immigrant collectivity is unstable and changeable, with its cohesion complicated by intergenerationality, by various degrees of identification and relation to a 'homeland,' and by different extents of assimilation to and distinction from 'majority culture' in the United States" (Lowe 1991, 27).

Lowe draws from Frantz Fanon to fully grapple with contrasting Asian American differences, as well as multivalences of oppression, histories of colonialism and neocolonial projects of nationalism and assimilationism that are integral to interrogations of multiplicity and Asian American politics. Lowe utilizes Fanon's critique of neocolonial bourgeois nationalism, which formulates identity around ethnicity and culture (thus inverting colonialism), to advocate for a more complex understanding of multiple positionalities in Asian America. Lowe states, "An Asian American subject is never purely and exclusively ethnic, for that subject is always of a particular class, gender, and sexual preference, and may therefore feel responsible to movements that are organized around these other designations. . . . [T]hese differences represent greater political opportunity to affiliate with other groups whose cohesions may be based on other valences of oppression." Thinking about the difficulties of ethnic and cultural markers that shape who we are, I push Lowe's articulation of multiple valences of oppression to crystalize an Asian American feminist praxis that can approach resistance movements from varying points of entry and belonging.

Throughout my research experience, once I began a more feminist activist approach with communities engaged in mobilizing efforts, I could see that the level of heterogeneity and multiplicity was unbound, everywhere, inherent, and inescapable. The levels of difference and complexity among those organizing in community-based organizations varied from lawyers, law students, legal aid workers, union workers, social service providers, elderly, alter-able-bodied Asian Americans and immigrants, college students, youth, wealthy, impoverished, citizens and noncitizens. Then there was me, a third/fourth-generation, monolingual English speaker who grew up in an inland town in San Diego's North County—where there were no other people of color (in my youth)—whose parents had been incarcerated in Japanese American internment camps as children during WWII, a single mother of a young school-age daughter, immersed in the immigrant rights movement in the San Francisco Bay Area during Clinton era welfare/ immigration reform. I frequently critiqued my own place as a researcher, as moments that illuminated my own privilege seriously put in question my role within this very complex movement. To make sense of unavoidable moments of contradiction, Lowe's piece, and her conceptualization of multiplicity specifically, in dialogue with Women of Color frameworks of difference, gave me the lens and tools to consider the necessity for an Asian American and Women of Color feminist praxis.

To illustrate the politics of multiplicity, I socially locate myself as a way to complicate my positionality as a scholar, researcher, and teacher, as I examine my own subject formation across multiple valences of power through my research experience. Language was a bit of a sore spot for my family of origin. My father failed kindergarten in Los Angeles because he could speak only Japanese. His grandparents had migrated from Japan to work on plantations in Hawai'i, where his parents were born (both in Hilo). Growing up surrounded by Japanese plantation workers, my father's parents spoke only Japanese until they left for the mainland. My father recounted the humiliation of failing kindergarten, and once he learned English, he lost his Japanese. My mother's parents had migrated from Japan in the early 1920s. My mother (sixth of eight daughters) knew enough "broken" Japanese to communicate with her parents, but at the age of five, she was incarcerated in Manzanar concentration camp during WWII. As she was growing up, her parents insisted that she speak English and assimilate into American culture by attending Christian churches, even though they were practicing Buddhists.

After my parents and their families were released from concentration camps at the end of WWII, they faced a postwar anti-Japanese racism they both described as horrifying and traumatizing. Beyond the racial epithets, getting spat on, racist teachers and schools, watching their parents struggle after losing everything during internment, there were deeper feelings of shame and embarrassment that caused confusion to them as children. Unlike the model-minority narrative, neither of my parents received college degrees, and in 1968 they ventured into a nursery business in a small, then rural, nearly all-white town in North County in San Diego, just eighteen miles south of the home of Tom Metzger, founder of the White Aryan Resistance. My parents had a hard time buying property, and we regularly experienced racist affronts growing up.

Like many other students of color from predominantly white communities, it was not until undergraduate classes that I was exposed to literature and scholarship by people of color and Women of Color. I had no plans to pursue a PhD; the idea was never suggested by any of my professors until my last year of college. I was a young mother in my last years of undergraduate studies at University of California San Diego when I stumbled on two courses taught by a visiting instructor, "Asian American

Women" and "Asian American Community Issues." The visiting instructor could see my excitement over the discovery of a personally driven intellectual and political consciousness, and she introduced the idea of graduate school to me.

Reflecting back on my political investment in studying the impacts of welfare and immigration reform and my attempt at interviewing noncitizen welfare recipients, I remain accountable to the harm caused by my failure to consider how English-only interviews would impact the women with whom I sought to connect. However, I think the reviewer's comments also warrant a critical analysis. The reviewer's critique is not incorrect, but her expression of disbelief and disgust (calling my misstep "unforgivable") at my attempt to interview in English from a transnational feminist primacy reflects a larger dynamic between transnational feminisms and US Women of Color feminisms. I do not wish to engage in an adversarial debate, as both fields are critical to broader feminist, antiracist, and global formations of power, oppression, and resistance. From a Woman of Color perspective, though, transnational feminisms have carried stronger institutional validation than Women of Color feminisms.[2] Though it has taken me some fifteen years to be in a position to rethink this discussion on feminist praxis in relation to research conducted twenty years ago, this opportunity to critically engage this tension is important for scholars of both fields. Multiplicity as a conceptual framework provides not only more complex ways of negotiating incommensurable differences in research and scholarship; it also provides a more complicated way to think about political struggles and a feminist praxis that strives for coalitional formations with accountability to differing, conflicted, and incommensurable positionalities. In the following section, I continue to examine multiplicity as a tool for unpacking incommensurable differences but push the conceptual framework to consider the potential for coalitional work.

COALITIONAL POSSIBILITIES AND MULTIPLICITY IN ASIAN/AMERICAN ORGANIZING

Michael Hames-García elaborates in *Identity Complex: Making the Case for Multiplicity* (2011, 13) a theoretical premise of social identity "as the mutual constitution and overlapping of simultaneously experienced and politically significant categories such as ability, citizenship, class, ethnicity, gender, race, religion, and sexuality. Rather than existing as essentially separate axes that sometimes intersect, social identities blend, constantly and differently, expanding one another and mutually constituting one another's meanings." Hames-Garcia's working of multiplicity synthesizes a racialized gender system that "reveals the extent to which the gender and sexual domination of racially subordinated peoples has roots in the legacies of modernity and coloniality" (106). For my purposes here, what is most illuminating about this framework is that it foregrounds the embedded colonial violence of white supremacy and racialized neocolonial systems of neoliberalism and globalization against which particular groups resist and empower themselves, without erasing the legacies and persistent oppressions among multiple valences of power and position.

To think about multiplicity as always embedded in (neo)colonial projects of white supremacy provides a logistical format for thinking about the incommensurabilities within intersecting sites of coalition. This framework gives me a more complex analytical tool with which to make sense of the multiple layers of conflict and collaboration in the brief example of my research experience and the subsequent review of my article that attempted to critically analyze my research experience. I developed my research project through a complex web of economic vulnerability, racism, and racialized gendered assumptions of need and entitlement. My own experiences of white supremacy and economic vulnerability shaped the foci and orientation of my research.

As a third/fourth-generation Asian American, I grew up very aware of my parents' incarceration as children. They were heavily scarred from this experience. Their families were very poor, but surrounded by community and family, they grew up to be proud, intelligent, and industrious. For me, growing up in that remote town in inland San Diego County with virtually no people of color, a town that prided itself on being a bastion of the American West, with a rodeo and an annual parade that included men in cowboy outfits shooting cap guns at Native Americans (white men in costumes) and a float featuring a sheriff and a jail cell with a bandit yelling for his release; I used to fear that one of those sheriffs was going to come and take my father back to camp, as both my parents often reminded me that "it could happen again." I recall walking into stores that refused to serve us and witnessing my parents negotiating with racist people with their heads held high in the moment, but what we saw in our home was quite devastating. My way of coping was to stay as small as possible, to not be seen, and to blend in as best I could.

I describe this neocolonial racial milieu of my formative years as a way to underscore the racialized gendered system of white supremacy that pervaded every aspect of my family's survival. Until I left home in my mid-twenties, as a mother, I never knew the feeling of acceptance, I never felt the comfort or assurance that I would be served in any given establishment. I witnessed the backlash against migrant Latinos as their presence increased in the 1980s, the stories and racist narratives of migrant crime, fear, sexual violence, and drugs. Thus, in the 1990s, as a single mother in graduate school in Santa Cruz, the attack on immigrants through Proposition 187 in 1994, then the Personal Responsibility Act and Illegal Immigration Reform Act of 1996, my anger over the blatant display of nativism and the move for exclusion heightened my political interests to focus on examining the nativist policy movement, hoping to make some contribution to advocacy efforts.

Yet the multiple layers of difference remained as I set out to do my research. The racist imperialist thread shaped by a long trajectory of American intrusion in Asia through militarization and capitalism held in common an understanding of exploitation and exclusion. However, I, having been shaped as monolingual by the internal colonial racialized gendered system of white supremacy, had never traveled outside the United States, and I struggled economically as a single mother, racking up major debt through student loans and credit card advances while attempting to do research entirely on my own with few resources. Looking back now, I am not utilizing this framework to excuse my mistakes in attempting to conduct interviews with immigrant and refugee women facing welfare cutoffs, but I can at least analyze the structures, systems, and cultural formations that shaped that unfortunate attempt and recognize that it was a product of something much larger than myself. My failures to communicate reflect my own heterogeneous subjectivity born through multivalences of power. English-only colonial and white supremacist US laws and the violence of assimilation shape monolingualism among US people of color.[3]

Although I abandoned my attempt to interview Asian immigrant and refugee women, I continued participatory feminist activist research methods in community-based immigrant rights organizations, advocacy campaigns, marches, and citizenship drives. I found myself immersed in community service and political campaigns that would ultimately lead me to engage in research where community needs and goals directed my research. Participatory research is characterized by the intent to implement social change not from the top down but rather by following the course of action led by community participants. Suspending the "legitimized" top-down mode of knowledge acquisition enabled a horizontal move that temporarily shifted the hierarchical connections across difference and allowed me to navigate the multivalences of power through a coalitionally minded feminist praxis. I worked side by side with immigrant and refugee women in ways I never could have under other conditions. Reflecting back, I can see that my own experiences of racialized class and gendered harm allowed me to understand, know, and feel the emotional harm I had caused to those few I tried to interview. Likewise, in a more horizontal approach to researching the welfare and immigrant rights movement, it was my emotional knowing of racialized and economic vulnerability that allowed me to connect with those I was working with. Hames-García argues that an expansion of political interests can occur through attending to multiplicity (Hames-García 2011, 27). A multiplicity through expanded interests can generate a feminist praxis and, in the case of my activist research, an Asian American feminist praxis that allowed me to connect with members of the immigrant rights movement based upon my political and emotional understanding of the racial, gendered, and classed harm inflicted by welfare.

As a volunteer positioned lower in the organization's chain of command, I often "took orders" from immigrant and refugee women during marches, workshops, or even citizenship drives. My work became useful for advocacy measures, as I found myself producing literature used in meetings with local county officials. As a community activist, I was operating in a world where women's voices were often raw, angry, and defiant. I was in constant correspondence with other activists sharing their own experiences, passing on the words spoken by the immigrants they worked with, and witnessing the collective work to pull these narratives together for advocacy purposes. As a result, I was able to examine how social policy affected immigrant women and their families at the community level. I was able to see how the power of the state operated on multiple levels (for individuals, families, and the community).

I will illustrate with an example from my field notes:

On a cool autumn Saturday afternoon in 1997, I sat around a table in the Northern California Coalition for Immigrant and Refugee Rights, with about twelve other organizers and immigrant activists. We were planning our march on Sacramento and legislative visits with our local representatives and senators to demand that they rescind the immediate cuts that were about to be implemented. Among these twelve people were activists, staff members, immigrants, and their translators from Vietnam, China, Laos, Mexico, and Russia. At one point an elderly woman from Vietnam spoke very passionately, looking at each of us younger appearing staff, pointing her finger at us, softly hitting the table to emphasize the significance of what she was saying: "You have to realize how hard it is to survive. You see we were forced to leave and come here. The US told us that we would be taken care of here because we fought for them. It has been very hard here, we didn't have the skills to get good jobs, and now we are too old. No one wants to hire me now. But we need our SSI to pay the rent. I don't know what we will do when we don't have it. We are not going to be able to get by, if they take our cash. We need to make them change their minds or we will not get by." We listened intently and promised that we would all work hard to get Congress to restore SSI and food stamps.

Another soft-spoken elderly man speaking Spanish talked about the decades he has worked in this country, working in the fields, the family he has raised. Now that he is older and unable to work, he is being told that he cannot collect his Supplemental Security Income, which pays for his housing. Through his translator he tells us, "I will be homeless. I have worked hard all of my life, I have never been homeless, and now that I can no longer work, I fear I will be homeless." Everyone around the table nodded in agreement and compassion, when the NCCIRR staff member leading the meeting, a Vietnamese American woman in her midtwenties, expressed in anger, "There we have it, we will march on Sacramento, we will bring folks from all over California in their wheelchairs, walkers, however we have to, to show these legislators who they are hurting!"

Shortly after, a Korean American woman said, "I'm in my fifties, and I work at a grocery store. My mother is about to lose her disability benefits. She has Alzheimer's and needs to live in her nursing home. If she loses her disability, she won't get the care she needs, and I can't both keep working and take care of her. She needs twenty-four-hour care." Many folks around the table had never thought of a situation like the one this woman spoke about. Middle-age children of elderly immigrant parents were finding themselves in a bind because they did not have the means to support their parents. This woman went on to explain that she is barely making ends meet for her and her two dependent children. She said apologetically that she does not have other family that she can rely on for help. She was fearful and upset at the idea of her mother being kicked out of her nursing home. The atmosphere of the meeting went from solemn and quiet to enraged and boisterous. Suddenly the room was full of energy, folks working on organizing legislator lists, signs, volunteer calls, and everyone was working together, mainly taking orders from the elderly immigrants who were seen as the experts of the group.

In this group, the most striking differences were generational, national origin, race, gender, social economic status, educational background, and language. The commonality that brought us together was a political invest-ment in challenging the anti-immigrant provisions in the welfare law. Like-wise, immigrants who would normally not interact were collaborating and supporting each other as they shared stories of economic deprivation and political marginalization. Though experiences varied and family structures differed, the complexity was understood and structured into a larger dia-logue and a platform for immigrant rights.

Through a feminist praxis that centered a lens of *multiplicity*, I was ulti-mately able to engage in the multiple valances of power through a multi-plicity that allowed me to recognize my own location in relation to those I was working with and for. It was only through this coalitional praxis that I was able to see the multiple layers of difference, struggle, and solidarity among and across the heterogeneous immigrant rights communities. My role as newcomer and volunteer de-elevated my status in the eyes of many immigrants—longtime community members who were very familiar with the staff—who felt a sense of belonging and ownership of the organ-ization or community center. Some immigrants acted as though they needed to educate me on the conditions they faced. No longer was I the distant, threatening, potential agent of the state. Rather, I was perceived as someone who needed to understand their situations to challenge Con-gress. And I was accountable to this perception that I needed to learn how to move in solidarity with these multiply different community members.

The leveling I experienced as a volunteer and immigrant rights activist went beyond the patient educational explanations that many immigrants felt compelled to teach us about their situations so that we could better fight Congress for the restorations. When immigrants utilized services at the Immigration Program of Santa Clara County or the Asian Women's Cen-ter, they expected me to provide assistance. Their sharing of their situations was not seen as an unwanted invasion or interrogation, but rather as an explanation to get the appropriate guidance or advocacy within and against the system. However, in some instances, immigrants became impatient with me and expressed their frustration and demands that I act more immediately and proactively. The following scene is from a volunteer experience at the Asian Women's Center in San Francisco Chinatown when I worked with a woman on a long and cumbersome application for naturalization:

> I was helping a woman in her early fifties with her N400. She began to get very frustrated with me as we went through each question. She especially got mad when I had to tell her that she would have a nearly two-year wait before she would even get an interview with the INS. In a very sharp and crisp tone she said, "Why can't you do it faster?" I tried explaining that all I was doing was helping her with the form, that I wasn't making any decisions or acting in any "official" capacity. "What am I going to do?" she started to yell. She was very upset, and I could see that she was feeling very panicked. I tried to explain that it looked like the law might change, and she might be able to keep her SSI because so many people will not be able to live. I said, "Many people are working on it so that the government will change the law again, so noncitizens will be able to keep their benefits." She responded, "Well you better make sure they change that law fast, because we are not going to be able to live if they take that away from us."

My ability to engage in these settings as a researcher as well as an immigrant rights activist proved critical, as my positioning marked me as an "insider" to the mobilization efforts. Although my presence in the immigrant rights movement was not necessarily through an intersecting point of commonality, I was identifiable as an Asian American woman who was there to do the political work. I often felt my ability to negotiate the generational relationship with fluency informed the deference and humility on my part that shaped our interactions and conversations. Although our differences were significant, and I had important privileges as a citizen with economic advantages, language skills, and education, I was still accessible through a familiarity born of shared struggles as an Asian American woman advocating for noncitizens facing exclusion from benefits. For economically vulnerable immigrants and refugees, the act of making their circumstances public for political purposes carried a familiar form of collective responsibility as politicized subjects. Thus, my connection with immigrants' rights community organizations and advocacy efforts positioned me as an ally across and within these multiple valences of power. However, it was not just a matter of finding a different research approach; my ability to engage with immigrant rights coalitional groups, citizenship drives, and advocacy efforts required a constant critical negotiation of my own positionality, both historically informed and in the present, through reading and understanding the terrain of the folks I was working with. While our political interests shaped the heterogeneous configurations of folks, we were clear of the legislative harm of the law and set out to challenge its implementation. Multiplicity was essential, though not simply articulated as an Asian American and Asian immigrant and refugee political praxis.

MULTIPLICITY AS A TOOL FOR
ASIAN AMERICAN FEMINIST PRAXIS

The heterogeneity that shapes Asian America complicates the ways we think about and enact solidarity. Claire Jean Kim recognizes that Asian Americans are roughly two-thirds foreign born and remain one of the most internally diverse racial minority groups in the United States (Kim 2004, 22). Either internally within an Asian American–identified community or broadly among communities facing other forms of political and structural marginalization, how we understand our positionalities requires a critical consciousness of the multiple valances of power that we occupy and/or resist. Chandra Mohanty's argument for political solidarity and common interests remains pertinent to how we mobilize politically across differences. Mohanty (1997, 8) states, "This idea of political solidarity in the context of the incorporation of Third World women into a global economy offers a basis for cross-cultural comparison and analysis that is grounded in history and social location rather than in an ahistorical notion of culture or experience."

Mohanty's argument illuminates the transnational feminist reviewer's critique of my article submission as an erasure of my own multiple struggles as an Asian American Woman of Color, which informed my cultural competency to be able to connect with immigrants and refugees who did not speak English. She reduces my cultural competency to linguistic knowhow in an erasure of my history and social location as enabling modes of complex communication that extend beyond shared linguistic codes. My own trajectory of struggles against racialized neocolonial systems of neoliberalism and globalization moved me to share common political investments with the refugee and immigrant women with whom I sought to connect.

This disposition to connect across struggles enabled me to shift to participatory action research where I became legible to these subjects through
on-the-ground organizing as someone to whom they could communicate
their experiences and needs. The eclipsing of Women of Color feminisms
in the review informed the pain I experienced as an epistemic subject
denied the lens of multiplicity in my attempt to center immigrant/refugee
women. The lens of multiplicity makes visible my positionality within
multiple valences of power and makes us conscious of embodied knowledge born of lived struggle, encouraging us to suspend legitimized frames
of knowing that disavow emotional forces shaping who we are and how we
relate. In suspending legitimized frames that presume singular and exclusionary modes of knowing, we can attend to the energies infusing a collective struggle so as to fuel solidarity. Attention to the complexity of
multiple valences of power helps one avoid presuming that a monolingual
Asian American is incapable of communicating and connecting with Asian
refugees and immigrants who cannot speak English—or that an Asian
immigrant/refugee cannot connect and communicate with an Asian American who knows white supremacy intimately, albeit differently than them.

    In line with Women of Color feminists who were challenging binary log-
ics in race and feminist studies, Lowe's articulation of multiplicity strives
to expand our analyses of counterhegemonic formations in minoritized
communities that account "for a multiplicity of various, non equivalent
groups, one of which is Asian Americans" (Lowe 1991, 29). In recognizing
the multiple valences of power in coalitional spaces, there is no pretense of
equivalency or an intersecting sameness. Rather, the commonalities that
bring people together are shaped through a Women of Color politics of
knowing oppression through our lived experiences while recognizing and
holding accountable our varying levels of privilege. In her 1996 revised version of "Heterogeneity, Hybridity, and Multiplicity" in *Immigrant Acts: On
Asian American Cultural Politics*, Lowe expands on multiplicity as a political framework where multiple levels of difference among the various actors
shape coalitional space, forms of solidarity, and resulting struggles. She
states, "We can make more explicit—in light of feminist theory that has
gone perhaps the furthest in theorizing multiple determined nations and
the importance of positionalities—that it may be difficult to act exclusively
in terms of a single valence or political interest—such as race, ethnicity,
or nation—because social subjects are the sites of a variety of differences"
(Lowe 1996, 73–74).[4] For Asian American feminisms, multiplicity provides

a way of engaging Women of Color politics through shared political investments and a consciousness of difference and power.

The issues I have explored here further crystalize how a framework of
multiplicity can be useful for resistant strategies, self-reflexive political
accountability, and mobilizing efforts. Multiplicity allows us to grapple with
the messy, contradictory, and incommensurable relationships that still find
us fighting on the same side. While numerous Asian American or Asian
immigrant communities may find few intersecting structural similarities
with the demands of the Black Lives Matter movement, a racialized consciousness of institutionalized racism that can see the oppositional
divide-and-conquer motifs can lead to the organizing of such groups as
Asians4BlackLives. The Asians4BlackLives movement uses a framework of
multiplicity to enact a form of solidarity that simultaneously recognizes
Asian Americans as racially privileged vis-à-vis Black Americans and as
racially subordinated by white supremacist foundations.

Strategies for solidarity require naming and grappling with *difference*,
conflict, and the potentials for enacting harm by those whose relative
privileges impose communicative obstacles in our attempts to unite with
differently oppressed people. From a politically resistant standpoint, the
stakes remain critical, as Asian American feminists often need to define
their common interests and political consciousness within cross-racial
social justice struggles. The tension of naming the multiple layers of difference within Asian America lends itself to the relative invisibility of Asian
Americans as coalitional subjects. In other words, when Asian American
feminists fail to account for the multiple differences within Asian America
itself, we reinforce the very homogenizing logics that render us invisible
as coalitional subjects in solidarity with other communities of color.
Multiplicity as a feminist praxis inserts complexity into any coalitional
space, where Asian American feminist activists share common political
interests, even though different social and historical processes bring them
there. Using a lens that accounts for and engages multiplicity is especially
urgent in "Trump's America" as Asian American feminists heed the call to
organize against the persistence of police brutality toward Black bodies, the
Muslim ban, anti-immigration, the attack on healthcare, the environment,
workers, and Mexico. In these trying times an Asian American feminist
praxis must always remain conscious of the multiple valances of power at
play, as well as our positions within and across those valances, to enter the
spaces in which to enact solidarity.

NOTES

1   Major thanks to Grace Hong, who in her audience comments at my talk at UCLA helped me to rethink my "failure," beyond my privilege and power, but more so to unpack the complexities and multiplicities from a Woman of Color feminist perspective that shaped such a critical encounter.

2   For a more elaborate discussion, see Soto (2005), Chowdhury (2006), Holloway (2006), and Roshanravan (2012).

3   Thanks to Shireen Roshanravan for helping me parse this out.

4   Here Lowe is discussing the work of Trinh T. Minh-ha, Chela Sandoval, and Angela Davis in challenging binary logics that place Women of Color on the margins of antiracist, antisexist struggles, pointing to the complexity and the need for an understanding of positionality that centers the specificities of particular struggles within its political context.

REFERENCES

Chowdhury, Elora Halim. 2006. "Global Feminism: Feminist Theory's Cul-de-sac." *Human Architecture: Journal of the Sociology of Self-Knowledge* 4 (3): 291–302.

Crenshaw, Kimberlé. 2015. "Why Intersectionality Can't Wait." *Washington Post*, September 24. www.washingtonpost.com/news/in-theory/wp/2015/09/24/why -intersectionality-cant-wait.

Hames-García, Michael. 2011. *Identity Complex: Making the Case for Multiplicity*. Minneapolis: University of Minnesota Press.

Holloway, Karla F. C. 2006. "'Cruel Enough to Stop the Blood': Global Feminisms and the U.S. Body Politic, Or: 'They Done Taken My Blues and Gone.'" *Meridians: feminism, race, transnationalism* 7 (1): 1–18.

Kim, Claire Jean. 2004. "Asian Americans are People of Color Too . . . Aren't They? Cross-Racial Alliances and the Question of Asian American Political Identity." *AAPI Nexus* 2 (1): 19–47.

Lowe, Lisa. 1991. "Heterogeneity, Hybridity, and Multiplicity: Marking Asian American Differences." *Diaspora* 1 (1) (Spring): 24–44.

———. 1996. *Immigrant Acts: On Asian American Cultural Politics*. Durham, NC: Duke University Press.

Mohanty, Chandra Talpade. 1997. "Women Workers and Capitalist Scripts: Ideologies of Domination, Common Interests, and Politics of Solidarity." In *Feminist Genealogies, Colonial Legacies, Democratic Futures*, edited by Jacqui Alexander and Chandra Talpade Mohanty, 3–29. New York: Routledge.

Ong, Aihwa. 1995. "Women out of China: Traveling Tales and Traveling Theories in Postcolonial Feminism." In *Women Writing Culture*, edited by Ruth Behar and Deborah A. Gordon, 350–72. Berkeley: University of California Press.

Peterson, Latoya. 2015. "Intersectionality Is Not a Label." *Washington Post*, September 21. www.washingtonpost.com/news/in-theory/wp/2015/09/21/how -intersectionality-lost-its-punch/?tid=a_inl.

Roshanravan, Shireen. 2012. "Staying Home while Studying Abroad: Anti-Imperial Praxis for Globalizing Feminist Visions." *Journal of Feminist Scholarship* 2 (Spring): 1–23.

Soto, Sandra K. 2005. "Where in the Transnational World Are U.S. Women of Color?" In *Women's Studies for the Future: Foundations, Interrogations, Politics*, edited by Elizabeth Lapovsky Kennedy and Agatha Beins, 111–24. New Brunswick, NJ: Rutgers University Press.

Visweswaran, Kamala. 1994. *Fictions of Feminist Ethnography.* Minneapolis: University of Minnesota Press.

Zavella, Patricia. 1993. "Feminist Insider Dilemmas: Constructing Ethnic Identity with Chicana Informants." *Frontiers: A Journal of Women Studies* 13 (3): 53–76.

CHAPTER 12

WEAPONIZING OUR (IN)VISIBILITY

Asian American Feminist Ruptures of
the Model-Minority Optic

SHIREEN ROSHANRAVAN

IN NOVEMBER OF 2014, PETER LIANG, A CHINESE AMERICAN
police officer employed by the New York City Police Department (NYPD),
was conducting a routine patrol in the dark stairwell of a predominantly
African American public housing unit in Brooklyn. With the elevator out
of commission, residents regularly used the stairwell to enter or exit the
unit. On this day, for an unknown reason, Officer Liang entered the dark
stairwell with his gun drawn and ready to fire; it accidentally went off. The
bullet ricocheted off a wall and killed Akai Gurley, an innocent unarmed
African American father who happened to be leaving his friend's seventh-
story apartment. Instead of immediately administering CPR and calling
for an ambulance, as professional protocol required, Liang left Gurley to
bleed, as he worried about his own fate instead of Gurley's imminent death.[1]
Consequently, Liang was indicted for second-degree manslaughter, a charge
that carries a sentence of up to fifteen years in prison, becoming the first
NYPD officer to be indicted in ten years for an on-duty shooting. In response
to Liang's indictment, Chinese Americans across the nation took to the
streets with signs that read "Racist Prosecution" and "Peter Liang Deserves
Justice Too." The first nationwide public protest led by Asian Americans in
decades sought public attention for what they believed was the racist prosecution or "scapegoating" of a Chinese American police officer (Wang

2016). Justice Danny Chun eventually reduced Liang's charge from manslaughter to criminally negligent homicide and sentenced Liang to five years of probation and eight hundred hours of community service but no jail time.

As the nationwide protests erupted against Liang's indictment, another Asian American mobilization took flight in support of Gurley's family and the larger Black Lives Matter movement. In New York City, the Committee Against Anti-Asian Violence (CAAAV) and Asians4BlackLives-NYC issued statements to the Chinese and larger Asian American community to declare solidarity with Gurley's family and demand police accountability for the systemic murder of Black people (Rao 2016). During a discussion hosted by the independent media outlet *Democracy Now!* CAAAV executive director Cathy Dang sat next to Akai Gurley's aunt, Hertencia Petersen, in vocal and visual solidarity with Petersen's demands for justice for her slain nephew. Dang's visual and ideological alignment with Gurley's aunt stood in stark contrast to that of John Liu, also present for the discussion, who sat opposite Petersen and persistently defended Liang's light sentence. While Liu, the first Asian American elected to the city council in New York City, argued with Petersen and at times talked over her, Dang entered the conversation infrequently but thoughtfully to support Peterson and the larger demand to hold all police officers accountable for murder. She never attempted to speak for Petersen or make her own display of Asian American solidarity the reason for being present. Instead, Dang made clear in her comments that Petersen's demands should also be Asian American demands, insisting that "all lives matter when Black lives matter" (*Democracy Now!* 2015). Her presence in the *Democracy Now!* segment offered a model of Asian American visibility inextricable from coalition with Black struggle.

This chapter analyzes these different post-Liang trajectories of Asian American public visibility to argue that Asian Americans can challenge what Mitsuye Yamada calls our "unnatural invisibility" only by enacting Women of Color coalition politics.[2] In both of her chapter contributions to *This Bridge Called My Back: Writings by Radical Women of Color,* Yamada (1981, 74) argues that silence in the face of injustice reinforces the Orientalist distortion of Asian American women as the "least political" among women of color. Yamada's call can be read as an echo of Frank Chin and Jeffrey Paul Chan's (1972, 75) claim that "the method of being not-black is to make a lot of silence for all the noise the blacks make." Yet, as the Peter Liang protests make clear, breaking silence and piercing the public shroud of a state-prescribed compliant invisibility is not sufficient to challenge the anti-Black logics of Asian American racial formation. Given Women of Color critiques of the racial state as a purveyor of violence in communities of color, what should a Women of Color political project of Asian American feminist visibility entail? If maintaining "cultures of dissemblance" is essential to Women of Color strategies for collective self-determination (Hine 1989), how do we need to rethink what visibility should mean for Asian Americans who have benefited from the model-minority racial project at Black Americans' expense?

As Grace Kyungwon Hong (2006, xvii) argues, the racial state's commitment to white supremacist neoliberal logics make "visibility a rupture, an impossible articulation," for women of color and our communities. Women of Color politics lives in this impossibility of legibility via the racial state's divisive logics and emerges as meaningful in coalitions across what Audre Lorde names our "non-dominant differences."[3] Anchored in cosmologies and histories of resistance that challenge Eurocentric accounts, nondominant understandings of the very differences used to justify systemic state violence against us emerge *within community*, by and for those committed to living beyond state logics of possibility. Constructed as the antipode to a pathologized defiant Blackness, with the primary points of distinction our obedience to authority (silence) and investment in heteropatriarchal tight-knit families (insularity), Asian Americans inhabit a powerful locus from which to understand the coalitional imperative of any struggle against state violence (Wu 2015, 171). The project of Asian American feminist political visibility, therefore, cannot seek representation through appeals to the state and its institutions, but rather must be communicative *beyond Asian America as a refusal and disruption of the state's divisive racist optics.*

Given the above, I engage Daphne Brooks's (2006) tactical strategy of "spectacular opacities" to map an Asian American communicative politics of visibility that respects opacity as integral to insurgent Women of Color coalition politics. I invoke Édouard Glissant's (1997, 67 and 49) understanding of *opacity* as "that which protects the Diverse" in its refusal to become legible according to principles of generalization that seek to assimilate or annihilate the other. The "spectacular" dimension of Asian American coalitional visibility is born from the intentional rupture of "model-minority" public transcripts that generalize Asian Americans as the silent and obedient racial-ethnic minority (invisible) who keep to themselves (insular). Exhibits of coalitional boundary crossing are thus central to this Asian American feminist praxis because they disrupt both state-prescribed hostility toward

other communities of color and the heteropatriarchal principle of indifference to those not legally defined as one's own community or kin. The Chinese Americans protesting Liang's indictment sought to rupture their
invisibility as the silent, obedient racial-ethnic minority while remaining
loyal to divisive principles of insularity to protect and advance their own
interests against state-imposed obstacles. As one Asian American participant at a Liang protest rally conceded to a Black woman who asked where
were Asian Americans during Black-led protests against the racist criminal justice system: "At the end of the day, if it's not your people, you do not
care" ("Christopher Kwok Defending Chinese Protestors" 2016).

The current #NotYourModelMinority pledge and Asians4BlackLives
mobilizations in support of the Black Lives Matter movement refuse this
closed insularity in a communicative exhibit of coalitional boundary crossing. By confounding, if not disarming, the model-minority scripting of
Asian Americans, Asian-Black solidarity projects enact "spectacular opacities" or "dark points of possibility that create figurative sites for the reconfiguration" of Asian American bodies "on display" (Brooks 2006, 8). Displays
of Asian-Black solidarity rupture model-minority constructions of Asian
Americans as insular, silent, and anti-Black. The disruption of these dominant expectations of anti-Blackness renders Asian Americans opaque in the
face of "hostile spectators' epistemological resistance to reading alternative
racial and gender representations" (8). This opacity in turn extends an invitation to (re)learn Asian American (inter)subjectivity in coalitional relation with Black communities against whom we are racialized.

ASIAN-BLACK ROOTS/ROUTES OF COALITIONAL VISIBILITY

I begin with Yuri Kochiyama and Grace Lee Boggs because they serve as
important anchors for understanding the historical legacy and dynamics
of what I am calling an Asian American feminist praxis of coalitional visibility. As two Asian American women activists well known within and
beyond the grassroots political and academic institutional circles of Asian
America, they are most recognized for their intimate and sustained commitment to movements for Black liberation rather than their political identification or work with Asian American communities. For this very reason
Kochiyama and Boggs exemplify a process of becoming Asian American
political protagonists through modes of relating and learning in relation to
those against whom we have been racialized. I highlight, in particular,
Kochiyama's and Lee's emphasis on learning about, and identifying with,

Black struggle without ever appropriating that struggle as their own, and the consequent confounding (or occlusion) of their Asian American identities via this coalitional immersion. The question of whether Boggs and Kochiyama are more models of freedom fighters for Black community than Asian American feminist resisters signals an epistemic investment in what Glissant (1997, 11) calls "root identity." Root identity reduces Asian American belonging to singular terms of linear descent from an originary mythic (geographic, familial, cultural) site of authentic and pure Asianness. If, however, we understand identity through Glissant's "Poetics of Relation," in which "each and every identity is extended in and through a relationship with the Other," then Kochiyama's and Boggs's Asian Americanness is not confounded by their deep and expansive relationship with Black communities and struggles; by contrast, it is only in and through these relationships that we can glimpse how, and with what meaning, they emerge as Asian American.

Yuri Kochiyama's activism is a key example of how cross-racial grassroots solidarity enacts "spectacular opacities" that make her simultaneously "invisible" or "opaque" to the public yet visible in her coalitional commitment to a politics of liberation across communities of struggle. In C. A. Griffith's and H. L. T. Quan's (2010) documentary film *When Mountains Take Wing*, Angela Davis and Kochiyama reflect on the lack of credit given to women of the civil rights and Black Power movements. Kochiyama states, "People know who almost all the big names were." Davis joins her in finishing the statement: "But not the women who did the *real* work." As Davis affirms this general statement on women's invisibility in the civil rights and Black Power movements, she does so as one of the few women famous for her activism in these movements and beyond. Kochiyama, on the other hand, is much less popularly known. Davis then continues, "If we want to encourage young people to continue to do the organizing work that will lead to social movement that will have a radical impact we have to legitimize the role of the organizer, which means, also, the work that women, that *you've* [*pointing to Kochiyama*] done."

In this exchange Davis at once legitimizes Kochiyama's legacy of doing the "real" work of organizing in social movements that have had a radical impact and characterizes this work as "women's work." Such work does not yield the kind of fame enjoyed by a public political activist whose name everybody knows, by Kochiyama and Davis's own account. Documentation of the details of Kochiyama's political legacy and the work she mobilized exposes her political work as decidedly grassroots, coalitional, and radical in its orientation. Kochiyama's political visibility was thus decidedly routed through and rooted in her commitment to coalitional boundary crossing and the relationship-building processes integral to sustaining a coalitional movement. The goal of coalitional boundary crossing is not vertical communication with the state or general public, but rather horizontal communication with those with whom one seeks to build new horizons of liberation. This "real" work of organizing in social movements remains invisible but generates a coalitional visibility that communicates solidarity across racial-ethnic boundaries of difference. Because the goal of this "real" work is not visibility to the public, Kochiyama's role in doing this "real" work renders her opaque except among those with whom she is mobilizing for social change.

That Kochiyama became radicalized through the Black Power movement serves as a model of Asian American feminist politics that affirms Asian American racial identity formation routed horizontally through people of color liberation rather than vertically toward model-minority assimilation. Her invisibility to the public lies in the rupture of Asian American root identity and the presumptions of insularity attached to model-minority racial formation. Within this rupture, however, we glimpse an Asian American coalitional visibility recognized and honored by the communities (Asian and Black) to whom she committed her life's work.

Similarly, Grace Lee Boggs (1998, xv) notes her own "habit of self-effacement" in the introduction to her autobiography: "As the only Chinese American present at political meetings, I tried not to draw attention to myself and was visibly embarrassed whenever I was singled out for praise. During the turbulent 1960s people used to joke about my 'passion for anonymity.'" She goes on to write specifically about the significance of her racialized gender identity as a Chinese American: "Had I not been born female and Chinese American, I would not have realized from early on that fundamental changes were necessary in our society. Had I not been born female and Chinese American, I might have ended up teaching philosophy at a university, an observer rather than an active participant in the humanity-stretching movements that have defined the last half of the twentieth century" (xi). Her statement echoes Lorde's emphasis on Women of Color coalition politics as happening through meaningful connection across our nondominant differences, in which we affirm the wisdom born of inhabiting these differences. Boggs makes clear that her identification with Black freedom movements does not happen *in spite of* her locus as a Chinese American female but rather because of it. The activation of her

Chinese American resistant subjectivity came through her becoming an "active participant in the humanity-stretching movements" led by African Americans (xi). That she calls the Black freedom struggles "humanity-stretching movements" is significant insofar as she recognizes the capacity to stretch her sense of being a Chinese American female self through identification with Black struggle. This sense of identification invokes María Lugones's (2003, 85) understanding of "identification" as a self-transforming epistemic shift that requires suspending one's familiar assumptions about one's identity to enable a faithful witnessing of one's self and the worlds one inhabits through the eyes of those differently oppressed. In Boggs's case, her immersion in Black struggle allowed her to read her own liberation as interdependent with that of Black peoples.

Identification, as Kochiyama and Boggs enact it, does not involve sameness or commonality and thus evades the dangers of mimicry. Boggs (1998, xi) notes the inability of the FBI to make sense of her presence as a non-Black Asian American in the Black movement, leading them to describe her "as probably Afro-Chinese." This FBI classification of Boggs illustrates what Brooks (2006, 8) describes as "the hostile spectator's epistemological resistance" to read Asian Americans beyond anti-Black insular model-minority racial representations. While Boggs admits to following her African American husband, Jimmy Boggs, in the early years of her involvement in Black community organizing in Detroit, she clarifies this process as part of the epistemic shift that transforms her and prevents superficial mimicry of Black identity in the struggle. Although not center stage in meetings, Grace Lee Boggs was working to understand the intimate connections between her liberation and those in the Black communities where she lived and learned about the world. She writes, "In the 1950s I rarely went to a community meeting without Jimmy and would usually just listen or ask questions" but goes on to clarify that later, "having worked in the city and socialized with Jimmy's friends and *Correspondence* readers for years, I felt I had something to contribute. I was beginning to feel comfortable with the *we* pronoun," (Boggs 1998, 118). Boggs, like Kochiyama, emerged into a coalitional "we" through the hard work of coming to see her Asian American female self as interdependent with Black struggle.

Kochiyama and Boggs exhibit resistance to state violence through coalitional connection where the jury to which they give themselves up to enact justice is the communities of color with whom they seek solidarity rather than the mainstream public and its racist, (hetero)sexist filters. Their visibility *as Asian American women activists* is routed through their intentionally resistant reach beyond the rigid state-defined racial-ethnic boundaries of who constitutes *their own people*, and thus involves a refusal to invest in the principle of noninterference as integral to their pursuit of justice and well-being. Boggs and Kochiyama thus remain opaque to those invested in the singularity and insularity of "root identity" and in model-minority racial and gender expectations of Asian Americans. They emerge as visible and intelligible *as Asian American* when we use an Asian American feminist lens grounded in the epistemic truth of Glissant's "Poetics of Relation" (1997, 11). Asian American racial positioning as always tangential makes us especially disposed to recognize the dangers of insular and singular "root identity" modes of resistance and to face the relational and interdependent reality of all struggles. The potential visibility of a truly resistant (rather than complicit) Asian American identification demands cross-racial alignment, and thus a process of coalitional self-making that can rupture the divisive public lens of model-minority insularity.

THE COALITIONAL IMPERATIVE OF THE RACIAL THIRD SPACE

A central premise of my argument is that Asian American racialization as "neither black nor white" arms Asian Americans with a grenade that can explode or reinforce racism's suicidal divisions. By *racial third space* I mean the *consigned* locus of Asian American racial subjects. Homi Bhabha (1994, 39) uses the term *third space* to refer to an unrepresentable in-between space that "eludes the politics of polarity" as it confounds the colonizing investment in boundaries erected to create and police fictive notions of purity. Gloria Anzaldúa (1999) similarly theorizes the *racial third space* as the site of concrete fleshy intersubjective negotiations that exceed and counter the racial state's reductive and normative abstract either/or logics. As an in-between space that explodes the fictions of institutional boundaries, all flesh-and-blood racialized subjects inhabit the *racial third space in their resistance against racial reduction.*

Asian Americans, however, inhabit the unrepresentable "third space" not only in their flesh-and-blood resistance but also *in their hegemonic racialization as neither-black-nor-white model minorities.* As Claire Jean Kim (1999) argues in her theory of racial triangulation, Black and white are two poles of the socially enforced US racial continuum of "relative valorization" with Blackness positioned as the hegemonic prototypical domestic symbol of nonwhiteness and racial degradation. Kim situates Asian Americans as racially indeterminate US subjects who become legible as US racial subjects when read in relation to the US black/white binary. The question posed in the title of Kim's 2004 article, "Asian Americans are People of Color Too . . . Aren't They?" captures this hegemonic consignment of Asian Americans to racial uncertainty between black and white and the corresponding suspicion of our capacity for cross-racial solidarity with other nonwhite peoples. How we respond or don't respond to this question either disrupts or reinforces our anti-Black construction in service of white supremacy. As Soya Jung (2014) so powerfully puts it, "We are either left or right of the color line. There is no sitting that out. . . . Our options are invisibility, complicity, or resistance."

Ian Haney Lopez's (1996) analysis of the so-called prerequisite cases for US citizenship at the beginning of the twentieth century demonstrates that racial legibility of US citizenry (in its legal sense) has been defined primarily through the portal of whiteness or Blackness. Before 1952, anyone seeking naturalization as a US citizen had to claim legal classification as either white or Black. While those who were neither Black nor white who brought their case for citizenship to the Supreme Court could have chosen to prove their eligibility through the portal of Blackness, only one did (Lopez 1999, 35). Lopez underscores the court's ultimate reliance on "common knowledge" for what constituted the boundaries of white identity to rule on one's citizenship eligibility. As the courts invoked "common knowledge" to define white as that which was *not nonwhite*, they concomitantly marked the specific boundaries of nonwhiteness, barring different ethnicities from US citizenship (20). The parameters for proving "Black" citizenship required a more restrictive criteria of demonstrating African ancestry (20), while proving a claim to white racial identity required proving that one was *not not-white*. As such, the failure of Asian appeals to state legibility as not-not-white not only blocks us from legibility as US citizen-subjects but also trains us into habits of active dissociation from, and devaluation of, Black people as a key strategy for achieving state recognition of US belonging.

I am thus invoking the consigned *racial third space* of Asian America to understand the voiced frustrations of Asian Americans about our sense of racial invisibility as US subjects of color (often expressed in relation to a hypervisible Blackness) and the particular communicative barriers toward a racial visibility that does not feed anti-Black state logics. Because the black/white binary is central to the construction of our racial ambiguity, it necessarily shapes our resistant possibilities both in maneuvering the model-minority construction to evade violent targeting by the racial state and in rupturing model-minority erasures of state-sponsored racism against us. To illustrate, Asian Americans who reject "honorary white" racist positioning reinscribe anti-Blackness when claiming visibility as aggrieved racial minorities just like Black people (Roshanravan 2018). The Peter Liang case referenced at the start of this chapter is instructive here. Asian American protests against Liang's indictment for Akai Gurley's murder challenged a criminal justice system that would indict an Asian American for a crime that white officers systemically commit without similar consequences. These protests thus name the criminal justice system as racist against Asian Americans *just like Black people* because the system failed to let Liang kill Black people without accountability *like other white police officers*.[4]

In short, Asian American hegemonic consignment to the *racial third space* in the United States compels us to face the ever-present choice between becoming legible to the US public either through a portal of whiteness that prescribes closed insularity away from other nonwhite peoples, or through a portal that effectively commits one to forge an identity in relation to those ejected from the purview of white inclusion. The model-minority racial project seduces Asian Americans to choose the portal of whiteness, inscribing and prescribing their insularity from Black community as innate to the "modelness" of Asian racial disposition. Liang, in his NYPD uniform, exemplifies performance of this model Asianness, as he became part of a state agency whose mission historically has been to "protect and serve" white supremacy.[5] Both Liang's murder of Gurley and his subsequent indictment protected and served white supremacy, not only in the destruction of Black life (the ultimate violent dissociation from Blackness), but also in offering the courts a nonwhite token through which to feign police accountability for the systemic state murder of Black people.

Wu Yiping, a coordinator for the protests against Liang's indictment, further evidences the anti-Black logic of this "model" Asianness in his suggestion that the Chinese immigrant community's insular focus on their careers accounts for Chinese-Black hostility over Liang's case (Wang 2016). In this statement, Yiping reinforces the model-minority construction of Asians as the respectable racial minority (who keep to themselves and focus on their own socioeconomic mobility) by invoking its corollary construction of Black people as the unruly racial minority (who lack the discipline to stay out of trouble and achieve careers that would lift them out of public housing). As Alex Quan-Pham and Kat Yang-Stevens (2016) document, news outlets wasted no time portraying Akai Gurley as a criminal with a prior record of arrests whose death at the hands of cops was justified if not inevitable. Gurley's constructed criminality amplified the model-minority portrayal of Peter Liang as a well-intentioned "rookie cop" who made an innocent "mistake" and thus did not deserve to be indicted or serve jail time (Quan-Pham and Yang-Stevens 2016). Yiping's coordination of the nationwide protests against Liang's indictment and his public comments about the ensuing Asian-Black intercommunity tensions reinforce these presumptions by dismissing and vilifying Black rage as based on a "misunderstanding" rather than the systemic state murder of Black people. Through Yiping's complicity with the institutionalized model-minority discourse, we see the animation of an authorized version of Asianness, portrayed as more disposed to rational civil discourse and state-prescribed insularity, which draws hostile boundaries against other nonwhite groups while "protecting and serving" white supremacy. The corollary construction of the irrational, raging, unruly Blackness of Akai Gurley's family and community is essential to animating this authorized version of model "Asianness."

Disrupting the anti-Blackness of model-minority logics requires exhibits of Asian-Black solidarity that explicitly counter weaponized state constructions of US Asians as insular "model minorities" that can be readily wielded against Black lives. As such, being seen in our specific racialized experience as Asian Americans who identify as US people of color requires an ever-evolving (self-)understanding of Asian American identity that is interdependent with (but not the same as) Black struggle. Accordingly, Asian Americans enter tricky terrain when attempting to express our need to be seen as active subjects in struggle against racial subordination. We can experience (with differing degrees of intensity) the seductive illusion of relative privilege in our model-minority racialization; and regardless of our (in)ability or refusal to give uptake to the illusion, we simultaneously suffer the psychic pain of not being seen in our struggle against racial subordination. Yet, as Kochiyama and Boggs demonstrate, the politics of not being seen is often a necessary aspect of doing the "real" work of organizing in movements for social justice. Remaining opaque to the public in one's resistance to state-sanctioned oppressions can also be and has been an important insurgent Women of Color strategy of survival against racist dehumanization and distortions. Let's turn to this infrapolitical avenue of survival and the obstacles it presents for Asian Americans seeking to undo our "unnatural invisibility" (Yamada 1981).

PERILS OF ASIAN AMERICAN INFRAPOLITICS

James Scott (1990, 19) defines *infrapolitics* as "a wide variety of low-profile forms of resistance that dare not speak in their own name." Infrapolitical resistance is thus operative through its capacity to remain unrecognizable as resistance to the oppressive systems being resisted. If, in Scott's terms, the "public transcript" presumes Asian Americans to be insular and obedient model minorities, Asian American infrapolitical resistance to white supremacy would rely on this "public transcript" to enact its "hidden transcript" of resistance (xii). Jid Lee's "The Cry-Smile Mask: A Korean-American Woman's System of Resistance" offers an important example of how infrapolitical resistance, when not combined with more publicly communicable disruptive modes of resistance, reinforces the anti-Black racist underpinnings of the model-minority racial project.

Lee begins her essay with an anecdote in which one of her former students, a forty-year-old white woman named Susan, who, in Lee's company, responds to a Black man's kindness with the comment, "I wish they were all like him. He's so nice. No bitterness or anger. If all Black people were like him we would be in heaven" (2002, 397). Uneasy, Lee responds to the incident by thickening her "cry-smile mask," which, in her words, she has "worn since she came to the United States in 1980" to cope with the racist "burden of smiling [that] always fell upon me" (397). After historicizing this "cry-smile mask" as a culturally specific reference to her Korean cosmology, Lee explains that the mask allows her to maneuver Orientalist expectations toward coalitional possibilities. She performs her expected smile in the face of racism, "opening a door" that, she hopes, will invite, even seduce, cross-racial perception of the "cry behind the smile" (398). This "cry behind the smile" signifies people of color struggles and suffering erased by racism's epistemic commitments to remain blind to the violence it enacts.

Lee acknowledges that the "cry-smile mask" risks feeding the "racist love" of those who expect Asian Americans to accept white racism cheerfully. She responds to this charge by insisting on the significance of "long-term" change that overrides any retrenchment of the model-minority stereotype (399–400). The dialogue enabled by the "cry-smile" mask, Lee argues, outweighs the racist stereotypes it seemingly reinforces to the extent that the dialogue is essential to inviting others to see the "cry" (oppression of people of color) behind the "smile."

The relational dynamics of racism generally, and the specific implications of her own in-between racial locus, however, are absent from Lee's account of the efficacy of her cry-smile mask in challenging racist logics among white people. This is particularly evident when she compares her "cry-smile" mask to the mask of survival described in Paul Lawrence Dunbar's "We Wear the Mask." She writes of her connection to African American literature, "I could identify with African Americans as a whole race, because I could feel what they felt, and because I had to wear a mask—*much like their own*—to survive" (400, emphasis added). Dunbar's poem describes the "mask" that African Americans have to wear to maneuver in white/Anglo racist culture while painfully communicating the "double consciousness" in the very act of wearing the mask. Dunbar, like Lee, suggests that white expectations shape the mask and that the decision to wear the mask is not about subordinating oneself to these expectations but instead about cultivating strategies to survive and maintain a resistant sense of self. Nevertheless, Lee's claim that she identifies "with African Americans as a whole race" because she "could feel what they felt" ignores how the very expectations that shape Lee's mask thicken the layers of the mask of racist expectations that African Americans have to wear.

This truth is particularly significant when one considers Lee's decision to wear the "cry-smile mask" instead of confronting Susan for her anti-Black racism. Susan's wish that all Black people were "kind" and "nice" (instead of bitter and angry) articulates institutionalized racist expectations that demonize Black people as bitter and angry relative to "model" Asian qualities of compliance and accommodation. The survival/resistant strategy of Lee's "cry-smile mask" relies on a closed insularity. As she explains, because Susan was no longer her student, she "could not correct her" (396). Lee's "cry-smile" requires and allows her to not interfere in the racism expressed by and toward people outside the institutional bounds of her *own people*. While Lee's felt connection with Black struggle aspires to coalition, she reduces Blackness to a source of inspiration from which she draws but to which she does not contribute. Her identification with Black people reduces the differences between Asian American and African American struggles to a generic ahistorical experience of racism that in turn presumes the capacity to utilize systems of resistance (like the infrapolitical smile in the face of racism) with similar consequence. This mode of identification contradicts the Women of Color politics of affirming and insisting on the specificity of our nondominant differences as a source of strength in coalition building. As such, Lee's system of resistance illustrates the perils for Asian Americans who use infrapolitical modes of survival that rely on the model-minority public transcript to stealthily maneuver in the face of racism.

Lee's strategic refusal of spectacular rupture of state-sanctioned racist optics is not accompanied by an inward turn to honor or foster the possibility of coalitional relations between Asian American and Black communities. While insularity may serve as one tool in the resistance/survival tool kit against white supremacy, its capacity to reinforce the model-minority racist optic of Asian Americans (and Black Americans) requires that its use be accompanied by exhibits of cross-racial coalitional boundary crossing. The current Asians4BlackLives mobilizations demonstrate this truth in their strategic disruption of public transcripts of Asian American model-minority insularity to enact an Asian American feminist praxis of coalitional visibility.

POETICS OF RELATION: IDENTIFYING WITH BLACKNESS

We have now established the following claims: recognition of Asian Americans as US racial citizen-subjects who suffer and resist state-sponsored racism requires collectively disrupting our public transcript as uncertain in our political orientation between whiteness and Blackness; and Blackness exists on this socially enforced US racial continuum as the hegemonic prototypical domestic symbol of nonwhiteness. Given both of these claims, it follows that Asian American racial visibility *as people of color* divested from anti-Black racism requires exhibiting Black identification. By "Black identification" I mean a process of recognizing one's interdependence with Black racial formation, which María Lugones (2003, 97) defines in terms of coming to see oneself through another's, in this case Black people's, eyes.

This process of identification is tricky because recognition of interdependence ought not be mistaken for an invitation to mimic, co-opt, or otherwise empty Blackness of its lived cultural specificity. The various mobilizations under the Asians4BlackLives campaign illustrate an important communicative shift toward Asian American demands for visibility. Instead of an "us too!" logic, the campaign makes Asian Americans visible as inextricably coalitional with other people of color—most explicitly, with the very Black communities against which Asian Americans are racially intelligible as model minorities in the United States. If "the problem of communication is primarily about recognition and disposition to communicate," as Gabriela Veronelli (2015, 122) states, then the Asians4BlackLives campaign tackles the problem head on. Not only does the campaign explicitly recognize the historical pain and resistance of the Black struggles motivating the Black Lives Matter movement, but it also enacts a coalitional disposition to intercultural communication by turning inward to self-definition in and through gestures that signal a commitment to learn about and understand Black lives.

That is, the Asians4BlackLives campaign ruptures the racial state logic that relies on nonwhite cross-racial antagonism and disconnection and instead issues a public cross-racial coalitional rescripting of Asian America. In the words of Audrey Kuo (2017) of Asian Pacific Islanders for Black Lives (Los Angeles), "We want to be visible but not for the sake of visibility but to call out to others to join us ... to build bigger coalition." To resist visibility for visibility's sake is to refuse transparency to a racial state rooted in white supremacy and to resist the divisive logics that structure its filters of public visibility. Instead, Kuo emphasizes that Asians4BlackLives actions seek a communicative visibility, one that issues a call for others disposed to end violence to join them in "building bigger coalition." The breadth and depth of these coalitional efforts are evident in the fact that many of the collectives and networks communicating Asians4BlackLives solidarity are queer identified and feminist and incorporate strategies for consciousness-raising about anti-Black racism in Asian American communities and the Black Lives Matter movement.[6] As such, the Asians4BlackLives campaign can be understood as emerging from a Women of Color coalitional feminist genealogy in which queer women of color have always led the way.

These collectives make Asian American struggles publicly visible as they issue a powerful and unequivocal statement of solidarity with Black Lives Matter. The public declaration of Asian-Black solidarity makes Asian Americans nonsensical to those unwilling to read beyond the state logics of model-minority racial and gender representation. However, their interlocutors are other Asian Americans and Asian immigrant communities and Black communities of struggle, not the racial state. They lay bare the state violence that structures communication from Asian America to Black America without reducing them to sameness. As the Queer South Asian National Network (QSANN) states, "We are committed to drawing connections between Islamophobia, caste-based oppression, privilege and complicity, xenophobia and profiling, and anti-Blackness in ourselves, our communities, and the imperial US" (2015, 1). As they go on to describe the horror of watching South Asians profiled as "terrorists" and murdered by police officers, they simultaneously call for a "model minority mutiny," recognizing that the racial project seduces us into complicity with the long history of surveillance, criminalization, incarceration, and murder of Black people. Calling forth the embodied knowledge of state and interpersonal violence in both South Asian and Black communities, QSANN enacts Women of Color feminist methodologies of doing "theory in the flesh . . . where the physical realities of our lives—our skin color, the land or concrete we grew up on, our sexual longings—all fuse to create a politic born out of necessity" (Moraga 2015, 19).

The call for solidarity demands that we remember Black freedom struggles from which Asian immigrants have benefited immensely. These statements circulate through public media, giving Asian Americans political visibility as accomplices in the struggle against anti-Black racism. By rupturing model-minority and Orientalist logics, the campaign generates an opacity of who/what Asian Americans are and thus creates space for us to turn back to our communities of place and "commit to undoing anti-Blackness at home, working against Islamophobia, and challenging our identity within the model minority myth" (Queer South Asian National Network 2015). These exhibits of Asian-Black solidarity are thus not about seeking recognition from the racial state or visibility as people of color *just like Black people* in the general public. The emphasis is on refusing insularity that promotes cross-racial antagonism and simultaneously enacting horizontal coalitional boundary crossing and relationship building, which (re)define what it is to be Asian American and to whom we must be accountable in our resistance against white supremacy. Exhibiting Asian-Black solidarity enables an Asian American feminist praxis of coalitional visibility that simultaneously ruptures the racist optics of the state and generates an opacity that creates space for Asian Americans to stretch our sense of self and possibility as interdependent with the Black community.

Because the model-minority myth solidified through an anti-Blackness coded in heteropatriarchal family-centered gender conservatism, model-minority mutiny must also refuse the heteropatriarchal gender ideologies that underwrite model-minority respectability (Wu 2015, 183). Freedom, Inc., a collective rooted in the Hmong and Black communities of Madison, Wisconsin, makes this indelibly clear as they actively generate public materials that feature Black and Southeast Asian American solidarity and coalition that center queer and trans experiences. In one of their youth organizing campaigns, two Freedom, Inc., leaders, one queer/trans and Black identified, the other a Hmong-identified woman, explain their definitions of leadership in terms of loving and creating family against what they've been told is family, against blood kin. In the last line of the video clip, they define Freedom, Inc., as "queer and trans Southeast Asian and Black leading so what we can get free because we know that our liberations are tied together" (Freedom, Inc. 2016). Their emphasis on championing modes of loving and building queer and trans family within Black and Southeast Asian communities embraces Cathy Cohen's (2004) call for "deviance as resistance" since the loving and building of coalitional community transgresses heteropatriarchal traditions and norms of respectability within both communities of color. In other words, the Freedom, Inc., leaders exhibit a commitment to coalitional boundary crossing rather than a closed insularity by redefining who constitutes family beyond rigid state-sanctioned heteropatriarchal boundaries. In doing so, they disable the racialization of Asian Americans as respectable relative to Black deviance and in turn create a bridge toward more liberatory definitions of love and family.

The opacity generated in these displays of Asian-Black solidarity is evident in the epistemological resistance to Asian American presence in solidarity acts with the Black community. In his *Politico* account of covering a Black Lives Matter protest in Milwaukee, Aaron Mak (2016) reflects on the Black readings of his Asian presence as communicating solidarity while others questioned his presence, asking, "You're Asian. . . . Why are you even here?" The latter question exposes the incomprehensibility of Asian-Black solidarity given the public transcript of Asian Americans as model minorities committed to an insularity that prescribes hostility or at best indifference to Black people and their struggles. Asian Americans showing up for Black lives is nonsensical when read through state logics. One must erase Asian presence from Black coalitional movements to keep dominant state constructions intact.

This explains Soo Ah Kwon's (2013, 75, 86) observations in her ethnography of Asian American youth organizing in the San Francisco Bay Area, where "campaign discourses about youth incarceration and criminalization rarely mentioned Asian and Pacific Islander youth," and "at many campaign actions, these youth were overlooked as targets of state incarceration or criminalization unlike their African American or Latino/a counterparts." The cloud of confusion generated in the rupture of state logics of representation renders Asian Americans opaque to the state in their coalitional presence, opening avenues beyond the halting grip of the racial state to generate coalitional conceptions of Asian American feminist (inter)subjectivity through the eyes of communities against whom we are racialized. Evidence of these avenues includes conference calls organized between members of Asians4BlackLives and the Black Lives Matter networks to strategize Asian-Black solidarity (Tom 2015). Such strategies rely on remaining opaque or invisible to the state and open to the diversity that opacity protects. As QSANN (2015, 3) explains, "Part of challenging anti-Blackness in ourselves and our communities is crafting a new narrative of what it means to be South Asian in the US." Without doing so, the survival/resistant strategy of infrapolitical insularity cannot but reinforce the model-minority racial project and its reliance on anti-Black racism.

TOWARD AN INSURGENT WOMEN OF COLOR EPISTEMIC LOCUS

Our racial positioning as always tangential makes us especially disposed to recognize the dangers of closed insularity and singular modes of resistance and to face the relational and interdependent reality of all community struggles. The potential visibility of a truly resistant (rather than complicit) Asian American identification demands cross-racial alignment and thus a process of coalitional self-making that can rupture the divisive public lens of model-minority insularity. The current Asians4BlackLives mobilizations build on the political legacies of Grace Lee Boggs and Yuri Kochiyama to illustrate a pathway toward Asian American feminist visibility through the "spectacular opacities" of coalitional boundary crossing. Becoming visible through participation in Black freedom struggles, these Asian American political subjects and movements reject an Asian American visibility routed through a "poetics of disconnection" seduced by and supportive of US racial state logics of legibility and insularity.[7] Asian American feminist visibility routed through a praxis of horizontal coalitional boundary crossing thus clarifies the racial third space of Asian America as an insurgent epistemic locus that opens toward a Women of Color consciousness of our interdependent realities and possibilities.

NOTES

1   Officer Liang testified that he did call for an ambulance when he discovered that Gurley had been shot. However, there is no evidence in the radio transcripts submitted to the court that he did indeed call for an ambulance (Nir 2016).

2   In "The Coalitional Imperative of Asian American Feminist Visibility," I use post-Liang manifestations of Asian American visibility to map the anti-Black traps of "us too!" appeals for Asian American visibility (Roshanravan 2018). This chapter focuses on the coalitional possibilities of an Asian American feminist visibility and strategies for achieving them.

3   Lorde (1984, 111) defines "non-dominant differences" as those positive life-giving differences constitutive of our complex (inter)subjectivity, which the racial state necessarily distorts to protect and promote the divisive logics of racism, (hetero) sexism, and other interlocking dominant structures of oppression.

4   For further elaboration of the anti-Black traps of Asian American uses of analogy to Black struggle against systemic racism, see Roshanravan (2018).

5   In "From the Convict Lease System to the Super-Max Prison," Angela Davis (2000) traces the history of policing and imprisonment as an ongoing legacy of white supremacy and its investment in the enslavement, exploitation, and disappearance of Black peoples.

6   These groups include Queer South Asian National Network; Freedom, Inc.; and National Asian Pacific American Women's Forum, to name a few.

7   Leslie Bow (2010, 127) coined the term *poetics of disconnection* to reference disavowal of a "self-implicating Blackness" experienced by Asian Americans in the segregated US South to affirm their greater proximity to valorized whiteness.

REFERENCES

Anzaldúa, Gloria. 1999. *Borderlands / La Frontera: Toward a New Mestiza Consciousness*. San Francisco: Aunt Lute Books.

Bhabha, Homi. 1994. *The Location of Culture*. London: Routledge.

Boggs, Grace Lee. 1998. *Living for Change: An Autobiography*. Minneapolis: University of Minnesota Press.

Bow, Leslie. 2010. *Partly Colored: Asian Americans and Racial Anomaly in the Segregated South*. New York: New York University Press.

Brooks, Daphne. 2006. *Bodies in Dissent: Spectacular Performances of Race and Freedom, 1850–1910*. Durham, NC: Duke University Press.

Chin, Frank, and Jeffrey Paul Chan. 1972. "Racist Love." In *Seeing through Shuck*, edited by Richard Kostelanetz, 65–79. New York: Ballantine.

"Christopher Kwok Defending Chinese Protestors at Peter Liang Rally (2-20-16)." *YouTube* video. www.youtube.com/watch?v=zwIEOtkLlaA. Accessed January 18, 2018.

Cohen, Cathy. 2004. "Deviance as Resistance: A New Research Agenda for the Study of Black Politics." *Du Bois Review* 1 (1): 27–45.

Davis, Angela. 2000. "From the Convict Lease System to the Super-Max Prison." In *States of Confinement: Policing, Detention, and Prisons*, edited by Joy James, 60–74. New York: Palgrave Macmillan.

Democracy Now! 2016. "As Officer Who Killed Akai Gurley Gets No Jail Time, Asian Americans Debate Role of White Supremacy." April 21. www.democracynow.org 2016/4/21/as_officer_who_killed_akai_gurley.

Freedom, Inc. 2016. "Leading So We Can Get Free." Freedom Inc. Queer Media Campaign 1.5. www.youtube.com/watch?v=iWBww6__Tqc.

Glissant, Édouard. 1997. *Poetics of Relation*. Translated by Betsy Wing. Ann Arbor: University of Michigan Press.

Griffith, C. A., and H. L. T. Quan. 2010. *When Mountains Take Wing: Angela Davis and Yuri Kochiyama—a Conversation on Life, Struggles, and Liberation*. Film. Quad Productions.

Hine, Darlene. 1989. "Rape and the Inner Lives of Black Women in the Middle West: Preliminary Thoughts on the Culture of Dissemblance." *Signs* 14 (4): 912–20.

Hong, Grace Kyungwon. 2006. *The Ruptures of American Capital: Women of Color Feminism and the Culture of Immigrant Labor*. Minneapolis: University of Minnesota Press.

Jung, Soya. 2014. "Why Ferguson Matters to Asian Americans." *Race Files* (blog), August 20. www.racefiles.com/2014/08/20/why-ferguson-matters-to-Asian Americans.

Kim, Claire Jean. 1999. "The Racial Triangulation of Asian Americans." *Politics & Society* 27 (1): 105–38.

———. 2004. "Asian Americans are People of Color Too . . . Aren't They?" *AAPI Nexus* 2 (1): 19–47.

———. 2016. "The Trial of Peter Liang and Confronting the Reality of Asian American Privilege." *Los Angeles Times*, April 21. www.latimes.com/opinion/opinion-la/la-ol -peter-liang-Asian-American-privilege-20160421-snap-story.html.

Kuo, Audrey. 2017. "Feminist Solidarities / Black Lives Matter." Roundtable, Association for Asian American Studies conference, Portland, Oregon, April 15, 2017.

Kwon, Soo Ah. 2013. *Uncivil Youth: Race, Activism, Affirmative Governmentality*. Durham, NC: Duke University Press.

Lee, Jid. 2002. "The Cry-Smile Mask: A Korean American Woman's System of Resistance." In *This Bridge We Call Home: Radical Visions for Transformation*, edited by Gloria Anzaldúa and AnaLouise Keating, 397–402. New York: Routledge.

Lopez, Ian Haney. 1996. *White by Law: The Legal Construction of Race*. New York: New York University Press.

Lorde, Audre. 1984. *Sister/Outsider: Essays and Speeches by Audre Lorde*. Freedom, CA: Crossing Press.

Lugones, María. 2003. *Pilgrimages/Peregrinajes: Theorizing Coalition against Multiple Oppressions*. Lanham, MD: Rowman and Littlefield.

Mak, Aaron. 2016. "'You're Asian, Right? Why Are You Even Here?'" *Politico Magazine*, August 23. https://www.politico.com/magazine/story/2016/08/milwaukee-protests -Asian American-black-lives-matter-214184.

Moraga, Cherríe. 2015. "Entering the Lives of Others: Theory in the Flesh." In *This Bridge Called My Back: Writings by Radical Women of Color*, 4th ed., edited by Cherríe Moraga and Gloria Anzaldúa, 19. Albany: State University of New York Press.

Nir, Sarah Maslin. 2016. "Officer Peter Liang, on Stand, Breaks Down as He Recalls Brooklyn Killing." *New York Times*, February 6. https://www.nytimes.com/2016/02 /09/nyregion/officer-peter-liang-in-emotional-testimony-describes-the-night-of-a -fatal-shooting.html.

Quan-Pham, Alex, and Kat Yang-Stevens. 2016. "Akai Gurley the 'Thug,' Peter Liang the 'Rookie Cop' and the Model Minority Myth." *Truthout*, February 26. www.truth-out .org/opinion/item/34988-akai-gurley-the-thug-peter-liang-the-rookie-cop-and-the -model-minority-myth.

Queer South Asian National Network. 2015. "South Asians for Black Power: On Anti-Blackness, Islamophobia, and Complicity." September 11. https://queersouthasian .wordpress.com.

Rao, Sameer. 2016. "Asian Americans Demand #Justice4Akai." *Colorlines*. www .colorlines.com/articles/Asian

American-activists-demand-justice4akai-protest-outside-major-chinese-language-papers.

Roshanravan, Shireen. 2018. "The Coalitional Imperative of Asian American Feminist Visibility." *Pluralist* 13 (1) (Spring): 115–30.

Scott, James. 1990. *Domination and the Arts of Resistance*. New Haven, CT: Yale University Press.

Tom, Alex. 2015. "Black Lives Matter Allies in Change." Interview by Margi Clarke and Preeti Shekar. *Reimagine!* www.reimaginerpe.org/20-1/clarke-shekar.

Veronelli, Gabriela. 2015. "The Coloniality of Language: Race, Expressivity, Power, and the Darker Side of Modernity." *Wagadu* 13 (Summer): 108–34.

Wang, Hansi Lo. 2016. "'Awoken' by N.Y. Cop Shooting, Asian American Activists Chart Way Forward." *Code Switch: Race and Identity, Remixed*, April 23. www.npr.org/sections/codeswitch/2016/04/23/475369524/awoken-by-n-y-cop-shooting-Asian American-activists-chart-way-forward.

Wu, Ellen. 2015. *Color of Success: Origins of the Model Minority Myth*. Durham, NC: Duke University Press.

Yamada, Mitsuye. 1981. "Invisibility Is an Unnatural Disaster: Reflections of an Asian American Woman." In *This Bridge Called My Back: Writings by Radical Women of Color*, edited by Cherríe Moraga and Gloria Anzaldúa, 35–40. New York: Kitchen Table Women of Color Press.

CONTRIBUTORS

MAILE ARVIN is assistant professor of history and gender studies at the University of Utah, where she is part of a growing Pacific Islander Studies Initiative. A Native Hawaiian feminist scholar who writes about Native feminist theories, settler colonialism, decolonization, and race, gender and science in Hawai'i and the broader Pacific, her work has been published in the journals *American Quarterly, Native American and Indigenous Studies, Critical Ethnic Studies, Scholar and Feminist,* and *Feminist Formations.* She serves on the board of the Critical Ethnic Studies Association and is at work on her first book, about settler colonialism and whiteness in Hawai'i and Oceania.

LYNN FUJIWARA is associate professor of ethnic studies at the University of Oregon. She is the author of *Mothers without Citizenship: Asian Immigrant Families and the Consequences of Welfare Reform* (University of Minnesota Press, 2008). She co-created the Women of Color Junior Faculty Project, "Women of Color, Borders, and Power: Mentoring and Leadership Development," at the University of Oregon and coordinated the project from 2008 through 2010. Her work in progress includes the book *Queering Asian American Feminisms: The Sexual Politics of Representation and Resistance.*

PRIYA KANDASWAMY is associate professor of women's, gender, and sexuality studies at Mills College. Her research focuses on the intersections of race, gender, sexuality, and class in the history of the US welfare state. Her articles have appeared in journals such as *Sexualities, American Quarterly,* and *Radical Teacher* as well as in numerous edited anthologies.

TAMSIN KIMOTO is a PhD candidate in philosophy at Emory University. Their primary areas of research are social and political theory, the metaphysics of gender, Women of Color feminisms, and trans studies, especially as these areas intersect in phenomena such as transphobic violence and trans liberation movements. Their work is informed by their own experiences and indebted to the women and femmes of color who have made living possible.

GRACE KYUNGWON HONG is professor of Asian American studies and gender studies at the University of California, Los Angeles. She is the author of *Death Beyond Disavowal: The Impossible Politics of Difference* (University of Minnesota Press, 2015) and *The Ruptures of American Capital: Women of Color Feminism and the Culture of Immigrant Labor* (University of Minnesota Press, 2006). She is coeditor of *Strange Affinities: The Gender and Sexual Politics of Comparative Racialization* (Duke University Press, 2011) and of the Difference Incorporated series at the University of Minnesota Press.

ERIN KHUÊ NINH is associate professor in the Department of Asian American Studies at the University of California, Santa Barbara. Her book on intergenerational conflict in immigrant families, *Ingratitude: The Debt-Bound Daughter in Asian American Literature* (NYU Press, 2011), explores the costs of so-called tiger parenting. She currently serves as the Southern California regional representative on the Executive Board of the Association for Asian American Studies.

SHIREEN ROSHANRAVAN is associate professor of American ethnic studies at Kansas State University. Her research focuses on Women of Color feminist methodologies as they inform and are informed by Asian American resistant negotiations of model-minority racial projects and legacies of colonial mimicry. Roshanravan's work can be found in journals such as *Hypatia: Journal of Feminist Philosophy*, *Meridians: Feminism, Race, Transnationalism*, and *Journal of Feminist Scholarship*. She is coeditor with Pedro DiPietro and Jennifer McWeeny of a collection on the work of Latina feminist philosopher and popular educator María Lugones (SUNY Press, forthcoming).

THOMAS XAVIER SARMIENTO is assistant professor of English and an affiliate faculty member of gender, women, and sexuality studies at Kansas State University. He specializes in diasporic Filipinx American literature and culture, queer theory, and cultural representations of the US Midwest and teaches courses on Asian American literature, feminist and queer thought, film adaptation, and queer cinema. His articles have appeared in *MELUS: Multi-Ethnic Literature of the United States* and *Women, Gender, and Families of Color.*

STEPHANIE NOHELANI TEVES is assistant professor of ethnic studies and women's and gender studies at the University of Oregon, where she teaches courses involving Indigenous feminisms, Pacific Island studies, and Native studies. She is coeditor of *Native Studies Keywords* (University of Arizona Press, 2015) and has published articles on Hawaiian hip-hop, film, and sexuality in the Pacific. Her articles have appeared in *American Quarterly,* the *American Indian Culture and Research Journal,* and the *International Journal of Critical Indigenous Studies,* and she is the author of *Defiant Indigeneity: The Politics of Hawaiian Performance* (University of North Carolina Press, 2018). She is a Kanaka Maoli feminist born and raised in Ewa Beach, Hawaiʻi, and a founding member of Hinemoana of Turtle Island, a collective of Pacific Islander feminists residing in California and Oregon.

SUNERA THOBANI is associate professor at the Institute for Gender, Race, Sexuality and Social Justice at the University of British Columbia. Her research focuses on critical race theory, postcolonial and feminist theory, globalization, citizenship, migration, Muslim women, the War on Terror, and media. She is the author of *Exalted Subjects: Studies in the Making of Race and Nation in Canada* (University of Toronto Press, 2007) and coeditor of *Asian Women: Interconnections* (Canadian Scholars' Press, 2005) and *States of Race: Critical Race Feminist Theory for the 21st Century* (Between the Lines, 2010). She is past president of the National Action Committee on the Status of Women (NAC), Canada's then-largest feminist organization (1993–96). She has helped organize, and spoken at, numerous international conferences, including the NGO Forum at the United Nations Fourth World Conference on Women in Beijing; the First International Women's Conference on APEC in Manila; the first Asian-Pacific Women's Conference in the United States; and the National Association of Black, Asian and Ethnic Minority Councillors conference and the Black Feminism conference, both in the United Kingdom. She is a founding member of Researchers and Academics of Colour for Equity (RACE), a cross-Canada network promoting the scholarship of academics of color and of Indigenous ancestry.

MA VANG is assistant professor and chair of critical race and ethnic studies at the University of California, Merced. Her interdisciplinary research advances a refugee critique of secrets, national history, and knowledge production. She specializes in critical Hmong studies to demonstrate how Hmong have been racialized through their history of involvement in the US "secret war" in Laos. Her book manuscript in process examines how secrecy structures both official knowledge and refugee epistemologies about war and migration. She is coeditor of *Claiming Place: On the Agency of Hmong Women* (University of Minnesota Press, 2016), and her writings have been published in *positions: asia critique* and *MELUS: Multi-Ethnic Literature of the United States*. She is a founding member of the Critical Refugee Studies Collective and coeditor of the collective's website. She is also actively engaged with community organizations such as the Hmongstory 40 Project and the Southeast Asian American Professionals Association.

GINA VELASCO is an assistant professor in the Women, Gender, and Sexuality Studies Program at Gettysburg College. Her research and teaching examine how gender and queer sexuality inform notions of nation, diaspora, and transnational belonging in a contemporary context of globalization. She is completing a book manuscript, *The Global Filipina Body: Gendered and Sexual Nationalisms in the Filipina/o Diaspora*, that explores how Filipina/o American cultural production queers the Philippine nation by unsettling the gendered and sexual politics of popular and state nationalisms. Her work has been published in *Women and Performance: A Journal of Feminist Theory*, the *International Feminist Journal of Politics*, and the *Review of Women's Studies*. She has been a member of the Critical Filipina and Filipino Studies Collective, a group of scholar-activists committed to interrogating and challenging imperialism. Prior to working in academia, she was the coordinator of a national network of student activists advocating for peace and justice.

JUDY TZU-CHUN WU is a professor in and chair of the Department of Asian American Studies at the University of California, Irvine. She is the author of *Dr. Mom Chung of the Fair-Haired Bastards: The Life of a Wartime Celebrity* (University of California Press, 2005) and *Radicals on the Road: Internationalism, Orientalism, and Feminism during the Vietnam Era* (Cornell University Press, 2013). Her current book project, a collaboration with political scientist Gwendolyn Mink, explores the political career of Patsy Takemoto Mink, the first woman of color US congressional representative and the cosponsor of Title IX. Wu is also coeditor of *Women's*

America: Refocusing the Past (8th ed.; Oxford University Press, 2015), *Gendering the Trans-Pacific World* (Brill, 2017), *Frontiers: A Journal of Women's Studies* (2012–17), and the online *Women and Social Movements in the United States, 1600–2000* (http://womhist.alexanderstreet.com).

INDEX

AAAS (Association for Asian American Studies), 4–5; feminist caucus of, 8

Abdulhadi, Rabab Ibrahim, 11

abortion: criminalization of, 219, 224, 232; and feticide, 218–19; laws, 236n2; pro-life pro-choice binary, 220, 233–34; self-induced, 219, 224, 235n1; sex-selective, 223

abortion rights, 29; and choice, 234; and fetal personhood statutes, 234; and reproductive justice, 221; and sterilization abuse, 29. *See also* reproductive rights

activism: and cultural production, 82; migrant worker, 204; and Pacific Islander studies, 131–32; refugee, 181–82, 189–93; and theory, 82

Adams, Romanzo, 127

Af3irm, 7, 199, 213n5, 214n11; Purple Rose Campaign, 200, 203, 214n11

Ahmed, Sara, 145

Aikau, Hokulani K., 131

Alexander, M. Jacqui, 9, 17, 183; on the "crossing," 182; on epistemology, 185; on re-membering, 11; on *This Bridge Called My Back*, 208

Alliance against Women's Oppression (AAWO), 29

Aloha (film), 132

American Sāmoa: and colonialism, 125; decolonization of, 118; and imperialism, 125

anti-Blackness, 107–8, 232; and Asian Americans, 133, 264, 267, 269, 275–76, 278; and incarceration, 235; and model minority myth, 18, 270–73, 276; and Pacific Islanders, 113, 133; and white supremacy, 112

anticolonialism: of Hmong feminism, 184; of Indigenous peoples, 171; and Islamophobia, 171; of South Asian Canadians, 166; and Third World women, 31; of TWWA, 31, 38; of Women of Color feminisms, 211

antihomophobia, 88–90

anti-imperialism, 27, 95; of Asian American feminists, 12, 47, 60, 210–11; in Canada, 158; of Filipinx feminisms, 88–89, 100, 199, 210–11; and queer politics, 95; of TWWA, 27–28, 30, 33, 35, 39; of Vietnamese women, 47; of Women of Color feminisms, 210–11

antiracism: and antihomophobia, 90; and Asian Americans, 60; in Canada, 158; and feminisms, 39, 83; and Filipinx, 88, 100; and heterosexism, 90; of Hmong feminism, 184; and Islamophobia, 171; of Women of Color, 170, 259n4

antiwar movement: Canadian, 158; US, 8, 30, 45; and Vietnamese women, 45

Anzaldúa, Gloria, 268

"API": Pacific, erasure of, 107, 114, 120–21, 124; and Pacific Islander marginalization, 124; as settler colonial construct, 114; as term, 14

Arab Americans: Asian American studies, marginalization in, 10; hypervisibility of, 140; invisibility of, 140; liberation movements of, 212; racialization of, 140, 151nn3,4; and South Asian Canadians, 164; and terrorism rhetoric, 140, 142

Arvin, Maile, 12, 13–14, 112, 123

Paltrow, Lynn M., 227, 229–30, 236n3
Parreñas, Rhacel Salazar, 4; on trafficking, 202, 205, 211
Partners in Healing, 7, 179–81, 184, 188, 189–90, 193
Patel, Purvi, 218–24, 226–27, 229; Asian American feminist defense of, 232; court appeal of, 219, 235n1; criminalization of, 21–22, 220, 227–28, 231–32, 234–35; media coverage of, 235n1; prosecution of, 222–24; stereotyping of, 222; as sympathetic victim, 232
patriarchy: and Asian American feminists, 224; and Asians, 233, 235; and diaspora, 91; Hindu, 223–25; and rape, 70. *See also* heteropatriarchy
peminism, 15–16, 82–83; as analytic, 83, 89; as antihomophobic, 88, 89–90; anti-imperialism of, 88–89; as antiracist, 88; and Asian American feminisms, 100; and class, 87; and decolonization, 83, 86–87, 89; definition of, 90; and empire, 85; and Filipinx subjectivity, 83; and identity, 17; and intersectionality, 87; and liberation, 89; marginality of, 89; and nation, 85; as Pinayism, 87–88; and queer affiliation, 16, 100–101; and queerness, 83, 90; and sexuality in, 17; and Women of Color feminisms, 100
people of color: and citizenship, 156; empire, complicity with, 34; and multiplicity, 245; as perpetual outsiders, 156; and prison industrial complex, 232; racialization of, 140. *See also* Women of Color
People's Coalition for Peace and Justice, 33
Philippines: colonization of, 16, 61n1; and globalized capitalism, 199–200; independence of, 93; and nationalism, 200; and neocolonialism, 16; and neoliberalism, 16; overseas labor migration of, 199–200; queer studies on, 83; and US empire, 200; and US imperialism, 199–200; and US militarism, 200
Pilipino Cultural Night (PCN), 198, 213n1
Pinayism: as antihomophobic, 88; as antiracist, 88; definition of, 90; and peminism, 87–88. *See also* peminism

Pinay Power, 86, 89, 92
politics: of accountability, 18; Asian American, 14; feminist, 7, 11, 43–44; Filipinx American, 86–88, 206; internationalist, 28; and intersectionality, 83; and model minority myth, 46–47; of multiplicity, 248; progressive, 83; queer, 95; of solidarity, 20; of visibility, 263; Women of Color, 6–7, 10, 257–58; working definition of, 6. *See also* coalitional politics
positionality, 259n4; of Asian Americans, 247, 256; and feminist research, 243; and intersectionality, 245–46; and multiplicity, 254, 257; and power, 256; and research, 255–56
pregnant women: criminalization of, 227, 230, 231–32, 233–34
prison industrial complex, 227–28; and people of color, 232
Puar, Jasbir, 4
Puerto Rican women, 8; sterilization of, 29; in *Triple Jeopardy*, 30, 32; in TWWA, 20, 27, 29, 35–36, 38

queerness: and family, 98, 276–77; and feminisms, 95; in Filipinx America, 92; in Filipinx culture, 90; and Filipinxness, 99; in Hagedorn, 86; and male subjective bias, 91; and peminism, 83, 90, 92; and solidarity, 17; and subjectivity, 12; and visibility, 92; white imperialist notions of, 92; and Women of Color feminisms, 86
queer of color critique, 90–91; and Women of Color feminism, 90–91
queer politics, 183; and anti-imperialism, 95; and Filipinx decolonization, 82–83; and nationalism, 95; and peminism, 99
Queer South Asian National Network (QSANN), 275–76, 278

race, 3; and authenticity, 246, 265; black-white binary, 87, 143, 269–70; and choice, 220; and citizenship, 4, 201; and coloniality, 250; and crime, 228; and criminalization, 232; and fetal personhood, 132; and feticide, 236n3;

DECOLONIZING FEMINISMS
Piya Chatterjee, Series Editor

Humanizing the Sacred: Sisters in Islam and the Struggle for Gender Justice in Malaysia, by Azza Basarudin

Power Interrupted: Antiracist and Feminist Activism inside the United Nations, by Sylvanna Falcón

Asian American Feminisms and Women of Color Politics, edited by Lynn Fujiwara and Shireen Roshanravan

CPSIA information can be obtained
at www.ICGtesting.com
Printed in the USA
LVHW051638251122
733910LV00002B/39